Making use of computerized data bases as
ll as the methodologies of social history
l anthropology, Barbara H. Rosenwein
e reassesses the significance of property
he tenth and eleventh centuries, a period
ransition from the Carolingian empire to
regional monarchies of the High Middle
es. In *To Be the Neighbor of Saint Peter*
explores in rich detail the question of
nastic donations, illuminating the hu-
n motives, needs, and practices behind
ts of land and churches to the French
nastery of Cluny during the 140 years
t followed its founding. Donations,
senwein shows, were largely the work of
ghbors, and they set up and affirmed
ationships with Saint Peter, to whom
uny was dedicated.

Cluny was an eminent religious institu-
n and served as a model for other monas-
ies. It attracted numerous donations and
was party to many land transactions. Its
charters and cartularies constitute perhaps
the single richest collection of information
on property for the period 909–1049. Analyzing the evidence found in these records,
Rosenwein considers the precise nature of
Cluny's ownership of land, the character of
its claims to property, and its tutelage over
the land of some of the monasteries in its
ecclesia. Using innovative techniques
afforded by the computerization of data,
Rosenwein untangles family relationships,
supplies statistical information on such
matters as donations, purchases, exchanges,
and quitclaims, and provides maps of property important to Cluny. She is able to show
in detail the ways in which local groups
interacted with one another and with the
monastery over the course of generations.
According to Rosenwein, property had
social and symbolic, as well as economic,
significance. It functioned as a social "glue"
to bind together monks, laity, and the saints
they served.

The conclusions Rosenwein draws from
the example of Cluny have implications
for much of Europe during the tenth and
eleventh centuries and should help to correct the view that medieval concepts of
property were similar to those that exist
today. *To Be the Neighbor of Saint Peter*
suggests that Western notions of private
property derive from a matrix of conceptions far more complex than has previously
been imagined. Historians of the church
and social, economic, and legal historians
are among those who will want to read this
remarkable new work by a leading medieval
scholar.

BARBARA H. ROSENWEIN is Professor of
History at Loyola University of Chicago.
Rosenwein received her B.A., M.A. and
Ph.D. degrees from the University of Chi-
cago and is also the author of *Rhinoceros
Bound: Cluny in the Tenth Century* (1982).

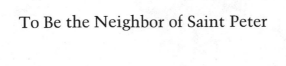

To Be the Neighbor of Saint Peter

Frontispiece. Saint Peter.
This figure dates from the twelfth century, when for the first
time monumental figural sculpture was produced at Cluny.
Nevertheless, certainly by the early eleventh century Cluny
had an *imago Petri*, which held relics and was used in the liturgy. Courtesy of the Museum of Art, Rhode Island School of
Design.

TO BE THE NEIGHBOR OF SAINT PETER

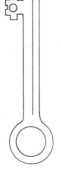

The Social Meaning of Cluny's Property, 909–1049

Barbara H. Rosenwein

Cornell University Press

ITHACA AND LONDON

Publication of this book was made possible, in part, by a grant from Loyola University of Chicago.

First published 1989 by Cornell University Press.

International Standard Book Number 0-8014-2206-x
Library of Congress Catalog Card Number 88-47912
Printed in the United States of America.
Librarians: Library of Congress cataloging information appears on the last page of the book.

The paper in this book is acid-free and meets the guidelines for permanence and durability of the Committee on Production Guidelines for Book Longevity of the Council on Library Resources.

To my children, Jessica and Frank,
and to my parents, Norman and Rosaline

Contents

Illustrations

Tables

Preface

THIS BOOK examines the significance of property in the tenth and eleventh centuries. It is based largely on the documentation for property transfers in the charters of the French monastery.of Cluny, which, in its own right, is an important topic. A prominent religious institution, Cluny was led by abbots who were called upon to institute reforms at other monasteries, and its way of life served as a model for many monks. Cluny was also, inevitably, a secular phenomenon. It attracted numerous donations, it was party to many land transactions, and it had an interest in the property of monasteries under its influence. More narrowly, then, this book also examines the precise nature of Cluny's ownership of land; the character of its claims to property and the way in which these claims related to other, overlapping claims; and, finally, the nature of its tutelage over the land of some of its churches and monasteries.

I began this work as a mapping project. Believing that historians and cartographers had not properly taken into account Cluny's property per se and that, for this reason, maps of Cluny presented a skewed picture of the monastery's importance, I entered charter information into a SAS (Statistical Analysis System) data set with the expectation of generating maps. With this computer program I reorganized the materials by location, thereby revealing new patterns. I was able, for example, to trace the history of particular pieces of property that were either recognized at the time to have had a distinct identity or that could be shown from boundary information to be identical. I was able to look at groups of properties at particular locations and to relate them to the social groups involved in these transactions. The outcome of these considerations is the present book, very different from the one I had intended to write.

In the materials from Cluny, some parcels of land recur in the charters over and over again. The vicissitudes of these properties and the social groups that owned, claimed, donated, and disputed about them tell us much about the uses of individual pieces of property and the meaning of property in general.

The context of these vicissitudes is the period between the fall of the Carolingian empire in the ninth century and the rise of relatively strong monarchies and principalities in the twelfth. During this time, much of western Europe was without government as we understand it today. Historians have traditionally called this period "anarchical" or "feudal," but recently historians have begun to look at the various ways in which people in this decentralized society continued to transact business, handle disputes, deal with violence, and, in short, regulate their social lives. The meaning of property within this society has not, however, been reassessed. In speaking, for example, of Cluniac property, which was usually land owned outright (alodial) rather than held in feudal tenure, historians have focused on the question of who—the individual or the family—was involved in the alienation. But these historians have not questioned the fact of alienation.

A careful examination of the charters of Cluny demonstrates that the transfer of property did not always result in a clear transfer of dominion. At times overlapping claims led to disputes, but overlapping claims were also tolerated. Ambiguous property ownership helped to keep the peace at a local level. Donors to Cluny, for example, often maintained an interest in the property they donated, as did, of course, the monastery. This does not signify that donations were meaningless but rather that they had, in addition to economic significance, also a social and symbolic one. They tied donors (and their families, often for generations) to the monastery and vice versa. At times this link was hostile, more often it was friendly, and sometimes these two aspects of the relationship were present at the same time.

Indeed, most of these relationships were those of neighbors, and, as people gave up portions of their land to Cluny, they became neighbors of Saint Peter, who was served by the monks there.

A reassessment of Cluny's property thus serves as a corrective to assuming modern property relations for that earlier period; it presents a more balanced view of so-called feudal society; and it suggests that Western notions of private property derive from a matrix of conceptions far more complicated than has previously been imagined.

Every book is ultimately a group effort. My own debts form, in themselves, a kind of history. In brief, this book is in good measure the result of a number of decisive and formative experiences.

In 1982 I attended a Summer Seminar in Cartography at the Newberry Library, Chicago, supported by a grant from the National Endowment for the Humanities. I hoped to learn there how to craft a new visual image of Cluny's importance by looking at its property rather than at the monasteries under its jurisdiction. I am grateful to the teachers of that seminar, particularly David Buisseret and David Woodward.

When it became clear to me that such a mapping project called for an information system more sophisticated than file cards, I turned to the Computer Center of Loyola University. I thank the staff of the center for its help, in particular Roger Addelson, John Bollweg, John W. Corliss, David Gabrovich, and Don Wee. A grant from the National Endowment for the Humanities for the summer of 1984 and a paid leave of absence from Loyola University for the fall of that year made it possible for me to enter the data from the charters into computer files.

To learn about place-name identifications, I traveled to Dijon, France, in the fall of 1984 on a grant from the American Philosophical Society. Mme Pierre Oursel-Quarré, Ancien conservateur of the Bibliothèque municipale de Dijon, did more than make available to me the place-name files on which she has been working for nearly thirty years. She accompanied me for every consultation; she insisted that *il faut vérifier*; she taught me her method. I am enormously grateful for her kindness. I would also like to thank M. Albert Poirot, Conservateur of the Bibliothèque municipale de Dijon, who made every resource of the library available to me.

As my initial project began to turn into the subject of this book, I was given the opportunity to try out my ideas at a seminar organized by Professor Patrick J. Geary and the Department of History at the University of Florida, Gainesville, in March 1985. It was a meeting of exceptional scholars: George Beech, Constance B. Bouchard, Fredric L. Cheyette, John B. Freed, Patrick J. Geary, Stephen Weinberger, and Stephen D. White. I am very grateful to all of them for their criticism, generosity, and support. Subsequently Professors Bouchard, Cheyette, and Geary read the entire book in draft, each correcting errors, suggesting alternative modes of exposition, and supplying me with new reading lists.

Finally, I was most kindly received in the summer of 1986 by Professor Joachim Wollasch and Frau Maria Hillebrandt at the University of Münster, who allowed me to make use of the materials on Cluny produced under Professor Wollasch's direction as part of Project B, "Personen und Gemeinschaften" of the Forschungsbereich 7. Frau Hillebrandt helped me consult the outprints of the *Gruppensuchprogramm* (about which, see the Introduction below); she gave me free use of the index of names produced by the *Lemmatisierungprogramm*; and she allowed me to cite a working draft of her book, *Studien zu den Datierungen der Urkunden der Abtei Cluny*, to be published as part of the series Münstersche Mittelalter-Schriften. She and I had discussions about Cluny at all hours during my stay at Münster, and I learned immeasurably. Above all, Frau Hillebrandt taught me to be sensitive to recurring groups in the charters. Later she read and commented on a draft of this book. I want to call particular attention to her role in Chapters 2 and 3. Thanks are due as well to many others at Münster, including Dr. Franz Neiske, with whom I had particularly illuminating discussions, Dr. Dietrich Poeck, and Herr Michael Curth.

But, in the end, it is not the extraordinary moment, but rather the *longue durée*—the context in which, bit by bit, a scholarly work gets done—that perhaps counts most in the creation of a book. There are many elements that make up this context. For me there is, first, Loyola University of Chicago, my colleagues there, and its library with, above all, Ms. Lorna Newman, surely the ideal interlibrary loan librarian. I have also to thank several extraordinary research assistants, especially Ms. Melinda A. Campbell and Sister Mary Ann O'Ryan.

I have also to thank my colleagues at other universities. Professor Lester K. Little of Smith College, in particular, has had a long-term and pervasive influence on my work. He read the present book in draft, and I am grateful for his comments. I am indebted as well to Professor Giles Constable, of the Institute for Advanced Study, Princeton, for his encouragement of this project in its early stages, and to Mr. Neil Stratford, Keeper of Medieval and Later Antiquities at the British Museum, and M. Jean-Pierre Aniel, Département des Manuscrits, Bibliothèque nationale, for their help in selecting illustrations.

Time itself must be acknowledged: the time to write was made possible by a fellowship from the National Endowment for the Humanities for the year 1986–87 and partial funding from Loyola University.

A generous subvention from Loyola University greatly facilitated publication; I want here particularly to record my thanks to Loyola's Research Services and its Director, Professor Thomas Bennett, whose support (financial and otherwise) on my behalf has always been unstinting.

Finally I turn to my family, without whom nothing at all would have been accomplished. My parents, Norman and Rosaline Herstein, read and commented on this book in draft (indeed, in more than one draft!). My husband, Tom, shared in all stages of its creation and gave it a careful, thoughtful, and critical reading. My children, Frank and Jessica, checked every day to see how many pages I had written. I thank them all.

It goes without saying that any errors that remain are mine alone.

BARBARA H. ROSENWEIN

Evanston, Illinois

Abbreviations

Angély   *Cartulaire de Saint-Jean d'Angély*, ed. Georges Musset, Archives Historiques de La Saintonge et de L'Aunis, nos. 30 and 33 (2 vols.; Paris: Picard, 1901–3).

AHR   *The American Historical Review*

Annales: ESC   *Annales: Economies, Sociétés, Civilisations*

BB   *Recueil des chartes de l'abbaye de Cluny*, ed. Auguste Bernard and Alexandre Bruel, 6 vols. (Paris: Imprimerie Nationale, 1876–1903). Cited by charter number, volume, and page(s), with month and year dates in parentheses.

Brioude   *Cartulaire de Brioude*, ed. Henri Doniol (Clermont-Ferrand: Thibaud, 1861).

Bibl. Clun.   *Bibliotheca Cluniacensis*, ed. Martin Marrier and André Quercetanus [Duchêne] (1614; repr. Mâcon, 1915).

Bull. Clun.   *Bullarium sacri ordinis cluniacensis*, ed. Pierre Simon (Lyon, 1680).

CCM   *Corpus consuetudinum monasticarum*, ed. Kassius Hallinger, 10 vols. (Siegburg: Schmitt, 1963–83).

Chaume, "Obs."   Maurice Chaume, "Observations sur la chronologie des chartes de l'abbaye de Cluny," *Revue Mabillon* 16 (1926): 44–48 (covering charters nos. 22–470); 29 (1939): 81–89 (nos. 471–875); 29 (1939): 133–42 (nos. 889–1710); 31 (1941): 14–19 (nos. 1747–2006) and pp. 42–45 (nos. 2007–43) and pp. 69–82 (nos. 2044–2234); 32 (1942): 15–20 (nos. 2267–2369) and pp. 133–36 (nos. 2370–2436); 38 (1948): 1–6 (nos. 2437–2776); 39 (1949): 41–3 (nos. 2806–2974); 42 (1952): 1–4 (nos. 2975–3124). (The last two sections prepared after Chaume's death by J. Marilier.) Cited (for dates

	and other information) after citations from BB, referring to the charter in BB.
Chaume, "En Marge 1"	Maurice Chaume, "En Marge de l'histoire de Cluny," *Revue Mabillon* 29 (1939): 41–61.
Chaume, "En Marge 2"	Maurice Chaume, "En Marge de l'histoire de Cluny," *Revue Mabillon* 30 (1940): 33–62.
Chaume, Origines	Maurice Chaume, *Les origines du Duché de Bourgogne*, 2 pts.; part II in 3 fascicles (1925–31; repr., Aalen: Scientia Verlag, 1977). Cited by part followed (if part II) by fascicle and page; thus II/3 = pt. II, fasc. 3.
Conques	*Cartulaire de l'Abbaye de Conques en Rouergue*, ed. Gustave Desjardins (Paris: Picard, 1879).
Gallia Christiana	*Gallia Christiana*, 16 vols. (Paris, 1715–1865).
Grand/Brioude	*Grand cartulaire du Chapitre Saint-Julien de Brioude: Essai de restitution*, ed. Anne M. Baudot and Marcel Baudot (Clermont-Ferrand: Imprimerie Générale, 1935). This supplies new charters in addition to those in *Brioude* and provides dates for the charters there. Cited by charter number and page, date in parentheses.
Hillebrandt, "Datierungen"	Maria Hillebrandt, "Studien zu den Datierungen der Urkunden der Abtei Cluny unter Verwendung des Gruppensuchprogramms." Preliminary draft of a book to be published: *Studien zu den Datierungen der Urkunden der Abtei Cluny*, Münstersche Mittelalter-Schriften. The dates cited from the working version are subject to further change or refinement.
JL	Philippe Jaffé with Samuel Loewenfeld, eds., *Regesta Pontificum Romanorum ab condita ecclesia ad annum post Christum natum MCXCVIII*, 2d ed., by William Wattenbach, 2 vols. (Leipzig: Veit, 1885). All references here are to vol. 1.
M	*Cartulaire de Saint-Vincent de Mâcon*, ed. M.-C. Ragut (Mâcon: Protat, 1864).
MGH	Monumenta Germaniae Historica
SS	Scriptores
MIÖG	*Mitteilungen des Instituts für Österreichische Geschichtsforschung*,
Erg.	Ergänzungsband.
Paray	*Cartulaire du prieuré de Paray-le-Monial*, ed. Ulysse Chevalier (Paris: Picard, 1890).
PG	*Patrologiae cursus completus: Series Graeca*, ed. Jacques-Paul Migne, 161 vols. (Paris, 1857–66). Cited by volume and column.
PL	*Patrologiae cursus completus: Series latina*, ed. Jacques-Paul Migne, 222 vols. (Paris, 1844–88). Cited by volume and column.
Raoul	*Recueil des Actes de Robert Ier et de Raoul, rois de*

	France (922–936), ed. Jean Dufour and Robert-Henri Bautier (Paris: Klincksieck, 1978). Cited by document number and page, with date in parentheses.
Romainmôtier	*Cartulaire de Romainmôtier*, ed. Frédéric Charles de Gingins-La-Sarra, Mémoires et Documents, Société de la Suisse Romande, 1st ser., vol. 3 (Lausanne: Ducloux, 1844). Cited by charter number and page, with date in parentheses.
Rudolfinger	*Die Urkunden der Burgundischen Rudolfinger (888–1032)*, ed. Theodor Schieffer and Hans Eberhard Mayer, MGH: Diplomata et acta. Regum Burgundiae e stirpe Rudolfina (Munich: MGH, 1977). Cited by document number and page, with date in parentheses.
Santifaller	*Quellen und Forschungen zum Urkunden-und Kanzleiwesen Papst Gregors VII*, ed. Leo Santifaller, pt. 1, Studi e testi 190 (Vatican: Biblioteca Apostolica Vaticana, 1957). Cited by document number and page.
Saint-Flour	*Cartulaire du prieuré de Saint-Flour*, ed. Marcellin Boudet (Monaco: Imprimerie de Monaco, 1910).
Sauxillanges	*Cartulaire de Sauxillanges*, ed. Henri Doniol (Clermont-Ferrand: Thibaud, 1864).
Zimmermann	*Papsturkunden, 896–1046*, ed. Harald Zimmermann, Österreichische Akademie der Wissenschaften, Denkschrifen 174, 2 vols. (Vienna, 1984). Paginated consecutively throughout the volumes. Cited by document number and page, with date in parentheses.

OTHER ABBREVIATIONS

arr.	*arrondissement*
B.N.	Paris, Bibliothèque nationale. Manuscripts in the *nouvelles acquisitions* Latin series are cited as MS nouv. acq. lat; those in the Bourgogne collection are cited as coll. Bourg.; those in the Latin series are cited as MS fonds lat.
ca.	*canton*
co.	*commune*
dép.	*département*
l.-disp.	a location that has disappeared
n. id.	not identified
S.-L.	dép. Saône-et-Loire

Note: All place names are dép. Saône-et-Loire unless otherwise noted. Place names in quotation marks refer to *villae* that do not correspond to any modern French place name. On maps, these have been placed at the location of the nearest modern French city, which is indicated in parentheses.

To Be the Neighbor of Saint Peter

A des degrés divers, dans tous les coins
de la ville, ces hommes et ces femmes
avaient aspiré à une réunion . . .

Camus, *La peste*

Introduction

THE PROCESSES of property transfers reveal much about the meaning of property in the tenth and eleventh centuries. The transfers under review here—for the most part gifts—were ordinarily of land alone or of land together with churches. Cluny is the focus because it attracted an outpouring of gifts; because it was considered an exemplary model of the religious life at the time, to which gifts were due; and because its extant documents are numerous enough to allow us to see the multitextured relationships between the cloister and its donors, of which gift giving was only one part.

Cluny's very foundation was a gift: in 909, Duke William the Pious of Aquitaine and his wife, Ingelberga, gave the villa of Cluny to the Apostles Peter and Paul, and then they established the monastery there.[1] In the course of the tenth and eleventh centuries Cluny was party to numerous donations, sales, exchanges, claims, and quitclaims (i.e., formal moments in which claims were given up) of both land and churches. As it became the head of a coalition of monasteries (commonly called the Cluniac order but termed more properly the *Cluniacensis ecclesia* by Joachim Wollasch), Cluny grew very famous.[2] At the end

1. BB 112;I:124–28: "res juris mei sanctis Apostolis Petro videlicet et Paulo de propria trado dominatione, Clugniacum scilicet villam." On the family and other connections of William and Ingelberga, see Chapter 5.
2. Joachim Wollasch, *Mönchtum des Mittelalters zwischen Kirche und Welt*, Münstersche Mittelalter-Schriften 7 (Munich: W. Fink, 1973), pp. 149–58. I have made use of Dietrich Poeck, "Die Klöster der *Cluniacensis ecclesia*," draft of a

of the eleventh century, indeed, Pope Urban II called Cluny "the light of the world."[3] Although in the course of the twelfth century its fame was eclipsed by monasteries such as Cîteaux, Cluny survived until the French Revolution, when it was pillaged, its monks evicted, and its buildings destroyed.[4]

In the hands of nineteenth- and twentieth-century historians, however, Cluny rose again as, at the very least, a significant exemplar of tenth- and eleventh-century Benedictine monasticism.[5] As part of this contemporary reassessment, the extent of its property was also considered and sometimes depicted in map form. The sort of map most commonly used, based on one first drawn by Simone Berthelier in 1938, showed Cluniac "houses," that is, the monasteries in Cluny's ecclesia, along with the many churches belonging to Cluny.[6] The clear implication of such maps—which showed late-eleventh-century Cluny dominating all of France, and which in some versions also had arrows pointing outward in graceful curves from Cluny to England, to Spain, and to Germany and Switzerland—was that Cluny was indeed a monastery of the world.[7] It was no accident that André Chagny wrote a book with the title *Cluny and Its Empire*.[8]

Yet there was a distinction, recognized already by Berthelier, between Cluny's "houses"—which were, after all, religious institutions with a spiritual life of their own—and Cluny's

study to appear in the series Münstersche Mittelalter-Schriften. I am grateful to Dr. Poeck for allowing me to see his work prior to publication.

3. Urban II, *Epistola* 214 (*PL* 151, col. 486), echoing Matthew 5:14.

4. On the later history of Cluny, see *Dictionnaire d'histoire et de géographie ecclésiastiques*, 13:115–35. Nearly all historians have noticed a decline in the spiritual leadership of Cluny in the twelfth century. John Van Engen argues to the contrary in, "The 'Crisis of Cenobitism' Reconsidered: Benedictine Monasticism in the Years 1050–1150," *Speculum* 61 (1986): 269–304.

5. See the bibliographical discussion in Barbara H. Rosenwein, *Rhinoceros Bound: Cluny in the Tenth Century* (Philadelphia: University of Pennsylvania Press, 1982), pp. 3–29.

6. Simone Berthelier, "L'expansion de l'ordre de Cluny et ses rapports avec l'histoire politique et économique du Xᵉ au XIIᵉ siècle," *Revue archéologique*, 6th ser., 11 (1938): 319–26. See my critique of maps of Cluny and the sources on which they are based in "Cartographic Patterns of Cluniac Monasticism," in *Monasticism in the Christian and Hindu Traditions: A Comparative Study*, ed. Austin B. Creel and Vasudha Narayanan (Lewiston, N.Y.: Edwin Mellen), in press.

7. For a recent such map, including arrows, see Geoffrey Barraclough, ed., *The Times Atlas of World History* (London: Times Books, 1978), p. 122.

8. André Chagny, *Cluny et son empire*, rev. ed. (Lyon: Emmanuel Vitte, 1938).

churches, which were often simply the centers of agricultural exploitations, comparable to Cluny's other landholdings. It would be useful, I thought at one time, to separate these two kinds of Cluniac empires, the one religious, the other landed, in order to see precisely what property Cluny held. The charters of Cluny, problematic as they were, appeared to lend themselves to such an enterprise. These charters recorded the transactions —gifts, sales, and exchanges, for example—that people made with the monastery. One might simply note the places obtained by Cluny—organize them by kind (land, church, or monastery), by date, and by transaction (donation or sale, for example)—and then produce maps of the different kinds of property of Cluny. There are, after all, thousands of charters; and there are also pancartes—long lists of Cluny's major properties along with its churches and monasteries—issued by popes and kings. Naturally, one would have at some point to draw the line between economic and religious "holdings"; this, I thought, would be the chief problem.

Monastic property has indeed been successfully mapped. A recent instance is Joan Wardrop's study of Fountains Abbey, a Cistercian monastery in northern England.[9] Yet the enterprise of mapping property has inherent problems. Charters are not as straightforward as they seem. Wardrop, for example, notes that charters of "donation" to Fountains often concealed sales. The

9. Joan Wardrop, *Fountains Abbey and Its Benefactors, 1132–1300,* Cistercian Studies Series 91 (Kalamazoo, Mich.: Cistercian Publications, 1987); a finely drawn map of Fountains' estates makes up the endpapers of the book. A somewhat different purpose is served by the study of Constance Hoffman Berman, *Medieval Agriculture, the Southern French Countryside, and the Early Cistercians: A Study of Forty-three Monasteries,* Transactions of the American Philosophical Society 76, pt. 5 (Philadelphia: American Philosophical Society, 1986), which includes maps of Cistercian granges on pp. 130-34. Berman's research shows decisively how closely Cistercian land acquisition resembled that of the black monks, although—in their programmatic statements—the Cistercians claimed to acquire "wilderness" lands only. See similar observations in Constance B. Bouchard, *Sword, Miter, and Cloister: Nobility and the Church in Burgundy, 980–1198,* (Ithaca, N.Y.: Cornell University Press, 1987), pp. 174–89. Monte Cassino's property is mapped in Luigi Fabiani, *La Terra di S. Benedetto: Studio storico-giuridico sull'Abbazia di Montecassino dall' VIII al XIII secolo,* 3 vols., Miscellanea cassinense, vols. 33–34, 42 (Montecassino, 1968–80). There is a series of fine maps of the property of Marcigny in Elsa Maria Wischermann, *Marcigny-sur-Loire: Grundungs-und-Frühgeschichte des ersten Cluniacenserinnen priorates (1055–1155).* Münstersche Mittelalter-Schriften 42 (Munich: W. Fink, 1986), pp. 472–81, with place identifications on pp. 482–91.

charters of Cluny—once I began to examine them in detail—led me to think that even more than that lay hidden behind them. In effect, they resisted mapping.

For maps imply a modern assumption about private property: that when property is given, it is alienated. When Dietrich Poeck made maps of Cluny's property, a dot served to indicate land given to Cluny at different periods; these culminated finally in a cumulative map, constructed, as it were, of all the dots from the past.[10] Yet, taken as a whole, the charters of Cluny do not describe a steady process of land acquisition. Instead, they reveal that land was given, taken back, and redonated; they show that the same or related groups were over and over involved with Cluny in disputes, sales, exchanges, and donations of land, sometimes simultaneously. Such giving and taking could last for several generations; memories connected with land were quite long. The "property of Cluny" was property in flux.

The maps in this book must not be misunderstood. They do not signify—at least not necessarily—the "property" of Cluny as we understand it today. They simply plot the places where the monastery and the world outside clearly intersected. Land acted as a bond between donors (or, for that matter, sellers) and the monastery.[11] Or rather, and more correctly, the land linked the donor (and groups of families, neighbors, and friends clustered around the donor) to Saint Peter and Saint Paul (but particularly to Saint Peter), to whom Cluny and its monks were dedicated and to whom, quite straightforwardly, donations were given.

I call this bonding the "social" meaning of Cluny's property; but in fact it might very well be called the "religious" significance. This is certainly what contemporaries considered it. Such religious meaning might apply as much to a simple land donation as to handing over a monastery to Cluny, a fact that makes

10. Dietrich Poeck, "Laienbegräbnisse in Cluny," *Frühmittelalterliche Studien* 15 (1981): 68–179. While Poeck's final map (p. 160) in fact shows only the properties most distant from the monastery, the assumption is that properties, once acquired, remained "Cluny's."

11. About concealed sales, Wardrop remarks that they, too, served "at least in part, their traditional function of expressing the benefactor's piety and his desire to attach himself to the house in some way" (p. 117).

it very difficult to separate neatly Cluny's agricultural landholdings from its ecclesia. Naturally, a monastery given to Cluny had a religious life of its own, which a piece of land did not. Yet the religious meaning of land, too, did not end with the final words of a charter. Land given to Saint Peter could have the character of a *locus sanctus* in that, like so much else in the period, it could mediate between the natural and supernatural world.[12] I have chosen to term this phenomenon property's "social" meaning, rather than religious, for two reasons. First, the word points to the importance of the *relationship* that property created or affirmed, a relationship that stretched beyond the mundane world. Second, it stresses the normalness of that association. For Saint Peter figured so prominently in most of the transactions with Cluny, as if a nearby landholder, that to "deal" with him was indeed to do business with a neighbor.[13]

Community Bonds

With the work of Marc Bloch, it became commonplace to speak of tenth- and eleventh-century society—the society that emerged in the hiatus between the Carolingian empire and the Capetian hegemony—as that of the "first feudal age." Here, in Bloch's words, "the characteristic human bond was the subordinate's link with a nearby chief."[14] Yet, it has been part of the

12. On the *locus sanctus*, see Steven D. Sargent, "Religion and Society in Late Medieval Bavaria: The Cult of Saint Leonard, 1258–1500" (Ph.D. diss., University of Pennsylvania, 1982), pp. 102–3. Historians have recently become interested in the cult of relics in the Middle Ages: e.g., Patrick J. Geary, *Furta Sacra: Thefts of Relics in the Central Middle Ages* (Princeton: Princeton University Press, 1978); Thomas Head, "Andrew of Fleury and the Peace League of Bourges," in *Essays on the Peace of God: The Church and the People in Eleventh-Century France*, ed. Thomas Head and Richard Landes, *Historical Reflections / Réflexions Historiques* 14 (1987): 513–30. At Cluny there was an *imago Petri* that contained various relics, including a part of the body of Saint Peter, a piece of the Holy Cross, and a portion of the garment of the Virgin; see the so-called *Liber tramitis* in *CCM* 10:260–61.

13. This is perfectly Augustinian: the City of God is a community; see Augustine *Civitas dei* xix.5, Corpus Christianorum, Series Latina 47–48, 2 vols. (Turnhout: Brepols, 1955), 1:669: "Nam unde ista Dei ciuitas . . . si non esset socialis uita sanctorum? [For how could the city of God come into being. . . . if the life of saints were not social?]."

14. Marc Bloch, *Feudal Society*, trans. L. A. Manyon (Chicago: University of Chicago Press, 1961), p. 444.

task of postwar scholarship to show how important and characteristic, on the contrary, were horizontal rather than vertical
ties. Already in 1958 Pierre Duparc was writing that community
confraternities were "the basic cells of medieval society."[15] In
the last two decades, such formulations have taken on new
meaning, as historians have begun to look at the nature of collective activities in early medieval communities.[16]

One of the most important issues that these new studies have
explored is the variety of mechanisms by which early medieval
societies handled disputes when no clearly superior power existed—or was wanted—to impose judgment.[17] Fredric Cheyette
and Stephen White, for example, point to the role of compromise in resolving quarrels in France, where each disputant won
something and (above all) no one lost face. Elsewhere disputes
were processed through arbitrators. The sibling communities
—the monks within the walls and laymen outside—met in the
liturgy, as monks sought to regulate the behavior of violent
magnates with curses.[18] Rather than exploring hierarchies of

15. Pierre Duparc, "Confréries du Saint-Esprit et communautés d'habitants au
moyen-âge," *Revue historique de droit français et étranger*, 4th ser., 36 (1958):
349–67 at 349; published in English in *Lordship and Community in Medieval
Europe: Selected Readings*, ed. Fredric L. Cheyette. (New York: Holt, Rinehart
and Winston, 1968), pp. 341–54.

16. See Susan Reynolds, *Kingdoms and Communities in Western Europe,
900–1300* (Oxford: Clarendon Press, 1984). For the tenth century, horizontal
relationships are similarly stressed in Heinrich Fichtenau, *Lebensordnungen des
10. Jahrhunderts: Studien über Denkart und Existenz im einstigen Karolingerreich*, Monographien zur Geschichte des Mittelalters 30, pts. 1 and 2. 2 vols.
(Stuttgart: Hiersemann, 1984). See also the essays in Richard C. Trexler, ed.,
*Persons in Groups: Social Behavior as Identity Formation in Medieval and Re-
naissance Europe*, Medieval and Renaissance Texts and Studies 36 (Binghamton,
N.Y.: Medieval and Renaissance Texts and Studies, 1985).

17. Patrick J. Geary speaks of "stateless France" in "Vivre en conflit dans une
France sans état: Typologie des mécanismes de réglement des conflits (1050–
1200)," *Annales: ESC* 41 (1986): 1107–33. In the conclusion to the illuminating
series of studies in Wendy Davies and Paul Fouracre, eds., *The Settlement of
Disputes in Early Medieval Europe* (Cambridge: Cambridge University Press,
1986), the editors suggest that it was not so much the objective ascendancy of
the state that brought people into public courts, but rather "the extent to which
people . . . were prepared to use public institutions when disputing rather than
fight or negotiate privately" (p. 238).

18. Fredric L. Cheyette, "Suum cuique tribuere," *French Historical Studies*
6 (1970): 287–99; Stephen D. White, "*Pactum . . . legem vincit et amor judi-
cium*: The Settlement of Disputes by Compromise in Eleventh-Century Western
France," *American Journal of Legal History* 22 (1978): 281–308; William Ian
Miller, "Avoiding Legal Judgment: The Submission of Disputes to Arbitration in
Medieval Iceland," *American Journal of Legal History* 28 (1984): 95–134; Lester

lords and vassals, such studies focus on the continuous ebb and flow of enmities and friendships and of community groups igniting and defusing quarrels.[19] The net cast by these studies is wide—from Iceland to Spain, Italy, England, and Byzantium —and the time frame has by now expanded to the sixteenth century and beyond.[20]

The questions that such historians pose are influenced by those put by anthropologists, particularly by legal anthropologists.[21] My own work, growing out of a similar interest in community interaction, falls historiographically within the penumbra of these studies. However, the present study is not of disputes per se, although these certainly arose when people laid claim to properties. Rather, its focus is on gift giving itself. Here, too, medievalists have already tested the waters; William Ian Miller, for example, has illuminated the world of the Icelandic sagas by discovering the connections between friendships, enmities, and gifts.[22]

K. Little, "La morphologie des malédictions monastiques," *Annales: ESC* 34 (1979): 43–60.

19. Geary, "Vivre en conflit," pp. 1113–26.

20. See Davies and Fouracre, especially articles by Rosemary Morris, "Dispute Settlement in the Byzantine Provinces in the Tenth Century" (pp. 125–48), and Jenny Wormald, "An Early Modern Postscript: The Sandlaw Dispute, 1546" (pp. 191–206). See the even wider net cast by the splendid essays in John Bossy, ed., *Disputes and Settlements: Law and Human Relations in the West* (Cambridge: Cambridge University Press, 1983).

21. E.g., Laura Nader and Harry F. Todd, Jr., eds., *The Disputing Process: Law in Ten Societies* (New York: Columbia University Press, 1978), and Simon Roberts, "The Study of Dispute: Anthropological Perspectives," in Bossy pp. 1–24; both have useful bibliographies.

22. William Ian Miller, "Gift, Sale, Payment, Raid: Case Studies in the Negotiation and Classification of Exchange in Medieval Iceland," *Speculum* 61 (1986): 18–50. One eagerly awaits the forthcoming study of Natalie Z. Davis on gifts in early modern Europe. Stephen D. White's *Custom, Kinship, and Gifts to Saints: The Laudatio Parentum in Western France, 1050–1150* (Chapel Hill: University of North Carolina Press, 1988) unfortunately appeared too late for me to take advantage of its insights here. See also Aron J. Gurevich, *Categories of Medieval Culture*, trans. G. L. Campbell (London: Routledge and Kegan Paul, 1985), pp. 221–39; Philippe Jobert, *La notion de donation: Convergences 630–750*, Publication de l'Université de Dijon (Paris: Société Les Belles Lettres, 1977); Jürgen Hannig, "Ars donandi: Zur Ökonomie des Schenkens im früheren Mittelalter," *Geschichte in Wissenschaft und Unterricht* 3 (1986): 149–62 (kindly brought to my attention by Sabine Reiter, Freie Universität, Berlin); and T. M. Charles-Edwards, "The Distinction between Land and Moveable Wealth in Anglo-Saxon England," in *Medieval Settlement: Continuity and Change*, ed. P. H. Sawyer (London: Edward Arnold, 1976), 180–87, who discusses the way in which gifts of moveables maintained friendships in Anglo-Saxon England,

The Mâconnais, where Cluny and most of its benefactors were located, was emphatically not a vertically organized feudal society in the tenth and early eleventh centuries. While there were a few lords and vassals (we shall meet some in the course of this book), there were hardly any fiefs. By and large, land was held by inheritance, gift, or purchase. This does not mean, however, that individuals were free to dispose of their property in any way. In the first place, groups—family groups and neighborhood groups—rather than individuals controlled the disposition of property. And, in the second place, the ways in which property was partitioned or handed down was determined largely by social purposes. In the course of this study we shall see some of these. Among other things, relationships were created, called into question, confirmed, and strengthened through land transactions.[23]

Transformations of the Eleventh Century

The social uses of property did not begin in 909, nor did they end in 1049. For our task, however, these moments are convenient. The first date is easily justified because it marks the foundation of the monastery of Cluny. The choice of the last date is more problematic. It is necessitated, however, by the conjunction of certain important transformations, some connected with wider historical developments and some with the nature of the documents and, indeed, of Cluny itself.

One of the more general contextual changes in the eleventh century was the church reform movement, which (among other things) ensured that churches formerly in lay hands would be transferred to ecclesiastical institutions.[24] Cluny felt the effects

---

arguing, however, that land was an exception, forging largely vertical relationships between lords and subordinates.

23. See the recent study by Emma Mason, "The Donors of Westminster Abbey Charters, ca. 1066–1240," *Medieval Prosopography* 8 (1987): 23–39, which reveals that many benefactors to that monastery were neighbors and that "preexisting ties were further strengthened by a conscious decision to patronize the abbey" (p. 25).

24. A brief recent summary of the movement with bibliography is Karl F. Morrison, "The Gregorian Reform," in *Christian Spirituality: Origins to the*

of the movement by mid-century. In the first twenty years of the abbacy of Saint Hugh (1049–1109), 40 percent of the donations to Cluny were of churches or partial churches, whereas in the twenty years preceding, they constituted about 17 percent of all donations (see Table 1).

In the Mâconnais, the period 980–1049 saw other important shifts: in settlement patterns, family structures, economic modes, and newly strengthened ties between vassals and lords.[25] The old system of multiple, sparsely populated villae in the region around Cluny began to disintegrate about 1000; slowly the settlements were either abandoned or transformed into villages that were (by comparison) populous, concentrated, and church-centered.[26] During the same period, families who manned the castles in the region, or who built new ones of their own, began to rise above other members of the regional aristocracy, subjecting humbler men to themselves as vassals or as tillers of the soil. At the same time, the character of the aristocratic family began to shift, from "amorphous" and open to tight and patrilinear. Finally, the economy was becoming increasingly monetary and market oriented.[27]

Twelfth Century, ed. Bernard McGinn and John Meyendorff, vol. 16 of *World Spirituality: An Encyclopedic History of the Religious Quest* (New York: Crossroad, 1985). On canonical thinking that directly affected lay rights over churches, see Peter Landau, *Jus Patronatus: Studien zur Entwicklung des Patronats im Dekretalenrecht und der Kanonistik des 12. und 13. Jahrhunderts* (Vienna: Böhlau, 1975). For Cluny and proprietary churches, see Georg Schreiber, "Cluny und die Eigenkirche," in *Gemeinschaften des Mittelalters: Recht und Verfassung, Kult und Frömmigkeit* (Münster: Regensberg, 1948), pp. 81–138, esp. 131–35; Hans-Erich Mager, "Studien über das Verhältnis der Cluniacenser zum Eigenkirchenwesen," in *Neue Forschungen über Cluny und die Cluniacenser,* ed. Gerd O. Tellenbach (Freiburg: Herder, 1959), pp. 167–217.

25. The classic discussion of all these developments is in Georges Duby, *La société aux XIe et XIIe siècles dans la région mâconnaise,* 2d rev. ed. (Paris: Jean Touzot, 1971).

26. François Bange, "L'*ager* et la *villa*: Structures du paysage et du peuplement dans la région mâconnaise à la fin du haut moyen âge (IXe–XIe siècles)," *Annales: ESC* 39 (1984): 529–69.

27. On the new banal powers of the aristocracy, see Duby, *La société,* pp. 141–44. On the patrilinear society of the twelfth-century Mâconnais, see Georges Duby, "Lignage, noblesse et chevalerie au XIIe siècle dans la région mâconnaise: Une revision," in *Hommes et structures du moyen âge: Recueil d'articles* (Paris: Mouton, 1973), pp. 395–422; this article was published in English in *The Chivalrous Society,* trans. Cynthia Postan (Berkeley: University of California Press, 1977), pp. 59–87. On the much-disputed issue of "amorphous" versus "linear" families in the early Middle Ages, the best introduction is Karl Schmid,

Table 1. Donations of land and churches, 1029–69

	Churches		Land		
	No.	%	No.	%	Total
1028–48	35	17	169	83	204
1049–69	45	40	68	60	113

Note: There were, in all, 327 transactions (for the definition of which see below, pp. 25-26), of which 10 land transactions are impossible to assign with certainty to either of the two twenty-year periods. (The charters which are counted for the period 1028–48 have variable FSTDATE greater than or equal to 1028 and less than 1049 and no SNDDATE, or SNDDATE less than 1050; those counted for the period 1049–69 have FSTDATE greater than or equal to 1049 and less than 1070 and no SNDDATE, or SNDDATE less than 1075. (For the definition of these variables, see Appendix A.) The figure given for churches here is a conflation of two kinds of gifts: those in which churches and monasteries are given with the intention of reforming their religious life, and those in which such gifts are given simply (as far as we can tell) as property. The breakdown is as follows:

	Church as property	Church for reform
1028–48	32	3
1049–69	33	12

The figures in Table 1 are rather different from those in Hans-Erich Mager, "Studien über das Verhältnis der Cluniacenser zum Eigenkirchenwesen," in *Neue Forschungen über Cluny and die Cluniacenser*, ed. Gerd O. Tellenbach (Freiburg: Herder, 1959), pp. 173 and 216, where the figure of 6.5 percent "aller Schenkungen" (before 1050) is contrasted with 16 percent (for the period 1050–75).

The net effect of these transformations was, by the twelfth century, to tie people into new and tightly woven networks defined by their parish, their family lineages, their lords or retain-

---

"Uber die Struktur des Adels im früheren Mittelalter" and "Zur Problematik von Familie, Sippe und Geschlecht. Haus und Dynastie beim mittelalterlichen Adel: Vorfragen zum Thema, 'Adel und Herrschaft im Mittelalter,'" both now reprinted in Karl Schmid, *Gebetsgedenken und adliges Selbstverständnis im Mittelalter: Ausgewählte Beiträge. Festgabe zu seinem sechzigsten Geburtstag* (Sigmaringen: J. Thorbecke, 1983), pp. 183–244 and 245–67; see also Constance B. Bouchard, "Family Structure and Family Consciousness among the Aristocracy in the Ninth to Eleventh Centuries," *Francia* 14 (1987):639–58, and the balanced review in John B. Freed, "Reflections on the Medieval German Nobility," *AHR* 91 (1986): 553–75, esp. 560–63. In my view, both familial strategies were used in the early medieval period, but by 1100 the patrilineal model, combined with the seigneurie, effectively put an end to the possibilities of "amorphous" organization. On the money economy, see Duby, "Le monachisme et l'économie rurale," in *Hommes et structures*, pp. 381–94.

ers, and their economic roles. Cluny was not simply affected by these movements but was itself part of them. Like the castellans, Cluny too became a seigneurial lord, holding a monopoly of command over particular men and lands. Its new political and economic position had far-reaching consequences: on institutions of peace, on the ideology of the three orders, and, indeed, on the very ideas about virtue that animated the monks.[28]

In part as a result of these changes, the nature of the documents used to record land transactions with Cluny also began to alter. The full, descriptive charters of the tenth century gave way to laconic notices in the mid-eleventh. Due perhaps to a new emphasis on oral custom, this transformation was also one symptom of an enhanced value placed on names and lineages rather than on land descriptions.[29]

It is appropriate, then, to end the discussion of the social meaning of Cluny's property with the mid-eleventh century. Certainly donations did not cease then, nor did sales or claims. But by 1049 many places involved in previous give and take had been consolidated as part of Cluny's seigneurie. Accompanying this development, certain transactions with the monastery ceased: exchanges, for example, virtually disappeared. Cluny itself, under Abbot Hugh, was a changed institution.[30] We should not assume that the meaning of familiar acts—of gifts, sales, and claims—remains the same simply because their forms persist. Indeed, it is one of my purposes in this study to show that each transaction is not only an individual act but also part of a larger system that is very particular to its time and place. The system under Abbot Hugh deserves its own separate study; but it does not belong to this one.[31]

28. Duby, *La société*, pp. 215–87; idem, *Les trois ordres ou l'imaginaire du féodalisme* (Paris: Gallimard, 1978), pp. 236–51; idem, "Recherches sur l'évolution des institutions judiciaires pendant le Xe et le XIe siècle dans le sud de la Bourgogne," in *Hommes et structures*, pp. 7–60, in English in *Chivalrous Society*, pp. 15–58; Dominique Iogna-Prat, "Continence et virginité dans la conception clunisienne de l'ordre du monde autour de l'an mil," in *Académie des Inscriptions et Belles-Lettres: Comptes rendus, 1985* (Paris: Boccard, 1985), pp. 127–46, and *Agni immaculati: Recherches sur les sources hagiographiques relatives à Saint Maieul de Cluny (954–994)* (Paris: Cerf, 1988) esp. pp. 344–49.
29. For further discussion of the transformation of the charters and its connection to modes of piety, see below, Chapter 5.
30. See Noreen Hunt, *Cluny under Saint Hugh, 1049–1109* (London: Edward Arnold, 1967), pp. 83–85, 124–61, and passim.
31. For a study of changing habits of largess, see Jennifer C. Ward, "Fashions

Nevertheless, the methodology used here may be applied to other monasteries. The results may reveal the same sort of social network as at Cluny; or they may point to a different view of land and its uses. In each place quite different mechanisms and motives may be at work. Hence it is that Wardrop can speak of sales concealed in gifts at Fountains Abbey, while I sometimes find at Cluny gifts concealed in sales.[32]

The Structure of the Argument

Chapter 1 surveys the several ways in which historians have handled the question of Cluny's patronage. Previous studies have concentrated largely on lay motives—generosity, anticipation of benefits, control over property—rather than on the social and neighborhood system in which gift giving to Cluny played a role. This last is, then, the focus of the present book.

In Chapter 2, I present two major theses about the neighborhood gift-giving system at Cluny. First, the same people who gave land to Cluny also took it away; the friends of Cluny were at the same time its enemies. This give and take constituted an important part of Cluny's property system. It involved not so much individuals as groups of people: friends, neighbors, family members, saints, and monks. Second, some places had special significance within this system. Certain places were donated only, others were continually claimed; some were used almost exclusively as a source of sales to the monastery, and still others were singled out by papal confirmations. In short, villae were not just economic exploitations or places to own or live in; they also had symbolic meanings.

While Chapter 2 is primarily about giving and taking, Chapter 3 is about apparently commercial transactions: exchanges and sales. These were much less frequent than donations, yet they were important because (as we discover) the same groups were

in Monastic Endowment: The Foundations of the Clare Family, 1066–1314," *Journal of Ecclesiastical History* 32 (1981): 427–51.

32. See also Chapter 5, which takes up in quick review some of the social networks surrounding the monasteries of Cluny's ecclesia.

involved in them. They cannot simply be dismissed as impersonal economic deals—at least not always—because they had other, less quantifiable, meanings as well. Indeed, they suggest that donations, too, had multiple meanings, shading from social to acquisitive. In short, Chapter 3 points up two contrary yet coexisting significances of land: first, as the exclusive property of Cluny, land was the foundation of its seigneurie; and second, as the distributable property of Cluny and certain of its friends, it was the glue of its social relationships.

In Chapter 4, I discuss the implications of these findings. Here the meaning of "ownership" as it emerges from the documents is explored, and the work of anthropologists on gift giving is brought to bear on materials from Cluny. Historians are rightly chary of using observations about other cultures as guides to the one that they are studying. Yet, if used flexibly, anthropological materials can be extremely helpful in unraveling the many strands of uses and traditions involved in societies as complex as those of the tenth and eleventh centuries. It is clear, in any event, that it is quite wrong to impose our own notions of property on earlier periods. At the very least, anthropologists can help shatter the fetters of our modern mental constructs and allow the historical materials to take their own shape. Above all, the work of anthropologists on gift giving alerts us to the reciprocal nature of gift giving to Cluny: gifts were part of a circle of giving, from God to people, from people to Saint Peter (who, like all saints, interceded with God), and then (sometimes) back again around the circle. Then, too, anthropologists point up the importance of asking about the *nature* of the thing given. This is one theme of Chapter 5, which deals in part with Cluny's "special" property.

Chapter 5 is, in effect, the long-deferred discussion of Cluny's land, churches, and monasteries. The deferral was necessary to avoid misunderstanding. Cluny's property cannot be discussed without first knowing its social meaning. Indeed, Chapter 5 is, essentially, an exploration of relationships once again. First, it takes up the relationship between Cluny and its churches and monasteries. The chief point here is that each of these ecclesiastical institutions was itself dedicated to a saint and could be part of a gift-giving nexus analogous to (but often separate from) the one at Cluny. Second, it takes up the pancartes and privileges that were issued on Cluny's behalf by kings and popes. These listed "special" properties, singled out over all others. This section addresses the question of choice: why certain properties were selected to be confirmed but not others. Finally, the discussion turns to the distribution of Cluny's property (or, more precisely speaking, of its property transactions). Most of these transactions were in its neighborhood, but some were not. These distant properties call for explanation. In fact we discover that they, too, were part of a network of relationships: the far-flung territories that Cluny acquired in its early years came from members of the highest aristocracy, for the most part connected with William the Pious, with Ingelberga, or with others associated with these founders.

The general reader who wishes simply to catch the gist of the argument of this book may elect at this point to turn directly to Chapter 1.

The Charters

Charters are today experiencing a kind of historiographical renaissance. Davies and Fouracre's group, for example, chose to look at such documents rather than at theoretical works or prescriptive law codes to discover legal practices.[33] What are the charters of Cluny? How reliable are they? How have they been used? What more can be done with them?

In 1770 a lawyer from Autun named Louis-Henri Lambert de Barive was appointed by the Comité Moreau to study the archives of the monastery of Cluny.[34] His task was part of a larger project, begun toward the middle of the eighteenth century under the twin impulses of intellectual enlightenment and

33. Davies and Fouracre, programmatic statement on pp. 2–4; see also Sawyer, p. 157.
34. Much of the following is taken from the useful discussion in the introduction to the first volume of BB. See also Jean Richard, "La publication des chartes des Cluny," in *A Cluny: Congrès scientifique, Fêtes et cérémonies liturgiques* 9–11 July 1949 (Dijon: Bernigaud and Privat, 1950) and Madeleine Oursel-Quarré, "A propos du chartrier de Cluny," *Annales de Bourgogne* 50 (1978): 103–7.

political absolutism, to study and systematize French history and law. Until the French Revolution put an end to his efforts, in 1790, Lambert de Barive copied the documents in the *Grand Trésor* of Cluny, carefully inventorying, annotating, and describing what he found. He copied about 5,000 charters, many of them (presumably) originals. Although many original charters were destroyed during the French Revolution, the copies made by Lambert de Barive survived.

Among the present collections of the Bibliothèque nationale at Paris are three groups of documents pertaining to land transfers at tenth- and eleventh-century Cluny: about 300 original charters; copies of charters made by Lambert de Barive; and four cartularies, that is, collections of charters, designated now by the letters A, B, C, and D, drawn up between the eleventh and the thirteenth centuries.[35]

The modern printed edition of the charters of Cluny drew upon and collated these three sources. The original editor, Auguste Bernard, died in 1868. He was succeeded by Alexandre Bruel, who, at his death in 1920, had not finished the task. The last volume, the seventh, was never completed. Nor was the index for the first six volumes, for which Bruel had planned and prepared hundreds of note cards. What was finished, however, was one of the most massive collections of documents for a single institution, especially for an institution of the tenth and eleventh centuries. For the period to 1049 they may be tabulated roughly as shown in Table 2. The challenge for subsequent historians was to figure out how to use this material.

35. Most of the relevant sources for Cluny are inventoried in Léopold Victor Delisle, *Inventaire des manuscrits de la Bibliothèque nationale: Fonds de Cluni* (Paris: H. Champion, 1884). The numbers of charters involved must be approximate because it is a matter of definition what is and is not a "Cluniac" charter. Many documents in the archives of Cluny are of only indirect importance to the monastery (e.g., charters that record some aspect of a piece of property before that property became Cluny's; or documents connected with a monastery that was part of Cluny's ecclesia). The important collections of original charters for the tenth and eleventh centuries are (all MSS at the Bibliothèque Nationale): fonds lat. 17715 (62 charters), nouv. acq. lat. 2163 (9 charters); nouv. acq. lat. 2154 (88 charters); coll. Bourg. 76 (32 charters); coll. Bourg. 77 (64 charters); coll. Bourg. 78 (58 charters).

The charters copied by Lambert de Barive—with care to preserve the original orthography and punctuation—are bound in 274 folio volumes: B.N. coll. Moreau 1–274. Lambert de Barive dated the charters, identified place names, and specified in which bin at Cluny he found his exemplar.

Table 2. Charters by abbacy

Abbacy	No.	%
Before 909	100	3.4
Berno (909–27)	99	3.3
Odo (927–42)	175	5.9
Aymard (942–64)	546	18.3
Maiolus (964–94)	1,021	34.2
Odilo (994–1049)	978	32.8
Uncertain date	64	2.1
Total	2,983	100.0

Note: Abbatial dates given here are those commonly accepted by historians. The dates for Maiolus have been carefully assessed by Dominique Iogna-Prat, *Agni immaculati: Recherches sur les sources hagiographiques relative à saint Maieul de Cluny (954–994)* (Paris: Cerf, 1988), p. 208. In brief, we may note that we have a notice about Maiolus's election as co-abbot with Aymard in 954 (see BB 883; II:1–2); sometimes this is given as the first date of his abbacy. He was sole abbot after Aymard's death, in 964. For the purposes of statistical manipulation, however, abbatial dates here and in other tables were in fact defined in the SAS job used to create them as they are in Appendix B, Illustration B.3, that is, without overlapping terminal dates. The dates of many charters are uncertain; some now included in the period before 1049 may indeed belong to the later period, while others now assigned after 1049 may need to be moved back. The dates of the charters counted in this table are as corrected by Chaume, "Obs." and Hillebrandt, "Datierungen," and as in Appendix F.

Cartulary A = B.N. nouv. acq. lat. 1497, dating from the late eleventh and early twelfth centuries (on the dating of the hands, I follow the attributions of Delisle); contains copies of charters believed *at the time cartulary A was redacted* to derive from the abbacies of Berno, Odo, Aymard, and Maiolus, although modern research has found that some of these attributions are incorrect; see esp. Chaume, "Obs."; Hillebrandt, "Datierungen."

Cartulary B = B.N. nouv. acq. lat. 1498, largely transcribed at the end of the eleventh and first half of twelfth centuries; contains copies of charters thought by the copyists to pertain to the abbacies of Odilo, and Hugh (1049–1109), and a few to Pons (1109–22) and Peter the Venerable (1122–56). The charters are organized by abbacies, and within each abbacy, by the nature of the donation: first monasteries, then churches, then land. For date changes see, Chaume, "Obs.," Hillebrandt, "Datierungen," and Damien Van den Eynde, "Remarques sur la chronologie du cartulaire de Cluny au temps de Pierre le Vénérable," *Antonianum* 43 (1968): 217–59.

Cartulary C = B.N. nouv. acq. lat. 2262 contains the most important papal bulls concerning Cluny; transcribed mainly at the end of the eleventh and first half of the twelfth centuries.

Cartulary D = B.N. nouv. acq. lat. 766. Delisle and BB thought this lost, but (according to a note on fol. 1) it was found in 1902. BB refers to this cartulary (e.g., BB 33;1:39), but obviously they did not use the original but rather drew from copies of the cartulary made by Baluze and others. See BB I:xxxi–xxxiv. The original was probably transcribed at the end of the thirteenth century; there are a number of different hands. It contains documents dating from 888 to the end of the thirteenth century.

Making Sense of the Charters

Indeed, Bernard and Bruel were the first modern historians of Cluny in the sense that, in the process of publishing its sources, they imposed (were forced to impose) an artificial organization on them. They chose a chronological presentation.[36] The charters that had been copied into the cartularies were wrenched out of context, as it were; those that had been attributed to Abbot Berno, for example, were published alongside other charters—originals and copies by Lambert de Barive—that could be dated to Berno's time. The coherence of cartulary A, which had (loosely) a geographic organization, and of cartulary B, which was organized by kind of property—monastery, church, land—was thus lost.

Bernard and Bruel were interested in preserving original orthography and archaisms; and they were careful not to impose modernized words or names. But because they assumed Lambert de Barive had had access to original manuscripts, they generally preferred his version to copies in the cartularies. Thus, ironically, they used the most modern copy to arrive at the most ancient source.[37] They also sometimes imposed a rectilinear order on witness lists not originally so organized but perhaps (for that reason) significantly organized.[38] For, as we shall see,

36. This was not the choice of every editor in the nineteenth century, even those publishing in the same series, the Collection des documents inédits sur l'histoire de France, which was sponsored by the ministry of education. See, for example, *M*, the edition of charters for the church at Mâcon, which retains the organization of its source, the so-called *Livre enchaîné*, decidedly nonchronological. On the various shapes that cartularies might take, see David Walker, "The Organization of Material in Medieval Cartularies," in *The Study of Medieval Records: Essays in Honour of Kathleen Major*, ed. Donald A. Bullough and Robin L. Storey (Oxford: Clarendon Press, 1971), pp. 132–50.

37. E.g., BB 2456;III:538–39, where Lambert de Barive's copy is considered (p. 539, n.1) to represent "l'original perdu." Most of the time, however, Bernard and Bruel provided footnotes to account for any differences, even orthographical, between the text of the cartularies and the text of Lambert de Barive. Nevertheless, the "originals" are not always what Bernard and Bruel take them to be. See Bernard F. Reilly, *The Kingdom of Castile under Queen Urraca, 1109–1126* (Princeton: Princeton University Press, 1982), p. 54 n. 31.

38. For example BB 23;I:27–28 (?5.880) allows the text of the witness list to run together, whereas its exemplar (B.N. coll. Bourg. 76, fol. 2r) has the principals on one line, and then a clear indentation, thus (with the text indicated here by ellipses all on the first line):

S. Vualdoni S. Sieradane, qui cesione ista . . . rogaverunt.
        Ego Erlenus roitus SSS [subscripsi] Ellulfus SSS
S. Felganto S. Siardo S. Elberto S. Monberto S. Gerardo [etc.]

coherent social groups were indicated by the order and grouping of names on the witness lists.

The published charters were immediately used to write histories of the monastery, a task first accomplished by Ernst Sackur. Their texts were mined by scholars such as Georg Schreiber, to discover Cluny's attraction in donors beyond the walls.[39] But above all, at least initially, they were exploited for studies of Burgundian geography and society.

These regional studies had not only a history but a kind of lineage: their "founder" was Canon Maurice Chaume, to whom homage was paid by André Déléage, whose work (in turn) served as a starting point for Georges Duby's studies. Though Chaume was an important figure in Cluniac studies, his magnum opus was a history of Burgundy.[40] Because the documents of Cluny provided so rich a mine of information about that region, Chaume worked carefully through its charters, making connections across volumes that Bernard and Bruel had not noticed. Chaume's memory was prodigious; because of the links that he saw, he was able to redate hundreds of charters and call attention to recurring witnesses and donors. He also identified thousands of place names.[41]

Ten years after Chaume's study appeared, Déléage published his detailed survey of the organization of the countryside of Burgundy prior to the year 1000.[42] Déléage was the first to quantify Cluny's charters and to subject them to an economic analysis. He used them to derive the price of a field, for example; and to count the quantity of land in the hands of churches.[43]

This particular charter was drawn up before the foundation of Cluny and probably entered its archives when the property in question became associated with Cluny.

39. Ernst Sackur, *Die Cluniacenser in ihrer kirchlichen und allgemeingeschichtlichen Wirksamkeit bis zur Mitte des elften Jahrhunderts*, 2 vols. (Halle an der Saale: Max Niemeyer, 1892–94); Georg Schreiber, *Gemeinschaften des Mittelalters*; and see below, Chapter 1.

40. Chaume, *Origines* I and II/1 and 2.

41. The date changes are mostly in his series of articles, referred to here as Chaume, "Obs," Place-name identifications are in *Origines* II/3, esp. pp. 1014–1170.

42. André Déléage, *La vie rurale en Bourgogne jusqu'au début du onzième siècle*, 2 vols. text, 1 vol. maps (Mâcon: Protat, 1941), (pages run consecutively throughout the text and therefore no volume number will be given henceforth).

43. For ecclesiastical possessions, see, e.g., ibid., app. 4, pp. 1024–57, which

A little more than a decade later came the work of Georges Duby. "I have chosen the Mâconnais because the important work of the late Déléage on rural life in Burgundy before the eleventh century offered a solid point of departure and greatly simplified the preliminary research," wrote Duby in the introduction to his book (first published in 1953) on the society of the Mâconnais.[44] This book revolutionized medieval regional studies and had major repercussions in other areas of medieval history as well. But from our vantage point for the moment, the great significance of Duby's work was the way in which he exploited the charters of Cluny. Besides building upon the analysis of land-ownership that Déléage had begun; besides continuing the exploration of family genealogies initiated by Chaume; besides pioneering a new approach to judicial institutions by looking at documents concerned with the counts of Mâcon, Duby used the charters to understand the very structure of society. Only the briefest illustration may be given here, for nearly the entire book—a study of social, economic, and political transformations over the course of three centuries—was documented by the charters of Cluny.

Thus, by way of example, among the many changes that Duby chronicled was a shift from a social classification that divided "free" from "unfree" to one that divided "knights" from "peasants."

In 971, *miles*, a Latin translation for the vernacular word knight, is, to our knowledge, employed for the first time by the scribes of the Mâconnais to designate the member of a particular social class. Certainly, the term had been in use for some time in the popular tongue, and its appearance as a title in the archives does not mean that a new social class was born at that precise moment. The redactors of the charters and notices had their own language, hallowed by tradition, and the new expression was imposed on them from the outside, by current practice.[45]

---

rely in part on Cluny's charters, or pp. 1059–84, which rely almost entirely on Cluny's charters to tabulate possessors of the soil; for prices, see pp. 983–1022, which rely mainly on charters from Cluny and Saint-Vincent de Mâcon.

44. Duby, *La société* p. 7. See Jean-François Lemarignier's review in *Le Moyen Age* 62 (1956): 167–84.

45. Duby, *La société*, p. 191.

Duby's source was precisely a charter by one Hugo, designated after his name as *miles*, who confirmed the provisions of a donation to Cluny.[46] If the vocabulary of the charters, tardily, reflected the social structure outside the monastery, then the charters could be used not just for monastic history, not just for a history of ideas, but above all for a history of the social life of the laity. Duby's pioneering work put the charters right into the laps of the social and economic historians.[47]

Ironically, for all their indisputable value for every aspect of medieval history, these social and economic studies still need to be integrated into the history of Cluny itself. For the monastery was more than simply a convenient repository for charters. It was the very institution on behalf of which most of the documents were drawn up. The charters tell us not only about "the world" but also (perhaps even more so) about the relationship between that world and the monastery.

The present study grows out of that consideration. This is equally true of the work now being done, under the direction of Joachim Wollasch, at the University of Münster. Both of these projects harness the computer to do some of the labor.[48]

Computer-Assisted Studies

The *Gruppensuchprogramm*

In order to identify Cluny's donors, historians needed a way to manage and correlate the names (ordinarily simply first names) that filled the charters. In Germany, computer programs to do

46. BB 1297;II:374–75.
47. See Duby's own work, as, for example, the studies in *Hommes et structures* (most of which are translated in *Chivalrous Society*). Bange's study, "L'*ager*," is also based on Cluny's charters.
48. David Herlihy must be called the pioneer of computer-assisted charter studies; see esp. "Church Property on the European Continent 701–1200," *Speculum* 36 (1961): 81–105, reprinted in *The Social History of Italy and Western Europe, 700–1500: Collected Studies* (London: Variorum Reprints, 1978), paper 5. More recent studies include those using the program *Famulus*; See John Blair and Philip Riden, "Computer-Assisted Analysis of Medieval Deeds," *Archives* 15 (1982): 195–208. The SAS program is used in the Domesday Database Project, designed to aid research in social history; see Robin Fleming, "A Report on the Domesday Book Database Project," *Medieval Prosopography* 7 (1986): 55–61.

this were created in the course of putting together synoptic editions of necrologies and confraternity books. These documents contained lists of the names of people for whom the monks prayed. Researchers at Freiburg and Münster needed to find a way to identify identical people on parallel lists.[49] Many first names were very common; spellings were not standardized. One solution that was adopted was to create a "lemma" or "key" spelling under which all variants could be organized. The *Lemmatisierungprogramm* was created to find these lemmata automatically. A second task was to match *groups* of names. The Bernardus in the cluster of names Andreas/Petrus/Rainaldus/ Bernardus in a document from Saint-Martin-des-Champs was parallel to the one in the cluster in the necrology of Longpont of Andreas/Petrus/Martinus/Rainaldus/Bernardus; very likely, then, the two Bernards in these groups referred to the same person.[50]

Wollasch and his team of researchers brought these solutions with them when they turned to the charters of Cluny, the single richest source for the study of Cluniac history. The lists of names potentially generated from the charters—including donors, sellers, family members, witnesses—would have been unmanageable without the aid of the computer. The *Gruppensuchprogramm* (GSP), the collective name for a series of programs, was devised to discover nonrandom, parallel groups of names.[51] The names and other information from the charters of

49. See Karl Schmid with Gerd Althoff et al., eds. *Die Klostergemeinschaft von Fulda im früheren Mittelalter*, 3 vols. in 5, Münstersche Mittelalter-Schriften 8 (Munich: W. Fink, 1978); Johanne Autenrieth, Dieter Geuenich, and Karl Schmid, eds., *Das Verbrüderungsbuch der Abtei Reichenau (Einleitung, Register, Faksimile)*, MGH, Libri Memoriales et Necrologia, n.s. 1 (Hannover: Hahnsche Buchhandlung, 1979). More recent work at Münster was on materials from Cluny: Joachim Wollasch, with Wolf-Dieter Heim et al., eds., *Synopse der cluniacensischen Necrologien*, 2 vols., Münstersche Mittelalter-Schriften 39 (Munich: W. Fink, 1982), in which see particularly articles by Franz Neiske, "Die synoptische Darstellung der cluniacensischen Necrologien" (1:19–27) and W.-D. Heim, "Lemmatisierung und Registrierung der Personennamen" (1:28–33). On the significance of names, see Stefan Sonderegger, "Personennamen des Mittelalters: Vom Sinn ihrer Erforschung," in *Memoria: Der geschichtliche Zeugniswert des liturgischen Gedenkens im Mittelalter*, eds. Karl Schmid and Joachim Wollasch, Münstersche Mittelalter-Schriften 48 (Munich: W. Fink, 1984), pp. 255–84.

50. Wollasch, *Synopse*, 2:290.

51. For a discussion of these programs, see Friedrich-Wilhelm Westerhoff, "Gruppensuche: Ein Verfahren zur Identifizierung von Personen und Personen-

Cluny have been entered onto computer tape at Münster for analysis by means of the GSP.[52]

One immediate result of the rapprochements afforded by the GSP is to make possible the systematic redating of the charters on the basis of their correspondence to charters for which dates are certain; the GSP brings together instantaneously and automatically potentially parallel charters out of the welter of more than 60,000 names. But the usefulness of this instrument obviously goes beyond redating the charters; it is also a tool for social history.[53]

The GSP could not work, or could not work very well, unless there were an underlying structure to the very placement of the names in the charters. Part of that structure has long been known and is dependent on the form of the document itself (see Fig. 1). For example, the *protocol* (the beginning) of the charter always contains the name of the principal; the *subscriptio* of the *eschatocol* (with which the charter ends) lists the principal first, then the names of witnesses, last the name of the scribe.[54] But nothing formally dictates that, for example, three witnesses be listed together.[55] Such clusters were expected in confraternity books—books of prayer brotherhoods in which members of

---

gruppen in mittelalterlichen Namen-Quellen," *Dokumentationsband zum EDV-Kolloquium, 1985,* Schriftenreihe des Rechenzentrums der Westfälischen Wilhelms-Universität Münster 59 (Münster, 1985), pp. 67–77. See Maria Hillebrandt, "The Cluniac Charters: Remarks on a Quantitative Approach for Prosopographical Studies," *Medieval Prosopography* 3 (1982): 3–25.

52. The information included is constantly being expanded; it includes the charter number, source of the charter (e.g., original, copy by Lambert de Barive, cartulary), names and function of the person in the charter (e.g., witness), and title (e.g., *rex*).

53. See, for example, the forthcoming study by Maria Hillebrandt, *Datierungen.* The chief document generated by the programs at Münster that was consulted for the present work was the index of lemmatized names produced by the *Lemmatisierungprogramm.* I was also able to consult at Münster part of the output of of the so-called GSP6, which gives a concordance of charters in which parallel groups of names are found. The degree of certainty about the randomness of the parallels can be adjusted.

54. There is a nice summary of, and bibliography for, diplomatics by Leonard E. Boyle, "Diplomatics," in *Medieval Studies: An Introduction,* ed. James M. Powell (Syracuse, N.Y.: Syracuse University Press, 1976), pp. 69–101.

55. On the order of names in charters, see Heinrich Fichtenau, "Die Reihung der Zeugen in Urkunden des frühen Mittelalters," *MIÖG* 87 (1979): 301–15, which deals with the ranking of clergy before laity, and for a more general discussion on order and disorder, see his *Lebensordnungen,* esp. "Ordo" in pt. 1, pp. 11–112, and "Confusio" in pt. 2, pp. 499–566.

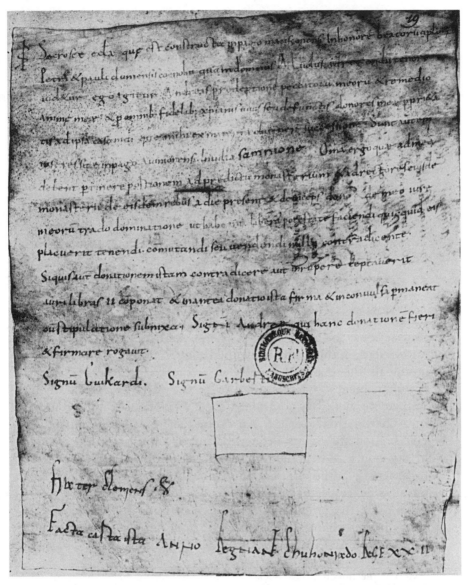

Figure 1. Tenth-century charter. This donation charter was drawn up in 958/9 by "frater Clemens," a scribe discussed in Monique-Cécile Garand, "Copistes de Cluny au temps de saint Maieul (948–994)," *Bibliothèque de l'Ecole des Chartes* 136 (1978): 5–36 (B.N. nouv. acq. lat. 2154, no. 19 = BB 1057; II:151–52). Courtesy of the Bibliothèque nationale, Paris.

communities or families were entered together—but it is remarkable to find (as the GSP alerts historians to find) that the
same is true in the charters. That is, names are often found
consistently in the context of a particular group of names, even
in charters that were drawn up at different times and by different scribes.[56] In some instances it is possible, through this and
other evidence, to discover what sort of relationship the people
in such a group had to one another. In some instances it is not;
and yet, the very existence and persistence of the group strongly
suggests that there is a relationship of some sort. Analyzing
these groups is a new way to study the society of the Mâconnais, or rather of those within the Mâconnais who chose to
associate themselves with Cluny.[57] Such analyses contributed
in important ways to the exploration, in the present study, of
the social meaning of property.

The SAS Program

Even beyond knowledge of the social groups involved in land
transactions, the completion of the present study depended on a
knowledge of the land itself and, above all, on the ability to
group all the charters concerned with the same place. Such
grouping meant that histories of pieces of property and their
immediate vicinities could be traced. Consider the information
in a charter from 947: "I, Anselmus, and my wife, Lantrudis,
give to God and Saints Peter and Paul at Cluny, for the remedy
of our souls, a field in the *pagus* Matisconensis, in the *ager*
Rufiacensis, in the *villa* Lornant, the whole of which is bounded
on all sides by land of St. Peter."[58] For the moment we may
leave aside the problems involved in defining the geographical
terms in this charter; it is sufficient to note that the field given
to Cluny by Anselmus and Lantrudis was thought to be located

---

56. On the importance of social grouping, see, for example, Otto Gerhard
Oexle, "Gruppenbindung und Gruppenverhalten bei Menschen und Tieren:
Beobachtungen zur Geschichte der mittelalterlichen Gilden," *Saeculum* 36
(1985): 28–45.
57. See Otto Gerhard Oexle, "Die 'Wirklichkeit' und das 'Wissen': Ein Blick
auf das sozialgeschichtliche Oeuvre von Georges Duby," *Historische Zeitschrift*
232 (1981): 61–91.
58. BB 1359;II:427–28 (2.974).

within a hierarchical arrangement of spaces, the largest of which was the *pagus* and the smallest of which was the *villa*.[59]

Already Duby, and even more so Déléage and Chaume before him, had managed to organize and make sense of this geographical information. But its sheer bulk invited the use of automatic methods. For the present study the SAS program, a standard statistical package, was chosen as a convenient way to enter, retrieve, and manipulate the information from each charter. The variables chosen—that is, the categories for the data that were deemed important—were the charter number, its date or range of dates, an index of the source and accuracy of the date, the type of charter (e.g., land transfer, royal confirmation), the type of transaction (e.g., exchange, donation, sale), and the outcome (e.g., whether Cluny "gained" or "lost" in the transaction). If a church was involved, as was often the case, its name (more precisely, its *patrocinium*) was recorded. Finally, a variety of geographical information was included: the pagus, the ager, the villa, and information about borders (e.g., that the property bordered on a river, that it bordered on other land of Saint Peter [i.e., Cluny], and so on).[60]

A few technical points are so important as to warrant their inclusion here. First, SAS deals in "observations" rather than charters. Many charters involve more than one villa; these were entered as two or more observations. For example, one charter spoke of the donation of land "in pago Lugdunensi" (i.e., the Lyonnais), "in villa Nonedis" and "in villa Merlerges."[61] These

---

59. Some charters locate property with even greater precision by mentioning the name of a part of a villa (a *locus* name) and/or a field name. But these are generally too rare to be useful in any attempt to group charters by place. Nevertheless, see the collection of charters concerned with Igé and Saint-Vincent-des-Prés, organized by locus names, in Déléage, pp. 1064–67 and 1080–84.

60. See Appendix A for details about the fields, or variables, that were chosen and how they were defined. Special attention should be called to the category "activity"; for the purposes of discussion in this book, the kind of transaction recorded by the charter has been simplified considerably. For example, that which is here called a "donation" refers principally to charters in which the gift giver used the word *dono*, but it includes as well those charters which utilized such verbs as *trado* and *cedo*. In the actual data entry, separate codes were used for these different verbs. A more nuanced understanding of "donation" may eventually be achieved by careful attention to the precise vocabulary of the charters.

61. BB 1097;II:190.

were recorded in the data set as one donation for each villa, resulting in two observations for this single charter.

Second, land at any one villa in any one charter was counted as one observation. Thus, for example, the donation of a field called Cavaniacus and a field called Pratum Manencum, both in the villa of Igé, resulted in one observation.[62] This method was chosen because the location was of paramount importance, and this could be known primarily by the villa name (the pagus and ager being useful particularly to identify the precise villa in question, since many are homonymous). But it was also chosen because only at the level of the villa were the charters comparable; some spoke of fields, others of *mansi* (a unit of exploitation)[63] *cum vineis et planta*;[63] some in great detail of mansi *cum omnibus ad ipsum pertinentibus, campis, vineis, pratis, silvis.*[64] It was impossible to know, for example, how many *campi* (fields) were meant in the latter, or the proportion of newly planted vineyard (*planta*) to those already cultivated (*vineis*); and it would have been misleading in the extreme to allow two observations for one charter because it mentioned specifically two aspects of the mansus while allotting four observations to another because it named four parts of the mansus.

Third, in a similar manner, separate observations were made when a charter contained more than one kind of transaction, as, for example, both a donation and a sale.

Fourth, in the case of exchanges, two observations were (usually) created: one for the land gained by Cluny and one for the land lost, even if all the land in question pertained to the same villa. (The exceptions are those instances in which only one side of an exchange was recorded.)

In this book, the term "transaction" refers to what SAS calls an "observation"; and the term "charter" refers to all the contents of a charter, which may include many observations.

Like personal names, place names too were spelled in a variety of ways in the charters. Rather than create "lemmata" for them, I instead identified them as far as possible by a single modern equivalent. The information for these modern place

62. BB 1380;II:443–44.
63. E.g., BB 1541;II:590–91.
64. E.g., BB 1480;II:534–35.

names, including the city, commune, canton, *département*, latitude, and longitude, were entered (along with information about the source of the identification and an index of its probable accuracy) in a separate SAS file. The two files could be merged for each observation on the basis of their identical villa, ager, and pagus (and church name in some instances). In the end, then, the material in the charters could be sorted by any one or more of the variables in either data set, and various quantitative procedures could be used with them.

Geographical Information

There are three recurring geographical terms in the charters: *pagus, ager,* and *villa.* The largest geographical division was the *pagus* (whence the word *pays* in modern French). The word itself derived from the same root as *paginus* and *pax* and meant (like a page and a peace treaty) something with fixed boundaries: a district. The Romans, who distinguished carefully between country and city, used *pagus* to refer to the countryside; hence its applicability to those backwaters, Gaul and Germany. From the first, then, Burgundy was divided into *pagi;* but for administrative purposes, it was divided into *civitates,* which might encompass more than one pagus. Later, in the course of the seventh century, after the Franks had established their rule in Gaul, the pagus gradually replaced the civitas as the basic administrative unit (see Map 1).

Yet, despite its etymology, the boundaries of the pagus were not as certain as some mapmakers would like to think. The charters of Cluny afford many instances in which the same villa was said (at different times) to be located in two different pagi.[65]

65. E.g., Ecussolles is in Mâcon in BB 891;II:8–9 but in Autun in BB 1516;II: 565–66. See maps in Auguste Longnon, *Atlas historique de la France depuis César jusqu'à nos jours* (Paris: Hachette, 1907), plates v–ix. The depiction of boundaries in Longnon's maps were criticized by Lucien Febvre, "Une enquête: La succession des circonscriptions," *Annales: ESC* 2 (1947): 201–4. The maps in Chaume, *Origines* II/3 (e.g., a map of the pagus of Chalon opposite p. 1000), have two border indications: a thick continuous black line and thin dotted lines. Neither of these refers directly to the boundary of the pagus (p. xv), but the thick line (which is meant to show the borders of the diocese) in effect is treated as the pagus boundary, as all places that fall outside of it are assumed to belong to

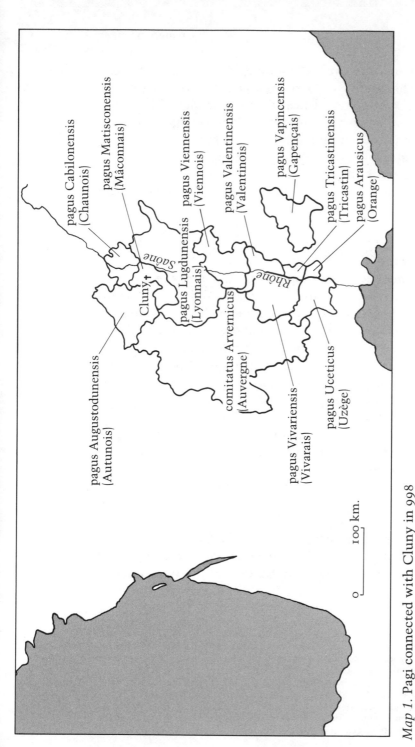

Map 1. Pagi connected with Cluny in 998

Note: The pagi outlined here are those subdivisions given in a privilege of Gregory V (998), for which see Table 9. For the most part, they follow the configuration of pagi in Auguste Longnon, *Atlas historique de la France depuis César jusqu'à nos jours* (Paris: Hachette, 1907), plate V: "Carte de l'empire de Charlemagne d'après le partage de 806," the base map for the one here. (See also ibid., plate VII.) However, the Auvergne of Gregory V was the larger *patria* and *comitatus* as well as the pagus, and it incorporated the pagi Brivatensis (Brioude), Tel-amitensis (Saint-Amand-Tallende), Tolornensis (Turluron), and Gabalitanus (Gévaudan), and so on. See the map "L'Auvergne de l'An Mil" in Christian Lauranson-Rosaz, *L'Auvergne et ses marges (Velay, Gévaudan) du VIIIe au XIe siècle: La fin du monde antique?* (Le Puy-en-Velay: Cahiers de la Haute-Loire, 1987).

Any depiction of pagi is bound to be criticized. The map reproduced here is meant only to present a schematic visual picture of tenth-century

Even less clear is the nature of the ager. In Chaume's view, the term *ager* "tends to have the vague meaning of the 'more or less immediate environs,' or sometimes even of a *'finage'* [i.e., the area around a city, rather like the present-day French commune], or of a *'lieu-dit'* [i.e., a place with a special, traditional name because of its historical or other associations]."[66] This view implies a vaguely concentric arrangement, with several villae fitting loosely into the larger area represented by the ager. More recently, however, François Bange has argued that the relationship between the ager and the villa was more "magnetic" than concentric. His model of the ager/villa shows the main city of the ager (i.e., the one after which it was named) in the center of a star, the rays of which reach out to its various villae. The agri had the spatial configuration of separate cells, their extent and shape defined by natural geographic boundaries, such as mountains or rivers.[67]

Implicit in all this is a definition of the word *villa* in the charters of Cluny, or at least of what the villa was not. It most certainly was not a "manor" in the classic sense implied by, say, the Carolingian *Capitulare de villis*, where numerous dependent peasants worked for one lord. In the Mâconnais there were many independent landowners in each villa.[68] Nor was it the equivalent of a village: the villa often had no church, and nothing in the charters points to a concentrated settlement. Instead, the term simply described space, within which was land of every sort (arable, unfarmed, woods), buildings, water, animals, and human beings. We know nothing more: we do not know its size;

---

neighboring pagi. Chaume himself was sensitive to the problem: "Mais cette limite de l'évêché est-elle identique à celle du *pagus* du dixième siècle?—Nous ne le croyons pas" (p. 1024). At times he appeared to think that the boundaries of the pagus, particularly at the frontier, were uncertain (e.g., pp. 1024–25), yet at other times, he assigned a place to one pagus in favor of another (as in the case of Ecussolles, which he assigned to the pagus of Autun [p. 1068]). For a discussion of the ambiguity of boundaries in the Middle Ages and of cartographic solutions to depict them, see Norman D. Schlesser, "Frontiers in Medieval French History," *International History Review* 6 (1984): 159–73.

66. Chaume, *Origines* II/3:1028.
67. Bange, p. 550.
68. Bange (p. 535) speculates that at one time the villae of the Mâconnais may have been economic units, each belonging to a family. As we shall see, those holding land in the same villa had important and close relations with one another.

we do not know if it included something like a village proper or if the population was widely scattered.[69]

Place-Name Identifications: Problems and Solutions

It is of the utmost importance, then, to recognize that any modern equivalent of a place name in the charters of Cluny is bound to be approximate, no matter how certain it seems. For the very organization of the countryside taken for granted by the charters was changing (the charters are, again, ironically, its witness) into a pattern which, however transformed by modern farming methods, probably remains nevertheless the underlying structure of the French city and its commune today.[70]

There is, then, essentially a hierarchy of uncertainties in the place-name identifications for Cluniac charters. Some villae, such as the villa Lornant in the charter quoted earlier, bequeathed their names to modern settlements, in this case Lournand (ca. Cluny). Others are like the villa Bieria, which left its name ("en Biérin" on cadastral maps) at a place near the modern Sainte-Cécile-la-Valouse (ca. Cluny).[71] A place such as the villa Vetus Curtis, however, has left no trace in modern names. Its approximate location may be fixed only if the charters give other information. In the case of Vetus Curtis, Déléage was able to locate *lieux-dits* belonging to it in various sections of five different present-day cities.[72] Clearly no single point on a modern map will suffice to locate Vetus Curtis, but for convenience Ravry (ca. Cluny) is used here (as in Déléage and Chaume) to in-

69. See the remarks of Henri Dubled, "Quelques observations sur le sens du mot *villa*," *Le Moyen Age* 59 (1953):1–9, and most recently, Elisabeth Magnou-Nortier, "A propos du temporel de l'abbaye de Lagrasse: Etude sur la structure des terroirs et sur les taxes foncières du IXe au XIIe siècle," in *Sous la règle de saint Benoît: Structures monastiques et sociétés en France du moyen âge à l'époque moderne*, Colloquium, Abbaye Sainte-Marie, 23–25 October 1980 (Geneva: Droz, 1982), pp. 235–64, esp. 235–53.

70. See, however, the remarks of P. D. A. Harvey in Sawyer, pp. 155–56, which caution against assuming continuity between even late medieval and modern settlement patterns.

71. Déléage, pp. 234 n. 3 and 409 n. 3. All places identified in the present book are dép. Saône-et-Loire unless otherwise noted. Chaume identified the villa Bieria as Le Nière (Chaume, *Origines* II/3:1097 n. 9 and passim), but Déléage found the trace of its name on the cadaster of Mazille.

72. Déléage, p. 235 n. 7, naming in fact seven present-day cities, of which the last two seem incorrectly linked to the charter in question.

dicate the approximate location. Yet Vetus Curtis is an example of the most precise identification possible for villae that have disappeared. There are other villae, such as Mons Betonus, which can be located only as being within the ager to which it is attached.[73]

The villae just described are the places most easily amenable to identification. Some villae appear in charters without any information about their ager or even their pagus. These places must be identified on a case by case basis. For example, if several villae are mentioned in such a charter, all with names familiar from a particular pagus, then one assumes that that is the pagus in question. Or, in other instances, if the people in the charter are known to have land in a particular pagus, and the name of the villa is homonymous with one in that pagus, then the places are assumed to be the same.

Finally, there are villae with such common names that, unless the charter gives more specific information, they cannot be assigned to any particular location. Such are, for example, the many villa Vals and villa Mons, which correspond to the many cities named Vaux and Mont in present-day France.

Given all these difficulties, it is quite extraordinary that scholars have managed to make the many identifications that they have. Unfortunately, there is not yet a *Dictionnaire topographique* for the Saône-et-Loire, to which many villae in Cluny's charters belong.[74] But the Mâconnais has had its local historians—most notably Chaume and Déléage—who have used the charters of Cluny (among others) to reconstruct the topography of ninth- and tenth-century Burgundy.[75] What remains is the identification of places farther afield.

In 1920, when Guy de Valous undertook a study of the domain of Cluny, he assigned identifications to places in the Lyon-

73. E.g., BB 967;II:63–64, Mons Betonus in ager Prisciaco, and therefore somewhere in the vicinity of *Prisciacus*, i.e., Pressy-sous-Dondin (ca. Saint-Bonnet-de-Joux). For lists of such villae, see, for example, Chaume, II/3, pp. 1086–89.

74. *Dictionnaire topographique de la France comprenant les noms de lieu anciens et modernes*, 37 vols. (Paris: Imprimerie Nationale, 1861–1979).

75. Mention should also be made of Gabriel Jeanton, *Pays de Mâcon et de Chalon avant l'an mille: Notes de géographie historique* (Dijon: Rebousseau, 1934).

nais, the Auvergne, the Viennois, and so on, as well as in the Mâconnais.[76] While his work on the Mâconnais was refined and completed by Chaume and Déléage, his work elsewhere was left unmodified. It formed the basis for many subsequent identifications. Yet, as Madeleine Oursel-Quarré has pointed out, many of Valous's attributions were incorrect.[77]

It is Mme Quarré herself who, for the last thirty years, has painstakingly gathered all the possible place-name identifications for the charters of Cluny, including those far from Mâcon. These are scheduled to be published as part of the index of Cluny's charters, begun long ago by Alexandre Bruel.[78] We will soon be in a position to see, with as great a precision as is likely possible (but recognizing the limitations of any identification), the locations of places named in the charters of Cluny.

The present work is indebted to multiple lines of historical research. If it poses any new questions and suggests any further answers, this is because many of the old issues have been resolved. What this study cannot do, however, is transcend the limitations of its sources. Nearly all the evidence for the prop-

76. Guy de Valous, "Le domaine de l'abbaye de Cluny aux Xe et XIe siècles," *Annales de l'Académie de Mâcon*, 3d ser., 22 (1920): 299–481, issued as a separate publication, under the same title, with the additional subtitle, *Formation, Organisation, Administration* (Paris: E. Champion, 1923); *Le monachisme clunisien des origines au XVe siècle: Vie intérieure des monastères et organisation de l'ordre* (1935; 2d ed., Paris: Picard, 1970); and *Le temporel et la situation financière des établissements de l'ordre de Cluny du XIIe au XIVe siècle*, Archives de la France monastique 41 (Paris: Picard, 1935).

77. Oursel-Quarré, pp. 103–7. For the reliance on Valous, see, e.g., Poeck, "Laienbegräbnisse"; Hubert Jedin, Kenneth S. Latourette, and Jochen Martin, eds., *Atlas zur Kirchengeschichte* (Freiburg: Herder, 1970), map. 47, with "Kommentare" by I. Liebrich, p. 36: "Die Identifizierungen basieren auf den Arbeiten von G. de Valous." Few cartographers reveal their sources so explicitly, but it is quite likely most of them have consulted Valous. See Rosenwein, "Cartographic Patterns."

78. A collaborative effort including Michel Petitjean, M. Oursel-Quarré, Jean Richard (Dijon), and J. Wollasch and M. Hillebrandt (Münster). The sources for the place-name identifications in this book, unless otherwise noted, are (for the pagi of Autun, Mâcon, and Chalon): Déléage; Chaume, *Origines* II/3; Jeanton. For places elsewhere the sources are: the files of Mme Quarré; Johann G. T. Graesse, F. Benedict, and H. Plechl, eds., *Orbis Latinus: Lexikon lateinischer geographischer Namen des Mittelalters und der Neuzeit*, 3 vols. (Braunschweig: Klinkhardt und Biermann, 1972); Laurence Henri Cottineau and G. Poras, *Répertoire topo-bibliographique des Abbayes et Prieurés*, 3 vols. (vols. 1 and 2, Mâcon: Protat, 1939, vol. 3, Paris, 1971); Longnon, *Atlas historique*; and various volumes of the *Dictionnaire topographique*.

erty of Cluny in the tenth and eleventh centuries, and for the people who gave or took or somehow participated in that property, comes from charters. Yet those charters are in many ways unsatisfactory (albeit the only available) sources. Let us set forth the problems in these charters in bold relief. They were written to record only major events in property transfers. Although some of these documents speak of the transfer taking place *per cartam* (by means of the charter), there is no certainty that a charter was always drawn up. The change about 1030–40 in the nature and precision of the charters (a change which led Georges Duby to speak of a decline in the value of the written act and François Bange to speak of the transformation of the countryside) sets these problems squarely in center stage.[79] Charters do not necessarily tell us what happened; they tell us how people wanted themselves and their actions to be recorded and perhaps remembered. They present us with a "public face."[80] To compound these difficulties, many of the charters are lost. Those that remain extant are, on the whole, copies (some very late copies indeed). Some are assigned a date with only moderate certainty and a few with no certainty at all.[81] They name people who may or may not be the same as others with their name. They contain places that, at best, correspond only approximately

79. Duby, *La société*, p. 9; Bange, p. 531. See below, Chapter 5, for further remarks on the changes in the charters c. 1040.

80. I am indebted to conversations with Professor Karl Brunner, University of Vienna, on this point. Most of the charters are, of course, classified in diplomatics as "private acts" because they were drawn up by "private" persons, i.e., persons in whom the *fides publica* was not vested. But they were public documents in the sense of being open and witnessed. See Arthur Giry, *Manuel de diplomatique: Diplômes et chartes—chronologie technique—éléments critiques et parties constitutives de la teneur des chartes—les chancelleries—les actes privés* (Paris: Hachette, 1894), esp. pp. 823–62; Alain de Boüard, *Manuel de diplomatique française et pontificale* vol. 2: *L'acte privé* (Paris: Picard, 1948). But even the distinction between public and private persons deriving from Roman conceptions is probably anachronistic when applied to the tenth and eleventh centuries. See Heinrich Fichtenau, *Das Urkundenwesen in Österreich vom 8. bis zum frühen 13. Jahrhundert* MIÖG, Erg. 23 (Vienna: Böhlaus, 1971), pp. 76 and 79.

81. For date changes that were made as a result of the studies done for this book, see Appendix F. Other date changes were adopted from Chaume, "Obs.", "En Marge 1" and "En Marge 2"; Hillebrandt, "Datierungen." I have only selectively used the changes suggested in Etienne Fournial, "La souveraineté du Lyonnais au Xe siècle," *Le Moyen Age* 62 (1956): 413–52, which are based solely on considerations of probable political jurisdictions of the kings named in the charters.

to present-day locations. These caveats must be borne in mind. It would be tedious if every identification or generalization in the ensuing chapters were to be followed by a question mark; but that is, in fact, what the reader is hereby invited to supply.

It is only fair, however, to balance these rather bleak caveats with the larger view. The charters of Cluny allow us to see in detail at least four aspects of the period in question: (1) the interactions between different groups of people: monks and donors, witnesses and neighbors, parents and children; (2) the flux of property as villae changed hands over time; (3) the long memories attached to parcels of land and to groups associated with them; (4) the general patterns of property transfer, distribution, and consolidation over time. Despite their problems, the charters offer us a precious glimpse into a process of give and take in the tenth and eleventh centuries.

CHAPTER ONE

The Problem of Donations

"THEIR SOLITARY CELLS in the hills were like tents filled with divine choirs—singing Psalms, studying, fasting, praying, rejoicing in the hope of the life to come, and laboring in order to give alms and preserving love and harmony among themselves. And truly it was like seeing a land apart."[1] Thus did Saint Athanasius describe the first monastic settlements. The idea of the monastery as a "land apart" from the rest of the world remained a constant—albeit continuously reinterpreted—goal within the many forms of Western monasticism.

Yet the monastery was always part of the world from which it stood aloof. It drew its recruits from that world, and it depended on the societies and economies in which it thrived. Saint Antony, Saint Athanasius's fourth-century hero, lived on the bread brought to him by an acquaintance. In the fifth and early sixth centuries, the monks at Lérins, who spread the ideals of ascetic monasticism through Gaul, were supported by the Gallo-Roman aristocracy. Later, when Columbanus came from Ireland to the Continent to found monasteries, at the end of the sixth century, Frankish aristocrats paved his way. From that time on, lay men and women were important patrons of monastic houses.

Indeed, by the late eighth century, those "in the world" had become some of the most important creators, disposers, and

1. Saint Athanasius, *The Life of Saint Antony*, trans. Robert T. Meyer (New York: Newman Press, 1950), p. 57. See Athanasius *Vita S. Antonii* 44 (*PG* 26, cols. 907–8).

active supporters of the "lands apart" from the world.[2] Under the Carolingians, monasteries were often established with royal support, but by the mid–ninth century the initiative for this, as for so much else, had again largely devolved into the hands of magnates. In the ninth century Gerald, self-styled "Count of Aurillac," founded a monastery, then looked for monks to inhabit it. A different count, Gerard, and his wife, Bertha, founded Vézelay in about 867.[3] There was, then, nothing especially extraordinary about Duke William the Pious and his wife founding a monastery at the villa of Cluny in 909.

Nevertheless, if Cluny's foundation was not exceptional, the sheer quantity of support that it subsequently received from the laity was quite extraordinary. This is one reason why it has received close scrutiny from medievalists. For the period 909–1049, nearly 3,000 charters of all sorts are contained in its archives.[4] Among other things, those documents allow us to ask

2. See Abbo's support of Novalesa in Patrick J. Geary, *Aristocracy in Provence: The Rhône Basin at the Dawn of the Carolingian Age*, (Philadelphia: University of Pennsylvania Press, 1985), and the monastic foundations chronicled in Heinrich Büttner, "Christentum und Kirche zwischen Neckar und Main im 7. und frühen 8. Jahrhundert," in *Sankt Bonifatius: Gedenkgabe zum zwölfhundertsten Todestag* (Fulda: Parzeller, 1954), pp. 362–87, esp. 371–79. This was part of the background for the reforms of Boniface. See Friedrich Prinz, *Frühesmönchtum im Frankenreich: Kultur und Gesellschaft in Gallien, den Rheinlanden und Bayern am Beispiel der monastischen Entwicklung (4. bis 8. Jahrhundert)* (Munich: Oldenbourg, 1965); Eugen Ewig, "Milo et eiusmodi similes," in *Sankt Bonifatius*, pp. 412–40; Theodor Schieffer, *Winfrid-Bonifatius und die christliche Grundlegung von Europas* (Freiburg: Herder, 1954), esp. pp. 130–33. On Pippin III, see Josef Semmler, "Pippin III. und die fränkische Klöster," *Francia* 3 (1975): 88–146.

3. For royal patronage, see Josef Semmler, "Karl der Grosse und das fränkische Mönchtum," in *Karl der Grosse: Lebenswerk und Nachleben*, ed. Wolfgang Braunfels, 5 vols. (Düsseldorf: Schwann, 1965) 2:255–89. On Gerald of Aurillac, see Odo of Cluny *De vita Sancti Geraldi* ii.4 (*PL* 133, cols. 972–73). On Gerard and Bertha, see *Monumenta Vizeliacensia: Textes relatifs à l'histoire de l'abbaye de Vézelay*, ed. R. B. Huygens, Corpus Christianorum, Continuatio Mediaevalis 42 (Turnhout: Brepols, 1976), no. 1 (dated 858–59), pp. 243–48. See Rosalind Kent Berlow, "Spiritual Immunity at Vézelay (Ninth to Twelfth Centuries)," *Catholic Historical Review* 62 (1976): 573–88. On Gerard, see René Poupardin, *Le royaume de Provence sous les Carolingiens (855–933?)* (Paris: Emile Bouillon, 1901), pp. 10–14, 36–38.

4. See above, Table 2. Cluny's charter materials are perhaps unrivaled for the tenth century. However, for the ninth century, there is the extraordinary collection of charters from Lorsch; see *Codex Laureshamensis*, 3 vols., ed. Karl Glöckner, (1929–36; repr., Darmstadt: Hesse historische Kommission, 1975), in which, for the period 755–855, for example, there are 3,427 charters (but for the period 856–956, only 150 charters); see tables in ibid., 1:66–261.

how transfers of property were understood and used in the tenth and eleventh centuries.

In an important sense, the uses made of property are part of a history of ideas and value systems. It is worth noting, for example, that in the twelfth and thirteenth centuries, the set of assumptions that permitted lay people to donate their land and serfs and to be involved in sales and exchanges with monks went out of favor as an ideal, even if it continued to be practiced without cessation.[5] But the way in which property is used is more than an idea. It is a fundamental part of economic, political, and social life. When we ask why and how people entered into land transactions with a monastery, and why monks entered into land transactions with people outside their walls, we are inquiring about the uses of a basic source of wealth and power.[6] What were the motives and circumstances that allowed, indeed fostered, land transfers? This is hardly the first time, inspired by Cluny, that a historian has posed this question, and the way in which it is to be answered in the course of this book relies in the first place on the solutions of the past. What follows is a brief summary of some of the most important formulations that have been adduced to explain donations to Cluny.[7]

5. On new attitudes toward property and the religious life, see Lester K. Little, *Religious Poverty and the Profit Economy in Medieval Europe* (Ithaca, N.Y.: Cornell University Press, 1978), esp. the discussion of the Cistercians, pp. 90–96. The overwhelming conclusion from the studies of Berman, esp. pp. 11–60, Wardrop, pp. 67–131, and Bouchard, *Sword*, pp. 173–89, is that the old sorts of property transactions remained a regular part of Cistercian monastic life despite legislation to the contrary.

6. See the discussion of monastic ambivalence toward benefactors in Emma Mason, "Timeo Barones et Donas Ferentes," in *Religious Motivation: Biographical and Sociological Problems for the Church Historian*, ed. Derek Baker, Studies in Church History 15 (Oxford: Blackwell, 1978), pp. 61–75; with, however, a rather jaundiced view of the monastic-patron relationship.

7. For a more complete and chronological survey of the literature on Cluny, see Rosenwein, *Rhinoceros*, pp. 3–29; for a discussion of motives for noble generosity to reformed monasteries in general, see Bouchard, *Sword*, pp. 225–46; for Fountains, see Wardrop, pp. 235–79; for la Trinité, Vendôme, see Penelope D. Johnson, *Prayer, Patronage, and Power: The Abbey of la Trinité, Vendôme, 1032–1187* (New York: New York University Press, 1981), pp. 69–102; for Montecassino, see Heinrich Dormeier, *Montecassino und die Laien im 11. und 12. Jahrhundert*, Schriften der MGH 27 (Stuttgart: Hiersemann, 1979), pp. 58–80. These constitute simply a sample of recent studies. For a bibliography on monasticism more generally, see Giles Constable, *Medieval Monasticism: A Select Bibliography* (Toronto: University of Toronto Press, 1976).

Salvation

Focus on the mutual motives of the laity and the monks of Cluny began in 1915, when Georg Schreiber published an article on donations to the church.[8] The crux of his thesis was that there was a clear relationship between the material gifts given by lay people and the spiritual gifts offered by clerics. Donations were from the first linked to liturgical services, Schreiber argued; and at Cluny the promise of prayers in return for gifts was developed to an unprecedented degree. The laity gave land and (above all) private proprietary churches because this assured their bodies a place in the monastic graveyard and their names a place in the monastic liturgy, particularly the masses for the dead. As part of a spiritual confraternity, lay people became, vicariously, members of the convent, participating in absentia with the abbot and the monks in the liturgy. All, in turn, were part of a larger community, formed by the saints, apostles, and martyrs.

Schreiber's ideas were given further elaboration in some of his later work and in the research of his student Willibald Jorden.[9] In their view, concern for the salvation of souls, for the commemoration of the dead, and for the spiritual confraternity of monks and laity was behind each gift to the monastery. The monastic liturgy was the key that opened the pocketbooks of the laity. As for the monks, their views were the same as those of the lay world, from whence, indeed, they were recruited. Inadvertently they grew to be even more like the laity by their accumulation of property. Eventually Cluny became a financial institution, playing a role in the new money economy and consolidating its holdings. But, in Schreiber's view, economic interests were the consequences, not the causes, of Cluny's wealth.[10]

---

8. Georg Schreiber, "Kirchliches Abgabenwesen an französischen Eigenkirchen aus Anlass von Ordalien," in *Gemeinschaften*, pp. 151–212, esp. pp. 162–82.

9. Georg Schreiber, "Cluny und die Eigenkirche," in *Gemeinschaften*, pp. 81–138, esp. 123–25; Willibald Jorden, *Das cluniazensische Totengedächtniswesen vornehmlich unter den drei ersten Äbten Berno, Odo und Aymard (910–954): Zugleich ein Beitrag zu den cluniazensischen Traditionsurkunden*, Münstersche Beiträge zur Theologie 15 (Münster: Aschendorf, 1930).

10. See esp. Schreiber, "Cluny und die Eigenkirche," in *Gemeinschaften*, pp. 121–22 and 134–36.

In an article published in 1965, H. E. J. Cowdrey refined this line of argument by locating the heyday of the confraternity during the abbacy of Saint Hugh (1049–1109).[11] Although Cowdrey continued to think that laymen had always given land to Cluny in order to "have a part in the prayers of the monks," he showed that the really decisive period for these liturgical benefits occurred after about 2,000 charters had been drawn up on Cluny's behalf, most of which involved laymen donating their lands.[12]

The problem posed by Cowdrey's work, then, is to understand why people before the abbacy of Hugh were involved in transactions with Cluny. Cowdrey convincingly pointed out the benefits accruing to them in the time of Hugh; but one cannot simply read the same motives back 150 years. At issue here are three conceptually separable considerations: prayer, confraternity, and commemoration of the dead at early Cluny.

The prayers for laymen in the *consuetudines*, the "customaries," of Cluny, do not appear to be much related to gift giving. When Cowdrey was writing, Cluny's earliest customaries had not yet been given the fine critical edition now available.[13] The so-called Farfa customary, the *Liber tramitis*, which probably dates from between 1020 and 1035 with later additions and changes, speaks of prayers for monastic benefactors in general; but laymen who were specifically named were of extremely high status.[14] There was a good deal of liturgy for the dead in general

11. Herbert Edward John Cowdrey, "Unions and Confraternity with Cluny," *Journal of Ecclesiastical History* 16 (1965): 152–62. See also Robert G. Heath, *Crux imperatorum philosophia: Imperial Horizons of the Cluniac "Confraternitas," 964–1109* (Pittsburgh, Pa.: Pickwick Press, 1976), esp. pp. 73–81. More recently, on confraternities in general, see Cowdrey, "Legal Problems Raised by Agreements of Confraternity," in Schmid and Wollasch, pp. 233–54.

12. See Appendix B, Illustration B.2. For the period 909–1049 there are about 2,983 charters, about 2,197 of which come under the heading of transfers of property to or from Cluny. The remainder consists in property not directly related to Cluny (including 100 charters from the period before Cluny's foundation), in confirmations and privileges, in requests for reforms (which, in terms of Appendix B are not considered property transfers per se), and in transactions not involving real property.

13. *CCM* 7/2: *Consuetudines Cluniacensium antiquiores cum redactionibus derivatis* and *CCM* 10: *Liber Tramitis aevi Odilonis Abbatis*, ed. Petrus Dinter.

14. E.g., prayers "pro imperatore" (*CCM* 10:285), or, as part of the martyrology, "Teudberga comitissa fidelis" (*CCM* 10:286); for certain laymen who die and are brought to the monastery for burial, there is an elaborate ritual, but for *mediocribus*, "eant [the monks] quanti prior iusserit" (*CCM* 10:284–85). During Rogation days, the monks chant *Deus auribus nostris* and fifteen psalms after

in this customary; but donors to the monastery did not automatically get more prayers than other departed faithful.[15] Liturgical benefits accrued far more to individual monks and clerics than to individual laymen, however generous.

As to confraternities, although it is beyond doubt that donors to Cluny thereby in some way became linked to its community, there is no trace of a confraternity book at Cluny.[16] It is true that some charters speak of a *societas* at Cluny, and the *Liber tramitis* speaks of a *liber vitae* there.[17] But these terms do not prove the existence of a true confraternity book. This kind of book—kept upon the altar and in which the names of monastic benefactors for whom the monks prayed were inscribed—was a ninth-century rather than a tenth-century phenomenon.

The sort of memorial book that was used at Cluny was the necrology, or *martyrologium*. It contained the names of the dead organized by date of death, and it was used during the chapter meeting, when the names appropriate to each day were read. Although no necrologies from Cluny survive, scholars working under the direction of Joachim Wollasch at Münster published in 1982 a concordance of nine necrologies from houses in Cluny's ecclesia. Taken together, they point to the contents of the one presumably in use at Cluny.[18] From the point of view of the problems posed here, the most important observation to be made about these synoptic lists is that they mainly concerned monks, not lay people. Of course, it is likely that some of the monks represented in the necrology were laymen who converted

---

Prime "pro omnium tribulationibus siue remunerationibus benefactorum necnon et pro defunctorum requiae." (*CCM* 10:102–3). On the date of the *liber tramitis*, see Dinter's discussion in *CCM* 10:xliii–lii.

15. Other early customaries speak of offices of the dead: "Uesperum et Officium Mortuorum et Matutinum eorum post Nocturnos" (*CCM* 7/2:127), psalms for the dead (ibid., p. 57), *psalmi familiares* for benefactors and the dead (ibid., p. 59, and see commentary in *CCM* 7/1:299.)

16. The argument here and the points below are outlined in Franz Neiske, "Communities and Confraternities in the Ninth and Tenth Centuries" (Paper presented at the 23d International Congress on Medieval Studies, Kalamazoo, Mich., 5–8 May 1988).

17. For the *liber vitae, CCM* 10:279.

18. Wollasch, *Synopse*; see above, Introduction. *CCM* 10:285 and passim. See Nicolas Huyghebaert and Jean-Loup Lemaitre, eds., *Les documents nécrologiques*, fasc. 4 of *Typologie des sources du moyen âge occidentale*, ed. Léopold Genicot (Turnhout: Brepols, 1972).

on their deathbeds. It is also likely that the names of *local* lay donors to Cluny were included in *its* necrology but are impossible to recapture now through a synopsis of "cluniac" necrologies. Finally, as Franz Neiske has shown, it is clear that the names of at least some outside benefactors lurk among those classified as monks in the necrology of Marcigny, the list closest to the one Cluny must have possessed.[19] By the time the list at Marcigny was drawn up, the true status of these benefactors had been forgotten. Nevertheless, donors were not the primary group memorialized in the necrologies; the evidence elsewhere suggests conclusions similar to the one argued here.[20]

It is striking that relatively few Cluniac charters for the period before 1049 ask for prayers. One cannot consider the words *pro anima* (a very common formula by which a donation was given on behalf of the soul of someone) as a petition for prayer. On the contrary (as will be seen in Chapter 4), the words are in fact shorthand for a longer preamble that expresses the redemptive effects of giving away worldly goods to gain celestial ones, of pious gift-giving per se, quite apart from intercessory prayers.[21] When Wollasch himself turned, as we shall soon see, to look at the relationship between lay patronage and monastic practice, his conclusions took him far from the the liturgical *Gegengaben* postulated by Schreiber. Naturally, Cluny's prayers and commemoration of the dead remain important for understanding why laymen wanted to associate themselves with the monastery. But they are not the complete explanation.

One other connection already noted by Schreiber, Jorden, and Cowdrey remained: burial in Cluny's grounds. A scholar working under Wollasch, Dietrich Poeck, put this motive at center stage in 1981. Noting that Cluny had a ritual for burial of the dead, Poeck undertook to discover precisely who was given this privilege. He inventoried all the donation charters containing

19. Neiske.
20. E.g., for Montecassino, see Dormeier, p. 121: "Der Kreis der Laien, die nach ihrem Tod auf das Gebetsgedenken des Mönche rechnen konnten, war—wie man sieht [pp. 114–20] ziemlich exklusive." See also his pp. 164–71. Dormeier sees a change in about 1038 (pp. 171–98).
21. See Heinrich Fichtenau, *Arenga: Spätantike und Mittelalter im Spiegel der Urkundenformeln*, MIÖG, Erg. 18 (Graz: Böhlaus, 1957), esp. pp. 141–44; Jobert, pp. 139–225, illuminates the history of the *pro anima* formula precisely as the development of a theme of redemptive giftgiving.

the formula *in locum sepulture,* (the right to interment in Cluny's grounds)—or formulas akin to it, such as donations *ad sepulturam*—listing the names of the donors and the nature of their gift, and making maps of the places that were given to Cluny. Poeck concluded that donors ad sepulturam came from every class; their donations ranged from major land grants to small plots. These gifts allowed Cluny to consolidate its holdings along a northwest axis and outward on all sides to a limit of about twenty kilometers from the monastery.[22]

Poeck's findings, significant as they are, cannot, however, account for all or even the majority of donations to the monastery. Using his own calculations, such donations constituted at most (under Abbot Odilo) 17.36 percent of the extant donation charters.[23] Under the other abbots, charters for burial were still more rare. It is true that Poeck found that, for many of the more well-to-do families that gave to Cluny, a gift in locum sepulturae was only one "link in a chain of donations."[24] But this need not mean that it was the most important aspect of their relationship to the monastery.

If the monks did not primarily pray for lay donors, and if donations ad sepulturam constituted only a small fraction of the donations made to Cluny, then salvation through the liturgy or

22. On the class of the donors, Poeck, "Laienbegräbnisse," p. 106; on consolidation, pp. 107, 129, and passim.

23. Ibid., p. 122. There are, of course, different ways to read the charters, so that every researcher will come up with a different number. For example, Poeck does not include as a "donation" charter BB 520,I:506, which speaks of a "werpitio seu donatio." This is a matter of interpretation. More serious is the fact that Poeck does not take note of the remarks of Chaume, "En Marge I" and "En Marge 2," regarding charters in BB I, so that, for example, at least eight (and possibly ten) of the charters in locum sepulture of the twenty-one that he places in Odo's abbacy probably do not belong there (BB 301;I:301; BB 313;I:308; BB 324;I:315–16; BB 326;I:317; BB 349;I:330; BB 338;I:324; BB 442;I:430–31; BB 465;I:451–52; and possibly also BB 304;I:303; BB 343;I:326). According to my own calculations (see Appendix B, Illustration B.2) there are 1,651 donation charters for the period 909–1049, and of these, 250 are ad sepulturam, or about 15 percent of the total. But, in my view, charters of donation were only one form of lay contact with the monastery, and donations ad sepulturam formed an even smaller percentage of all charters documenting lay/monastic transactions.

24. Poeck, "Laienbegräbnisse," p. 105. There is an illuminating discussion of the relationship between donation and liturgy for the dead in Molly Megan McLaughlin, "Consorting with Saints: Prayer for the Dead in Early Medieval French Society" (Ph.D. diss., Stanford, 1985), pp. 58–67, 188–89; for the relationship between donation and intercessory prayer, pp. 166–89. I am grateful to Professor McLaughlin for sending me a copy of her dissertation.

burial in hallowed monastic grounds cannot be the whole answer to the question of why the world outside and the world
inside the cloister met over property.

Economic Insurance

The motive of acquisition was, it would seem, the most obvious one to ascribe to the monks, but, by the same token, the
most perplexing *not* to ascribe to the laity. What possible economic purpose could monastic patronage have for lay people? In
Schreiber's view, there was an economic method to the mad-
ness of giving away one's property: the monastery was so beset
by disputes about what belonged to it and what to its patrons
that in the end it made payments back to the laity.[25] In the
1950s, in his book on the Mâconnais, Georges Duby spoke of
precarial donations, that is, gifts made by the abbey of Cluny *to*
laymen, that helped to create some of the great lay fortunes in
the region.[26]

But what of those not so favored? Joachim Wollasch suggests a
new answer.[27] He argues that the spate of monastic conversions
at the end of the eleventh century were (ironically) a way in
which families retained their patrimony. By that time, generous
donors to Cluny had depleted much of their resources; but by
the conversion of one of their sons, accompanied by a sizeable
donation, they could, through their child, continue to adminis-
ter the patrimony that they had given away.[28]

Yet, the great age of conversions was late: by then families
and groups—few of whom actually entered the cloister—had

25. Schreiber, "Eigenkirche," in *Gemeinschaften*, esp. pp. 123–25.
26. Duby, *La société*, pp. 57–58. For precarial donations (gifts of land made by
the monastery for the life of the recipient), see Chapter 4.
27. Joachim Wollasch, "Parenté noble et monachisme reformateur: Observations sur les 'conversions' à la vie monastique aux XIᵉ et XIIᵉ siècles," *Revue
historique* 264 (1980): 3–24.
28. See Eric John, "'Secularium Prioratus' and the Rule of Saint Benedict,"
Revue Bénédictine 75 (1965): 212–39, esp. pp. 224–27; John argues that because
of the connection between families and their land, monasteries to which families donated "came in turn into the family" (p. 225), for example, by the de facto
arrangement that all abbots would come from the founder's family. But John
exempts Cluny from this pattern.

been making donations to Cluny (and Cluny had been accepting them) for nearly two hundred years. The search for motives thus continues.

Economic Systems

One of the most fruitful approaches has grown out of a relatively new view of the economy of the tenth and eleventh centuries. Chapter 4 will take up in detail the genesis and subsequent history of the idea of the "gift economy." At this point, a few remarks may suffice. It was Georges Duby who, in the 1970s, popularized the use of this anthropological formulation to describe a noncommercial system of exchange in the early Middle Ages. Gold and silver were plentiful and goods changed hands, but they did so because of social systems and mental attitudes that dictated that plunder be taken, gifts be given, and prestige be measured in terms of display and generosity.[29]

This economic model helped to illuminate the meaning of property transactions at Cluny. Lester K. Little, whose primary interest was the commercial period, nevertheless best postulated the mechanisms involved in cases such as Cluny.[30] Rich laymen outside the monastery walls demonstrated their status and retained their prestige by their largess to the monks. Meanwhile the monks could live in good conscience with all their wealth and potential wealth because they, too, accepted the view that gifts denoted prestige and were an appropriate tribute to their spiritual life. From the historian's point of view, the monks' use of wealth (in commerce, in building projects) helped to create a money economy; but from their own point of view such wealth was the source of new gifts and fitting display. Land was given out in precarial arrangements, precious liturgical vessels were commissioned, and a huge and sumptuous church was built to

29. Georges Duby, *The Early Growth of the European Economy: Warriors and Peasants from the Seventh to the Twelfth Century*, trans. Howard B. Clarke (Ithaca, N.Y.: Cornell University Press, 1974), pp. 48–57.

30. Little, *Religious Poverty*, esp. pp. 3–8, 61–69. See also McLaughlin, pp. 169–72, who uses the notion of the gift economy to talk about the way in which donations helped define the social status of the giver.

house monks splendidly attired. Was this not the proper way to petition the gift-giving Lord in heaven?

And yet, this is only a part of the story. For the gift economy implies a certain kind of social system. It formed an essential component (in various marriage gifts, for example, and gifts to children) of the most basic building blocks of the social fabric, the family. And it helped in complex ways to define friends on the one hand and enemies on the other. If those who participated in the gift economy did not calculate monetary values, that was because the social meaning, rather than the thing given or traded or taken, was paramount. Thus one cannot simply say that Cluny fit into the context of a gift economy, but one must ask how it fit into the social network in which such an economy made sense. In short, what place did Cluny have in the society of the tenth and eleventh centuries, to command so much "necessary generosity"?

Social Motives

About ten years before his death, Maurice Chaume wrote what he called a "marginal" piece.[31] It was a two-part article on the first two abbots of Cluny, showing that the personal ties of the abbots and the major officers of the monastery were responsible for Cluny's material success. Because of their familial and geographical ties, the abbots and priors attracted major donations from afar; because of their importance in the immediate vicinity of Cluny, they commanded petty donations in the neighborhood.[32] The ties might be at one remove: many donors in the time of Abbot Berno (909–27), for example, were connected not so much to him as to his patron, William the Pious.

31. In Chaume, "En Marge 1" and "En Marge 2." In fact, Chaume had annotated his personal volumes of the charters of Cluny right on their margins, with suggestions about dates, places, and personal connections. He may have had this literal reference, as well as the more general one, in mind when making up the title. Mme Quarré kindly allowed me to consult Chaume's volumes, which are now in her keeping.

32. For Berno, for example, Chaume, "En Marge 1," p. 46: "En dehors des limites du *pagus Matisconensis*, Bernon fait des acquisitions infiniment plus importantes."

But this did not dilute their obligation to the monastery. For Chaume, personal relations explained the outpouring of lay donations during the period 909–42. And, Chaume suggested, his conclusions applied even more perfectly to the abbots to follow. Unfortunately, he never pursued the thesis further.

There are many merits to Chaume's argument, not the least of which was his stress on personal relations to explain property transfer. The present work will bear this out, though not as an argument about abbatial contacts as such. But there are also problems with Chaume's study. First, by limiting his discussion to relations with the first two abbots of Cluny, Chaume of necessity dealt with a very small sample of charters. Donation charters from the abbacies of Berno and Odo together number about 103. This figure must be compared with 272 for the abbacy of Aymard, 620 for the abbacy of Maiolus, and 613 for the abbacy of Odilo.[33] However suggestive his thesis was, it remained to be refined and elaborated.

Second, Chaume's pioneering efforts in the then relatively new field of prosopography has been superseded by subsequent scholarship.[34] Chaume was limited, in the main, to discussing members of the very highest aristocracy: kings, counts, ancestors of castellan and episcopal families. "Let us continue [he wrote in his survey] to descend the degrees of the feudal hierarchy and let us stop at the personages whom it has been possible to situate historically."[35]

I found a similar limitation when I argued several years ago that anomie, engendered by the experience of social mobility and the disjunction between social goals and social norms, led people to support Cluny, a model of well-regulated, changeless, normative behavior.[36] That study concentrated mainly on those

33. See Appendix B, Illustration B.2. There are forty-three charters of donation with dates so uncertain as to preclude assigning them to any abbacy.
34. For a discussion of the field, an overview of its history, and a useful bibliography, see George Beech, "Prosopography," in Powell, pp. 151–84. A journal devoted to the subject, *Medieval Prosopography*, is published by the Medieval Institute, Kalamazoo, Mich.
35. Chaume, "En Marge 2," p. 58.
36. Rosenwein, *Rhinoceros*. While the term "anomie" will not be used, and is not necessary here, it clearly might still apply to some of the findings to be presented: land transactions created social networks in a period that saw important transitions in the nature of the family, neighborhood, and social structure.

who handed monasteries over to Cluny for reform, a very small, if significant, sample of lay contact with Cluny. Now, however, new techniques and new questions are prodding historians to look not only at the highest levels of the aristocracy but also at persons of lesser rank.[37]

Crisis as a Motive

The lifestyle and the moral problems posed by the life of the warrior cut across social distinctions between knights and aristocrats. This was the perspective of Constance Bouchard's thorough study of the interrelationships between knights, nobles, and monasteries in Burgundy. For Bouchard, long-term careers and moments of personal crisis helped to explain lay patronage: "the life of the reformed monastery appealed exactly because it was so diametric to the normal noble [i.e., both knightly and aristocratic] life in the world."[38] Noble men and women, who believed in the reality of the next world, believed also in their own sinfulness, particularly at those critical junctures in their lives when the threat of death loomed. At these moments they became active monastic benefactors.[39]

The Thesis of This Book

The hour in which people made major donations may very will have been determined by turning points in the life cycle — we shall see some examples in the chapters that follow — but it must be admitted that the majority of charters are mute on

---

The claim in *Rhinoceros* that men of about the year 1000 were impoverishing themselves because of their donations to the monastery and because they subdivided their land among their children needs to be refined. At one level (from the hindsight of our modern point of view) this is true. But as we shall see, it was an unanticipated result of land donations that had a very different significance originally: that of retaining or forging social ties.

37. See the study of peasant donors in Wardrop, pp. 213–34; on knights, see Johnson, pp. 85–90; for Bouchard, *Sword*, see remarks below.

38. Bouchard, *Sword*, p. 244; and for the larger argument, pp. 238–46.

39. See also a similar argument in Alexander Murray, *Reason and Society in the Middle Ages* (Oxford: Clarendon Press, 1978) esp. pp. 350–82.

the matter. In any event, lay involvement with monks did not begin and end with a gift. Donations were only one part of the relationship that certain people outside the walls of the monastery had with those inside.[40] We find the same men and women not only witnessing donations but participating in sales, claiming and quitting their claims to land, and receiving grants from the monastery in turn. In brief, ongoing transactions with monks were part of the very fabric of social life, particularly in the neighborhood around Cluny.

Thus, donations had social meaning: they created and reinforced personal ties, with all the ambivalence inherent in such relationships. The links were with the monks of Cluny, of course; but they were above all with the saints that they served, and particularly with Saint Peter, heaven's doorkeeper. At the same time, donations, sales, and quarrels over land also had their secular social uses. They functioned to define groups and to enforce social cohesion. The entire process of property exchange created a web of interconnections and relationships. It was a primary social mechanism for uniting a society too often seen as simply fragmented and disorderly.

40. Bouchard, *Sword*, pp. 99–100 and passim, makes this point as well. McLaughlin, p. 180, argues that the primary goal of donation was to create a relationship with a community of "those who pray"; intercessory prayer was, then, a by-product of this relationship.

CHAPTER TWO

Givers and Takers: Land Donations as Social Events

IN 981 OR 982, Abbot Maiolus and the monks of Cluny made an exchange of land with a lady named Eva and her children (see Genealogy 1). Maiolus and the monks relinquished a mansus with a flour mill, fields, meadows, woods, and water at a villa named "Fontana."[1] In return, Eva, along with her sons, Girbaldus, Antelmus, and Bernardus, gave to the monks a mansus at Ciergues including fields, meadows, a serf and his wife; and they added a vineyard elsewhere in the same villa. At the same time, Eva and her sons gave a donation to Cluny of two fields at Ciergues, half of a curtilis at Bézornay (both ca. Cluny), and a flour mill. (For all places in this chapter, see Map 2.)

Genealogy 1. The family of Eva

```
                               Eva
                                |
        ┌───────────────┬───────┴───────┬──────────────────────┐
        │           Antelmus        Bernardus                   │
Gerard [2] = Rana = [1] Girbaldus          Adelaida [1] = Gauzfred = [2] Eve
```

Note: BB 2678;III:707–8 with Adelaida; BB 2090;III:283–84, with Eve. Evidence for the husbands and wives depicted here is discussed below and, in the case of Eve, in Appendix C.

This chapter and Chapter 3, as well as their corresponding Appendixes, C and D, make much use of the printout of the *Lemmatisierungprogramm* and of Hillebrandt, "Datierungen," both generously provided to me by Maria Hillebrandt. The substance of, and the methodological discussions in, her forthcoming book will be of the greatest importance for further research.

    1. For the exchange of land with Eva, BB 1584;II:628–29 (981–82). Chaume, "Obs.," for BB 572 says Fontana is near Charolles, but Chaume, *Origines* II/3:826 and 840, says it is not identified. Eva and her family are discussed in

"Grandmont" (St.-Gengoux-le-National)▲

•Vaux

Chevagny-sur-Guye
•

Grosne

Guye

Taizé▲

Flagy □

Massilly □

Farges▲ ▲Bézornay

"Vissandon" (St.-Vincent)▲

Collonge □

□ Merzé

"Vetus Canava" (La Chaume) □Varanges

Ciergues▲ ▲"Mons" (Donzy) ▲Lournand

Bassy▲

Chiddes▲

□Cotte

▲"Mailly" (Carrière des Moines) □

Cluny †

▲Buffières

•Château

AUTUNOIS

MÂCONNAIS

▲ Ste.-Cécile-la-Valouse

La Valouse

Villae not identified
(All in Autunois)
"Fontana"
"Mons"
"Clericorum"

•"Tissiacus" (St.-Point)

Grosne

KEY

Place names connected with:
▲ Family of Antelmus
□ Family of Arleus
• Other places

0   2 km.

Base map: Michelin 1:200,000 #69

Map 2. Places connected with Antelmus and his associates

Figure 2. The history of Fontana

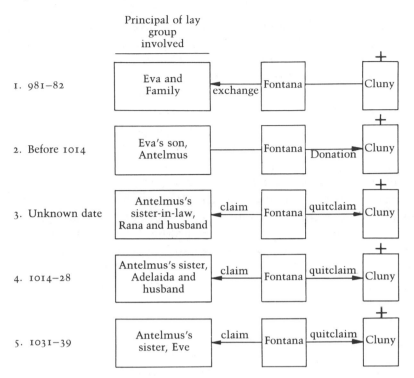

This exchange marked the beginning of a series of gifts and of revocations of gifts of Fontana that ended in about 1040. The give and take of Fontana may serve as a window onto the social nature of land transactions with Cluny up to the mid–eleventh century. (See Fig. 2.) The system that we shall describe, just as the place called Fontana, no doubt continued to exist after mid-century. But after that time this particular place disappears from the record, as does the family with whom it was formerly associated.

Chaume, *Origines* 1:413 n. 3, but Chaume incorrectly considers Eva identical to a woman of the same name who was married to a Count Gauzfredus, e.g., in BB 446;1:464 (4.936). On the terms *mansus* and *mansus indominicatus* (a demesne mansus), the units of exploitation most frequent in the charters, which included a "core"—*curtilis*—as well as outlying lands economically attached to it (the *appendicia*), see Duby, *La société,* pp. 38–41, and, more generally, his *Rural Economy and Country Life in the Medieval West,* trans. Cynthia Postan (Columbia: University of South Carolina Press, 1968), pp. 28–36.

The Give and Take of a Place

We do not know how Cluny came to have Fontana; the charter of exchange with Eva is the first time it appears in the extant documents. But after the monks at Cluny gave it to Eva, they did not lose sight of the property nor end their contact with her and her family. On the contrary, the transaction of 981/82 was apparently the beginning of a relationship that lasted for more than three generations and involved property far beyond the villa Fontana. For the moment, however, let us trace the history of this single piece of property.[2]

First, Antelmus, Eva's son, gave Fontana back to Cluny. This happened at some point between 981/82 and 1014, the date of Antelmus's death.[3] The donation was for the salvation of Antelmus's soul and the souls of his brothers, Girbaldus and Bernardus, and other members of his family.[4] Thereafter followed a series of events, all of which took place after Antelmus's death, in which three separate claims to Fontana were brought and then quit (in other words, quitclaimed) by three different women. In the process, the claimants, along with their families, became important associates of Cluny.

All of the women were related to Antelmus. The most remote was Rana, Antelmus's sister-in-law. She had been married to his brother, Girbaldus, for whose soul Fontana had been given to Cluny. But at the time she made claim to Fontana, she had been widowed and remarried. Her new husband, Gerard, joined her in

2. The reconstruction of events depends on dating the charters, which at times must remain uncertain. The notes will provide the interested reader with the pieces of the puzzle and the many questions that are involved in interpreting the charters.

3. In BB 2689;III:717–18 (8.1014), Antelmus gives a donation but is not present. It is one Hugo, instead, "qui firmavit et aliis firmare rogavit," the formula normally used for the principal. The donation is given ad sepulturam. BB III:718 n. 1 suggests Antelmus had died and Hugo made the donation in his name, the interpretation adopted here.

4. BB 129;I:140–41 (Chaume, "Obs.," after 1014). This was not the original donation but rather a quitclaim, in which Antelmus's donation is mentioned. However, the phrase here "sicut Antelmus in carta quam fecit Sancto Petro annotavit," implies that there once was a written document that is now lost. See also BB 2678;III:707–8.

the "quitclaim or donation" (the ambiguity is significant) of the land at Fontana.[5] The history of the gift of this land and its pious significance were recounted at the proceedings of the quitclaim: Fontana was "the alms which Antelmus made for himself and for his brothers Girbaldus and Bernardus at Fontana and at Farges."[6] But now Rana and Gerard tied the gift to their own welfare as well. They were granted, in return for their quitclaim, burial in Cluny's cemetery.

Rana's claims to the land were, thus, not so much denied as satisfied; for she and her husband were said to donate Fontana at the same time that they quitclaimed it. Their rights to the land were not utterly rejected, nor was that necessary. The proceedings of claim and quitclaim created, through a piece of land already charged with the significance of a pious donation, a second set of associations. The quitclaim bound Rana and her new husband to the monks, or more specifically to Saint Peter, whom the monks served, in ways that the original exchange had not made explicit and in other ways that it had not envisaged at all. Invoking the donation that Antelmus made to Saint Peter, their quitclaim affirmed at one stroke a model of piety and a set of relationships: between Antelmus and his brothers, between Antelmus and Saint Peter and the monks of Cluny, between Rana and her new husband and these others. In this way, the quitclaim created a chain of relationships with Saint Peter that

5. The following observations may be made about Rana's marriages. BB 2392;III:488 (997) appears to record the time of Girbaldus's death, for the document involves a donation by Antelmus and Bernardus for the soul of their brother Girbaldus; but whereas Antelmus, Bernardus, their mother, Eva, and Girbaldus's wife, Rana, are present, Girbaldus himself is not. Yet gifts were often made pro anima for those who were still alive (see below). In BB 129;I:140–41, Rana is married to Gerard. It is unlikely that Gerard is simply another name for Girbaldus because (1) in all other charters that refer to him, he is called nothing other than Girbaldus; and (2) even in BB 129, Gerard and Girbaldus are kept distinct: "ego Gerardus et uxor mea Raina facimus vuerpitionem necnon, si aliquid habemus rectum, donationem de [helemosina quam Antelmus fecit pro se et pro fratribus suis Girbaldo et Bernardo . . .]" (There are two copies of this charter in cartulary A, and the brackets add the material from the first.) Gerard may be the same as the Gerard who appears in BB 127;I:139 (Chaume, "Obs," groups together BB 127, 128, and 129 and dates them all after 1014).

6. The villa Fargias here has two possible identifications: la Fâ (ca. Tramayes) or Farges (ca. Cluny); see Chaume, Origines II/3:1123–24 n. 22 and 1130 n. 3. Its inclusion as part of Antelmus's donation is unique here. It is clear, however, that Antelmus had property there, some of which he donated in BB 2689;III:717–18 (8.1014).

extended from the past of Girbaldus and Antelmus, to the present of Rana and her new husband, to the future of their death
and burial.

Antelmus's two sisters, Adelaida and Eve, also claimed Fontana. Adelaida's claim was made between 1014 and 1028.[7] It
was made quit through the good offices of Landric, count of
Nevers:

> I always wanted the monks to have a tranquil life and to fulfill
> their vows to God day and night without impediment. There is a
> claim which a certain noble lady, named Adelaida, the wife of
> Gauzfred, has against Saint Peter and the monastery at Cluny over
> the land . . . at Fontana which her brother Antelmus gave to Saint
> Peter for the salvation of his father and mother, his brothers and all
> his relatives. I am redeeming this land [i.e., paying Adelaida] for the
> sum of three pounds, and if the woman in question seems to have
> any rights in that land, then I receive her assent.[8]

Adelaida not only agreed to the arrangement worked out by
Landric, but she also gave to Cluny a mansus at "Mons" (near
Donzy-le-National), "for the redemption of the souls of herself,
her husband, and her sons," Girbaldus and Rotbert.[9] Girbaldus

7. BB 2678;III:707–8. It is dated about 1010 by BB but that is simply a guess.
It can be dated certainly between 992 and 1028 because it involves Landric,
count of Nevers, who appears as count in 992 and who died in 1028. But, since
the charter speaks of land Antelmus had given to Cluny, Antelmus most likely
is dead.

8. BB 2678;III:707–8: "Ego Landricus, gratia Dei comes, semper obtavi mo-
nachos tranquillam vitam habere, et absque impedimento vota sua Deo persol-
vere die noctuque. Ideoque querelam quandam quam habet quędam nobilis fem-
ina, nominę Adelaida, uxor Gotfredi [= in the same document, Gautfredus and
Gauzfredus], contra Sanctum Petrum et Cluniacense cenobium, ex terra que est
sita in pago Augustudunensi, in villa quę vulgo dicitur Fontinellulas [= Fontana],
quam dedit frater ejus Antelmus Sancto Petro, pro salute patris et matris, fratrum et omnium parentum suorum, quam terram ego precio trium librarum
redimo; et si quid predicta mulier in eadem terra rectum habere videbatur, inde
accipio astipulationem." On Landric, see BB 2781;III:805–7, BB 2811;IV:13– 14,
and the discussion in Bouchard, Sword, pp. 341–43.

9. BB 2678; III:707–8. The document, which we know through its copy in
cartulary A, is rather unclear regarding these sons, but it seems that Adelaida
had one child of her own, named Girbaldus, and her husband, Gauzfred, had one
of his own, named Rotbert: "S[ignum]: Adeleidis, que hanc donationem fecit. S.
Girbaldi filii ejus. S. Gauzfredi ejus mariti. S. Rotberti filii sui." BB have here in
fact changed the order of cartulary A, which had the names of Adelaida and
Girbaldus at the end of the act. The villa Mons referred to here, which was in
the pagus of Mâcon, was not the same as the villa Monte in BB 127;I:139, 128;
I:139–40, and 2689;III:717–18, but was the same place as the villa Mons given
by Antelmus himself in BB 2489;III:570 (999–1000).

was no doubt named after his uncle. Adelaida's quitclaim afforded benefits and associations that had not been made explicit in Antelmus's act. The redemptive effects of the original donation of Fontana now, through the quitclaim, fell particularly on Adelaida, her husband, and her sons.

The third quitclaim, that of Eve, another of Antelmus's sisters, took place at some time between 1031 and 1039.[10] At a solemn meeting, which included representatives from Cluny as well as laymen and members of the secular clergy, Eve and her sons, recorded as Wichard, Hugo, Jocerannus, G—— and L—— "quit every claim and challenge" that they had against the monks. Fontana's associations were duly recalled: it was the land "which my brother Antelmus, the uncle of my children, gave to Saint Peter at Cluny." And Eve's quitclaim, like the others, was also a donation and in this case a sale as well: Eve and her sons accepted fifty solidi for it. But that was only the beginning. They and other relatives, both living and dead, became participants and partners, *participes ac consortes*, in the society and charity of the monks. In addition, at her death, Eve was to be received in Cluny's burial grounds without paying any fee, unless one were freely given by one of her heirs. A lay woman could not associate more completely with a monastery. It must have been a heady moment when Eve and her son Wichard presented themselves before Abbot Odilo, to be received by him formally into Cluny's *societas*.[11]

Thus ended the *werpitiones*, or quitclaims, regarding Fontana. As a whole, they show us various members of Antelmus's family quarreling and negotiating with the abbey over a piece of land and tying themselves ever more firmly to the monastery in the process. Were these events isolated ones, there would be justification in seeing in them simply the sort of battle over land and rights—with rapacious heirs and monks patiently amassing their patrimony with the spiritual "weapons" at their disposal —that has long been the interpretation of such events.[12] But a closer look reveals something more.

10. BB 2090;III:283–84. See Appendix C, n. 1, for problems and solutions connected with this charter.

11. The ceremony is described in BB 2090.

12. E.g., Bloch, pp. 131–33; Duby, "Evolution des institutions judiciaires," in *Hommes et structures*, pp. 38–39 and n. 222; Stephen Weinberger, "Les conflits entre clercs et laïcs dans la Provence du XIᵉ siècle," *Annales du Midi* 92 (1980):

Antelmus and Cluny

A closer look requires the exploration of two related issues. First, gift taking was not one generation's way to recoup the losses of its fathers but rather was simultaneous with gift giving.[13] The same persons, or, in any event, the same groups, were involved in both. This leads to the second issue. Giving and taking were social events in which relatives, associates, and neighbors participated. These people were involved not in rapacity per se, but rather, quite literally, in an ongoing process of give and take with each other and with the monks of Cluny and the saints they served.

In order to demonstrate this, we need first to reconstruct what donors did with land, and where and when they did it. In other words, we need to look at donations by plotting them, as it were, in space and time. Let us first follow Antelmus in order to show the scope of his transactions and the extent of his associations to both people and properties.[14] Throughout much of his life, Antelmus was actively involved in giving to and taking away from the monastery of Cluny. He usually did so in tandem with at least one of his brothers, whether he was the principal in

---

269–79; but for a more nuanced view, see Bouchard, *Sword*, pp. 209–17. Johnson, pp. 76–85, speaks of the counts of Vendôme as predators and patrons of la Trinité, but this is handled as a special case.

13. See Gurevich, *Categories*, p. 336, on the linguistic connection between "to give" and "to take."

14. The name Antelmus appears in eighteen extant charters before 1050: BB 129;I:140–41; BB 495;I:480–81, BB 572;I:551, BB 603;I:566–67, BB 1225;II:306, BB 1584;II:628–29; BB 1619;II:656–57, BB 1657;II:690–91, BB 1764;III:27; BB 2000;III:213; BB 2090;III:283–84; BB 2115;III:301–2; BB 2317;III:438; BB 2351; III:461; BB 2392;III:488; BB 2489;III:570; BB 2678;III:707–8; BB 2689;III:717–18. Four of these pertain to an Antelmus in the pagus of Lyon (BB 1225, BB 1764, BB 2000, BB 2317), probably a different Antelmus from the one who interests us. One (BB 603) concerns an Antelmus who was the son of Eve, that is, a nephew of "our" Antelmus. Most of those that remain appear to apply to the Antelmus of villa Fontana. However, BB 2115 concerns land at Massy (ca. Cluny) that borders on land of one Antelmus. None of the other names in this charter is familiar from the corpus of Antelmus charters, nor is Massy a place that is associated with him. BB 495, listing an Antelmus as a witness, dates from 939. It concerns an exchange of land at Sainte-Cécile-la-Valouse, where (it is revealed in BB 2392), our Antelmus and his brother had land to give. Assuming Antelmus died about 1014, he could just possibly have been alive and witnessing an act in 939; but none of the other names in the charter connects it with the charters of the 980s and 990s, when our Antelmus was particularly active.

the affair or simply present at a transaction by someone else. He was most active during the 980s and 990s, and the last we hear of him is in a charter ad sepulturam in 1014.

At first, in the 980s, Antelmus did not play a principal role in relationships with Cluny. Rather, at about the time that he and his mother and brothers were exchanging land with Cluny and acquiring Fontana, he and his brother Girbaldus were among the witnesses to a donation at Taizé (ca. Saint-Gengoux) to God and his Apostles Peter and Paul at Cluny.[15] Part of this donation was made by a man named Odilo, and part by the widow of Odilo's brother Wichard. Gathered together as witnesses were Gauzerannus, a neighbor whose land bordered on the land that was donated, and his sons Maiolus Poudreux and Israel. These men were part of the family that would later become castellans known as the Grossi. We shall return to them repeatedly.[16] Present as well were four men who remain unidentified;[17] then Girbaldus and Antelmus (the brothers whom we are following in detail); and, finally, two brothers named Arleus and Bernardus.[18] Arleus, who was the vassal of Gauzerannus, was there partly because of that tie and partly because he held a good deal of land at Taizé.[19]

The next year Antelmus and Girbaldus witnessed another donation. This time the gift to Cluny concerned land at Chiddes (ca. Saint-Bonnet-de-Joux) and land and forests at "Grandmont" (near Saint-Gengoux). The donor was Teodericus, levita (deacon); among the witnesses were Antelmus, his brother Girbaldus, and (once again) Arleus.[20]

The third time that we find Antelmus, in 997, he is solidifying his links to the monastery at the time of the death of Gir-

15. BB 1619;II:656–57 (8.982).
16. They are the subject of much discussion: notably in Duby, La société, pp. 336–39, and Bouchard, Sword, pp. 300–307. See Genealogy 2 and, in Chapter 4, Genealogy 7.
17. Anselm, Grifo, Oddo, and Rodulf.
18. The charter has "Berrardus," but this likely should be emended.
19. BB 2827;IV:31 (1030?) (where Jotserannus = Gauzerannus).
20. BB 1657;II:488 (983–84). I am considering this Girbaldus to be Antelmus's brother because the two are grouped together, but in the cartulary A version of an earlier donation by Teodericus (BB 1154 [963]), a Girbaldus is identified as a brother of Teodericus. This earlier donation does not include Antelmus in the witness list.

baldus. On this occasion, Antelmus, his brother Bernardus, and their mother, Eva, acknowledged that they had "a quarrel against Saint Peter and the monks serving him." They quit their claim to land at Bassy "which our relatives gave to Saint Peter. Therefore, if we have any title to this land, we give it to Saint Peter for the salvation of our souls and of our brother Girbaldus. And we give to Saint Peter a curtilis in the pagus of Mâcon, at 'Vissandon' [near Saint-Vincent] . . . and at Buffières . . . and at Sainte-Cécile-la-Valouse [all ca. Cluny]. . . . We make this donation for our souls and the soul of our brother Girbaldus, so that the Lord may snatch us from the punishments of Hell and make us his heirs in paradise."[21] This quitclaim was witnessed by Rana, the widow of Girbaldus. We have already seen how, at a later time, she and her new husband would attach themselves to Cluny through a different quitclaim. In the same way, the quitclaim of land at Bassy had the purpose of strengthening the family's association with Saint Peter and assuring its members a place with God after death.

Claiming land from Cluny was (undeniably) a hostile act, but this enmity must itself be seen as part of an ongoing relationship which, in due course, produced a renewed friendship between the donors and the monks.[22] The alternation—indeed, simultaneity—of enmity and friendship was a continuous social

21. BB 2392;III:488 (4.997): "vurpitionem facimus ab hodierno et deinceps de terra quę est in Basiaco, quam propinqui nostri Sancto Petro dederunt. Si quid igitur in eadem habemus directum, Sancto Petro damus pro remedio animarum nostrarum et fratris nostri Girbaldi; damus etiam Sancto Petro quoddam curtile in pago Maticensi, in villa Visandono, et quicquid in eadem villa habemus quesitum, ad inquirendum totum. Et damus in villa Buferias curtile unum quod de Nazareno conquesivimus, et in ipsa villa vineam quam de Aydoardo conquesivimus, quesitum, ad inquirendum, totum ad integrum. Et damus in villa Bieria [Sainte-Cécile-la-Valouse] medietatem mansi qui erat inter Girbaldum at Letbaldum, et quicquid ad ipsam medietatem aspicit vel aspicere videtur, quesitum, ad inquirendum, totum ad integrum. Donamus etiam servum, nomine Abraam, cum uxore et infantibus suis. Facimus autem hanc donationem pro animabus nostris et anima fratris nostri Girbaldi, ut Dominus de penis inferni nos eripiat, et paradisi faciat heredes." On "Vissandon," Déléage identifies it as a l.-disp. near Saint-Vincent-des-Prés, ca. Cluny (p. 179 n. 3), while Chaume identifies it as Sandon, ca. Cluny, co. la Vineuse (Origines II/3:1135 n. 9). These two possibilities are in any event very close to each other. On Bieria, see Introduction, n. 71.

22. Cowdrey, in "Unions and Confraternity," pp. 153–56, notes that entrance into Cluny's societas generally was associated with charters of quitclaim.

process; neither one was a permanent stance begun or ended by a donation or a quitclaim.[23]

Thus, three or four years after his quitclaim, Antelmus renewed his association with Cluny in a simple donation to God and Saints Peter and Paul of "some of my own property for the soul of my brother Bernardus and for his burial there." It is likely that this donation marked the occasion of Bernardus's death. Part of the land was in the pagus of Mâcon, at Mons, and part of it was in the *comitatus* of Autun, at villa Clericorum (n. id.). Later, as we have seen, Antelmus's sister Adelaida would give Cluny more land at Mons.[24]

Sometime later, Antelmus witnessed the donation of land at Lournand by a man named Oddo.[25] Oddo, known as a *legis doctor*, was probably a relative of the Grossi—Gauzerannus and his sons, Maiolus, Israel, and Bernard—all of whom were present at the donation, and the last of whom, with his wife, Emma, consented to Oddo's gift (see Genealogy 2.)[26] Maiolus himself had

23. Geary, "Vivre en conflit," makes a similar observation about the handling of disputes, which are less "settled" than temporarily defused. Terms of friendship and enmity are sometimes used in documents connected with Cluny; e.g., Doda says she and her son want to be *amici* of Cluny in BB 802;I:754–56 (3.951). Walter, a donor to Cluny (e.g., BB 2802;IV:5–6 [10.1027–10.1028], BB 2869;IV: 66–67 [Chaume, "Obs" 1049], BB 2965;IV:163 [c. 1047]), is, nevertheless, among the "crudeliores persecutores" of Cluny in a letter of Benedict VIII, in Zimmermann, no. 530 (4.1021–1023), p. 1009. (On this letter, see below, Chapter 5.)

24. BB 2489;III:570 (10.999–10.1000). The term *comitatus* (county) was often used interchangeably with "pagus" in the charters. Patrick Geary has postulated that donations pro anima are given on behalf of those who own the property in question. See "Echanges et relations entre les vivants et les morts dans la société du haut moyen âge," *Droit et Cultures* 12 (1986): 3–17. While his rule generally appears to hold, here and elsewhere there are exceptions, for Antelmus and Bernardus do not appear in other transactions at Mons and Clericorum. For Mons, see BB 465;I:451–52, BB 914;II:26–27, BB 1427;II:483–84, BB 1676;II:703–4, BB 1677;II:704–5, BB 1238;II:327, BB 1268;II:348–49, BB 1749;III:16–17, BB 1810; III:61–62, BB 1819;III:66–67, BB 1914;III:136, perhaps BB 2095;III:288–89, BB 2261;III:392, BB 2388;III:485, BB 2389;III:486. See Chaume, *Origines* II/3:1116 n.13. For Clericorum, see BB 993;II:87–88 and Chaume, *Origines* II/3: 826.

25. BB 2351;III:461 dating from the reign of King Robert (996–1031) narrowed by Chaume, "Obs.," to 996–1005 for reasons that are not entirely convincing. The terminus ante quem here is the presumed date of Antelmus's death, 1014. The witnesses were, in order: Bernard and his wife, Emma (who consent), Maiolus, Israel, Milo, Antelmus, Aydoard, Ingelelmus, Ledprannus, Bernard, Odilo, Gauserannus, Arleus, Sivuinus, Sofredus.

26. Oddo is *legis doctor* in BB 2406;III:497–98 (Chaume, "Obs.," c. 1002). In BB 1577;II:622–23 (981–82), Rotrudis and Gauserannus "ac reliqui filii mei"

Genealogy 2. The Grossi (much simplified)

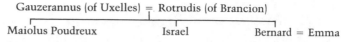

Gauzerannus (of Uxelles) = Rotrudis (of Brancion)

Maiolus Poudreux   Israel   Bernard = Emma

Note: The family tree of the Grossi is discussed in Duby, *Société*, p. 337 n. 85; in Bouchard, *Sword*, pp. 300–307; and in Chapter 4 below. In BB 1845;III:88–89 (990–91) Maiolus names his father and mother: Gauzerannus and Rotrudis; on the witness list are Arleus and Bernard. The brothers Maiolus, Israel, and Bernard are identified as such in BB 2486;III:568–69 (7.999); Arleus and Bernard are also present here. The brothers are again named, as well as Bernard's wife, Emma, in BB 2617;III:664–65 (11.1005).

land near Lournand, which is reason enough for his presence.[27] But many of the other witnesses came to draw up the charter because of their association with him and his family rather than because they held land there. Antelmus, as we have already seen, was closely associated with the Grossi; and he was preceded by Milo, probably his brother-in-law.[28] Aydoard, who followed Antelmus, was an associate of Arleus (whom we met at Taizé); indeed, Arleus, one of his brothers, Siguinus, and their father, Ingelelmus, along with Siguinus's son, Soffredus, were all witnesses to the transaction (see Genealogy 4).[29] Finally, the Odilo who was present here was undoubtedly the same man we met at Taizé, where he was similarly surrounded by the Grossi family.

The net result of these occasions is a chronicle mainly of giving, but also of taking and regiving. Antelmus both quarreled with the monastery of Cluny and donated to it; and he associated with others who were doing the same thing. He did not follow the expected scenario of an heir reclaiming his inheritance or of an original donor who would be followed by such heirs. Rather, he was both. If we knew only that he had made one do-

---

gave land at Curtil-sous-Buffières (ca. Cluny) to Cluny. These are certainly the parents of Bernard, Israel, and Maiolus, and the founders of the Grossi (see Genealogy 2). Those present in BB 1577 included an Odo, possibly the same as the Odo, canon of Saint-Vincent de Mâcon, who was a relative *(consanguineus)* of Leutbald, brother of Rotrudis. See *M* 406;233–34. Very likely he is the Oddo of BB 2351;III:461 and BB 2406.

27. At Lourdon, in BB 2406;III:497–98 (Chaume, "Obs.," 6.1002) and BB 2552;III:617 (3.1002).

28. See Appendix C.

29. Aydoard appears in association with Arleus in BB 443;I:431–32 (Chaume, "Obs.," 987): BB 460;I:448 (Chaume, "Obs.," 986–89).

nation, or (on the other hand) if we had only a record of his quit-claim, we would be misled. Antelmus (and, as we shall see, the generation after him and others as well) had an intense, ambivalent, and mutual relationship with Saints Peter and Paul and their servants, the monks of Cluny.

In August 1014, one Hugo, acting in Antelmus's name, gave Cluny alodial land with serfs and slaves at some unspecified place for the privilege of burial; more land and serfs at Mons; and freemen at Farges.[30] Antelmus was not present, and it is likely that he had just died. But the people that acted in his name are unfamiliar.[31] Their identification leads us to a new generation.

A Third Generation of Givers and Takers

The key to the new group standing in Antelmus's stead were the brothers Hugo and Jocerannus and their half brother Bernard. The two brothers were among the adopted sons of Eve, Antelmus's sister. Their entrance into the story brings with it a host of other characters, for Eve's marriages linked her and her family to many other families. The complexities of these connections are set forth in Appendix C. Here we may simply follow the activities of this third generation, which, like the older generation of Antelmus and Eve, was involved in giving to and taking from Cluny.[32] The cast of players includes the sons and stepsons of a man named Witbert, who became Eve's husband. The stepsons were generally grouped together as a quartet of brothers (Ber-

30. BB 2689;III:717–18 (8.1014), "in villa Forgias" = Farges, ca. Cluny; see Chaume, *Origines* II/3:1130 n. 3. The name Hugo appears in the witness list of BB 2392;III:488 (997). This could be the same as the Hugo who stands in for Antelmus in BB 2689. Chaume identifies a Hugo, *filius Lebaldi* (BB 572;I:551 [Chaume, "Obs.," c. 981–97]) as an associate of the family of Antelmus. I do not think this is the same Hugo as the person in BB 2689, for reasons explained in Appendix C.

31. The witnesses were Aia, Rotbert, Antonius, Bernardus, Jocerannus, another Rotbert, Ansedeus, Walterius, Josfredus.

32. Eve's donations are in BB 2477;III:555 (for the date, see Appendix C); BB 2911;IV:111–12 (Chaume, "Obs.," 1039): a donation of land at "Tisiacus" (l. -disp., near Saint-Point, ca. Tramayes) and Praye; and BB 554;I:537–38 (Chaume, "Obs.," c. 1010–20): a donation by Gauzbert (Eve's husband at the time) with Eve's consent, of land in exactly the same places, with the addition of land at Trades, from Gauzbert's maternal inheritance.

Genealogy 3. The family of Witbert

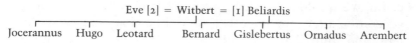

Eve [2] = Witbert = [1] Beliardis

Jocerannus	Hugo	Leotard	Bernard	Gislebertus	Ornadus	Arembert

nard, Gislebertus, Ornadus, and Arembert), and the sons as a trio (Jocerannus, Hugo, and Leotard). Bernard's position was, however, pivotal, as he joined with both groups as occasion demanded.[33] The family configuration, in its simplest form, is shown in Genealogy 3.

Let us follow the foursome, the brothers Bernard, Gislebertus, Ornadus, and Arembert. About 994 they quit their claim to land at Ruffey, which had been donated to Cluny originally by Bishop Mainbodus.[34] Then, in April 995, with the brothers Arembert and Bernard present as witnesses, Ornadus and Gislebertus made a donation to Cluny "in emendation for all the things we have done against the holy apostles there and on account of the place which we have violated."[35] At that time, they gave a curtilis in "Vetus Canava" and another in Château. At some other time, Gislebertus and Arembert gave more land at Vetus Canava and part of a field at Château "for the remedy of the souls of our brothers, Ornadus and Bernard."[36] This was a

33. E.g., Bernard, Hugo, and Jocerannus appear in tandem in BB 583;I:556–57. The terminus for this triplet occurs in BB 2098;III:291, where Bernard and Jocerannus donated to Cluny land at Ciergues (ca. Cluny) "for our brother, Hugo, of blessed memory." On the other hand, Bernard was part of the quartet with Gislebertus, Arembert, and Ornadus in BB 1835;III:79 and BB 3152;IV:312. See Appendix C, n. 10.

34. BB 1835;III:79(Chaume, "Obs.," c. 994). In BB 667;I:620–21 (3.945), Mainbodus, bishop of Mâcon, made an exchange with Cluny by giving some property at Ruffey to the monastery, while the monks, led by Abbot Aymard, gave the bishop land at "Vetus Canava" (near La Chaume). Only very limited circumstantial evidence ties the fraternal quartet who quitclaimed Mainbodus's gift to the family of the bishop. Mainbodus had a brother named Arembert (BB 374;I:352 [1.929]). Beliardis had land at Ruffey and Vetus Canava (e.g., in BB 2293;III:420–21 and BB 320;I:313–14). Nevertheless, Chaume, "Obs.," for BB 2507;III:584–85 calls our quartet of brothers "issues de la lignée de l'évêque Maimboeuf."

35. BB 2296;III:422–23 (4.995).

36. BB 311;I:307 (Chaume, "En Marge 2," p. 51 n. 7, calls into question the date of BB, who put it in Odo's abbacy following cartulary A). It records the same donation as BB 3152;IV:312 (dated by BB 1049–1109? because it is in cartulary B for Hugh's abbacy), where, however, only the local names and not the villa

"simple" donation, but it was recorded twice, with entirely different witnesses each time. Perhaps this is a matter of textual transmission, but it is also possible that the land was registered as a donation on two different occasions. There are examples of redonations in other charters (see Chapter 4).

The brothers also appeared as witnesses for a quitclaim by Maiolus Poudreux, one of the Grossi brothers, who gave up his claim to woods at Grandmont. This was a major social event, at which were present an assemblage of eight monks and six *nobiles viri*. The latter included Witbert and his sons Gislebertus, Bernard, and Hugo. The charter drawn up to record the meeting was quite explicit, not about who owned the land but about its placement and who was (and remained) associated with it:

> in the first place, [Maiolus] quitclaimed the land which Oddo designated for us and which Teza, Oddo's daughter, handed over to Saint Peter by charter, namely the woods at "Grandmont," with borders [as follows]: on the east [it borders on] the same inheritance, through the middle of the mountains, the ravine, and the castle of Teodoricus; on the south, [it borders on] the land of free tenants; on the west and north, [it borders on] land of Saint Peter. He draws up this notice at this time so that he may reunite himself with the favor of Saint Peter and the brothers, and so that he may remain in the future as a faithful servant in the service of Saint Peter.[37]

Thus were set forth a complex mélange of claimants, witnesses, donors, and recipients. The purpose of bringing them together

---

names are given. The two charters ought to be dated c. 990–1013 (the latter date marking Ornadus's death. See n. 38 below).

37. BB 2508;III:585 (Hillebrandt, "Datierungen," 1004–35): "in primis verpivit hoc quod Oddo nobis destinavit et Teza, filia ejus, Sancto Petro per cartas tradidit, et silvam in Grandi Monte, sicut terminatur a mane de ipsa hereditate, per medios montes, et per medium crest [cartulary B: *per mediam crepidinem*] et per castellum medium Teodorici, a medio die terra francorum, a sero et a cercio terra Sancti Petri. Facit autem hanc noticiam in presenti, ut gratiam Sancti Petri et fratrum sibi reconciliet, et in futuro devoto famulamine in servitio Sancti Petri permaneat." On the term *terra francorum*, see Déléage, pp. 378–80. We have a charter from Teodoricus (BB 1657;II:690–91 cited above, since Antelmus was among the witnesses) also donating land at Grandmont, where, apparently, he had a fortification (castellum). See also an earlier donation by Teodoricus, in BB 1154;II:243–44. On the identity of Oddo, see n. 26 above.

was, according to the charter, a reconciliation and a renewed relationship between Maiolus, Saint Peter, and the monks of Cluny. The social links thus forged extended from present to future, from earth to heaven.

Ornadus probably died in 1013, when Gislebertus and Arembert, thinking of their souls and that of Ornadus and other relatives, manumitted a slave and her four children.[38] Ornadus was not present then; nor was he with his brothers when Eve, Antelmus's sister, made a donation witnessed by Witbert, Gislebertus, and Arembert.[39]

There are other examples of givers and takers. There is no need to explore the histories of all of them (even if we could). Let us simply set forth a few bald facts: Maiolus, as we saw, quitclaimed land at Grandmont after 994; but he had donated land to the monks in the comitatus of Lyon in 990–91.[40] Achard, with his brothers, gave a mansus in Chevagny-sur-Guye (ca. La Guiche) to Cluny but he took half of a mill from Cluny at Merzé (ca. Cluny).[41] Gotefredus and Alexandra, major donors to Cluny, were nevertheless also involved in a quitclaim at "Tisiacus," in 1002–3.[42] This is not to deny that heirs were frequently involved in quitclaims. Teuza consented to the donation of villa Vallis (probably Vaux, ca. Saint-Gengoux) in 956, but she later claimed it and finally quitclaimed it.[43] Andreas claimed and then renounced his claim to land that had been given to his father by the prior of Cluny "as long as he lives."[44]

---

38. BB 2686;III:715–56 (4.1013).

39. BB 2477;III:555 (probably to be dated 1013–26 because of the absence of Ornadus and the dates of the reign of King Robert).

40. BB 1845;III:88–89 (990–91).

41. Gift in BB 3155;IV:313–14; werpitio in BB 3290;IV:390–91; both dated ? 1049–1109.

42. Tisiacus is near Saint-Point, ca. Tramayes. Gotefredus and Alexandra were the founders of Berzé-la-Ville; among their donations was BB 1554;II: 601– 2; the werpitio is in BB 2567;III:628. It netted the couple six *modii* of bread and wine and a blanket worth ten solidi. On Berzé-la-Ville and its donors, one awaits the forthcoming study by Maria Hillebrandt.

43. In BB 1001;II:95–96 (dated 6.956), Teuza consents; in BB 1496;II:548–49 (dated 8.979), she renounces her claim. For the place identification, see Chaume, *Origines* II/3:1075 and 1108 n. 9.

44. BB 926;II:37–38 (Chaume, "Obs.," c. 1006–8): the land is given to Adalgisus; BB 927;II:38 (written on the back of BB 926): the land is quitclaimed by his son.

Nevertheless, it is clear that quitclaims were not simply cease-fires; they were part of enduring relationships.

Group Connections

Thus far we have followed Antelmus, his family, and the groups that surrounded them as they gave and took. It is time now to focus systematically on these groups. What determined the cluster of people involved in transactions? The answer lay in a combination of factors: family bonds, neighborhood attachments, the prestige of particular groups, and, finally, connections with Cluny.

Let us use, by way of example, the rather complicated quitclaim of 997 made by Antelmus, his brother Bernardus, and their mother, Eva.[45] The land that was returned—on behalf of their own souls and that of another brother, Girbaldus—was at Bassy. At the same time, the brothers gave gifts: of land at Vissandon; of a curtilis at Buffières and a vineyard there that they had acquired from Aydoard; and of half of a mansus at Sainte-Cécile-la-Valouse that had been shared by Girbaldus and Letbaldus.

In short, there were four places involved in the quitclaim of 997: Bassy, Vissandon, Buffières, and Sainte-Cécile-la-Valouse. None of these places was more than ten kilometers from the monastery. Yet, as it turns out, most of the witnesses were connected with Buffières alone. A glance at Map 2 will show that this one place marked a kind of border region between Antelmus's activities in the Autunois—at Mons, Fontana, and Clericorum, none of which, unfortunately, may be mapped with precision—and his activities in the Mâconnais. Buffières was a key location, then, at least in part because of its strategic importance in the context of Antelmus's other landholdings.

The first witness to the werpitio in question was (1) Rana, the wife of Girbaldus. The others were, in order: (2) Bernard, (3) Rotbert, (4) Hubert, (5) Atto, (6) Lanbert, (7) Wilelmus, (8) Hugo,

---

45. BB 2392;III:488 (4.997)

(9) Ainardus, (10) Eldricus, (11) Bernardus. Who were these people and why were they assembled for the recording of this event? Let us seek to answer this question in some detail.

The first three people after Rana were connected to the brothers Maiolus, Israel, and Bernard and to Bernard's wife, Emma, who owned land at Buffières. In about 1000, for example, Bernard and Emma gave land and serfs there to Cluny, as pledge for a loan.[46] Three signatories for this event were (in slightly different order) the same as the first witnesses for the quitclaim of 997: (2) Bernard, (3) Rotbert, (4) Hubert.[47]

The next four people present at our quitclaim—Atto, Lanbert, Wilelmus, and Hugo—were also landowners at Buffières. In 1013 Atto would give to Cluny his share of property there.[48] About the same time, a man named Wichardus quit his claim to land once belonging to Atto's brothers at Buffières, and "gave it again" to Cluny.[49] In the quitclaim of 997 that we are following in detail, the names that follow that of (5) Atto, are three of the brothers of Wichardus: (6) Lanbert, (7) Wilelmus, and (8) Hugo. We know a little about Wichardus's family, which gave a good deal of land in the Autunois to Cluny: the mother was Blismodis, the father Blisardus; and one brother, Wigo, may have been viscount of Mâcon.[50]

The last three witnesses were (9) Ainardus, (10) Eldricus, and (11) Bernardus. It is not clear who Eldricus was or why he was

46. BB 2532;III:603–4 (1000–1001).
47. Hubert (Ubertus) and Rotbert (Rotbertus) were also witnesses for Teodericus, levita, in BB 1657;II:690–91 (983–84), at which Antelmus was also a witness.
48. BB 2685;III:714–15 (3.1013). Note that in BB 611;I:571 Atto quitclaimed land at Buffières.
49. BB 924;II:35. The brothers of Atto, Vuinibaldis, Oddo, and Ugo, were named in this donation/quitclaim. BB followed cartulary A and dated this in the abbacy of Maiolus (954–94). But cartulary A is notoriously inaccurate in its grouping of charters with abbacies. Chaume, "Obs.," suggests c. 990. I suggest a time about 1013 because of the apparent connection to BB 2685;III:714–15.
50. See BB 1775;III:33–34, BB 1859;III:97, BB 1934;III:152. The most revealing is BB 1859, which specifically names as brothers Wigo, Lanbert, Berardus, and Wilelmus. This must be added to the information in BB 924;II:35, namely that Hugo was the brother of Wilelmus as well. The relationship between Wichardus and Atto is not clear. Chaume connected Wichardus with the family of Wigo, viscount of Mâcon. In my view, the donor may clearly be shown to be the brother of a Wigo, but the charters are inconclusive as to whether this Wigo is identical to the viscount.

interposed between Ainardus and Bernardus. But the latter were two brothers who were associates of Aydoard elsewhere—at Tourniers—and were possibly brought in as witnesses because the vineyard at Buffières had been acquired from Aydoard.[51]

The place where Antelmus's quitclaim was recorded was Cluny. The witnesses had to be chosen beforehand; a short trip had to be made to the monastery. Out of all the possible arrangements that one might envisage, the least likely is that the witnesses were picked randomly. We may expect members of Antelmus's family, which is precisely what Rana represents. We may expect, given what we know about early medieval society from other contexts, groups of "retainers," vassals, *fideles* or *amici* or, indeed, lords. These are probably represented by the first three witnesses, associates of Bernard, Maiolus, and Israel. Finally, we may expect neighbors. There were many potential choices here. Perhaps neighbors from Buffières were chosen because that was a central point in Antelmus's power; but Buffières was a villa—not a manor, nor a village, but rather a "township territory." It contained a good bit of land and, one must assume, a fair share of the population. It is proper to ask, then, What criteria were operating in the choice of particular neighbors as witnesses? There appear to be at least two answers: first, social prestige was a factor, for the families of the Grossi and of Wichardus were important ones in the region. And, second, the neighbors chosen were those who themselves transacted business—sales, donations, quitclaims—with Cluny. In-

---

51. BB 1664;II:695–96 (984): an Aydoard is among the witnesses. An Aydoard had also been present at Wichardus's donation in BB 924;II:35 at Buffières. In BB 2191;III:345–46 (Chaume, "Obs.," 994) Ainardus and Bernardus gave Cluny land at "Misy" (near Saint-Vincent and Donzy) and at Ciergues, where Antelmus, too, appeared. Ainardus and Bernardus occur in the charters of Cluny generally in connection with land at Turniacus (= Tourniers, ca. Mâcon-Nord); see BB 1650; II:683–84, 1664;II:695–96, 1817;III:65, 1853;III:94, 2321;III:441–42 and possibly BB 1907;III:130–31. The connecting link with BB 2191 is BB 1650, which concerns land at both Tourniers and Ciergues. It is possible that the Ainardus of this group is also the Ainardus, father of Arembert, who appears in connection with charters for Besorniacus (= Bézornay, ca. Cluny) in BB 1876;III:108 and BB 1877; III:108–9. An Arembert appears in connection with Bernardus and Girbaldus, the brothers of Antelmus, in BB 1906;III:129–30 and BB 1907;III:130–31. The latter concerns land in Besorniacus and Herniacus, which, if Herniacus = Terniacus, may imply that the Ainardus of the two groups— Ainardus/Bernardus at Tourniers and Ainardus/Arembert at Bézornay—is the same person, with connections to Antelmus at several places.

deed, Eldricus was the only witness to the quitclaim of 997 who was not clearly a Cluny "regular."[52]

Werpitiones in the Context of Donations

Thus, networks of friends, neighbors, and relations were involved in giving and taking and regiving. But they gave much more often than they took. In the period before 1050, donations constituted 69 percent to 80 percent of the land and church transactions with Cluny recorded in the charters (see Table 3.)

Yet there is justification in speaking of a system of give and take. For although there were thousands of gifts to Cluny, there were not so many thousands of donors. Certain groups and

Table 3. Donations and quitclaims

Years	Donations		Quitclaims		Other transactions	
	No.	*%*	*No.*	*%*	*No.*	*%*
909–41	155	72	5	2	54	25
942–63	429	69	27	4	165	27
964–93	836	72	46	4	274	24
994–1048	950	80	64	5	179	15
Unknown	55	75	13	18	5	7
Total	2,425	74	155	5	677	21

Note: The figures here are, in effect, a summary of the same material in Appendix B, Illustration B.1. For the definition of "transaction," see the Introduction. "Other transactions" include exchanges, loans, precarial gifts, and sales. The percentages cover all transactions during the given time period, rounded off to the nearest whole number. The intervals correspond roughly to the abbacies of Berno and Odo, Aymard, Maiolus, Odilo. To look at the matter from the point of view of the *charters* (see Appendix B, Illustration B.2), there are 102 charters between 909 and 1048 that may be classed as werpitiones, as compared with 1,651 charters of donation for the same period.

---

52. Assumptions to the contrary, by Chaume and Valous and to some extent by Wollasch, have led to the view that the whole charter tradition was orchestrated by their monastery, a view that attributes far too much power and social control to the monastery, and that begs the question of lay interest and lay initiative in the documentation. Charters of donation were drawn up in the name of the donor and say nothing at all about the monastery wanting the land in question, but rather a good deal about the donor wanting to give the land. The abbot and monks were rarely present.

certain families gave repeatedly. Indeed, the evidence suggests that a relatively limited number of overlapping groups, particularly family groups, were responsible for most of the transactions with the monastery. Each charter represents, then, only part of the transactions of larger "networks" of families, friends, and neighbors. Werpitiones cannot be seen as isolated cases, but rather as part of a larger matrix of gift giving and taking.

Moreover, some places were never taken but were always given. For giving and taking were rituals, and land was, among other things, a highly charged ritual object. To be sure, land in many villae was both given and taken, sold and given in gage. But some villae had meanings more concentrated and precise. Fontana was above all a place to reclaim. Flagy, however, as we shall see, was a place to give.[53]

A "Donopolis" at Flagy

One group of lay men and women, an extended yet definable group, was involved as principal or party to almost every transaction pertaining to Flagy in the charters of Cluny.[54] We may, for convenience, call them the Arlei.[55] Arleus and Bernardus, whom we have already met, were two of the sons of Ingelelmus. They had five other brothers: Ornadus, *presbyter;* Siguinus; Gaufredus; Wichard; and Achard, *clericus.* These brothers and their father and mother held land at Flagy, Merzé, and Massilly

53. Flagy, ca. Cluny, about seven kilometers to the north of Cluny, between Taizé and Bézornay.

54. The documents (with dates only if certain) are BB 155;I:156, BB 173;I:165–66, BB 227;I:217–18, BB 878;I:833–34 (4.954), BB 879;I:834–35, BB 1458;II:512–13 (978–79), BB 1522;II:571–72 (4.980), BB 1588;II:631–32 (1.982), BB 1691;II:715–16 (5.984), BB 1702;II:725–26 (10.984), BB 1865;III:100–101 (990–91), BB 2120;III:305–6, BB 2196;III:348, BB 2202;III:351, BB 2290;III:417–18 (3.995), BB 2338;III:453–54, BB 2430;III:517–18, BB 2555;III:619–20 (1002), BB 2566;III:627–28 (1002–3), BB 3159;IV:315, BB 3244;IV:365. Two "exceptions" to the identifiable group are hardly that: in BB 1588 and BB 1691 names appear that cannot be directly linked to it, but in another charter (BB 1458) the same people appear along with known members of the family under study. BB 878 and its counterpart BB 879, BB 1702, and BB 2566 appear to be wholly unrelated. Of course, the archives of Cluny are no longer complete; there may have been other charters concerned with Flagy.

55. Duby, in *La société,* pp. 200 n. 33 and 336–38 mentions "Les Arlier, ancêtres des Merzé," and their holdings appear in his "Croquis IV," p. 509.

(all ca. Cluny), some of the brothers associating more closely with one or another place in their relations with Cluny. Arleus's lord was Gauzerannus, the father of Maiolus Poudreux, Israel, and Bernard. Arleus also had a *consanguineus*, probably a nephew, named Arleus, the son of Eve (not any Eve we have already met). (See Genealogies 2, 4, and 5).[56] The nephew Arleus was also involved with Cluny, especially through land at Cotte, Varanges, and "Mailly" (l.-disp., near Carrière des Moines).

These intertwined families dominated the transfers of land to Cluny at Flagy. And almost all of that land was given away in donations. We have only to trace the transactions generation by generation to see that gift giving at Flagy was a family tradition. About 980, Oda, Arleus's aunt or grandaunt, gave Cluny a mansus with the consent and approval *(laudatio)* of her son, Upertus.[57] In April of that year she gave Cluny a curtilis, vineyard, and mansus indominicatus there.[58] Ingelelmus and his family donated a mansus "for the redemption of my soul, so that the Lord, by his piety, and the holy apostles, too, may deign to succor me on the day of judgment and receive me into the delightfulness of paradise."[59]

In the next generation, Tetsa, the wife of Achard (Arleus's brother) gave two pieces of arable land and a forest for her husband's soul.[60] Arleus himself gave his inheritance at Flagy: a mansus and a family of serfs.[61] He and other members of his family witnessed the gift by Sievertus (a neighbor, possibly related to the family) of a vineyard at Flagy, and later of a field nearby which bordered on land held by Arleus.[62] Ornadus, Achard, and Arleus gave a vineyard at Flagy that was part of the inheritance of their sister Teza, for her soul and her burial at Cluny.[63] Siguinus, another brother, gave a curtilis at Flagy for

56. In BB 2555;III:619–20 (4.1002) Arleus gave some of his property to his "dilectus nepos Arleius" (as the orthography of cartulary A has it) with the provision that it go to Cluny after his nephew's death.
57. BB 155;I:156–57 (Chaume, "Obs.," c. 980).
58. BB 1522;II:571–72 (4.980).
59. BB 2338;III:453–54 (Chaume, "Obs.," 996–1007).
60. BB 173;I:165–66 (probably to be dated 990–91 by rapprochement with BB 1865;III:100–101).
61. BB 227;I:217–18 (Chaume, "Obs.," c. 960–90).
62. BB 1458;II:512–13 (11.978–79); BB 1691;II:715–16 (5.984).
63. BB 1865;III:100–101 (990–91) : "pro anima sororis nostrę Tezę, sicut ipsa

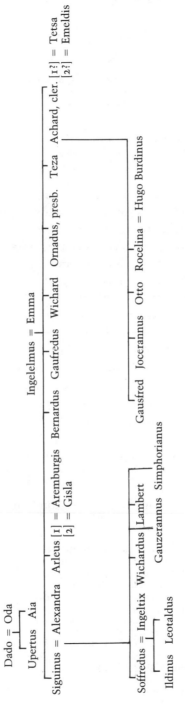

Genealogy 4. The Arlei

Note: See Appendix D.

Genealogy 5. The family of Arleus, son of Eve

Eve
|
Arleus = Gundrada
┌──────┴──────┐
Ornadus   Girbertus

Note: In BB 2331;III:448–49 (Chaume, "Obs.," 1005–7) and BB 2625;III:669, Eve is identified as the mother of Arleus. In BB 2144;III:322–23 (Chaume, "Obs.," 1005–20) this Arleus's wife is identified as Gundrada and his sons as Ornadus and Girbertus.

the salvation of the soul of his son, Lambert, who had been killed.[64] He and his brother Ornadus witnessed the gift of a vineyard and field there.[65] In 995 he gave some of his property at Flagy to Cluny "on account of a horse which I stole from them."[66] Arleus gave a vineyard and a field there named Curbatillea (the significance of which will become clear shortly), reserving the usufruct until his death.[67] Maiolus, brother of Israel and Bernard, who witnessed that gift by Arleus, himself gave Cluny part of a mansus at Flagy.[68]

A charter drawn up at the end of Arleus's life was particularly revealing. It was a donation, not to Cluny, but to Arleus's "dear nephew Arleus" of a good deal of land, some of which was in Collonge, some in Merzé, and some, finally in Flagy. But the land at Flagy was clearly associated with Cluny as the land elsewhere was not: "and I give to you some arable land, the half [that is mine], except for the field named Curbatillea, which I gave to Saint Peter."[69] The rest, too, apparently went to Cluny in the end.[70]

Finally, in the following generation came a change. It is true

---

deprecata est, donamus Deo et sanctis apostolis Petro et Paulo, ad locum Cluniacum, aliquid de hereditate ipsius et in locum sepulturę."
64. BB 2120;III:305–6 (Chaume, "Obs.,"1022–30).
65. BB 2196;III:348 (Chaume, "Obs.," c. 995–1007), reading "Givuinus" as = Siguinus. The form Sivuinus for this same person is in BB 2290;III:417–18.
66. BB 2290;III:417–18 (5.995).
67. BB 2430;III:517–18 (Chaume, "Obs.," 996–1007).
68. BB 2202;III:351–52 (Chaume, "Obs.," 994–1007). Maiolus also gave land in BB 2175;III:337, where no location was given, with Arleus as witness along with a Stephanus, who appeared on the witness list of BB 2202. It is very likely that the place meant in BB 2175 is Flagy.
69. BB 2555;III:619–20 (5.1002).
70. BB 2775;III:796–97 (1022–23).

that Gausfred and Jocerannus, two of the sons of Achard, witnessed the donation of a mansus at Flagy.[71] But the only other time in which this generation concerned itself with Flagy is when Gausfred and Jocerannus quit their claims to a mansus at Flagy that had been given to Cluny by their uncle Arleus and had been given back to them in turn, *in beneficio* (as a benefice), by the prior of Cluny.[72] This was the first quitclaim associated with Flagy. The family had used the place exclusively as a source of donations, though *elsewhere* they were engaged in other kinds of transactions.[73] In return for their quitclaim Gausfred and Jocerannus accepted "a very good and expensive horse."

This effectively marked the end of the story of Flagy. Very likely the family had run out of plots to give there. By the same token, Cluny had now consolidated its hold at Flagy. Henceforth Flagy was not part of a nexus of give and take.

Although there was a period when Flagy was a focus for the donations of the family of Arleus, they clearly held (and gave) land elsewhere: at Cotte, at Merzé, at Varanges, at Massilly, and at Collonge.[74] In none of these other places did they have the monopoly on donations that they maintained at Flagy. Did this reveal a family strategy? It is suggestive of self-conscious decisions that, in the charters, witnesses were grouped by their relationship to the land in question; that the pro anima formula was often used on behalf of the owner of the land; and that a family such as Arleus's continually gave land from one particular place to Cluny even though it held and on occasion gave land elsewhere. This does not demonstrate a self-conscious dynasty consolidating itself around a certain piece of property. It shows a different use of land: precious parcels were broken off bit by bit to build incrementally a family association with Saint Peter and his monks.

71. BB 3244;IV:365 (?1049–1109).

72. BB 3159;IV:315 (?1049–1109). See BB 227;I:217–18.

73. E.g., Achard, "miles et clericus," claimed a mill at Merzé (BB 2975;IV: 170–71 [Chaume, "Obs.," 1049–64] and BB 3290;IV:390 [?1049–1109]); Arleus and Aremburgis made an exchange with Cluny regarding lands at Chassange, Collonge, Toury, and Merzé (BB 1616;II:653–54 [982]); and see the other places noted in Appendix D.

74. See Appendix D.

Duby has shown that castellans were consolidating their patrimony around fortifications about A.D. 1000. The family of Arleus was also consolidating, but not around Flagy. The epithet "de Marziaco," associated with Achard and Wichard, shows us that the identity of the lineage was coalescing at a different location, at Merzé.[75] This familial identification with a particular place involved both the redefinition of the family and the redefinition of property, for lineages consolidated around the stable center of a castle stronghold or of a seigneurie. This consolidation is a different notion of stability from that involved in give and take, where the stable center was the relationship set up and affirmed, where the land itself was held, given away, reclaimed, given again. The give-and-take system suggests that donations in which the usufruct was explicitly reserved were not in any significant way different from other donations.[76]

75. For Wichard de Marziaco, see BB 3255;IV:371; in BB 3290;IV:390–91: "Achardus clericus de Marziaco."

76. See also the remarks of Ernst Levy, *West Roman Vulgar Law: The Law of Property* (Philadelphia: American Philosophical Society, 1951), pp. 39–40. It may nevertheless be of interest to see the proportion of donations with reservation of usufruct to those that were made "outright." In the table here the percentage figure is of total donations in the row. Under the category "reservation of usufruct" are included as well other delayed transactions, e.g., a donation to a son after whose death the gift is to revert to Cluny. The intervals for the dates correspond approximately to the abbacies of, respectively, Berno and Odo, Aymard, Maiolus, Odilo.

Donations with and without reservation of usufruct

Years	Simple Donations		Donations with reservation of usufruct	
	No.	%	No.	%
909–41	97	63	58	37
942–63	261	61	168	39
964–93	499	60	337	40
994–1048	722	76	228	24
Unknown	41	75	14	25
Total	1,620	67	805	33

It thus seems that donations in which the usufruct was reserved became less common in the eleventh century, when, it appears, Cluny's own new seigneurial status competed with the give-and-take property system that had hitherto been paramount.

Terra Sancti Petri

Transactions with Cluny were neighborhood and family affairs. For if we ask precisely what sort of social event was involved in a donation, the answer must center on the community surrounding the land, not on the monastery. The transactions that took place with Cluny tended to be dominated by certain key members of the local community, around whom clustered family and neighbors. The monks of Cluny—even the abbot or the prior or just one representative—were present only rarely when donations were recorded. The place where the documents were drawn up was only occasionally Cluny, and that only when Cluny was fairly conveniently close by. The scribe, who most certainly at times was a monk from Cluny, was on other occasions a neighborhood priest.[77] Above all, the donation itself created a new neighbor: Saint Peter. All land given (or, indeed, sold) to the monastery became part of Saint Peter's property. Thus Saint Peter became a neighbor in the vicinity. This must be understood (as it was at the time) as a literal fact, one that could be entirely routine: "We give to you a field . . . which is bounded on the east and west by the same inheritance, on the south by a wall, on the north by land of Saint Peter."[78] Saint Peter was a neighbor, as much a fixture of the countryside as the *murus manufactus* that ran to the south of the field. This was no pious locution; the document from which the quote is taken is not a donation to the monastery of Cluny but the gift of a layman to his brother. The land that Cluny held was rarely referred to as the *terra Cluniacensis*.[79] To have Saint Peter, the

77. See the ingenious articles by Monique-Cécile Garand, "Copistes de Cluny au temps de saint Maieul (948–94), *Bibliothèque de l'Ecole des Chartes* 136 (1978): 5–36, and "Le scriptorium de Cluny carrefour d'influences au XIᵉ siècle: Le manuscrit Paris B.N. nouv. acq. lat. 1548," *Journal des savants* 4 (1977): 257–83, where MSS from the scriptorium of Cluny are shown to be in the hand of particular scribes identifiable from original charters. Yet other scribes, as, for example, Deodatus (below, Chapter 3), were apparently drawn from the local, rather than the monastic, community.

78. BB 1278;II:357–58 (1.970).

79. The Council of Anse (BB 2255;III:384–88 at 385 [c. 994]) calls Cluny the *locus Cluniensis sanctissimus* when confirming its possessions and prohibiting anyone from violating its property. On the context of this decree, see below, Chapters 3 and 5.

doorkeeper of the kingdom of heaven, as a neighbor was one immediate effect of any land transaction with Cluny.[80]

Sometimes, indeed, Saint Peter became a next-door neighbor. Of the 1,426 transactions in which Cluny gained land in the period 909–1048 and in which borders were specified, 408 (about 29 percent) involved land with at least one border on other property belonging to the original owner or described as terminating "on the same inheritance."[81] But this led—ironically but inexorably—to a less sociable meaning of property, as Cluny consolidated its hold on the land of many neighbors.[82]

For a long time, these two processes—gaining Saint Peter as a neighbor and consolidating Saint Peter's territory—were complementary. The memory of families that had once held land given to Cluny persisted over many generations. Among other things, the land operated as a token or reminder of those who gave it. At times, often at moments of crisis or change, such as Rana's marriage out of Antelmus's family, the links that such memories forged broke down. Then they needed to be reinforced by renewed claims on the land, by the ceremonies of quitclaims and redonation, and often by new (and carefully articulated) integrating mechanisms, such as entry into Cluny's societas and burial in its grounds. But for the most part there was an equilibrium in which the claims and the memories of the original family were balanced with the claims and needs of Saint Peter. And there was good reason for this. To have the property of Saint Peter in one's midst was to be close to his *patrocinium*,

80. BB 635;1:592–93 (5.943): Peter is the *clavigerus aethereus*. Paul, who was more rarely named, is in the same charter the *egregius doctor*.

81. I.e., land *de ipsa hereditate*. The phrase is ambiguous. It may mean that the gift was broken off from the rest of the inheritance (so that, of course, it shared a border with it); or it may mean that parts of the inheritance were already fragmented but still remembered as having belonged originally to one single "inheritance." There is an extraordinary document in the cartulary of Lérins that traces the partition and then the reconstitution of a single demesne (*dominium*) at Vallauris (ca. Antibes, dép. Alpes-Maritimes) over the course of five generations; see Henri Moris and Edmond Blanc, *Cartulaire de l'abbaye de Lérins*, 2 vols. (Paris: H. Champion, 1883), 1:119–20, no. 132. I thank Patrick Geary for this reference. We have seen (e.g., at Fontana) long-lived memories connected with lands and families; the phrase *de ipsa hereditate* may point to a similar sensibility.

82. Of those same 1,426 transactions, 782 (or about 55 percent) had one or more borders with other land of Saint Peter.

that is, his protection and his aid. It was in the interest of everyone.

Thus donations to Cluny brought with them many intangible advantages: prayers, to be sure, but also links with neighbors and with Cluny; the prestige of giving gifts to Saint Peter; and the benefits (especially for the hereafter) of his proximity. Did people benefit in other ways? The model of the "gift economy" postulates a system of gifts and of countergifts. Did Cluny give away property? The answer is that it did do so on precisely three kinds of occasions: during exchanges, when the monastery gave land for land; during sales, when it paid a price (usually in money) for land; and during donations *in precaria* and other fixed-term donations, when Cluny voluntarily divested itself of property. What was involved in these transactions? Leaving precarial donations for Chapter 4 (for reasons which will become clear in the course of that chapter) let us turn now to some instances in which Cluny gave as well as received.

CHAPTER THREE

Consolidating Property: Exchanges and Sales

"FOR THOSE WHO are not limited in their love, [exchanging] a part for a part offers convenient benefits. For one judges himself not depleted in his own property at all. Rather he receives it back in greater measure."[1] Thus opened a charter of 825 in which the villa of Cluny changed hands. Hildebaldus, the bishop of Mâcon, gave it to Count Warinus and his wife, Alba, at the bidding of Emperor Louis the Pious. It went to Warinus and Alba along with another villa, this one in the pagus of Nevers. In return, Hildebaldus received land in the pagi of Mâcon and Nevers, and in the Auvergne.

Then, in 893, the villa of Cluny was once again part of an exchange. The "humble servant of Christ" (*humilis Christi famula*), Ava, exchanged it for some property belonging to her brother, William the Pious of Aquitaine, who would later found the monastery on the land she gave up.[2] What she traded, precisely, was the promise that Cluny, "that certain villa of mine," would be his after her death, in return for her use, while alive, of William's alod in the county of Chaumont.[3]

---

1. *M*, 55, p. 42 (825): "Inter quos caritas inlibata permanserit pars cum parte beneficia opportuna prestantur, quia nihil sibi de rebus propriis censuit minuendum, quod e contra recipitur in augmentis."

2. BB 53;1:61–63 (893). Ava, sister of William, is called *comitissa* in BB 856;1: 810–1 (10.953). Constance B. Bouchard suggests that Ermengard, mother of William and Ava, was the daughter of Warinus; in that case Cluny would have come to Ava through her maternal inheritance; see Bouchard, "Family Structure," pp. 655–58.

3. BB 53;1:61–63: "in comitatus Calmontensi," today dép. Meurthe-et-Moselle. For William's possessions and control, see, Christian Lauranson-Rosaz,

Thus, even before the monastery was built, the place called Cluny was associated with mutual uses and benefits. It was not fought over; it was not donated outright; it was, rather, part of a strategy of accommodation.

From the first, Cluny was involved in a nexus of exchange, one different in some ways from that created by donations and werpitiones. The exchange was potentially the most mutual of transactions; but it could also be impersonal and economically acquisitive. Within the coexisting gift and commercial economic modes of the tenth century, exchanges were the most flexible of instruments, useful for both.

Relatively few of Cluny's transactions were exchanges.[4] Nevertheless, they form a most interesting subset of documents. By their very nature they involved both giving and taking at the same moment. They were also among the most precise documents in the archives of Cluny; they often supplied land measurements as well as border information. The land measurements are less helpful than we might hope, because they generally involved lateral lengths, while land parcels were not necessarily square or rectangular. Without knowing the angle between two sides, we cannot calculate area.[5] More useful are

---

L'Auvergne et ses marges (Velay, Gévaudan) du VIIIe au XIe siècle: La fin du monde antique? (Le Puy-en-Velay: Les Cahiers de la Haute-Loire, 1987), pp. 66–72, which includes a map.

4. For the period 909–1048, 356 transactions (or, about 11 percent of all transactions) took place as part of an exchange, including those in charters describing precarial arrangements or quitclaims. The criteria by which an exchange was judged to be among the purposes of a charter must be made clear. I have designated as exchanges all charters that use the word *commuto* (or a variant thereon); or charters that speak of transactions *in escamgio* (*cambio, scamium*) in which, from the context, it is clear that an exchange is envisioned. The term *in escamgio* is used very frequently in the charters of Cluny and, while it may refer to a sale, it often refers generally to any transaction at all, even a gift (as in BB 1027;II:122). At times editorial comments in BB use the term "commutation" to refer to documents that do not, from the vocabulary used in the charter, warrant the appellation by the criteria above; and these I have not included. On exchanges at Cluny I have been unable to consult Nicole Renevey-Boulouis, "L'échange dans les chartes de Cluny," Mémoire pour le diplôme d'études supérieures d'histoire du droit et des institutions, 1e année de 3e cycle (Dijon, 1974).

5. Déléage, pp. 963–1022, calculated areas by multiplying length by width. (Metric equivalences for the documents of Cluny are discussed ibid., pp. 964–65; there were twelve feet to a perche.) It goes without saying that the length of the foot in the Mâconnais is quite speculative. On the Carolingian foot see Walter Horn and Ernest Born, *The Plan of Saint Gall,* 3 vols. (Berkeley: Univer-

the borders. As we shall see, exchanges apparently often allowed both parties to consolidate their holdings. At the same time, they appear very often to have allowed both parties to intermingle, with the land once again serving as intermediary. This requires some explanation.

"Mutual" Exchanges

The notions of "gift" and "commercial" economic modes of exchange can be seen as "ideal types" constructed by anthropologists and (now) by historians (see Chapter 4). They form the extreme ends of a continuum of economic behavior that, in reality, generally partook (and continues today to partake) of both modes. On that continuum, some exchanges may be plotted at the extreme and of the personal, gift-giving mode. A charter from 989 illustrates the way in which an exchange could serve essentially as an event of mutual gift giving:

> It was pleasing and convenient that venerable Abbot Maiolus and the brothers at Cluny should make an exchange of land with a certain man named Eldinus, levita; and they did so. In the first place, Eldinus, levita, gives to Cluny and to the brothers some of his land: i.e., a vineyard which is in the pagus of Mâcon, in the ager of Ruffey, in the villa Vetus Canava, which is bounded on the east by [land of] Eldinus, levita, on the south and west by [land of] Saint Peter, on the north by land of Otbert. It is 12 perches in length, and in width on one side measures 7 perches, on the other side, 5 perches. Within these boundaries, I give this, whole and complete, to the just-named monastery. And, for his part, the said abbot and the brothers of Cluny give to Eldinus, levita, a different vineyard in the same ager and in the same villa, which is bounded on the east and south and west by the land of Eldinus, levita, and on the north by Saint Peter. It is 12 perches in length, and in width on one side

sity of California Press, 1979), 1:94–97. Only rarely do the charters appear to refer to area, rather than side measurements: e.g., in BB 590;1:560 (942–54), Cluny received a vineyard of 36 perches, and it gave in return two vineyards and a little field (*agellus*) that together totaled 36 perches. In BB 571;1:550–51 (942–54), Cluny received a vineyard of 29 perches while it gave up two vineyards that together totaled 50 perches.

measures 6 perches and on the other side, 4 perches. Within these boundaries they give it whole and complete. And let each one do with what he has received whatever he wants to do.[6]

This is an uncomplicated transaction. It involves the exchange of the same kind of land—vineyard—in the same villa. Both pieces of vineyard were uneven quadrilaterals; the dimensions suggest that Eldinus got the worst of the deal: he gave a parcel measuring $12 \times 7 \times 5$ ($\times 12$?) perches, while the monks gave him one measuring $12 \times 6 \times 4$ ($\times 12$?). But (as noted above) these numbers may be misleading. What is certain is that the transaction gave both parties the chance to consolidate their holdings, to fill in gaps. Eldinus already held land on three of four sides of the vineyard that he received from Cluny. In turn, Saint Peter, served by the monks of Cluny, already held land on two sides of the portion that the Cluniacs received from Eldinus. At the same time, consolidation was not at all the same thing as isolationism. On the contrary; the exchange made clear that Eldinus and Saint Peter would continue to be neighbors. The land that Eldinus received was bounded by other land belonging to Saint Peter to the north; the land that Cluny gained was bounded by land of Eldinus to the east. Boundary information helped to identify the land, to objectify it, and to show its connections. In this instance it made explicit the association of the land of Eldinus and the land of Saint Peter.[7]

6. BB 1809;III:60–61 (12.989); taken from the copy made by Lambert de Barive with additions and notes from cartulary A: "Placuit adque convenit inter venerabilem abbatem Maiolum et fratres Clunienses, necnon etiam cuidam viro, nomine Eldino levita, ut inter se quasdam terras scamiarint, quod ita fecerunt. In primis donant Eldino levita ad locum Cluniaco et ad fratres quamdam suam terram, oc est vinea que est in pago Matisconense, in agro Rufiacense, in villa Veskanevas [A: Vetus Kanavas]; qui terminad a mane Eldino levita, a medio die et a sero Sancti Petri, a cercio terra Otbert, et abet in longo perticas xii, in uno fronte perticas vii, in alio fronte perticas v. Infra istas terminio, totum ad integrum donant ad jam denominatum cenobium. Et contra predictus abba et fratres Clunienses donant Eldino levita alia vinea in ipso agro, et in ipsa villa; qui terminat a mane et a medio die et a sero terra Eldino levita, a cercio Sancti Petri, et abet in longo perticas xii, in uno fronte perticas vi, in alio fronte perticas iiii. Infra istas terminio, totum ad integrum donant. Et faciatis unusquisque de suo quod accipit quitquit facere voluerit."

7. Of course, such boundary information was also useful as a reminder of precisely which piece of land at Vetus Canava was in question. David Herlihy used just such boundary information in his path-breaking study, "Church Property," in Herlihy, *Social History*, paper 5, where he calculated the proportion of

How representative was this transaction? Of the 356 exchange transactions with Cluny, we have boundary information for 247.[8] Even without considering gains and losses, it is immediately apparent that Saint Peter was the single most frequent "neighbor" of every such parcel of land: 62 percent of the transactions for which border information was supplied had Saint Peter on at least one side. This contrasts with exchanges in which one or more borders were contiguous with land of the other party, which occurred in 27 percent of the cases: a bit over a quarter of the land fits the model of social linkage implied by the example of Eldinus. And we may add that about 28 percent of the parcels had borders neither with Saint Peter nor with the other principal.

But statistics can befuddle as well as clarify, and in this instance (as in all) they must be used with care. It is true (we shall argue the point later) that many exchanges did not have the function of mutual give and take, or, at least, that was not their primary purpose. But it is also true, as we saw in Chapter 2, that each transaction with Cluny involved a social network that reached beyond the principals involved in it. Land which did not

---

developed land owned by the church. Because of his purposes, he deliberately excluded information mentioning borders with the principals involved in the transaction (p. 85). It is there, however, that the *interaction* between laymen and saint is to be found.

8. It should be kept in mind that here "transactions" are involved, not charters. Nearly every exchange charter involves at least two transactions, since Cluny will always both gain and lose. However, owing largely to accidents of textual transmission, some information is missing. In particular, if the two parts of an exchange were drawn up on separate pieces of parchment, one might be lost. But this seems not to have been an entirely random process. It is interesting that the "lost" portion was always that which recorded Cluny's countergift. As we shall see, by the time cartulary A was drafted, ideas about property had shifted; the exchange was by then a relatively unfamiliar form of land transfer. As always, VILLA and OUTCOME information (see Appendix A) determined the way in which material was entered into the data set. Thus, sometimes, Cluny gained two pieces of land in two different villae: this was considered as two separate transactions. On the other hand, sometimes an exchange involved more than one piece of land at the same villa. As long as these were part of the same charter and part of the same OUTCOME, they were effectively merged as one transaction. If boundary information was given for one piece but not for another *at the same villa*, this was nevertheless coded as BORDERS = 1. If boundary information was given for both pieces at the same villa, the information was merged: e.g., if piece no. 1 bordered on all sides on land of Saint Peter, but piece no. 2 bordered on a river, the information would be entered as BORDERS = 1, STPETER = 1, RIVER = 1.

border directly on land of a principal may, nevertheless, have had important social associations.

Let us take the relatively simple example of an exchange at Sainte-Cécile-la-Valouse. In August 962, Bernart and his wife, Berrels, gave to Saint Peter a field there that bordered on two sides on land of Saint Peter and on two other sides on land of Rainald and Tedeno.[9] This field was 47 perches by 2 perches. In return, Abbot Maiolus and the monks of Cluny gave a different field, one that bordered, on three sides, on land belonging to Rainald and Tedeno and, on the fourth side, a road (*via publica*). This field was 47 perches in circumference.

It seems fairly clear that these two pieces of land were meant to be comparable at least at a symbolic level, since the number 47 is invoked in both. But here the mutual and social character of the transaction appears to end. The territory of Saint Peter at Sainte-Cécile was consolidated by means of this exchange; on two sides, the land received by Cluny was contiguous with other land of Saint Peter. But what of the other two sides that bordered on land of Rainald and Tedeno? Were these simply random people, now to become neighbors of Saint Peter? And what of Bernart and Berrels? What did they gain? The land that Cluny gave up (diminishing but, be it noted, apparently not dismembering any larger holding of Saint Peter) did not afford them a link with the monastery. Did it have any social significance for them at all?

The evidence suggests that it did. Rainald and Tedeno are the keys to the exchange at Sainte-Cécile. We find them involved in an exchange with Cluny in a charter from 949, thirteen years before the exchange of land at Sainte-Cécile.[10] In this earlier exchange, they gave Cluny land at Vaux-sous-Jalogny in return for land at Château (both ca. Cluny). Both sides, in this instance, used the occasion to consolidate their holdings.[11] Then, in a

9. BB 1134;II:225 (8.962; a *notitia* of an act that had taken place); I am standardizing the spelling of the names. Rainald (as in the text of BB 1170;II:258–59 in cartulary A) appears as Rannalt and Rainbalt (BB 1134) and Annalt (BB 1170); he is possibly the same person as Ramnald in BB 744;I:699–700 and as Ramald and Ramalt in BB 886;II:4–5. Tedeno (as in BB 1170 and BB 886) appears as Teteno (BB 1134) and is probably the Tetidinus of BB 744.
10. BB 744;I:699–700 (6.949).
11. The land gained by Cluny: two fields, each bordering on the land of Saint

charter dated two years after the exchange at Sainte-Cécile, Rainald and his wife along with Tedeno and his wife gave to Cluny land at villa "Casellas" (n. id.), while Tedeno and his wife gave in addition a newly planted vineyard (*plantata*) at Sainte-Cécile that bordered on land of Saint Peter on two or three sides, and on a fourth side with land of Bernart and his heirs.[12] Bernart was among the witnesses. In sum, Rainald and Tedeno were well known, both to the monks of Cluny and to Bernart (and, presumably, Berrels). Rainald and Tedeno were at least modest donors to the monastery, and they were neighbors of Bernart and Berrels at Sainte-Cécile. The exchange of land at Sainte-Cécile, at one and the same time, affirmed links among neighbors (including Saint Peter) and helped both laymen and saint consolidate their territory.

Consolidation certainly appears to be a major motive in exchanges with Cluny. Seventy-five percent of the villae that were *gained* by Cluny (in exchange transactions that tell us anything about borders) had at least one border with land belonging to Saint Peter.[13] That contrasts with parcels that the monastery gave up; of these, only 47 percent had a border with Saint Peter.[14] Turning to the other party to the exchange, the numbers suggest similar conclusions. Only 22 percent of the land that was given to Cluny in exchange bordered on land associated with the donor, while, on the other hand, 33 percent of the land that was received from Cluny bordered on one or more sides with land of the recipient.

Peter on two sides. The land gained by Rainald, his wife, Edvera, and Tedeno (Tedeno's relationship to Rainald is not indicated; possibly they were brothers): two fields, one bordering on one side with land of the "filia Ranuardi," which I take to refer to the daughter of Rainald; one bordering on three sides with land of "Ramnaldi cum heredibus," which again I take to refer to Rainald.

12. BB 1170;II:258–9 (1.964); the text copied by Lambert de Barive apparently had the piece of property bordering on land of Saint Peter on two sides, and on land of Pedrono on a third. But cartulary A has in place of Pedrono, "terra Sancti Petri de ipsa plantata vel non plantata."

13. The total number of transactions in which Cluny gained land (and borders are indicated) is 134; in 100 of these, the acquired land bordered that of Saint Peter, in 29 it bordered that of the other principal party, and in the rest it bordered land of neighbors, roads, rivers, etc.

14. Total transactions in this case are 113. For the discrepancy (Cluny gained in 134 instances, but lost in 113), see above, n. 8. Of the 113 transactions, there were 53 in which the lost land bordered that of Saint Peter, and 37 in which it bordered that of the other principal.

Seigneurial "Incorporation"

The push for consolidation evident in these charters was not a constant. It was, rather, a historical process. Duby and others have dated the formation of the seigneurie about the year 1000. In the case of Cluny, we may trace the contours of this process quite precisely, above all through charters of exchange and sale. These were closely related transactions, both being clearly initiated by the monastery in tandem with other parties. While we shall later adduce some figures for donations as well, these cannot be considered so sensitive a barometer of Cluniac designs, since—as we have seen—they were more likely to be initiated by the donor.

Unlike donations, which often began with a pious preamble and generally named Saint Peter as the recipient of the gift, exchanges and sales were mundane transactions between the living: they named the parties to the transaction, including the Abbot or the monk representing the monastery, but *not* the saints that they served.[15] This underlines their mutual nature; but it also signals their worldly and potentially commercial character. From the point of view of periodization, as well, such charters are exceptionally useful. Let us first consider charters of exchange, which were used to consolidate Cluny's property during a fairly narrow band of time.

There are extant ninety-eight charters of exchanges in which Cluny gained land that bordered on one or more sides with Saint

---

15. I have made some calculations for charters of exchange: only one speaks of Saint Peter as a party to the transaction (BB 2580;III:637–38, [1003–4]): "In primis donant monachi Clunienses. . . . Econtra donat jam dictus Teobaldus partibus Sancti Petri." The abbot alone or with the monks of Cluny was the representative of the monastery most often cited. On occasion, the prior was the representative; such as Heldebrannus in BB 466;I:452–53 (936–54 in BB; but in his unpublished marginal notes for the charters, Chaume suggested c. 940). The monks as a whole, without mention of their abbot, were cited frequently only beginning in 987 (BB 1758;III:23, *seniores* in BB 1767;III:28, etc.; between 987 and 1028, thirteen charters cite the "monks" as the Cluniac party). On two occasions an exchange was made with a particular, named monk; it is not even entirely certain that these monks represented the monastery. In BB 2216;III:359 (Chaume, "Obs.," c. 995), Acfredus, the monk of the charter, is the name of a monk at Cluny who often represented it—in tandem with others—as a witness in other sorts of transactions; see Hillebrandt, "Datierungen"; but in BB 2500; III:579 (c. 1000), Lanfredus, *monachus*, does not correspond to any name in the usual roster of Cluny's representatives.

Peter. Between 910 and 940, there were twenty such charters, mostly dating from the abbacy of Odo.[16] There were nineteen such charters under Abbot Aymard, beginning in 942 and extending until 957, after which time Maiolus (who had been made coadjutor of the monastery in 954, a position he held until 964, when Aymard died) began to represent Cluny in charters of exchange.[17] With Maiolus came an expansion in the number of such instruments, along with a comparable increase in the total number of charters. Between 959, when he was first named in a charter of exchange, and 991 (three years before his death), there were thirty-nine or forty such charters in which Cluny gained land bordering with Saint Peter.[18] However, in the abbacy that followed, under Odilo, there was first a continuation, and then a marked decrease in such instruments, although the total number of charters during his abbacy was about the same as during his predecessor's. Odilo held the abbacy of Cluny from 994 until

16. Note that here *charters* are in question, whereas in n. 13 *transactions* are involved. In chronological order: BB 113;I:128–29 (910–11), BB 193;I:180–81 (913), BB 220;I:209–10 (920), BB 259;I:251–52 (926), BB 278;I:273–74 (926), BB 279;I:274–75 (926), BB 280;I:275–76 (926) (all under Berno), BB 375;I:353 (929), BB 376;I:354 (929), BB 381;I:362–63 (930), BB 383;I:364–65 (930), BB 452;I:441–42 (936), BB 473;I:459 (937), BB 477;I:463–64 (937), BB 495;I:480–81 (939), BB 466;I:452–53 (940), BB 506;I:491–92 (940), BB 513;I:499–500 (940), BB 337;I:323–24 (927–42) (under Odo). BB 309;I:305–6 is of uncertain date (Chaume, "En Marge 2," p. 52 n. 2).

17. In chronological order: BB 571;I:550–51 (942–54), BB 590;I:560 (942–54), BB 610;I:570–71 (942–54), BB 703;I:657–58 (947), BB 744;I:699–700 (949), BB 753;I:710 (949), BB 760;I:716–17 (950), BB 761;I:717 (950), BB 762;I:718 (950), BB 769;I:724–25 (950), BB 795;I:746–47 (950–51), BB 830;I:785–86 (952), BB 831;I:786–87 (952–53), BB 851;I:806 (953), BB 852;I:806–7 (953), BB 881;I:836–37 (954), BB 886;II:4–5 (954–55), BB 1024;II:119–20 (957). To these should be added BB 650;I:605–6 (943–64).

18. In chronological order: BB 1058;II:152–53 (959), BB 1059;II:153–54 (959), BB 1063;II:156–57 (959), BB 1086;II:179 (960) (citing Aymard as Cluny's agent), BB 1134;II:225 (962), BB 1142;II:232–33 (962–63), BB 1173;II:260–61 (964), BB 1217;II:298–99 (966), BB 1255;II:338–39 (969), BB 1259;II:341–42 (969), BB 1260;II:342 (969), BB 599;I:564–65 (970), BB 1315;II:391 (972), BB 1339;II:412–13 (973–74), BB 1340;II:413 (973–74), BB 1360;II:428–29 (974), BB 1374;II:439–40 (974), BB 1463;II:517-18 (978–79), BB 1464;II:518–19 (974), BB 1468;II:521–22 (979), BB 1486;II:539 (979), BB 984;II:80–81 (978–85), BB 896;II:11–12 (Chaume, "Obs.," 980–86), BB 1570;II:615–16 (981–82), BB 1612;II:649–50 (982), BB 1616; II:653–54 (982), BB 1653;II:686–87 (983–84), BB 1693;II:717 (984), BB 1758;III:23 (987–96), BB 1767;III:28 (987–96), BB 1797;III:51–52 (988–89), BB 1809; III:60–61 (989), BB 1816;III:64–65 (989–90), BB 922;II:34 (Chaume, "Obs.," 990–94), BB 959;II:58–59 (990), BB 1839;III:83–84 (990), BB 1847;III:89–90 (990), BB 1874;III:106–7 (991), BB 1902;III:127 (991–92). To these should perhaps be added BB 573;I:552 (Chaume, "Obs.," 980–1000), which might equally well fall under Odilo's abbacy.

Table 4. Exchanges in which Cluny gains land bordering on land of Saint Peter

Decades	No. of charters	Decades	No. of charters
910s	2	980s	12
920s	7	990s	11
930s	6	1000s	7
940s	9	1010s	2
950s	15	1020s	2
960s	8	1030s	0
970s	10	1040s	0
		Uncertain	7
		Total	98

his death in 1049. During that time, only nineteen or twenty charters of exchange contributed to the consolidation of Saint Peter's lands.[19] Almost all of these were drawn up in the 990s or between 1000 and 1010. The last such exchange occurred in 1028. After 1032 there was a hiatus of seventeen years before another charter of exchange of *any* sort was drawn up.[20] Such facts point to policy rather than chance. Table 4 summarizes the results by decade.

In part, these numbers are symptomatic of a shift from "sociable" ideas about property. Exchanges always were part of a system of gift and countergift. But every piece of property given away by Cluny was a piece of Saint Peter's territory (whether or not it bordered on any other land of Saint Peter). About the year 1010, Cluny stopped giving out the property of Saint Peter. About fifteen years before this, it had declared some of its property inviolable. At the council of Anse in 994, Cluny begged for and received a special privilege:

19. In chronological order: BB 580;I:554–55 (Chaume, "Obs.," c. 990–1000), BB 2017;III:228 (Chaume, "Obs.," c. 995), BB 2134;III:315 (Chaume, "Obs.," c. 994–1008), BB 2216;III:359 (Chaume, "Obs.," c. 995), BB 2387;III:484–85 (997), BB 2214;III:358 (Chaume, "Obs.," c. 994–1016), BB 2234;III:370–71 (Chaume, "Obs.,"c. 1000), BB 2500;III:579 (c. 1000), BB 2553;III:618 (1002), BB 2565;III:627 (1002–3), BB 2580;III:637–38 (1003–4), BB 2610;III:659 (1005), BB 2048;III:253 (Chaume, "Obs.," c. 1010–15), BB 2092;III:285–86 (c. 1010), BB 2762;III:783–84 (1022), BB 2023;III:234 (Chaume, "Obs.," c. 1028). To these should be added three charters of uncertain date, but falling within Odilo's abbacy: BB 2127;III:311 (993–1048), BB 2214;III:358 (994–1016), BB 2434; III:520–21 (997–1031).

20. Of course, in every instance, such statistics can count only extant charters.

that no one might presume to [claim] any of their churches, with tithes and *servitia*, that belonged to their monastery; nor any fortification belonging to that holy place, inside or outside, without the order and consent of the Abbot or the brothers of that place. Indeed, we [Fathers of the Council] decree [Cluny's] exemption by conceding and entirely confirming the estates of that holy place. They [the Council members] have interdicted most forcefully, excommunicating and anathematizing by their pontifical authority [anyone] who infringes or violates or takes away booty from the churches or the buildings and cellars pertaining to that place [Cluny], or who takes or robs at Lourdon mountain in the pagus of Mâcon [where Cluny had a castle]; or at Blanot, or at Bézornay, with the curtis and villa attached to it; or at Mazille, Péronne, Chevignes, Solutré, Ecussolles, and Clermain with their appurtenances, or at Saint-Victor, constructed on the Rhins river; and also at [Sainte-Marie de] Beaumont-sur-Grosne in the pagus of Chalon.[21]

We shall have occasion to consider carefully the places named in this document, which had come, by 994, to make up the core of Saint Peter's holdings (see Chapter 5 and Map 5). At this point, let us look in detail at one of them: Bézornay. Cluny's acquisitions there may serve as a "case study" of the consolidation of the lands of Saint Peter.

A "Vendopolis" at Bézornay

About the year 995, Cluny made an exchange of fields at Bézornay with a man named Walter. Cluny received three fields.

---

21. BB 2255;III:384–88 (994): "scilicet omnia eorum ecclesias cum decimis et servitiis ad eundem cenobium pertinentibus vel burgum ejusdem sancti loci, infra et extra, sine precepto et consensu abbatis vel fratribus ejusdem loci aliquam personam nullus presumat. Sancimus etiam privilegium concedendo et in omnibus confirmando potestate[m] sancti loci superius dicti infringere aut violare vel predam auferre vel ęcclesiis cum domibus et cellariis ad eundem locum pertinentibus, scilicet in pago Matiscensi, Lordonem montem capere vel depredare, sua pontificali auctoritate excommunicando, anathematizando, vehementissime contradixerunt; Blanoscum scilicet et Besorniacum, curtem et villam sibi adherentem; Macerias et Peronnam, Cavinias, Solestriacum, Scociolas et Claromane cum apendiciis suis; Sanctum Victorem constitutum supra fluvium Remis; Belmontem etiam in pago Cabilonensi sito. . . ."

Two of them were surrounded by land belonging to Saint Peter. One ˜of them had a border with Saint Peter on only one side. In return, Walter got one field: on one side it bordered on a via publica, on another side it was bounded by land of Bertard, on a third side by land of Landricus and Rothard.[22]

Like all transactions, this exchange was not an isolated event. In this instance it involved economic and political interests as well as personal associations. Walter's exchange came right in the middle of what might be called a campaign on Cluny's part to consolidate Saint Peter's land at Bézornay. Unlike Flagy, where land was parceled out to Cluny in gifts, Bézornay was a "vendopolis," a place dismembered (by its inhabitants) and consolidated (by Cluny) through exchanges and above all through sales.

Bézornay did not appear in the documents of Cluny until 957, when Ricfredus donated a mansus there.[23] Two years later

22. BB 2017;III:228–29 (Chaume, "Obs.," c. 995).

23. BB 1038;II:131–33 (10.957). There are fifty-eight charters connected with Bézornay for the period 909–1048, dating from 957 to 1037. At first glance, there appear to be documents connected with the place from before 957: BB 340;I:325 is dated 927–42 because it appears in cartulary A under the rubric of Odo's abbacy. Chaume recorded his doubts about it in "En Marge 2," p. 51 n. 7. The document concerns a donor named Acardus (= Achardus) who gives land at Bézornay that, on one side, borders land of Landricus. We find an Achardus who witnesses land transactions at Bézornay c. 990 (in BB 1850;III:92, BB 1863;III:99) and an Achardus, miles, who exchanges land there with Cluny in a charter (BB 3246;IV:366) dated in Hugh's abbacy because it is placed there in cartulary B. Landricus is the name of a landowner at Bézornay who appears in charters of the 980s and 990s (BB 1519;II:568–69 [dated 980], BB1735;III:7 [dated 11.987], BB 902;II:17 [dated by Chaume c. 990]). The best guess for the date of BB 340, then, is probably c. 990. BB 298;I:299 and its companion BB 299;I: 300, concerned with Bézornay and "Veroliae" (near Massy, ca. Cluny), are also dated 927–42. But these texts must be redated. Because BB 298 cites an Odo, monachus, it was taken by both the redactors of cartulary A and by BB as referring to Abbot Odo. But the same donors, Artaldus and Gauzfredus (in BB 298, Guisfredus; in BB 2114;III:301, Gausfredus and Gaufredus), exchange with Cluny *the same pieces of land* in charter BB 2114;III:301 (dated 993–1048 because it names Odilo abbot and because it appears in cartulary B under that abbacy). BB 2114 makes clear that Odo is a monk representing Cluny along with Odilo: "Ego Odilo abba monachorum Sancti Petri Cluniacensis monasterii, et omnis congregatio ejusdem aecclesiae, et ego Oddo monachus." This text also gives a witness list, which helps us to date it, along with the fact that Artaldus and Gauzfredus are referred to as *milites*, a fact that speaks against a date much before c. 1000. Two charters appear closely related: BB 2080;III:275–76 (Chaume, "Obs.," 1034–39) and BB 2895;IV:97–98 (1034–35), both of which concern Veroliae. These, in turn, relate to BB 2326;III:444–45 (Chaume, "Obs.," c. 1000), which makes precise family connections: Artaldus and Gauzfredus are brothers, the sons of

Abbot Maiolus was involved in two closely related exchanges at Bézornay.[24] These exchanges had the mutual character that we explored at the beginning of this chapter. In the first, Cluny received land from Bernoldus, presbyter, in a variety of places (but not at Bézornay), all abutting land of Saint Peter. In return, the monks gave Bernoldus a field at Bézornay that bordered on land of Saint Peter and, on another side, land of Bernard, who (as we shall see immediately) was closely associated with Bernoldus. In the second exchange, Bernard and his wife gave a field at Bézornay that bordered on land "of Saint Peter and of Bernoldus, presbyter," while Maiolus gave Bernard a field, also at Bézornay, that had borders with Bernard himself and, on two sides, with Saint Peter. About two years later, Cluny received an apparently unrelated donation of some land at Bézornay.[25] Then all activity involving Bézornay ceased for nearly twenty years.

We shall take up in a moment the period in which that hiatus ended. But it is important to point out that there was a similar pause later on. Only two charters concerned with Bézornay, both donations, are extant for the period between about 1010 and 1049.[26] The facts then, are these: four charters document land transactions with Cluny at Bézornay before 962; two are extant for the period after 1010. But in the thirty years between 980 and 1010, fifty-two charters recording Cluny's activities at Bézornay were drawn up.[27] Nine of these were exchanges; their

Hupert and Humberg; their uncle on their father's side is Witbert. Thus BB 298, 299, and 2114 must all be dated 1000–35. For reasons that will become clear shortly, I favor the earlier end of these dates; most activity involving Bézornay occurred before 1010.

24. Exchanges are in BB 1058;II:152–53 and BB 1059;II:153–54 (both dated 959); these have nearly the same witness lists and were both drawn up at precisely the same time by Berardus. They show that Cluny had land at Bézornay to exchange, but the process whereby this was amassed is not revealed by the extant documentation.

25. BB 1119;II:210–11 (II.961–62).

26. BB 2887;IV:81 (dated 1032–33) and BB 2919;IV:119–20 (1037). To these may perhaps be added BB 2225;III:365–66 (993–1048), with a range of dates too broad to be enlightening.

27. Most of these will be discussed in due course. The few that do not come under the categories of exchanges, sales, and donations are: BB 926;II:37–38 (Chaume, "Obs.," 1006–8), a temporary donation *by* Cluny *ad medium plantum* (for which term, see n. 79); BB 927;II:38 (after 926), the werpitio of the land given in BB 926 by the son of the recipient; BB 2093;III:286 (993–1048), another werpitio; BB 2255;III:384–88 (994), the Council of Anse; BB 968;II:64–65 (990), land given to Cluny as pledge for a loan; BB 455;I:444 (986–87), land "donated"

Table 5. Exchanges at Bézornay, 909–1049

Years	No. of charters
909–79	2
980–89	1
990–99	5
1000–49	3
Total	11

distribution over time, including two from before 980, is summarized in Table 5.[28]

So spare a sample can only tease. Yet, as we shall see from the other charters, the bulge in the 990s is significant. Exchanges were not a major factor in land transactions at Bézornay; but they revealed their flexibility there, and because of this, they provide a nice microcosm of what was occurring in general. In the last chapter, we saw how the exchange of Fontana led to a long history of gifts and countergifts. At this point we may recall that that exchange, which took place in 981–82, included some of Eva's land at Bézornay. This coincided with the beginning of the campaign of consolidation of the land of Saint Peter at Bézornay that will be traced here.[29] But the real push there began in the 990s.

In 990 and 991, a man named Livo gave a field to Cluny. In exchange he received a field, not at Bézornay but rather at Donzy, about four kilometers to the south. We see the same phenomenon in an exchange about 1000, when Manno gave Cluny land measuring $36 \times 6\frac{1}{2} \times 6$ perches at Bézornay, while he received land with exactly the same dimensions at "Misy."[30] This kind of calculated transaction easily shaded into a sale. In the case of Livo, the field at Donzy came to him from Cluny

---

to Cluny as a penalty for default on a loan.

28. In order by (approximate) date: BB 1584;II:628–99 (981–82); BB 902;II:17 (Chaume, "Obs.," c. 990); BB 1850;III:92 (990–91); BB 1874;III:106–7 (991); BB 2017;III:228–29 (Hillebrandt, "Datierungen," c. 994–c. 1004); BB 2216;III:359 (Chaume, "Obs.," c. 995); BB 2233;III:370 (Chaume, "Obs.," c. 1000); BB 2500; III:579 (c. 1000); BB 2062;III:262–63 (Hillebrandt, "Datierungen," 1004–19).

29. BB 1584;II:628–29.

30. BB 2233;III:370. "Misy" is l.-disp., near Saint-Vincent-des-Prés.

Figure 3. Line drawing of Christ, probably made at Cluny in the early eleventh century. (B.N. nouv. acq. lat. 1455, fol. 112 v.) Courtesy of the Bibliothèque nationale, Paris.

along with six solidi. This is the first of several instances in which the mechanism of exchange came quite close to a purchase at Bézornay.[31]

In 991, for example, Rotart and Doda made an exchange with Cluny of fields at Bézornay. There was nothing remarkably acquisitive about the exchange proper: Cluny was given a field with one border with Saint Peter; it gave away a field with one border with Saint Peter and two borders with neighbors and associates of Rotart and Doda. But in the same charter was also a sale: Deodatus sold to Cluny a different field at Bézornay for two solidi and one denarius.[32] In 995, in another exchange, Arembert gave Cluny a field measuring two and one-half perches, while he received from Cluny land totaling one and one-half perches and, "over and above the exchange," eight denarii.[33] The most mutual of transactions thus became a money matter. At Bézornay exchanges were used to further interests that (from one point of view, at any rate) superseded social purposes. The same was true, too, of sales there.

Sales to Cluny, indeed, constituted a near majority of transactions at Bézornay. Twenty-five extant charters, or 43 percent of the total, record purchases made there by Cluny during 980–1010.[34] This is quite extraordinary in view of the general picture for this thirty-year span, where sales form about 7.5 percent of the total number of land transactions with Cluny.[35] From the very first, the land purchased by the monastery at Bézornay had at least one border with other land of Saint Peter. Thus, in 980, Landricus, Maingaudus, and their wives sold to

31. The exchange is BB 1850;III:92 (990–91).
32. BB 1874;III:106–7 (4.991).
33. BB 2216;III:359: "super scamium vero ipse monachus (Acfredus, who represented Cluny in the transaction) octo denarios dedit."
34. In order by (approximate) date: BB 1519;II:568–69 (980), BB 1598;II:639 (982), BB 470;I:456–57 (987), BB 1729;III:2–3 (987), BB 1815;II:64 (989), BB 1818; II:65–66 (990), BB 1820;II:67 (990), BB 1822;II:68–69 (990), BB 1860;III:98 (990), BB 1863;III:99 (990–91), BB 1874;III:106–7 (991), BB 1876;III:108 (991), BB 1877; III:108–9 (991), BB 1904;III:128–29 (991–92), BB 1905;III:129 (991–92), BB 1907; III:130–31 (991–92), BB 1938;III:155 (992–93), BB 1980;III:192–93 (993–96), BB 1928;III:147–48 (994–96), BB 2248;III:380 (994), BB 2249;III:380–81 (994), BB 2252;III:382–83 (994), BB 2629;III:672 (1006); BB 2631;III:673 (1006); BB 2632; III:674 (1006).
35. The total number of land transactions during the period were 1,437: there were 1,074 donations and 107 purchases, other transactions making up the difference.

Table 6. Purchases at Bézornay, 909–1049

Years	No. of charters
909–79	0
980–89	5
990–99	17
1000–49	3
Total	25

Cluny a field that bordered Saint Peter's lands on three sides.[36] In 982, Amandus sold a field that was surrounded by Cluny's land.[37] In 987, Arembert and Alaria sold to Cluny a vineyard that bordered on three sides with Saint Peter; at the same time they gave the monastery a meadow that had one border with Saint Peter.[38] The first years of the 990s saw a veritable flood of sales: Walter (doubtless the same man who was involved in the exchange with which we began this section) and his wife sold Cluny land that had two borders on Saint Peter's land; Arembert sold the monks land with two such borders; Guntard and his wife sold a field one side of which bordered the saint's land; Amblardus, who had already sold Cluny a vineyard in 989, now sold the monks two fields, all sides of which bordered Saint Peter's land, and one field with a single border in common with the land of Saint Peter; Bovo sold a field with one border in common, and so on.[39] The 990s were clearly the critical years for purchases at Bézornay (see Table 6). In fact the effective end of this campaign of consolidation coincided with the Council of Anse in 994.

Certainly, at the same time that this systematic consolidation was taking place through purchases, people made donations of

36. BB 1519;ii:568–69; in BB 1735;iii:7 (dated 11.987), Landricus and his wife gave Cluny property at Bézornay as a gift; by contrast to the sale, it bordered on three sides with a via publica and on the fourth side with the land of one Bernaldus. It is difficult to know what to make of the varying prices of land and their significance.

37. BB 1598;ii:639 (3.982): "terminat terra supradictae ecclesiae."

38. BB 470;i:456–57.

39. In the order mentioned in the text: Walter, BB 1818;iii:65–66 (1.990); Arembert, BB 1820;iii:67 (2.990); Guntard, BB 1822;iii:68–69 (4.990); Amblardus's first sale, BB 1815;iii:164 (989), and second sale, BB 1860;iii:98 (990–91); Bovo, BB 1863;iii:99 (990–91).

Table 7. Donations at Bézornay, 909–1049

Years	No. of charters
909–79	0
980–89	2
990–99	9
1000–49	4
Total	15

Note: BB 2225, dated 993–1048 is here included in the period 1000–49.

land at Bézornay; but these were unusually infrequent. While donation charters make up 75 percent of the total number of charters for the period 980–1010, they constitute only 26 percent of the charters concerned with Bézornay. There are fifteen donation charters for the period 980–1010.[40] Their distribution suggests the same pattern as the purchases (see Table 7).

Taken together with purchases and exchanges, these donations seem part of calculated economic policy rather than part of social give and take. But in the affairs of men, such exclusive categories rarely obtain. Rather, in addition to having clear economic purpose, the transactions we have seen here had *at the same time* social significance. In order to demonstrate this, we must look at the social networks involved in transactions at Bézornay.

Bézornay in the Social Scheme

In the first place, at Bézornay (as elsewhere) the people who sold Cluny land, or who were involved in exchanges, were also donors. Landricus sold Cluny land at Bézornay in 980; in 987 he was a donor there.[41] In the 980s Arembert and his wife

40. In order of (approximate) date: BB 470;I:456–57 (Chaume, "Obs.," 987); BB 1735;III:7 (987); BB 1843;III:86 (c. 990); BB 340;I:325 (c. 990; see above, n. 23); BB 1906;III:129–30 (991–92); BB 1912;III:134–35 (992); BB 1918;III:139–40 (992); BB 1935;III:152–53 (992–93); BB 1838;III:82–83 (992–93); BB 2225;III:365–66 (993–1048); BB 2404;III:496 (997–98); BB 2456;III:538–39 (998); BB 332;I:320 (Chaume, "Obs.," c. 1000); BB 2667;III:699–700 (1008); BB 2098;III:291 (c. 1000; see Appendix C, n. 10).
41. Donation: BB 1735;III:7; sale: BB 1519;II:568–69. He witnessed the exchange recorded in BB 902;II:17.

gave two meadows to Cluny at the same time that they sold the monks a vineyard bordering Saint Peter's land on three sides.[42] He did the same thing in 991–92, when he sold Cluny a field and then at the same time gave the monks a meadow.[43] Aynard, Arembert's father, followed suit in 992–93, when, in one transaction, he sold the monks two perches of a field and gave them one perch.[44]

Thus Cluny had ongoing and multifaceted relationships with the people at Bézornay. Moreover, its links with people there were part of a larger picture, extending to past and future generations, and broadening out beyond Bézornay to other villae in the countryside around Cluny. Let us look, for example, at the case of Deodatus.

Deodatus had important relations with Cluny at Bézornay. We glimpse him selling a field to Cluny in 991 and giving the monks a field (presumably a different one) about 1000.[45] More important, perhaps, he was actively involved in a gift-giving network with his neighbors there. Guntard, who gave Cluny land at Donzy and Bézornay in 992, specifically included a vineyard "for the soul of Deodatus, who gave it to me on condition that I give alms for his soul every day of my life. But I am doing something even better by giving it for his soul to the brothers [at Cluny] so that they may add [his soul] to their prayers."[46] At about the same time, Odulfus gave another vineyard to Cluny "which Deodatus gave to us."[47] Odulfus's wife and son witnessed Guntard's donation, along with Deodatus himself. Gir-

42. BB 470;I:456–57 (Chaume, "Obs.," 987).
43. BB 1906;III:129–30 (991–92).
44. BB 1938;III:155.
45. Sale in BB 1874;III:106–7, part of a charter of exchange between the monks of Cluny and Rotart and his wife, Doda (4.991); gift in BB 332;I:320 (Chaume, "Obs.," c. 1000). A Deodatus with a wife named Liva was involved in a donation of land at Fuissé and Pouilly that was drawn up at Bézornay (BB 1567;II:613–14 [11.981–82]; but ten years later we find a Deodatus with wife Gaultet at Bézornay, where they make a sale to Cluny (BB 1818;III:65–66 [1.990]). Perhaps these refer to the same man, who appears as well in BB 1918;III:139–40 and BB 1935;III:152–53.
46. BB 1918;III:139–40 (2.992): "dono vineam unam in villa Besorniaco, pro anima Deodati, qui mihi illam donavit, eo tenore ut omnibus diebus vitę meę elemosinam facerem pro anima ejus; sed ego melius agens, dono eam pro anima ejus jam dicti loci fratribus, ut ipsi in orationibus suis eam aggregentur."
47. BB 1935;III:152–53 (992–93).

bald, *sacerdos*, was present at both transactions. He had bought a field in 987 that was surrounded on all sides by land of Saint Peter.[48] The lines between neighbors at Bézornay and Cluny were tightly intermeshed; and Deodatus was embraced all the more closely when his soul was added to the flock (*aggregare*) for whom the monks at Cluny sent up prayers.

But Deodatus's connections with Cluny extended beyond heaven and Bézornay. He came from a family with land scattered throughout the region (much like Antelmus, in the previous chapter); and he and his family used their land and their relations with their neighbors to tie themselves to Cluny as donors, as sellers, as witnesses, and as scribes.

In fact, the history of Deodatus's relations with Cluny extended back to the 930s, with his father, also Deodatus. The elder Deodatus was a scribe who drew up numerous charters between about 930 and 960. In 949 or 950, he himself donated a vineyard to Cluny in villa "Dias" (n. id.; perhaps near Joncy).[49] One of his sons, Malguin, signed the witness list directly after him, and it appears that he himself drew up the charter. Similarly, at about the same time, he signed as a witness and was the scribe for the charter of a donation by Malguin and his wife involving land at "Bussiacus" (near Saint-Huruge?) and *in villa Tonaio* (n. id.; in vicinity of Aynard).[50] In 953, in tandem with one Berengerius, Deodatus père gave land to Cluny at Chevagny; he also wrote up the document "with the fullest good will."[51]

Deodatus the younger was old enough to write in 979 or 980, when his father made a major donation to Cluny of land in the pagus of Autun.[52] In this transaction the younger Deodatus was paired with one of his brothers, Anselmus. Because of their association we can relate other land transactions with Cluny to

48. BB 1729;III:2–3 (10.987): Bernulf and his wife, Eldeart, sold the field to Girbaldus.

49. BB 756;I:712–13; villa Dias is discussed in Chaume, *Origines* II/3:1126. Joncy is ca. Mont-Saint-Vincent.

50. BB 757;I:713–4. Saint-Huruge and Aynard are both ca. Saint-Gengoux-le-National.

51. BB 839;I:794–95 (4.953): "Ego Deodatus rogatus et plinissima [*sic*] voluntate escripsit."

52. BB 1505;II:555–57 (11.979–80). The places in the Autunois that are mentioned in the charter are not identified.

this same Deodatus. For example, we know that he gave land at Villards in the pagus of Autun to Cluny in 982, because the charter recording this transaction shows Anselmus signing directly after him.[53] The document was drawn up at Bézornay, and the scribe was Girbald, *sacerdos*, whom we have already met. Similarly, Deodatus and his brother were present at Bézornay when a charter was written up for Heldricus, who gave land at Farges, first to his son, Durannus, and then to Cluny upon Durannus's death.[54]

To sum up: were we to take in isolation the seemingly simple sale of a field at Bézornay to Cluny, we would miss the multi-textured relationship that existed between Cluny and those with whom it dealt. In the case of Deodatus, a long history of familial associations with the monastery at many different places in the neighborhood of Cluny made his sale part of a series of social events. And yet, at the same time, it was a transaction finely calculated for its economic benefits. Was this the rule?

The Significance of Sales

Historians have tended to think that cash renders a transaction impersonal: all sales are final. As we shall see in detail in the next chapter, clear and useful distinctions have been made between the systems of a "gift economy" and a "commercial economy." Yet, while conceptually clear, these systems remain intellectual constructs. Leaving theoretical considerations for the most part to the next chapter, we need nevertheless to consider two points here before exploring the significance—both to the monastery and to those with whom the monks dealt—of Cluny's purchases.

First, there is nothing intrinsically impersonal about a sale, which is (after all) like the exchange, a simultaneous giving

53. BB 1586;II:630 (1.982): "in villa Vilaris," perhaps Villards (dép. Allier), ca. Moulins. See Chaume, *Origines* II/3:828 n. 10.

54. BB 1903;III:128 (991–92). It seems possible that the Deodatus we are following here is the Deodatus, levita, who appears, for example, in BB 1660; II:692–93 (11.983–94), accompanied on the witness list by Durannus and Aldulfus (= Odulfus? as above). It is also possible that he continued his father's work as a scribe: BB 1871;III:105 (3.991), drawn up at Igé, has "Deodatus scripsit".

and taking. Indeed, in some cultures, such as that on the Truk Islands, a sale is as much a social event as any gift giving.[55] And in eleventh- and twelfth-century Languedoc, where mortgage contracts were given out in cash, social standings were as much on the line as loans.[56] Even in our own archetypically commercial culture, salesmen know the importance of "contacts," and the "old boy network" may bind as tightly as kinship ties. The question for the historian, then, is not, Is it a sale? but, What purposes are served by a particular transaction in a particular instance? If relationships are cultivated to make a sale, then economic motives predominate. If sales are made to effect relationships, then social needs are to the fore.

Second, purchases and bequests in a "commercial society" may be made to demonstrate social prestige, power, and virtue, just as much as stores of gold were accumulated in the "gift economy system" to be distributed in orgies of generosity. The chief distinction to be made between these two uses of wealth is that in the commercial system the social relationship between the suppliers of material goods and their purchasers are, by and large, incidental to the primary economic goals of both; whereas in the gift economy, it is the social relationship that counts.[57]

In the case of Cluny, therefore, the fact that the monastery purchased land tells us little unless we know why these purchases were made, whether they set up or affirmed ongoing social relationships, and what uses the monks made of them.

Sales to Cluny

Between the time of its foundation and 1049, Cluny made about 206 purchases of land.[58] In comparison with land gained

55. Ward H. Goodenough, *Property, Kin, and Community on Truk* (Hamden, Conn: Archon, 1966).

56. Fredric L. Cheyette, "Mortgage and Credit in Eleventh and Twelfth Century Languedoc" (Paper presented at the workshop, "The Structure of the Aristocracy in Feudal Europe," University of Florida, Gainesville, March 1985).

57. Nevertheless, there is a "culture" of salespersons and customers that varies from store to store and that implies a social meaning in the very act of purchase.

58. This figure is based, once again, not on the number of charters per se but rather on the number of transactions, as defined in the Introduction.

in other ways, mostly through donations, land obtained by sales was insignificant, forming about 6 percent of the total number of transactions. Purchases were clearly used sparingly and selectively. We have already seen one place, Bézornay, in which the monks chose to use the strategy of purchase to consolidate their holdings while at the same time confirming the social links—with Landricus, Arembert, and Deodatus, for example—that they had with their donors. In some ways Bézornay was exceptional; it was singled out by the Council of Anse as part of the inviolable property of Cluny. It was, therefore, special: sacred like Cluny's most personal belongings—its cellars and buildings—and prestigious as well as economically advantageous.[59] The number of purchases at Bézornay as compared with donations was unusually high. By amassing the land of Saint Peter there, the monks were creating a special locus for Saint Peter, a seat for him in the Mâconnais. There were more purchases at Bézornay, both in absolute numbers and in proportion to other transactions, than at any other single place in the charters of Cluny.

Yet, in other important ways, Bézornay was typical. For us, it may serve as a paradigm, indeed, for the kind of consolidation of the land of Saint Peter that could be effected through sales. Although no other purchases were part of so vast a campaign as that which was put into effect at Bézornay, on the whole they followed a similar model. At Bézornay 81 percent of the land that was purchased by the monks bordered at least in part the property of Saint Peter.[60] For sales as a whole, this was true for 70 percent of the transactions. Of the sales at Bézornay, 33 percent of the land purchased bordered land of the seller. This corresponds to 25 percent for sales in general. Thus some kind of consolidation and/or neighborly linkage was involved in most of the purchases Cluny made. But to what avail?

The distribution of Cluny's purchases may be readily seen from Map 3, which indicates all places at which Cluny made more than a single purchase. The purchases were concentrated in the region to the north of Cluny, somewhat more toward the

59. Cluny's special property is discussed in detail in Chapter 5.
60. A calculation based, of course, on extant charters where border indications are given.

Map 3. Places connected with sales

west than the east. On the whole their pattern compares nicely with the contours of Cluny's banal property (over which Cluny had both economic control and political power), the boundaries of which were set forth clearly at the end of the eleventh century. It is important to realize that the purchases we are discussing took place before 1049.[61] The answer to the question "To what avail were these purchases?" is, precisely, to create a banal territory and to cement social bonds at the same time. We have already seen both of these processes at work at Bézornay.

But not all places on the map fall within the *bannum* Cluny was creating; and these require explanation. The four pieces of land purchased so far away from the monastery, at Châtel-de-Neuvre, in the Auvergne, puzzling as they may appear at first glance, all involved the same group, which sold land to Cluny between 966 and 974.[62] These purchases were possibly related to Cluny's acquisition of Souvigny in 954.[63] Certainly, the concentration of land to the north of Cluny, around Sennecey-le-Grand, was part of activity set in motion by the donation, in 980, of the church of Sainte-Marie at Beaumont-sur-Grosne along with a great deal of land and many serfs to work it.[64] All the purchases in the area around Beaumont came in the wake of that donation, mostly in the first decade of the eleventh century.[65] Very likely Cluny was creating here terram Sanctae Mariae, an inviolable zone around the church at Beaumont, which (like Bézornay) was named at the Council of Anse.

61. The *designatio sancti banni*, i.e., the area in which Cluny had banal powers, appears in a privilege of Urban II (10.1095; = JL 5583; = *Bull. Clun.*, p. 25). But it was already anticipated at the Council of Anse and in other, earlier, privileges. See Chapter 5. The outlines of Cluny's *bannum* are in "Croquis VI" in Duby, *La société*, p. 512.

62. BB 1204;II:286–87 (966), BB 1284;II:362 (5.970), BB 1302;II:379 (5.971), BB 1368;II:434–35 (3.974). The recurring names are so numerous as to preclude doubt that the same group is involved. They are: Rainbaldus (Raimbalt), Ebrard, Martin, Girard, Garinus (Garin), Nichran (Mebran, Nisbran, Nicbran), Calter (Alterius, Walter), Teotbert (Otbert, Tetbert, Teetbert).

63. See Chapter 5. However, none of the people associated with Souvigny seems to have been involved in the sales at Châtel-de-Neuvre.

64. BB 1525;II:574–75 (5.980). For further discussion, see Chapter 5.

65. Two purchases at "Ariengae" (l.-disp. near Beaumont-sur-Grosne, ca. Sennecey-le-Grand; see Chaume, *Origines* II/3:1011 n. 8): BB 2640;III:680 (1006–7), BB 2645;III:683–84 (1007); three at Beaumont (see Chaume, *Origines* II/3: 1008 n. 7): BB 572;I:551 (Chaume, "Obs.," 981–97), BB 2638;III:678–79 (1006–7), BB 2644;III:682–83 (1007); five at Vieil-Moulin (ca. Sennecey-le-Grand; see

La Chize

In La Chize the monks made seven purchases.[66] Fifty-five charters in Cluny's archives pertain to La Chize before 1049, six of which do not directly involve Cluny. About 14 percent of the charters, then, document sales to the monks. This is a figure much above the norm. Compare it with Igé, for example, for which there is a comparable number of charters but only one sale (hence it does not figure on our map). Why were there so many sales at La Chize? It was not on the list of places drawn up at the Council of Anse, nor did it later come under the sway of Cluny's banal power. The church of Saint-Vincent de Mâcon had a good bit of land at La Chize, but its relationship with Cluny was not at all parallel to that of Sainte-Marie de Beaumont: the church of Saint-Vincent did not belong to Cluny.[67] Saint-Vincent was the seat of the bishop of Mâcon. The monks of Cluny could never hope to create terram Sancti Vincenti et Sancti Petri at La Chize.

But, in the instance of La Chize, the purpose of sales was not to consolidate territory but rather to cement relationships with prominent individuals. We shall see that one man, Adalbaldus, and two others closely associated with him, Adalricus and Johannes, presbyter, participated in most of the sales and exchanges—and in many of the donations—that took place there over the course of the tenth century. They, and a few others, were largely responsible for the anomalous position of La Chize on our map.

Transactions at La Chize began in May of 943. They neatly

Chaume, *Origines* II/3:1005 n. 2; Déléage, pp. 1036–37): BB 2372;III:474–75 (1000–1007), BB 2593;III:647–48 (1004), BB 2598;III:651 (1004–5), BB 2602;III: 654–55 (1004–5), BB 2624;III:668–69 (1005–6); four at Sennecey-le-Grand (see Chaume, *Origines* II/3:1008 n. 10): BB 2325;III:444 (1002–4), BB 2330;III:448 (1002–4), BB 2376;III:477 (1000–1007), BB 2592;III:646 (1004).

66. Generally "Segia" or "Seia" in the charters. Chaume identifies it positively as La Chize (ca. Mâcon-Nord) (*Origines* II/3:1101–2); and Déléage, while suggesting the alternative of La Chaize, ca. and co. Sologny, agrees. The two possibilities, in any event, are not far apart.

67. That Saint-Vincent owned land at La Chize is shown in the documents of Cluny, not in those in the cartulary of Saint-Vincent. For land bordering on Saint-Vincent's land, see, e.g., BB 645;I:600–601, BB 760;I:716–17, BB 1545;II: 593–94, etc.

Table 8. Land transactions at La Chize, 909–1049

Interval	No. of charters
909–39	0
940–49	5
950–59	2
960–69	6
970–79	6
980–89	5
990–99	13
1000–1009	5
1010–19	4
1020–29	3
1030–49	0
Total	49

Note: See Appendix E for the documentation.

coincided with the accession of Abbot Aymard, which might be considered significant except for the fact that Cluny's involvement at La Chize afterward remained fairly steady over the decades, aside from a marked bulge in the 990s (see Table 8).

Aymard made at least two purchases in May 943, one from Martin and his wife, Osanna, and one from Gontard and his wife, Etva.[68] These people would remain closely associated with Cluny, as we shall see in a moment. But they were only bit players in the drama that took place around the land at La Chize. For the star, we must look at Adalbaldus.

Adalbaldus was present at those two sales to Cluny in 943. His importance is clear, as in the first his name followed those of the principals; and in Gontard's sale, Adalbaldus joined the list of sellers.[69] In 966 he sold a vineyard to Cluny. His witnesses included Johannes, presbyter; Martin, whose sale in 943 we have just discussed; Rothard, who reappeared at two later sales transactions; and Gontard.[70] To sum up: there were seven

68. BB 636;I:593 (5.943), BB 638;I:594–95 (5.943): here I take Gonerio and his wife, Etva, to be the same as the Gontart and his wife, Sayra, who, in 950, made an exchange with Cluny of land partly at La Chize (BB 760;I:716–17 [1.950]).

69. BB 638;I:594–95: "Gonterio et Etva, et Adalbor et Joan." Joan was probably identical to Johannes, presbyter, who quite regularly was paired with Adalbaldus. The land at La Chize in this charter had a border with terra Joan.

70. BB 1203;II:286, BB 1930;III:149 (992–93) and BB 1936;III:153 (992–93). In BB 1930, Adalbaldus sells a vineyard; present are (in order) Aalbaldus (= Adal-

sales at La Chize to Cluny in the tenth century; Adalbaldus, in tandem with a group of associates, was involved in all but two of these.[71]

We might be tempted to call Adalbaldus a medieval land salesman, with only cash on his mind, were it not for the fact that he also participated in other sorts of transactions with Cluny. He (or possibly his son) witnessed, for example, a donation by Adalricus at Sologny.[72] He was present, with Adalricus, when Gontard and his wife made an exchange with Abbot Aymard in 950.[73] He was present again when Maimbodus exchanged land at La Chize with Cluny with the consent of David, presbyter.[74] And when David himself purchased land from Adalgart and his son Adaldrannus, in 968, Adalbaldus was present again, as the first person on the witness list, with Johannes, presbyter, drawing up the document.[75] A year later Osepia made an exchange

---

baldus), Aaldricus, Rothardus, Bernardus, Johannes, Mainardus, Vuidradus, and Gontardus. In BB 1936, Mainard sells a *petiola de vinea* that borders on one side with Rothard, and another piece of land that borders with the seller's and with Adalbaldus's land. Present are (in order) Mainardus, Widradus (= Vuidradus), Aaldricus, Guntardus, Rotardus, Bernardus, Aalbaldus, Johannes. In a closely related transaction at Sologny (BB 1917;III:139 [3.992]), Adalricus and his brother and wife give a vineyard and a mansus; present were Adalricus, Widradus, Tellendis (the principals), Mainardus, Rothardus, Bernardus, Adalbaldus, Gontardus, Johannes, Durannus. This donation offered exceptionally rich possibilities for social contact: the land given to Cluny (with reservation of usufruct) bordered on land of Saint Vincent, Saint Ciricus, Saint Peter, land *de ipsa hereditate*, and on land of Adaldricus's brother, Widradus.

71. The other sales are BB 2503;III:581 (975–87; see Appendix E, n. 2), BB 615;I:573–74 (942–54), a sale by one Ermelaus and his wife, Benedicta. There are also ambiguous charters: BB 2433;III:519–20 (Chaume, "Obs.," c. 998), involving Livo, who speaks of a donation ("dono in elemosina") but also receives thirty solidi; and BB 1769;III:29–30 (987–96), where Ranaldus speaks of making a donation but also receives a horse worth one libra. It seems the latter two should be taken as an indication of the fluid meaning of money: as both cash and countergift. BB 1072;II:166–67 (959–60) mentions *two* Adalbalduses. The witness list reads in part: "S. Martino. S. Alio Martino. S. Atalbol. S. alio Atalbol." Because they are grouped together, and because Adalbaldus and Martin were at times grouped together, it seems likely that the two Atalbol (= Adalbaldus) names refer to father and son.

72. BB 1917;III:139 (2.992).

73. BB 760;I:716–17 (1.950).

74. BB 1072;II:166–67 (11.959–60).

75. BB 1234;II:324 (3.968). Given the rules of naming patterns, rules which were (admittedly) pretty much out of use by the tenth century, the names Adalgart, Adaldrannus, and Adalbaldus suggest that there was a family relationship between these people, the precise nature of which it is not possible to reconstruct.

with Cluny that was witnessed by Adalbaldus and by Johannes.[76] And Adalbaldus was first among the witnesses of a transaction that accompanied Osepia's, in which David, presbyter, gave a vineyard to Cluny.[77]

In the 970s, Adalbaldus continued to be associated with Johannes and Adaldrannus at La Chize. When Johannes bought a field from Adaldrannus, Adalbaldus was first on the witness list.[78] When Johannes gave Cluny, in a very generous donation, a number of different kinds of land at La Chize, Adalbaldus was not only on the witness list (along with Adaldrannus) but also was directly and intimately involved with the lands that were donated: the curtilis and mansus given to Cluny bordered, on the south and west, with land of Adalbaldus and the donor, Johannes; and the vineyards *ad medium plantum* had come to Johannes from Adalbaldus.[79]

Adalbaldus was present at five more land transactions, all but one of them donations to Cluny, in the period 979–87.[80] However, he was not present when Dominica gave Cluny a curtilis at La Chize in 979, though, interestingly, he was a witness (along with Martin and Johannes as scribe) for her gift to her husband of land *in Suplinniago* (near Laizé, ca. Mâcon-Nord).[81] Nor was he a witness when, about 980, Aldegardis and her son, Mainard, gave a curtilis, two vineyards, and a field to Cluny, though his

76. BB 1259;II:341–42 (5.969). Osepia made the exchange with "Johannem, monachum, vel potius donnum Maiolum, abbatem de Cluniaco," so it is possible that the Johannes directly following Adalbald's name is the representative from Cluny rather than Johannes, presbyter, who, in any case is present as the scribe of the document.

77. BB 1260;II:342 (5.969). The charter, from cartulary A, is apparently defective, recording only David's part of the exchange.

78. BB 1369;II:435–36 (3.974): the sellers also included Adaldrannus's wife and Ingelbert and his wife.

79. BB 1361;II:429–30 (3.974): "Et dono vobis mea parcionem de medium plantum qui de Adalbaldo mihi advenit." In the *méplant* or *complant* contract (*ad medium plantum*), a newly planted vineyard was divided into two at the end of five years, half becoming that of the peasant who had transformed it into vineyard, half going to the original lord of the land. See Déléage, 239–40; Duby, *Rural Economy*, p. 139.

80. BB 1486;II:539 (5.979), exchange between David and Cluny; BB 1487;II:540 (5.979), donation with reservation of usufruct by David; BB 1489;II:541 (5.979), donation by Eusebia (David's mother?); BB 1724;II:747–48 (986–87), donation by David.

81. BB 1350;II:421 (1.974): Dominica gives land to Hiradus, her *senior*. BB 1485;II:538 (5.979): Dominica donates land at La Chize.

association with Mainard is documented, and others from his group—Martin, Rothard, Widrad, and Adalricus—were present.[82] In brief, Adalbaldus was not physically present at every transaction. But he was a leading figure around whom clustered men and women who, taken as a whole, dominated land transactions with Cluny at La Chize.

Adalbaldus was a purely local "star." If the very first donation to Cluny at La Chize, which took place just after the very first sale in 943, had nothing to do with him, it was probably because the donors had more far-flung connections. Arlebald and his wife Alindrada, those early and initial donors,[83] had land at Marchiseuil, Ruffey, and Mons (all ca. Cluny) in the Mâconnais, and at Thoissey (dép. Ain; ca. Trevoux) in the pagus of Lyon.[84] Similarly, in the 960s Adalbaldus's name was absent from two large donations to Cluny that were only partly concerned with land at La Chize, involving as well more remote territories: Bladinus and his wife gave land at La Chize, at Purlanges (ca. Cluny), and at "Avalosus" (n. id.); Teudrada and her amici gave property at La Chize and at Joux (ca. Tramayes) and land that stretched from the villa "Treticus" (n. id.) to Joux.[85] Similarly dispersed was the donation by Gotefredus and Alexandra in 981.[86]

By the 980s, successors to Adalbaldus were appearing at La Chize. They did not so much displace the people who had surrounded Adalbaldus as they rearranged them, adding some

82. BB 1545;II:593–94 (c. 980). On Mainard, see n. 70 above.

83. BB 645;I:600–601 (10.943). The witness list includes Raimund, who consents; Hildibald; Aygulf; Alberic; Ramnulf; and Rotard. The name Rotard alone is not sufficient to warrant identifying him with the Rotard in Adalbaldus's group. On the other hand, the presence of the name part -baldus in both Adalbaldus and Arlebaldus may indicate some blood relationship.

84. BB 519;I:504–5 (c. 940), BB 557;I:540–41 (942–54), BB 1008;II:103–4 (12.956). None of the names on the witness lists here is that of a person known from La Chize. And yet when Landrada, possibly the daughter of Alindrada (she cannot be Alindrada herself, since her husband was named Maiolus), gave land to Cluny in the pagus of Chalon, present were Arlebaldus (as we would expect) and Johannes, clericus, who may be the same man as the Johannes, presbyter, of the Adalbaldus group; see BB 697;I:651–52 (1.947).

85. Bladinus in BB 1117;II:208–9 (11.961–62); Teudrada in BB 1190;II:274–75 (11.965–66).

86. BB 1554;II:601–2 (5.981): donating land at "Curciacus" (near Igé, ca. Cluny) and Verzé (ca. Mâcon-Nord) as well as at La Chize. Gotefredus and Alexandra were, in any event, major donors to Cluny, the founders of Berzé-la-Ville. See above, Chapter 2, n. 42.

(doubtless younger) new ones. These successor groups clustered around a few new foci: around, for example, Odila or Livo or Rannaldus.[87] What we see at La Chize, throughout the tenth century and into the eleventh, is not groups formed solely for the purposes of commerce, but rather commerce affirming local groups and helping to form new alliances, particularly—in the cases we know about—with Cluny. The complex and over-lapping motives at work in Adalbaldus and the people around him, so intensely local in their relations, to reach out beyond La Chize to that monastery eleven kilometers to the north, or—its corollary—the motives of Cluny to forge alliances with people in that particular place, must remain largely hidden from the historian. But it cannot be doubted that, in so reaching. the people of La Chize were including Saint Peter in their world and themselves in the world of Saint Peter. The sales at La Chize form part of a series of social acts that, to be sure, had many important economic motives and consequences, but also ce-mented affiliations. It is not surprising that a man from La Chize, Gyso, would give his son to Cluny to become a monk and thus "to serve the Lord with them for all time."[88]

We have seen that social bonds were formed and affirmed by land transfers of every sort. It is time now to ask why this should have been the case.

---

87. For Odila, BB 1954;III:171 (Chaume, "Obs.," 994–96), BB 2320;III:441 (Chaume, "Obs.," 1005–20), BB 2706;III:729 (1016); for Livo, BB 2295;III:422 (995), BB 307;I:304–5 (Chaume, "Obs.," c. 995), BB 2810;IV:13 (1028–29); for Rannaldus and Robert, BB 2019;III:230–31 (Chaume, "Obs.," c. 1020), BB 2739; III:763–64 (c. 1020).

88. BB 1625;II:662 (982–83): "cum eis omni tempore Domino serviat."

CHAPTER FOUR

Landed Property and the Gift Economy

"WITHIN THESE BOUNDARIES [at La Val] we give everything, whole and complete, on this day, to God and his apostles, for the salvation of our souls. . . . And from this day forth let those who live at [Cluny] do whatever they want with these properties. But if anyone should want to usurp this donation, let him not be able to appropriate what he claims."[1] On the face of it, nothing could be more straightforward than a transfer of property. The formula just quoted was repeated, more or less in the same form, in nearly every charter of Cluny. But what did it mean?[2]

1. BB 1341;II:413–4 (11.973–11.974): "Infra istas terminationes, totum ad integrum a die presenti donamus Deo et prelibatis apostolis, pro remedio animarum nostrarum . . . et faciant post hac die de his rebus supradicti loci habitatores quidquid facere voluerint. Si quis autem hanc donationem voluerit usurpare, non valeat vindicare quod repetit." The place in question is La Val, ca. Monsols (dép. Rhône); see Chaume, *Origines* II/3: 839.

2. Aron J. Gurevich, in "Représentations et attitudes à l'égard de la propriété pendant le haut moyen âge" (*Annales: ESC* 27 [1972]: 524), argues that "Les masses populaires demeurèrent longtemps une 'majorité silencieuse,' non seulement parce qu'elles n'avaient pas d'interprètes de leurs idées et de leurs états d'esprit, mais aussi parce que la langue de la culture officielle était vraisemblablement incapable de transmettre les représentations profondes du monde conservées par le peuple." See, further remarks on p. 525. Against this view, at least in the instance of the Cluniac charters, may be adduced the following: (1) the charters were public "self-declarations" of the principals, articulated before witnesses (see Herwig Wolfram, "Einleitung," in *Intitulatio II: Lateinische Herrscher- und Fürstentitel im neunten und zehnten Jahrhundert*, ed. Herwig Wolfram, MIÖG, Erg., 24 [Vienna: Böhlaus, 1973], pp. 7–18, esp. p. 8, where the titles used by rulers in charters, whether public or private, are called "herrscherliche Selbstaussage"; (2) the scribe who drew up the charters was sometimes a neighbor of the monks; (3) the property system that is revealed in the charters of Cluny was shared—presumably along with the mental constructs that gave it meaning and

Ownership

Within the mélange of notions, expectations, and assumptions about ownership in the early Middle Ages, historians have abstracted two sets of ideas—or more precisely they have constructed two "models"—which for the moment we may set forth in bold relief.[3] In one model property was legally controlled by individuals or corporate groups. It could be alienated by its owner in return for money (in sales) or in order to make a gratuitous offering (in donations). When seisin was transferred, the property came under the *dominium* of the new owner, who in turn had the right to alienate the land as he saw fit. We may say that this model was already in place in the late Roman Empire, as it was revealed in the law books of that period. It has been, therefore, associated with Roman norms, although it represented an attenuation and simplification of classical Roman law.

The second model, which was, indeed, an inspiration for the anthropological notion of the "gift economy," also involved private property. Here, too, property could be alienated in a sale upon payment of a price. But it could not be alienated gratuitously.[4] Rather, gifts were made in return for, or with the expectation of, a countergift. Or they were made between people who had a relationship of dependence; the donee's ownership was contingent on the maintenance of this relationship, and the donor retained certain rights in the land. Hence, gifts did not

---

the terms that expressed them—by the monks of Cluny and the laity alike; (4) it is unlikely that the donors to Cluny ordinarily represented the "silent majority." Nevertheless, Gurevich is right to call attention to the problem of language. The meaning of the charters must be understood from the context, from the ways that the words are used, and certainly not from a dictionary of classical Latin. For a similar problem in the interpretation of English documents, see Eric John, *Land Tenure in Early England: A Discussion of Some Problems* (Leicester: Leicester University Press, 1960): "Discussions of book-right usually start with the assumption that what the charters mean and what they say have at most a tangential relationship" (p. 2).

3. The following discussion is drawn largely from Levy, pp. 21–43, 84–99, 127–49. See also Jobert, pp. 51–136.

4. See Frederick Pollock and Frederic William Maitland, *The History of English Law*, 2 vols. (1898; repr. of 2d ed., Cambridge: Cambridge University Press, 1968), 2:213: "Every alienation of land, a sale, an onerous lease in fee farm, is a 'gift' but no 'gift' of land is gratuitous; the donee will always become liable to render service."

constitute an irrevocable transfer of property. A classic, albeit relatively late, instance of such a gift was the fief.

This second model is sometimes associated with original Germanic law, but, because of the lateness of any sources purporting to describe pristine German customs, it is probably best simply to recognize that the two models were, even initially, roughly contemporaneous.[5] In the formulas of later documents and law books, it appeared that the "Roman" idea of *donatio* triumphed: "The very institution then of a purely lucrative and unrestricted gift," wrote Ernst Levy, "bears witness to the reception of Roman law."[6] In the charter quoted at the beginning of this chapter, the phrase *quidquid facere voluerint* ("whatever they want to do with it") and the *si quis* clause ("but if anyone . . ."), for example, are clearly based on Roman forms. Yet if Roman terms triumphed, the patterns and expectations of the second model did not disappear. The documents from Cluny suggest that both models were part of a pool of traditions upon which people drew as they gave, took back, negotiated, and wrote charters about property transfers.[7]

When Cluny exchanged property at Fontana for land elsewhere, its original hold still operated; and in the next generation it received Fontana back as a gift. In turn, the family that had once received the property and had given it back in donation continued to consider it to be within their purview. Between the years 1014 and 1039, at least four groups claimed the same place. There were, of course, the monks of Cluny. There was Rana, the widow of Antelmus's brother, and her new husband. There were the claims of the family of Adelaida, Antelmus's sister. There was a similar claim by another sister of Antelmus, Eve, along with her sons. Cluny's ownership of the land was

---

5. On the contrasting pair of Germanic and Roman models, see the cautionary remarks regarding medieval judicial procedures but equally applicable to notions of property ownership, in Davies and Fouracre, speaking of "the impossibility of neatly separating early medieval judicial procedure into Roman and Germanic traditions, the two elements conventionally seen as its components. Instead we have seen procedures grow out of a pragmatic accommodation of traditional practices to present needs" (p. 215).

6. Levy, p. 167.

7. The argument in John, "'Secularium prioratus,'" pp. 124–27, begins with a similar observation but sees the consequences in the abuses of the proprietary monastery rather than in a system of gift giving.

never proved; that was not the point of the werpitio. The point was to adjust claims so that an equilibrium among them, satisfactory to all, could be achieved. Rana made a "quitclaim or, if we have any right [in the land], a donation." Eve's was couched in similar terms. Adelaida's claims were paid off by Landric, count of Nevers, who possibly himself had some claim on the land (about which we know nothing, however).

Thus land could intersect with a number of groups, all of whose claims were, from time to time, recognized. Consider the formulation of property "ownership" in a charter of Duke William the Pious, the founder of Cluny:

> Be it known to all who will hear or read this that the aforesaid duke, within the time set by law, summoned Anscherius to question him because the latter held the villa of Aine against both civil and public law. . . . When this Anscherius was able to offer neither a will nor a document of inheritance . . . he returned that villa and restored it legally to its legal owner, namely Count [i.e., Duke] William. Then he [Duke William] was immediately zealous to restore [the villa] to Cluny, where it had long been and to which it pertained by the testamentary document which Abbess Ava [William's sister] made in favor of Cluny.[8]

Here at least three different parties "owned" the land at Aine: Duke William, the "legal possessor" (legalis possessor); his sister Ava, who had already given Aine *per testamentem* to Cluny; and finally Cluny itself, to which the land "pertained" (*pertinebat*).

There remained the claim of Anscherius, which might at an-

8. BB 192;I:179–80 (10.913). The text of the entire charter reads: "Noticia quo ordine vel qualiter Willelmus comes quandam villam nomine Aionam, lege favente, super Anscherium conquisivit. Noverint igitur omnes qui hoc vel audituri vel lecturi sunt, quod prefatus dux, infra tempora legibus prestituta, eundem Ansgerium interpellavit, quia scilicet villam Aionam contra jus vel civile vel publicum teneret; nec vim aliquam inferens, nec potestatem quamvis princeps exercens, concessit locum et tempus, ut si posset sese legaliter tueretur. Causa vero diu multumque discussa ac tandem ad sui finem ordinarie perducta, cum isdem Anscherius neque testamentariam neque hereditariam valeret obtendere, recredit se et in magno ut erat placito, in villa Anaziaco, iiii kalendas novembris, cunctis videntibus, reddidit eandem villam, et suo legali possessori, Willelmo videlicet comiti, legaliter restituit. Tunc ille mox Cluniaco, unde dudum fuerat et ad quam per testamentum pertinebat, quod Ava abbatissa, de eodem Cluniaco eidem fecerat, reddere studuit, atque Bernoni abbati et Cluniensibus monachis ad honorem Dei sanctorumque apostolorum Petri et Pauli perpetualiter possidendam recipere fecit."

other time have been recognized. For Anscherius almost certainly held property at Aine. We know that his son, Hubert, the prior (*praepositus*) of the church of Saint-Vincent de Mâcon, was a landowner there. In 951 Anscherius witnessed Hubert's donation of a mansus at Aine to Cluny for the remission of the sins of (among others) his father (namely Anscherius) and his mother, Engela.[9] This was not the first donation to Cluny from this family, however, which in fact supported Cluny for at least three generations. Anscherius's father, Ranald, and his mother, Alexandra, had given Cluny an alod at Ruffey in 935.[10] Ranald knew Ava, the sister of Duke William, who had given Aine to Cluny: she had at one time given land at villa "Belna" (n. id.; near Igé) to him. In 943 Ranald's grandson, Hubert, recounted this history of Belna, and then gave property to Cluny, along with other land there that came from his paternal inheritance.[11] At the same time, Hubert gave Cluny land at Igé for the souls of his father and mother. The family of Anscherius, then, like the family of Antelmus, was tied to Saint Peter, the *princeps apostolorum* (as one of Hubert's charters noted) through land. In this instance, the family was also closely bound to the church of Saint Vincent. Hubert was, after all, its *praepositus*, the office just below that of the bishop and second-in-command over the canons, who at Saint-Vincent lived together in common.[12] Sometime during the period 943–58, Hubert gave land to Saint-Vincent that he held at Avittes.[13] The donation was for the souls of Anscherius and Engela, and also for a man named Autgarius, who had originally given the property to Hubert's parents (see Genealogy 6).

Ownership overlapped in a similar manner in a donation *in precaria* given by Cluny to the bishop of Apt.[14] We shall take

9. BB 807;I:761–62 (4.951).
10. BB 427;I:414–65 (1.935). Anscherius witnessed the donation.
11. BB 633;I:590 (5.943): "rebus meis . . . in villa Belna, quicquid in ipsa villa Ava abbatissa dedit avo meo Ramnoldo vel quod pater meus [Anscherius] in ipsa villa." The donation was important enough for the monks to draw up a separate confirmation, in BB 635;I:592–93.
12. See *M*, pp. xxii–xxv.
13. *M* 317:185; the donation was confirmed in *M* 70:59. Villa Avistas in the pagus of Lyon is identified in *M* as Avittes (dép. Ain), ca. Pont-de-Vaux, arr. Bourg (p. 551).
14. BB 1071;II:164–66 (959–60). There are twelve villae named in the redaction of cartulary A. See the list of villae given by Fulcharius (Maiolus's father) to

Genealogy 6. The family of Anscherius

Ranald = Alexandra
|
Anscherius = Engela
|
Hubert

up precarial donations in detail below. For now it needs only to
be noted that in this instance the direction of the gift giving was
away from the monastery. Some of the *res sanctis apostolis
Petro et Paulo* (as the charter put it) in ten different *villae* were
given in life estate to Arnulf, bishop of Apt, and his consanguineus, Teotbertus. Yet the same charter, which was drawn up in
the name of Abbot Maiolus, went on to explain that

> all this [land] came to me and my brother Eyric by way of inheri-
> tance from our parents. We, that is I, Maiolus, abbot of the said
> monastery of Cluny, and my brother, for the salvation of our souls
> and those of our parents and all Christian faithful, handed it over to
> God and his holy apostles, Peter and Paul, at the monastery of
> Cluny. We cede, therefore, everything in those *villae* just named,
> or whatever my grandfather Fulcherius and my father, also named
> Fulcherius, held or acquired in the county of Apt, to the said
> bishop.[15]

Maiolus, who had given the property to Cluny, now with his
brother alienated this *res sanctis apostolis*.[16]

Thus the conveyance of a piece of property into the possession
of another did not irrevocably suppress the claims and rights of

---

Raimodis (Maiolus's mother) in BB 105;I:117–19 (9.909), and see also the list of
Fulcherius's alods in BB 106;I:119–20.

15. BB 1071;II:164–66: "Ista omnia [michi] et fratri meo Eyrico ex successione
nostrorum parentum nobis obvenerunt. Nos vero, ego videlicet Maiolus, prefati
coenobii Cluniacensis abbas, et predictus frater meus, pro remedio animarum
nostrarum, nostrorumque parentum, omniumque fidelium christianorum, Deo
et sanctis ejus apostolis Petro et Paulo in Cluniaco coenobio tradidimus. Omnia
itaque in denominatis villis conjacentia, sive quantum avus meus Fulcherius
et genitor meus ejusdem nominis Fulcherius, in comitatu Aptensi tenuerunt
vel conquisierunt, totum predicto episcopo et ejus consanguineo Teotberto concedimus."

16. On Maiolus, see Jean Barruol, "L'influence de St. Mayeul et de sa famille
dans la renaissance méridionale du XIᵉ siècle d'après une documentation nouvelle du Cartulaire d'Apt," in *Cartulaire de l'église d'Apt* (835–1130?), ed. Noël
Didier (Paris: Dalloz, 1967), pp. 67–86, and Iogna-Prat, *Agni immaculati*, esp. pp.
118–121.

former owners. On the contrary, these were recognized in memorials such as the pro anima formula, in claims such as the werpitiones, in consents to further alienation, and as we shall see, in more tangible ways as well.

Donations in Precaria

No series of documents better illustrates the enduring rights of all claimants to a piece of property than those in which Cluny itself gave a gift in precaria, that is, as a life estate.[17] The importance of such donations has long been recognized. Schreiber and Duby considered them economically significant: "The generosity of the princes and of the Church [including Cluny] created in large measure these great fortunes [of the four great castellan families of the Mâconnais]."[18] Yet, as we shall see, most precarial donations *gave back* hereditary lands that had once belonged to the family of the recipient.[19] Gifts of land, shifting from neighborhood magnates to Cluny and then back again, continually reinforced the links between the monastery and the rich.

17. In Appendix B I have included all estates given out by Cluny for a fixed term under the heading *Precaria*. Strictly speaking, however, precarial arrangements are probably best limited to those so denoted in the text of the charter. Quite unlike these truly precarial arrangements, which were made, by and large, with the rich, the monastery also gave out to presumably humbler folk a few gifts of uncultivated vineyards with the expectation of receiving back half, now planted and productive, after a fixed period. For these donations ad medium plantum, see BB 826;I:782, BB 926;II:37–38, BB 963;II:61, BB 1900;III:126, BB 2459; III:541, BB 2575;III:634, BB 2726;III:750, BB 2764;III:785–86, and see the provisions in BB 3089;IV:263: a grant of "terram . . . deserta [sic], ad hedificandum et construendum, et ut teneat in beneficium quandiu vixerit, et post mortem ejus totum ad integrum in dominicatum Sancti Petri perveniat [deserted land, for the purpose of reclaiming and working it, and so that it is held as a benefice as long as (the donee) lives and after his death it reverts wholly and completely to the demesne of Saint Peter]." Concessions ad medium plantum have not been included in Map 4. A donation *by* Cluny to a supplicant, but not for a fixed term, is BB 372;I:349; but this is entirely unique. BB 2195;III:348 concerns the concession of bread and wine for life.

18. Duby, *La société*, p. 57.

19. See Bouchard, *Sword*, pp. 98–101, who makes much the same observation. For a study of the language of Cluny's precarial arrangements, see Michel Petitjean, "Remarques sur l'emploi de la précaire par l'abbaye de Cluny, d'après les chartes éditées par A. Bruel," *Mémoires de la Société pour l'Histoire du Droit et des Institutions des anciens pays bourguignons, comtois et romands* 41 (1984): 121–28.

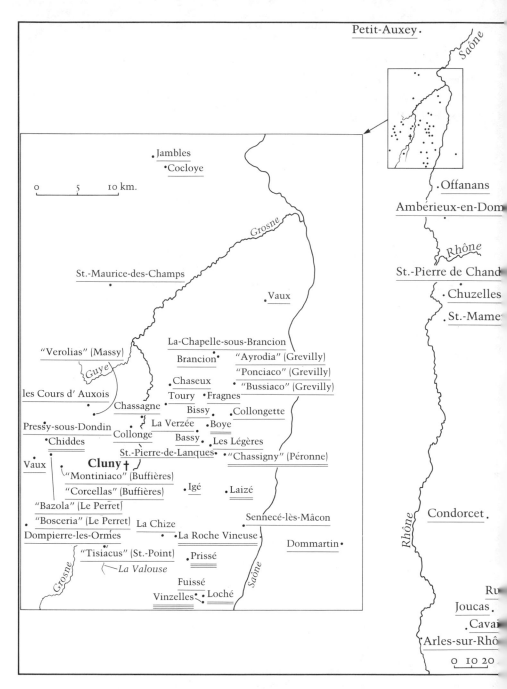

Map 4. Precarial and other fixed-term grants

Note: Each underline indicates a precarial donation involving that place.

For our period there are forty-six charters in which Cluny gave land away as a life estate.[20] (For the locations of such donations, see Map 4.) In seventeen of these, Cluny's gift was part of an exchange in which the monks received land at the same time as they gave some away.[21] Here their grant was explicitly a "countergift." But the same was true, if at times less obviously, of most of the others.

Take, for example, the instance of a donation in precaria to the cleric Leutbald of land in thirteen different villae in 978 or 979.[22] Leutbald, who would become bishop of Mâcon (993–1016), and who was the brother of Teuza, heiress of Brancion, no doubt was an important person in the region (see Genealogy 7). Handing these lands over to a magnate such as Leutbald was certainly in part Cluny's way to protect land that it could not otherwise defend.[23] The power of the rich could be harnessed to help the church.[24] But there was more to precarial transfers than that. Leutbald had a claim to the particular properties he received. His uncle Leutbald, his father, Warulf, and a man named Raculf, who appears to have been a relative, had given most of them to Cluny in the first place.[25]

---

20. In addition to those cited n. 21 are: BB 834;I:788–89, BB 907;II:20–21, BB 917;II:29–30, BB 919;II:31–32, BB 920;II:32, BB 935;II:42–43, BB 941;II:47, BB 1064;II:157–58, BB 1071;II:164–66, BB 1073;II:167–68, BB 1088;II:181–82, BB 1186;II:271, BB 1271;II:351, BB 1389;II:451–52, BB 1423;II:479–80, BB 1460; II:513–15, BB 1501;II:552–53, BB 1953;III:170, BB 2050;III:254–55, BB 2087; III:281, BB 2217;III:360, BB 2661;III:695–96, BB 2314;III:436, BB 2581;III:638–39, BB 2594;III:648–49, BB 2742;III:765–66, BB 2853;IV:53–54, BB 2883;III:77, BB 2950;IV:150. Some of these charters involve more than one location.
21. BB 299;I:300, BB 325;I:316, BB 852;I:806–7, BB 880;I:835–36, BB 912;II: 24–25, BB 942;II:47–48, BB 1322;II:397–99, BB 1396;II:456–57, BB 1464;II: 518–19, BB 1497;II:549–50, BB 1500;II:551–53, BB 1529;II:579–80, BB 1813; III:63, BB 1852;III:93 (in return for a quitclaim), BB 2014;III:226–27, BB 2480; III:557–58, BB 2517;III:591–92.
22. BB 1460;II:513–15 (11.978–11.979).
23. See Johannes Fechter, "Cluny, Adel und Volk: Studien über das Verhältnis des Klosters zu den Ständen (910–1156)" (diss. Tübingen, 1966), pp. 27–36.
24. See Rosenwein, *Rhinoceros*, pp. 79–81; Edmond Ortigues and Dominique Iogna-Prat, "Raoul Glaber et l'historiographie clunisienne," *Studi Medievali*, 3d ser., 26 (1985): 537–72, esp. 570.
25. Previous ownership of the land was acknowledged in the charter recording the precarial transfer, BB 1460;II:513–15: "Has ergo res, sicut nobis jam dictus Raculfus per testamentum condonavit, ei [Leutbald] concedimus. . . . Concedimus ipsi etiam et alias res que sunt ex parte domni Leudbaldi, avunculi ejus [We grant these properties to Leutbald just as Raculf handed them over by written deed to us. We grant to him also the other properties which are from

Genealogy 7. The Grossi

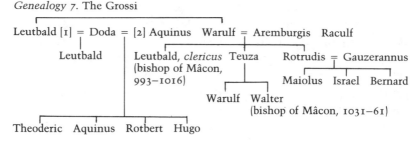

Note: The brothers Warulf and Leutbald are in BB 283;1:278–79 (4.927), where Doda, Leutbald's wife, also appears. Their son Leutbald appears in BB 370;1:348 (12.928) and BB 802;1:754–56 (3.951), discussed below. Doda later married Aquinus and had four sons (BB 798;1:750 [1.951]). Leutbald, son of Warulf and Aremburgis, appears in BB 1088;II:181–82 (8.960). Teuza appears in BB 2719;III:741–43 (10.1019). The link with Rotrudis is less certain, but in BB 2827;IV:31 (1030?) Maiolus Poudreux, who without doubt was the son of Rotrudis, calls Leutbald *avunculus meus*. Rotrudis was a family name; it had been the name of the mother of Leutbald, husband of Doda. See the discussion in Bouchard, *Sword*, pp. 295–300. This branch of the family is discussed in Chapter 2, above. See also Duby, *La Société*, pp. 336–46.

In 950 or 951, Raculf gave Cluny land at (1) Collongette, (2) Boye, (3) "Ayrodia" (near Grevilly), (4) "Chassigny" (near Péronne), (5) "Bussiacus" (near Grevilly), and (6) "Ponciacus" (n. id.) (all others ca. Lugny).[26] Leutbald, then *levita*, was present. About ten years later, Warulf, Leutbald's father, appeared before Count Alberic (with Raculf as a witness) to quit his claim to some of this land—at Boye—as well as to land that did not appear in the charter of Raculf: half of the church of Saint-Germain at Igé, land at Bissy-la-Mâconnaise, and at Bonzon; and, over and above that, the church of Saint Saturninus at Mazilly, and land at Dombine.[27] During the very same month, presum-

Lord Leutbald, his uncle]." Bouchard, in *Sword*, p. 100, suggests that Raculf may have been Doda's brother.

26. BB 793;1:744–45 (950–51); places identified by Chaume, *Origines* II/3: 1127: Colonicas may be Collonge, ca. St.-Gengoux, co. Cruzille, or Collongette, ca. and co. Lugny.

27. BB 1087;II:180–81 (8.960). For the identification of the places, see Chaume, *Origines* II/3:1135. From the way in which villae are grouped in this charter, it would appear that property at Mazilly and Dombine was considered to be part of a set of claims different from those on the other land: "vuirpivit contra illos ipsas res [i.e., at Boye, etc.]; alias res in ipso pago, quas ipse Vuarulfus super eos reclamavit, hoc est ecclesia in honore sancti Saturnini [etc.] [He quitclaimed on their behalf those properties (at Boye, etc.); Warulf quitclaimed in the same pagus the other properties that he claimed against them, namely the church of

ably slightly after this, Abbot Maiolus gave back in precaria to
Warulf, his wife, Aremburgis, and his son Leutbald the property
at Igé (except for the church), at Boye, and at Bissy.

The donation of Raculf in 950 was the basis for the precarial
donation the monks of Cluny made in 978/79 to Leutbald. This
gift involved the land at (1) Collongette, (2) Boye, (3) "Ayrodia,"
(4) "Chassigny," (5) "Bussiacus," and (6) "Ponciacus," named
in precisely the same order as they had been listed in Raculf's
donation over a quarter century earlier. But the precarial donation involved more land as well: at (7) La Verzée, (8) Les Légères,
(9) Fragne (all ca. Lugny), (10) Chaseux (ca. St.-Gengoux), and, in
the pagus of Autun, (11) Dompierre-les-Ormes (ca. Matour) and
(12) villa "Vallis."[28] Were these also return gifts?

The answer must be in the affirmative, for these same properties, too, appear in an earlier donation, one again dating from
a quarter-century before. The donation was by another Leutbald, the son of Doda and her first husband, yet a third Leutbald,
the uncle of Leutbald, clericus, Cluny's precarist donee. In the
course of this important donation, first by Doda and then by
himself, Leutbald *fils* took the monastic habit and then disposed
of his paternal inheritance: land at (7) La Verzée, (9) Fragne, (11)
Dompierre-les-Ormes, and (12) villa "Vallis" in Autun. At the
same time, Doda gave land at (10) Chaseux.[29] Of the property

Saint Saturninus, (etc.)]." According to BB 856;I:810–11 (10.953), half of the
church at Igé was given to William the Pious by Ava, his sister; William then donated it to Cluny. The charter is a werpitio or *reditio* of this and another partial
church by Hugo, son of Donana (= Doda), which claimed she held the land "per
donum et per cartam quae Leutbaldus senior ejus incartavit [by the gift and by
the charter which Leutbald, her husband, recorded in writing]." In 962 (BB 1124;
II:215–16) Count Alberic also gave Cluny half the church at Igé, presumably the
other half.

28. BB 1460;II:513–15; the place names as given in the charter were: "(ex
parte Raculfi) in pago Matisconense, in agro Griviliaco . . . villa . . . Colonicas . . .
in villa Boyaco . . . in Bassiaco . . . in villa Ayrodia, in loco qui dicitur Rocca . . .
in villa Cassiniaco . . . in Bussiaco . . . in villa Ponciaco. . . . (ex parte Leudbaldi,
avunculi ejus) in Virziaco . . . in Bassiaco. . . . in Lescherias [= Les Légères?] . . .
in Fraxno . . . in Casotis . . . in pago etiam Augustodunensi, in villa Domni Petri
. . . et in Vallis." I have taken identifications for this charter from Chaume, *Origines* II/3:1127, but it seems to me equally likely that "Virziaco in agro
Griviliaco," which Chaume gives as La Verzée, may refer to Verzé, since Bishop
Leutbald's uncle, also Leutbald, held property at Verzé already in the 920s, as BB
248;I:239–40 (924–25) shows.

29. BB 802;I:754–56 (3.951): Doda gave land *in Casoto*; Leutbald gave land to
his brothers with the provision that it then revert to Cluny: at "Fraxnedo villa

given to Leutbald in 978/79, there remains, then, only the property at (8) Les Légères to account for. This was almost certainly also land that once belonged to his family; in 985 Raculf gave "what I have" at Les Légères, along with land at Ayrodia and at Bussières (ca. Mâcon-Sud), to Cluny.[30]

The history of this gift did not, of course, end with its precarial donation to Leutbald. That donation was given only as a life estate, after which it was to revert to the monastery.[31] But other expectations and claims besides those of Cluny were also operating. The case of Chaseux, for example, nicely illustrates the way in which that piece of property, originally Doda's gift to Cluny, continued to be used to forge links and mend fences within a circumscribed social circle. For Leutbald did not hold onto it until his death. Rather, he gave it to a man, Gauzerannus, whose relative he had killed.[32] This did not take the property out of the purview of Leutbald's family, however. For Leutbald's nephew, Walter, at the time prepositus and soon to be the bishop of Mâcon, was the lord (senior) of Gauzerannus. The land remained in Gauzerannus's family for a time; it was inherited by his son, Wichardus. Upon his death, his widow, with the consent of her new husband, Wichardus's own brother, Ansedeus, "gave or rather gave again" the land at Chaseux to Cluny.[33]

The lessons from the precarial donation to Leutbald are the lessons to be drawn from many of the other gifts made by Cluny.

. . . in Vertiaco . . . in Aeduensẹ vero pago alodum, qui dicitur ad Domnum Petrum . . . et in Vallis."

30. BB 1708;II:729–30 (3.985), where land "in villa Roccas" clearly refers to the same place as BB 1460: "in villa Ayrodia, in loco qui dicitur Rocca."

31. See Zimmermann, no.530 (4.1021–23), pp. 1007–10 at 1009 (= BB 2703; III:27; = JL 4013) for a bull of Benedict VIII naming Warulf and his brother Walter as among the enemies of Cluny because they held on to the precaria granted to Leutbald.

32. For the relationship between property and wergild, see Karl Hans Ganahl, "Hufe und Wergeld," Zeitschrift der Savigny-Stiftung für Rechtsgeschichte, Germanistische Abteilung 53 (1933):208–46.

33. The story is partly told in BB 2946;IV:146–47 (Chaume, "Obs.," 1018–30) where Raimodis, wife of Ansedeus and widow of Wichardus, "dono vel potius reddo" the land "que vocatur Casoia." Raimodis gave it "pro anima senioris mei Wichardi et patris ipsius supradicti Gauzerannus." Walter, prepositus of Mâcon, is called the senior of Gauzerannus in BB 2784;III:809–10 (10.1023–10.1024). The sons and wife of Gauzerannus are named in BB 2848;IV:48–50 (1026–30). Other parts of Raculf's property continued to have an extended history. In 1019 (BB 2719;III:741–43), Teuza and her sons, Warulf and Walter, quit their claim to Collongette, Ayrodia, Les Légères, and so on.

Most often in the neighborhood (see Map 4), they gave back as gifts properties to which families already had some initial claim. In turn, Cluny had a claim, when the life of the precarist was over, to the return of the land. Ownership was no less real and no less important for involving, as we are suggesting, the participation of landholders past and present and (by expectation) future. The land still was "owned"; it was not public or shared out communally or indiscriminately. But its ownership intersected a number of groups, linking them through the intermediary of the land.

Thus Ugo, clericus, received in precarial donation a vineyard that had been given to Cluny by his uncle.[34] David, presbyter, was given back land at La Chize that he himself had given to Saint Peter.[35] Maiolus Poudreux received the church of Saint-Sorlin (today La Roche-Vineuse) in precaria from Cluny; the church had had a long tradition in his family. It had originally been given to Doda by her husband, Leutbald; subsequently it was donated to the monks at Cluny by the children Doda had with Aquinus, her second husband; later it was quitclaimed by Warulf, Doda's brother-in-law.[36] Interestingly, just before the precarial donation to Maiolus, the monks of Cluny had exchanged this church (for the lifetime of the donee) with Adalbertus, presbyter, for land in Verzé.[37] This apparently took it for a time out of the circle of the family of Leutbald, though Leutbald had property at Verzé, and the land that Cluny gained in the exchange with Adalbertus bordered on land of a Leutbald.[38] In any event, in the end, the exchange with Adalbertus did not extinguish the association of the church with Leutbald's family.

These examples suggest that the monks at Cluny as well as their contacts outside the monastery shared the view that gifts

34. BB 2050;III:254–55 (Chaume, "Obs.," 1008–26).
35. BB 935;II:42–43 (954–78).
36. BB 254;I:245–46 (925–26), BB 798;I:750 (1.951), BB 1087;II:180–81 (8.960). The donation in precaria to Maiolus is BB 941 (980–94).
37. Recorded in two charters, BB 942;II:47–48 and BB 1529;II:579–80, the latter dated quite certainly 6.980.
38. Leutbald's property at Verzé in BB 248;I:239–40 (924–25); borders of the land given by Adalbertus in BB 942;II:47–48 and BB 1529;II:579–80. Adalbertus was a major donor to Cluny, at Verzé and elsewhere (e.g., BB 1530;II:580–81 [7.980], redonated in BB 1681;II:708–9 [5.984] with different witnesses; BB 1555; II:602–3). He served as a scribe for many charters from the vicinity (BB 1027;II: 122, BB 1340;II:413, BB 1342;II:414–15). His son, also Adalbertus, became a monk at Cluny (BB 2368;III:472 [Chaume, "Obs.," 1000–1015]).

created ongoing social links. The giver did not sever himself from his gift but rather, to the contrary, used the gift to tie one social circle to another. In turn, the donee (as for example, Cluny) might use the same gift to forge or reinforce bonds with others, thus adding new claims to old. It is not surprising, given this significance of property transactions, that certain gifts were made repeatedly.

Redonations

> To the sacrosanct basilica in honor of God most high and the holy apostles, Peter and Paul, where Lord Odilo presides as abbot: let all sons of the church know that I, Milo, give in God's name, for the salvation of my soul and that of my wife, Ermengardis, some of my inheritance which is in the pagus of Mâcon, in the villa of Laizé, in the ager of Salornay, namely the church of Saint-Sulpice. And I hand over to you whatever I may hold in that villa or that pertains to the church: fields, meadows, woods, mansi and whatever pertains to that villa. And I also give to you male and female serfs and everything acquired or to be acquired that I have at Mornay and at another place called Sept-Moulins.[39]

There is nothing odd about this donation charter. Yet we happen to know that the church of Saint-Sulpice had already been given to Cluny along with land at Laizé, Mornay, and Sept-Moulins about a half-century before, in a donation made by Leotald, the count of Mâcon.[40] Clearly it was not absurd to give that which had already been given. Indeed, on the contrary, King

39. BB 2267;III:398–99 (c. 994): "Sacrosanctę basilice in honore summi Dei et sanctorum apostolorum Petri et Pauli, ubi domnus Odilo abba preesse videtur. Noverint omnes filii ecclesię, qualiter ego, in Dei nomine, Milo dono, pro remedio anime mee et uxoris meę, Ermengardis, aliquid de mea hereditate quę residet in pago Matisconense, in villa Laisiaco, in agro Solorniaco, hoc est unam ecclesiam in honore sancti Sulpicii, et quantum in ipsa villa mihi habere videtur, vel et ad ipsam ecclesiam pertinet, vobis trado: campos, prata, silvas, mansos et quicquid ad ipsam villam pertinet, et totum quantum habeo in villa que vocatur Maornag, et in altero loco quę Septem Molendinos vocant, cum servis et ancillis, quesitum et inquirendum, totum vobis dono." Laizé is ca. Mâcon-Nord, Mornay is ca. Lugny, and Sept-Moulins, now l.-disp., was near Igé.

40. BB 768;I:723 (5.950): "Ego Leotaldus comes . . . dono . . . in agro Laliacense [read: Lasiacense; see, Chaume, Origines II/3: 1126], in ipsa villa; haoc [sic] est ecclesia in honore beati Sulpicii, confessoris Christi, et alias res ibidem pertinen-

Robert and his son, Hugh, subsequently confirmed the two donations, granting "the church at Laizé named in honor of Saint-Sulpice with everything that pertains to it, just as count Leotald and later on Milo, miles, handed it over to Saint Peter."[41]

There are other examples of redonations.[42] In April 936, Ava

tibus: in Lasiaco mansos ii, in Madornaco mansi vii, et quicquid ibi habeo, et in Setmulinis mansum unum, a Sancto Mauritio [= Saint-Maurice-de-Satonnay, ca. Lugny; this place is not mentioned in BB 2267] mansum i."

41. William Mendel Newman, *Catalogue des actes de Robert II, roi de France* (Paris: Sirey, 1937), no. 59, pp. 76–77 (6.1017–11.1023) (= BB 2711;III:733–35). See the bull of Benedict VIII in Zimmermann, no. 530, p. 1009:"potestatem de Lasiaco . . . sicut dive memorię comes Leotaldus primum, deinde Milo religiosus miles per testamentum litterarum olim contulerunt sancto Petro." It is not at all clear how Milo came to give as "his inheritance" that which had been given by Count Leotald. It is tempting to speculate that the connection is through his wife, Ermengardis. The first wife of Leotald was Ermengardis, daughter of Ermengardis and Manasses (BB 432;I:420–21 [935]); is it possible that a girl in a later generation of this family was given the same name? The donation by Milo was witnessed by an Alberic, otherwise unidentified; Alberic was the name of the son (Count Alberic, 962–80) and the grandson of Count Leotald (see Bouchard, *Sword*, p. 263–64). Also present at Milo's donation was Count Otto-William (981–1026), who had married Count Alberic's widow (see Bouchard, *Sword*, pp. 265–69, and below, Genealogy 12). Bouchard discusses yet later redonations of this same church at Laizé (*Sword*, pp. 213–14). As Bézornay was a place to sell, so Saint-Sulpice at Laizé appears to have been a church to give again.

42. It is not possible at this point to estimate what proportion of donations are redonated. First, problems of textual transmission for the charters of Cluny have led to a number of duplicate charters which may or may not be records of the same event. E.g., BB 990;II:85–86 (3.955–86, derived from cartulary A) is nearly identical to BB 1370;II:436 (3.974, derived from a copy of Lambert de Barive), where the differences are probably due to textual rather than social reasons. (This identity was noted by Constance Bouchard among her many useful marginal annotations on one set of BB at the University of Chicago Libraries.) Or, again, BB 2780;III:804–5 is equivalent to BB 2750;III:774. Second, some redonations are, in effect, the equivalent of werpitiones, so that the categories blur. See, for example, BB 871;I:824–26 (1.954), in which Aimo of Bourbon gives (*dono res meas*) Souvigny and land supporting it that his father, Aymard, gave to Cluny (in BB 217;I:206–7 [3.920]) and which Aimo "ego miser et peccator tot diebus, propter cupiditatem meam, malo ordine retinui, unde nunc me culpabilem recognosco; et hec omnia eidem beato Petro inpresenciarum prompta et bona voluntate reddo [Miserably and sinfully I kept it in bad order for a long time on account of my greed. But now I see that I was wrong; and now, readily and willingly, I give again all these things to the same blessed Peter]." Third, redonations at times represent the return of property given by Cluny ad medium plantum. See, for example, BB 121;I:135–36 (Chaume, "En Marge 1," p. 44 n. 3: uncertain date), where this is clearly the case. Fourth, some charters may be redonations or they may be confirmations. See BB 1832;III:76–77 (11.990), which may be interpreted as a redonation of BB 1831;III:75–76 (11.990), as a confirmation (or *une analyse*, as Bruel suggests), or as a textual variant. Fifth, redonations may masquerade as donations, many of which no doubt will be uncovered by subsequent researchers.

and her husband, Gauzfredus, *comes* (not related to the Eve and Gauzfred we discussed in Chapter 2), gave their property at Ecussolles and the church of Saint Peter (today Saint-Pierre-le-Vieux) to Cluny.[43] In June of the same year, they repeated the gift.[44] The two donations were distinct events, the first taking place in front of sixteen witnesses, the second in front of nineteen, only six of whom appeared at the first.[45] Another example is the gift, in 1002, of a vineyard at Mazilly by a man named Rodolfus: the vineyard was one "that my father and mother, Telsaidis, once delegated to Saint Peter." Unfortunately, the earlier donation cannot be traced. But Rodulfus handed over the vineyard again as a pious act, for the salvation of his soul and the souls of his father and mother.[46]

Like the land at Fontana, then, the church at Laizé, the property at Ecussolles, and the vineyard at Mazilly were given to Cluny more than once. In some instances regivings were restitutions, the sequel to quarrels about ownership. The quitclaims of Fontana are good examples of this. In a few instances (as we have just seen), they appeared as acts of apparent generosity. In both cases, they were public social and ritual events that affirmed the relationship between the donor, Saint Peter, and a piece of land; they bestowed honor and prestige on people who, through their donation, associated themselves with places already charged with pious meaning. Very often they affirmed other relationships as well: with neighbors, *seniores*, executors, and so on.[47] That donations should not "alienate" but rather "garner" is in accord with much that we know about medieval

43. BB 446;I:434–36 (4.936). See above, Chapter 2, n. 1.
44. BB 449;I;438–40 (6.936). Bernard and Bruel call this a confirmation, but that is simply to explain the existence of two separate documents making the same donation. A genuine confirmation of the donation is to be found in a bull of Leo VII, in Zimmermann, no.74 (end of 936), pp. 126–28 (= JL 3598).
45. The six that are repeated are: Elpericus (in BB 446;I:434–36) (= Elfericus [in BB 449;I:438–40]), Girbertus (= Gyrbertus), Ugo, Antigius, Narduinus, Unbertus.
46. BB 2557;III:621–22 (6.1002). The villa Masiriaco in which the vineyard was located is not positively identified. It may be Mazilly (ca. Cluny), or possibly Massilly (same canton), or indeed a place that has now disappeared near Saint-Vincent. For all of these, see Chaume, *Origines* II/3:1134 n. 16, 1101 n. 8, and 1103 n. 10.
47. On the public and ritual character of the court, see Davies and Fouracre, pp. 234–35.

society and with much else that we can conjecture about it with the aid of anthropological studies.

The Gift

Bronislaw Malinowski was the first ethnographer to argue that gift giving constituted a system. Indeed, he treated the Kula trade—a ceremonial exchange in which certain objects changed hands in a particular direction, ultimately describing a circle— as the very source of all other aspects (from magic and myth to social organization) of the islanders he was studying.[48] Eschewing a narrow definition of "economic" activity, Malinowski became the founder of economic anthropology.[49]

The classic synthesis of the gift exchange in "primitive" or "archaic" societies was the 1923 study of Marcel Mauss.[50] In point of fact, Mauss was speaking of his own time and his own society as well: "People, classes, families and individuals may become rich, but they will not achieve happiness until they can sit down like the knights [of Arthur's round table] around their common riches. There is no need to see far for goodness and happiness. It is to be found in the imposed peace, in the rhythm of communal and private labour, in wealth amassed and redis-

48. Bronislaw Malinowski, *Argonauts of the Western Pacific* (1922; repr., New York: Dutton, 1961), esp. pp. 83–86. See Raymond Firth, "The Place of Malinowski in the History of Economic Anthropology," in *Man and Culture: An Evaluation of the Work of Bronislaw Malinowski*, ed. Raymond Firth (London: Routledge, 1957), pp. 209–27.

49. See Raymond Firth, *Elements of Social Organization* (1951; 3d ed. Boston: Beacon Press, 1963), p. 124. From the beginning, Firth unabashedly applied modern notions of economy to "primitive" societies, as in his *Primitive Economics of the New Zealand Maori* (New York: Dutton, 1929), esp. pp. 2–5, and *Primitive Polynesian Economy* (1939; 2d ed. London: Routledge, 1965). Some sociologists began to follow out the consequences of an anthropological approach to modern economic systems as well; e.g., see Talcott Parsons and Neil J. Smelser, *Economy and Society: A Study in the Integration of Economic and Social Theory* (1956; repr., New York: Free Press, 1964), esp pp. 14–16, for a programmatic statement. The economist Karl Polanyi introduced the idea of the "embedded economy" in *The Great Transformation: The Political and Economic Origins of our Time* (1944; repr., Boston: Beacon Press, 1957), pp. 43–55.

50. Marcel Mauss, "Essai sur le don: Forme et raison de l'échange dans les sociétés archaïques," *L'Année Sociologique* 1 (1923): 30–186. Published in English, as *The Gift: Forms and Functions of Exchange in Archaic Societies*, trans. Ian Cunnison (New York: Norton, 1967).

tributed."[51] Indeed, for Mauss, the gift held out hope for the moral regeneration of postwar France.[52]

In Mauss's view, the peace and the richness in the gift consisted in its obligatory, ongoing, and social character. Initial gifts, given for reasons ranging from the need to confirm family relations to the necessity of setting up intertribal links, had to be met by a countergift, and this second gift had to be reciprocated by its own return, and so on. A prolonged round of gift giving was the result. The "master concept" ensuring the mutual obligation of the parties was the idea of *hau*, which Mauss took to be the "spirit," indeed the "person" of the thing given.[53] Hau had to be returned to the original giver or the receiver could expect it to wreak calamity. The giver, therefore, never entirely alienated his gift because he never alienated its hau, to whom he remained related. Through hau, he had power over his recipient. And hau, itself, was driven by the desire to return home and to its original owner. Thus, in Mauss's scheme, gift and countergift set up a personal bond not only between the donor and recipient but, more precisely between the donor, the recipient, and the "person" in the thing.

Since the gift was, for Mauss, a mechanism for making peace, it hid (but sometimes expressed in ritual) aggression and rivalry. The overt expression of this hostility emerged in such institutions as the potlatch.[54] The potlatch ceremony ordinarily consisted of a feast and the distribution of gifts to guests. Its purpose was to mark and, indeed, ratify some important event in the life of a chief.[55] Rivalries were expressed on two levels. The

---

51. Mauss, "Le don," p. 185–86 (*The Gift*, p. 81).

52. See the useful discussion of Mauss's political philosophy in Marshall Sahlins, "The Spirit of the Gift," in *Stone Age Economics* (Chicago: Aldine-Atherton, 1972), pp. 149–53, esp. 168–83.

53. The term "master concept" is Sahlin's in his critique of Mauss's *hau* in "Spirit."

54. See Philip Drucker, "The Potlatch," in *Tribal and Peasant Economies: Readings in Economic Anthropology*, ed. George Dalton (Garden City, N.Y.: Natural History Press, 1967), pp. 481–93. See also Helen Codere, *Fighting with Property: A Study of Kwakiutl Potlatching and Warfare, 1792–1930*, Monographs of the American Ethnological Society 17 (New York: J. J. Augustin, 1950); Codere argued that contact with Europeans effected a change from physical warfare to "fighting with property," i.e., enhanced potlatch (an argument summarized by Codere on pp. 125–29).

55. Drucker, pp. 481–82.

first was on the vertical plane of the donor and donee: the giver attempted to place the receiver in his power, and the receiver countered with a gift that, in turn, placed the original donor in the subordinate position, and so on. The second was on the horizontal plane of the donor and other potential donors. Mauss spoke about Trobrianders, for example, whose Kula had elements similar to the potlatch: they strove with one another to woo the best donee in another tribe, to offer him the finest initial gift. If he accepted, an ongoing relationship had begun; he became a partner of the lucky donor.[56]

The potlatch and the Kula of the Trobrianders involved particular and very specific sorts of gifts. At the potlatch, for example, copper tablets of great rarity and preciousness were displayed and then broken, the shards distributed to the highest ranking guests. Each copper had its "own name and individuality."[57] For Mauss, the copper was hau, a kind of person.

With the lag that so often accompanies interdisciplinary borrowing, Mauss's formulation was drawn upon by historians only in the 1950s. Moses Finley found its applicability to the world described by Homer.[58] Philip Grierson suggested using the model to explain the nature of the economy of the early Middle Ages.[59] Grierson wanted to show how money and luxury goods could continue to change hands in the "dark ages" without postulating the existence of professional traders or, indeed, of trade. In brief, in his view, things were distributed by theft and by gift: "last but not least, though perhaps the most likely to be overlooked is the survival in early medieval society of the phenomenon known to anthropologists as gift-exchange."[60]

Because of his interests, Grierson stressed only selected as-

56. Mauss, "Le don," e.g., p. 78 (*The Gift*, pp. 5–6). See Malinowski, pp. 322–27 and on the partnership, pp. 85–86, 274–81.

57. Mauss, "Le don," p. 120 (*The Gift*, p. 43). Similarly, the necklaces and arm shells of the Kula had their own names and histories. See Malinowski, p. 322: a necklace named Gumakarakedakeda.

58. Moses I. Finley, *The World of Odysseus* (New York: Viking Press, 1954), esp. pp. 46–73; 102–8; 131–34. See Pierre Vidal-Naquet, "Economie et société dans la Grèce ancienne: L'oeuvre de Moses I. Finley," *Archives européennes de sociologie* 6 (1965): 111–48.

59. Philip Grierson, "Commerce in the Dark Ages: A Critique of the Evidence," *Transactions of the Royal Historical Society*, 5th ser., 9 (1959): 123–39.

60. Ibid., p. 137.

pects of Mauss's thesis: the mutuality of gift exchanges, the kind of objects given ("valuable and easy to transport"), the motives of social prestige involved in "generosity." When, in 1973, Georges Duby took up the model for his enormously influential overview of the medieval economy, he stressed these and other themes: the relationship between taking and giving, the obligatory nature of generosity, the glory derived from the display of accumulated wealth, and a new theme: wealth used to consecrate. Duby lay stress on the "supernatural consumer," who demanded gifts in the grave (in pagan rituals) or at the altar (in Christian ceremonies). For the first time, too, Duby considered the function of land donations within this system: "As for monks and clerks associated with bishops in serving cathedrals, they occupied a truly seigneurial position as idle consumers. The universal practice of giving, of making ritual sacrifices to Divine authority, went on adding to their landed estates. We have already recognized in the flow of gifts of land to the Church one of the broadest and most regular economic currents of this period."[61] For Duby the church's countergifts were alms to the poor and prayers for the donors.

But by the time that Duby and Grierson were writing, anthropologists had begun to modify Mauss's observations and the formulations that necessarily were based on them. First, some anthropologists refined or revised some of his interpretations. Firth, for example, began the long series of challenges and refinements of Mauss's view of hau.[62] Second, influenced by the work of Polanyi, some anthropologists drew a line of demarcation between the "formal economy" of market societies and the "substantive economy" of nonmarket societies. "There is a gulf between the Western and the primitive; types of *economic orga-*

61. Duby, *The Early Growth*, p. 56.
62. Firth, *New Zealand Maori*, pp. 411–15, and see pp. 268–71, the relation between *mauri* and *hau*. Subsequent commentaries include J. Prytz Johansen, *The Maori and His Religion in Its Non-ritualistic Aspects* (Copenhagen: Musksgaard, 1954), pp. 117–18; Claude Lévi-Strauss, "Introduction à l'oeuvre de Marcel Mauss," in M. Mauss, *Sociologie et anthropologie* (Paris: Presses Universitaires de France, 1966), pp. ix–lii, esp. xxxviii–xl; Sahlins, "Spirit," esp. pp. 157–68; Peter Gathercole, "*Hau, Mauri,* and *Utu*: A Re-examination," *Mankind* 11 (1978): 334–40; G. MacCormack, "Mauss and the 'Spirit' of the Gift," *Oceana* 52 (1981–82); 286–93; and Annette B. Weiner, "Inalienable Wealth," *American Ethnologist* 13 (1985): 210–27.

nization do not shade imperceptibly one into another; and it is not impossible to say where the usefulness of economic theory ends [i.e., precisely where the Western economy ends]."[63] While Grierson spoke of the "survival" of a "primitive Germanic pattern," anthropologists such as Dalton were viewing such systems as separate and contemporaneous, the one (monetary) as formally economic, the other (gift) as not.[64] Economic anthropologists who did not adopt the argument of the "substantivists" argued for the comparability of various economic systems, not for an evolution from one to another.[65]

For our purposes it is useful to consider Mauss's "gift economy" not as a description of any particular reality but rather as an anthropologist's mental construct derived from a variety of ethnographic observations. However "embedded" the gift economy may be in the whole social and political matrix, anthropologists can, nevertheless, dispute parts of it without destroying the whole. For this reason it has withstood both attacks and changes of emphasis. Those who criticize Mauss's spiritual interpretation of hau, for example, still find other elements of his discussion useful.[66] Grierson stressed a particular aspect of the Maussian formula—the redistribution of goods—because it

63. George Dalton, "Economic Theory and Primitive Society," *American Anthropologist* 63 (1961): 1–25, reprinted in *Economic Anthropology: Readings in Theory and Analysis*, ed. Edward E. LeClair, Jr., and Harold K. Schneider (New York: Holt, Rinehart and Winston, 1968), pp. 143–67, at p. 162.

64. LeClair and Schneider, p. 164: "It should be emphasized that no economic 'system' is of one piece. Rather, that in any society—including our own, and most certainly the primitive—there exist spheres of economy with different principles of organization." See the remarks of Little, *Religious Poverty*, p. 4, and Patrick J. Geary, "Sacred Commodities: The Circulation of Medieval Relics," in *The Social Life of Things: Commodities in Cultural Perspective*, ed. Arjun Appadurai (Cambridge: Cambridge University Press, 1968), p. 174; Natalie Davis argued similarly in "From Alms to Bribes: The Gift in Sixteenth-Century France" (paper presented at the Newberry Library, Chicago, Ill., 2 December 1985).

65. Edward E. LeClair, Jr., "Economic Theory and Economic Anthropology," *American Anthropologist* 64 (1962): 1179–1203, reprinted in LeClair and Schneider.

66. The principal exponent of a "rational" hau is Sahlins, who sees it as the fruit of an investment. The most recent defender of the spiritual meaning of hau is Weiner in her "Inalienable Wealth," pp. 220–23. It is, of course, possible that even in the culture of the Maori, hau has both economic and spiritual significance. It seems theoretically possible that the sort of force that Mauss saw in hau might exist in one culture but not in another, and that, even so, Mauss's formulation would remain a useful analytic tool.

suited the phenomena he was looking at. Mary Douglas and Daryll Forde, on the other hand, emphasize the amicable character of the gift economy, thus putting to the side, for example, Mauss's stress on competition: "The crucial difference between gift and sale is that the first object of gift exchange is the building up of a social relationship, whereas in buying and selling, any continuous social relation between the parties is merely incidental."[67] In contrast, C. A. Gregory sees the crucial element of gift exchange in reproductive strategies: systems of exchange of women establish the domination or subordination of clans to one another.[68]

The "gift economy" and the "market economy" as well are "systems" because economists, anthropologists, and historians conceptualize them as such. They are useful abstractions.[69] But it is also important that the models not be reified, as if the gift economy, for example, were more than a way of making sense of, and seeing the relationships between, certain acts and ideas.

But if the two systems are conceptualizations, they are conceived in relation to one another.[70] Indeed, it is useful to imagine them as two ends of a continuum. The continuum assesses the purposes of interactions that involve exchanges of any sort.[71] It begins at one end with "pure" profit and at the other

67. Daryll Forde and Mary Douglas, "Primitive Economies," in Dalton, pp. 13–28.

68. C. A. Gregory, "A Conceptual Analysis of a Non-Capitalist Gift Economy with Particular Reference to Papua New Guinea," Cambridge Journal of Economics 5 (1981): 119–35, esp. 128–34.

69. Anthropologists are, of course, keenly aware of this distinction: see, the differentiation between the "folk image" and the "model constructed by the anthropologist from the observed facts," in Jacob Black-Michaud, Cohesive Force: Feud in the Mediterranean and the Middle East (New York: St. Martin's Press, 1975), p. 63. Malinowski himself noted (p. 83), "Not even the most intelligent native has any clear idea of the Kula as a big, organised social construction, still less of its sociological function and implications."

70. Strictly speaking the gift economy was formulated as a counter to the commercial economy, whereas economic theory had been elaborated long before with reference only to Western commercial economy. There is no need to enter here into the substantivist-formalist debate, i.e., a debate about whether or not Western economic theory can be applied to primitive economies (see Dalton, "Economic Theory," in Economic Anthropology, esp. p. 164). The issue is simply that the gift economy is itself a theoretical construct.

71. The choice of "purpose" here rather than other criteria is due to its usefulness in the context of the documents from Cluny. Other criteria have certainly been proposed: e.g., the rank of the object exchanged (Gregory, "Conceptual Analysis," p. 125, argues that like-for-like is characteristic of the gift economy,

with "pure" honor; that is, at one end with material motives and at the other end with social. But it should be obvious that any real moment of exchange in any society may have elements from both ends, albeit in different measures, and often admixtures of other motives as well.[72] We need not argue with Marx that economic forces underlie all social and political relationships; nor with Weber that ascetic religious antecedents lurk behind capital investment; nor with Freud and Erickson that the psychology of compulsive accumulation lies behind the profit motive, to observe that calculated capitalist maneuvers also involve images of self-worth and strategies for social recognition and prestige. And gifts, in turn, however removed from prices and precisely reckoned profits, nevertheless are the result of calculations about return gifts, material benefits, and/or services.[73] The gift-exchange "system" and the commercial economic "system," therefore, are two conceptions, or ideal types, of exchange behavior. They can function together, and economic activity of every sort is produced by their mix in greater, lesser, or equal degrees. What predominates in a given culture at a particular mo-

---

unlike-for-unlike is characteristic of commodity exchange; but at p. 127 it becomes clear that Gregory's chief concern is motive); or the attitude toward the object (see Weiner, "Inalienable Wealth," pp. 215–20). The "new" economic anthropologists object with many good reasons to the stress placed on the categories of distribution and trade, which are dictated by the concerns of capitalism. Hence their parody: "any transfers of goods including stealing and giving, are 'exchanges' . . . if not 'trade'" (John Clammer, "Concepts and Objects in Economic Anthropology," in *The New Economic Anthropology*, ed. J. Clammer [New York: St. Martin's Press, 1978]; Clammer also includes a critique of the substantivist-formalist argument as "philosophical rather than anthropological," much the same point as my own.

72. The discussion in Weiner, "Inalienable Wealth," is particularly useful in suggesting the nuances and multiple meanings involved in giving affectively charged gifts.

73. A useful model that incorporates this entire continuum is the "maximization model." In this model, that which is "economic" is that which allocates limited resources in some chosen direction. The direction may be social prestige or higher wages; in either case the matter is an economic one, and resources are used to maximize it. See LeClair, "Economic Theory," and his concluding remarks in *Economic Anthropology*, pp. 456–59. Interestingly, in eleventh-century Normandy, the *forms* for gifts, sales, and exchanges were nearly identical, *motive* being the chief factor in distinguishing one from the other. See Emily Zack Tabuteau, *Transfers of Property in Eleventh-Century Norman Law* (Chapel Hill: University of North Carolina Press, 1988), pp. 41–43. I am very grateful to Professor Tabuteau for making a copy of her manuscript available to me prior to its publication.

ment of exchange is an empirical matter. Hence the society of the early Middle Ages, which most certainly did not mirror that of Polynesian islanders, may nevertheless be elucidated by a consideration of anthropological findings without necessarily adhering to every element of the model.[74]

It is time to sum up what we have discovered thus far about the giving, taking, exchanging, and buying of Cluny's property in light of the model and, rather more incidentally, about the model in the light of our findings.

In the first place, there is the social nature of land transactions of whatever sort with Cluny. The donation, in particular, was a family, a neighborhood, and a celestial event; the people that participated in it were the donor or donors; those for whose souls the land was given; Saint Peter (and sometimes, in various combinations, God, Saint Paul, the abbot of Cluny, and the monks of Cluny collectively); neighbors; and witnesses, who might be family members, neighbors, and (rather more rarely) individual monks. Occasionally men of high rank appeared (e.g., a count or the *senior* of the donor); often enough fideles, milites, and executors. There was a scribe. The sale and the exchange, by contrast, were less often otherworldly: they were rarely transacted with Saint Peter, a fact that suggests that at Cluny some distinctions were made between "commercial" and "social" transactions. Nevertheless, even at exchanges and sales, Saint Peter was often present as the owner of a piece of land.

What is striking in all instances is that these transactions were part of a series of events. The people involved in a sale at one villa were very often involved in another there or elsewhere, or in a donation or exchange. And if we think of groups rather than individuals, it is fair to say that there was a continuous social relationship between many laymen and Saint Peter that cut across villae and stretched over the course of several generations.

One of the reasons for this phenomenon was that the people who gave up their property did not thereby alienate their associ-

74. Similarly, modern market researchers are interested in the dynamics of gift exchange; see, John F. Sherry, Jr., "Gift Giving in Anthropological Perspective," *Journal of Consumer Research* 10 (1983): 157–68; the article includes an elaborate scheme for gift-giving behavior.

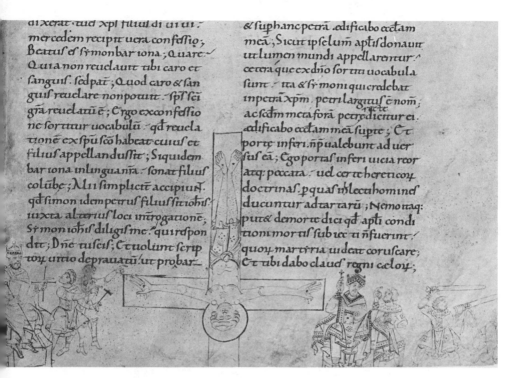

Figure 4. Martyrdom of Saints Peter and Paul. This representation of Saint Peter on the cross and of events in the martyrdom of Saints Peter and Paul was made in a hand contemporary with the lectionary in which it was drawn, that is, in the first half of the eleventh century. The lectionary is discussed in Raymond Etaix, "Le lectionnaire de l'office à Cluny," *Recherches augustiniennes* 11 (1976): 91–153; see also Charles Samaran and Robert Marichal, *Catalogue des manuscrits en écriture latine portant des indications de date, de lieu ou de copiste* 4, pt. 1 (Paris: Centre national de la recherche scientifique, 1981): p. 245 (B.N. nouv. acq. lat. 2390, fol. 32). Courtesy of the Bibliothèque nationale, Paris.

ation with it. We need not invoke Mauss's concept of hau; the fact emerges from the Cluniac texts themselves. The groups associated with particular pieces of land were remembered, and this memory was, in turn, based on notions of ownership.[75]

75. Gurevich, in "Représentations et attitudes," p. 532, finds certain aspects of medieval concepts of property that mirror Mauss's original formulation of hau: "Au Moyen Age, la relation particulière envers la nature en général et en-

People knew perfectly well the sources of their land, and they named them in the charters quite routinely, as when the Eva whom we met in the giving and taking of Fontana specified that the mansus at Ciergues that she was exchanging with Cluny had been acquired from someone named Ildearga.[76] Or, people made clear that their land was their own inheritance (hereditas), emphasizing its descent through a bloodline. Borders were given not by centuriation or other grid (though there may have been remnants of that system) but by the names of neighbors.[77] Social relations thus helped to define a piece of land. In one sense, the werpitiones may be understood as signaling a breakdown in this system in which overlapping claims to land were normally tolerated and expected. If so, then precarial donations represent the system at its most functional: a claim that had become more pressing—for whatever reason: perhaps economic need, perhaps a crisis in relations between the monastery and the potential precarist—was recognized and met. But it is immediately obvious that werpitiones in fact were symptomatic not so much of the breakdown of the system as its reconstruction. For they marked not a dispute but its handling.[78] Many of them were settled by compromise: by a tacit recognition of the disputed claim and by a strengthening of ties (of prayer and par-

---

vers la terre en particulier, la sensation qu'avait l'homme de sa communion avec elle, s'exprimait également dans le fait qu'il estimait les qualités sociales en fonction des possessions foncières. . . . La terre possédait des qualités magiques particulières et le lien avec son possesseur était étroit et vivant." G. MacCormack, in "Mauss," suggests that the notion that the "primitive mind" sees no distinction between person and thing is traceable to Lucien Lévy-Bruhl, *Les fonctions mentales dans les sociétés inférieures* (Paris: Felix Alcan, 1910), published in English as *How Natives Think*, trans. Lilian A. Clare (1910; repr., Princeton: Princeton University Press, 1985). Weiner, in "Inalienable Wealth," argues that a family's identity might adhere within an object, and in these cases the object was never really given up but rather "on loan" to the recipient.

76. BB 1584;II:628–29 (981–82).

77. See Fredric L. Cheyette and Claudie Duhamel-Amado, "Organisation d'un terroir et d'un habitat concentré: Un exemple Languedocien," in *Habitats fortifiés et organisation de l'espace en Méditerranée médiévale*, ed. A. Bazzana, P. Guichard, and J. M. Poisson, Table ronde, Lyon, 4–5 May 1982 (GIS—Maison de l'Orient, 1983), pp. 35–44. In Cluny's documents measurements were often given in charters of sales and exchanges, less often in gifts. This may in itself indicate different motives for the transactions.

78. See, Geary, "Vivre en conflit"; Geary shows that conflicts were just one part of ongoing group interactions.

ticularly of confraternity) with the monastery. Since this happened regularly, it must have been an anticipated outcome.[79] Hence newly intense claims, revealed by the werpitiones, themselves may be seen as strategies for renewed social ties rather than for the land per se.

Social ties, in any event, are not all amicable, and rivalries and ambivalences too were expressed by the werpitiones.[80] They were expressed in other ways as well. Many donations in precaria cast the precarist in the role of humble supplicant, begging land. This was part of a ritual of reversal: the precarist's subordinate position flew in the face of his real power; his request— which, had it not been humbly made, was potentially extortionate—was "without danger," indeed, "favorable" to the monks.[81]

Even donations to Cluny had rivalrous elements, though these appeared more between benefactors themselves than between benefactors and Cluny. We can see, for example, the traces of social ranking in the way certain individuals or families dominated the transactions that took place with Cluny in particular

79. On compromises in disputes, see Cheyette, "Suum cuique tribuere," and White, "*Pactum*." In England, beginning in the mid-twelfth century, compromises over questions of rights in land brought to the king's court were written up as "final concords." Three copies were engrossed and one (the so-called foot of the final concord) was placed in the treasury. But in fact these "feet of fines" often recorded feigned litigation; the *ritual* of dispute was used, presumably in this instance in order to stave off potential future claims, as the recording prohibited further litigation. See Wardrop, pp. 125–26; Charles Wilmer Foster, *Final Concords of the County of Lincoln from the Feet of Fines Preserved in the Public Record Office A.D.* 1244–1272 (Lincoln: Lincoln Record Society, 1920), 2:ix–xlvii. I am grateful to Dr. Brian Golding, University of Southampton, for bringing these fictive disputes to my attention.

80. Alfred Reginald Radcliffe-Brown, in *Structure and Function in Primitive Society: Essays and Addresses* (1952; repr., New York: Free Press, 1968), pp. 90–116, points out that "joking" relationships maintain equilibrium between friendliness and antagonism. Werpitiones may be described as one of the "modes of organising a definite and stable system of social behavior in which conjunctive and disjunctive components [i.e., friendly and unfriendly] are maintained and combined" (ibid., p. 95). See Davies and Fouracre, p. 235, where feuds may be understood "as a negative of the [social] links represented by the exchange of gifts." See also Davies and Fouracre, pp. 234–35, on the uses of formal courts in dispute settlements.

81. BB 372;I:349–50: "humiliter deprecati sunt." BB 1389;II:451–52: "Cognoscens . . . pater [Maiolus] illius petitionem non esse gravem neque fratribus dampnosam, eisdem omnimodis faventibus." Yet the social status of the precarists was high; e.g., BB 919;II:31–32: "cuidam viro illustrissimo." For further examples and discussions, see Petitjean, esp. pp. 123–24.

areas; those transactions declared the social positions of and the relationships among neighbors. Members of the family that would become the Grossi were present at many such events, cutting across villa boundaries. Deodatus and his family at Bézornay, more local in their ties, formed the center of all other networks of association between that place and Cluny.[82] Adalbaldus and his group dominated the transactions at La Chize.

Yet, it is necessary immediately to acknowledge that the rivalry rather often observed by ethnographers between givers and recipients was *not* a regular feature of the world portrayed by the documents from Cluny.[83] The paradigm for ethnographers was, of course, the potlatch, where the receiver was demeaned until he countered with a yet more splendid gift, forcing the original donor to exceed the countergift, and so on. We shall discuss countergifts from Saint Peter in a moment; but it is obvious that endless displays of rivalrous generosity did not characterize property relations with Cluny. It is, therefore, useful to note that Mauss's conception of the potlatch was derived from particular cases; other observers have found different institutions. Philip Drucker, for example, has located the Maussian potlatch in a particular historical period.[84] According to Drucker, the potlatch was ordinarily a once-in-a-lifetime public ceremony organized by a chief to announce his accession to that position. The gifts that he gave were designed to convince his guests that

82. See the stimulating comments of Gurevich, "Représentations et attitudes," pp. 538–47, regarding the prestige attached to gift giving and generosity. Even if no direct return were expected, this alone could account for donations. See also Murray, pp. 355–62. Orderic Vitalis (*Historia ecclesiastica*, iii.1, in *The Ecclesiastical History of Orderic Vitalis*, ed. and trans. Marjorie Chibnall, 6 vols, [Oxford: Clarendon Press, 1969–80], 2:10) speaks of the rivalry among Norman nobles in the good work of endowing monasteries: "Vnus alium in bono opere festinabat praeire.' elemosinarumque largitate digniter superare [One used to hurry to outdo the next in good works and to best the other honorably in the generosity of his alms]." See Gregory, "Conceptual Analysis," p. 129, on the "big-man" in Papua New Guinea: "The more debtors a person can accumulate through gifts, the more status, prestige and power he acquires as a 'big-man.'" On the other hand, in some societies the mechanism works entirely in the reverse; see Fredric Cheyette, "Mortgage and Credit," and similar observations about the power of the debtor and the weakness of the creditor in Black-Michaud, pp. 80–81.

83. Contrast this with Miller, "Gift, Sale, Payment," p. 49, who finds in the Icelandic context that gifts of land so subordinated the recipient that—to save face—he would sometimes try to reclassify the gift as a sale.

84. Drucker, pp. 488–89.

he had the right to his power and to put his guests under the obligation of ratifying his new position. If they did not do so, he
could not make good his claim. Generally the guests made the
ratification, and they normally attempted to reciprocate for the
gifts given to them; but the potlatch was neither an endless
round of obligatory gift giving, nor was the rivalry between giver
and receiver its essential characteristic. Only when extraordinary outside pressures were brought to bear on this system did it
become transformed into a kind of gift warfare.[85] Thus, it is not
essential for us to find active rivalry in a gift-giving nexus; and,
indeed, while there certainly were disputes between donors and
the monks of Cluny, the essential point of gifts appears to have
had little to do with rivalry with the monastery.

The general absence of rivalry may be explained by the fact
that gifts ordinarily were not to Cluny—the documents make
this abundantly clear—but rather to God and most often directly to Saint Peter, and only secondarily to the monks who
served them.[86] Still more precisely, gifts given to Saint Peter—
Christ's apostle, his chosen representative and the keeper of the
keys of heaven—were themselves countergifts. Property was
given by God in order to be given again to gain the kingdom of
heaven. God was the original source of all land: it was "His
property, ceded by the author of all good things" (as one of a
number of charters of donation begins).[87] And it was ceded by

85. Ibid., 488. The rivalry, which had particular historical causes, was, in any
event, between opposing claimants to the same position, rather than between
the donor and the donees (unless one of the donees happened to be the other
claimant). See also the extremely stimulating discussion of feuds in Black-Michaud, pp. 80–85: endless homicides serve, in a society of great scarcity, as a sociological equivalent to gift-giving networks; and on this scarcity, see pp. 160–
207. Such poverty was clearly not the case in the tenth-century Mâconnais.

86. The gift system at Cluny should be compared with the one analyzed in
C. A. Gregory, "Gifts to Men and Gifts to God: Gift Exchange and Capital Accumulation in Contemporary Papua," *Man* 15 (1980): 626–52, where the primary
purpose of gifts to the church "is to achieve the ranking of class and men" (p.
647), and where the actual recipient of the gift matters less than the simple fact
of its alienation, which removes the gift object from the power of others.

87. BB 141;I:148–49 (date uncertain; see, Chaume, "En Marge I," p. 44 n. 4):
"Pietas misericordissimę divinitatis compaciens humanę infirmitati, concedit
unicuique suorum fidelium quatenus ex rebus sibi concessis ab auctore bonorum
omnium valeant sibi mercari perpetuum regnum." See Cluny's foundation charter, BB 112;I:124–28: "Pernecessarium duxi, ut ex rebis quae michi temporaliter
conlata sunt, ad emolumentum animę aliquantulum inperciar [I have consid-

God precisely to give weak men the opportunity to return it: "By divine piety it is conceded to Christian faithful to be able to acquire, from the temporal property that they possess, a resting place eternal and without end. Wherefore we . . . give, in the name of God, to God and his holy apostles, Peter and Paul, and at the place called Cluny where Lord Maiolus, abbot, presides, something from our property."[88] Thus, like the Kula exchange, in which necklaces always moved in a clockwise direction, so too donations to Cluny formed a circle: from God to men and back to God again. The completion of the circle, one that touched both earth and heaven, was behind the *topoi* of the *arengae* of the charters. These documents expressed, in various ways, the view that gifts of temporal property were connected to eternal salvation. The pro anima formula so frequently used in them is, in fact, a shorthand way of expressing the idea of *do ut des* (I give so that you will give); it evolved as a convenient substitute for a longer introductory flourish about gifts and their rewards during the eighth century.[89] There is no need, therefore, to invoke prayers or entrance in confraternity or burial in Cluny's grounds in order to explain donations to Cluny. The social meaning of gift giving alone is enough. Those other benefits

---

ered it essential to give some of the property that was given to me temporally, for the benefit of my soul]." There is a parallel in the ceremony of presentation of the firstborn and its redemption for a price; see, Exod. 13:2, 12−13; Num. 18:15−16. See Jobert, pp. 182−84, for a discussion of Salvian's view that men hold their possessions from God in precarial tenure.

88. BB 1343;II:415−16 (11.973−11.974): "Divina pietate fidelibus christianis concessum est, ut ex rebus temporalibus quas possident eternam et sine fine mansuram valeant requiem adquirere. Quapropter nos, in Dei nomine, Bernardus et Berardus donamus Deo et sanctis apostolis ejus Petro et Paulo et ad locum Cluniacum, ubi donnus Maiolus, abba, preesse videtur, aliquid ex rebus nostris." A study of the *arengae* (the opening flourishes) of the Cluniac charters would prove very useful for certain purposes, but there is no doubt that the sentiment above was quite general, though other formulas were used to express it as well. See the biblical "Date et dabitur vobis" (Luke 6:38); the classification and discussion of arengae in Karl Glöckner and Anton Doll, *Traditiones Wizenburgenses: Die Urkunden des Klosters Weissenburg, 661−864* (Darmstadt: Hessischen Hist. Kommission, 1979), pp. 79−82; and Fichtenau, *Arenga*.

89. Fichtenau, *Arenga*, pp. 143−44: where he shows that the *pro remedio anima* is a "Kurzform" of the "Lohnarenga." See also Jobert, esp. pp. 205−30. On p. 205, Jobert defines the donation *pro anima* as a gift in return for prayers; but in fact nothing in his discussion leads to this conclusion but points rather to the view that the *pro anima* formula expresses the salvific effects of charity.

existed of course, and they were indeed of social, economic, and religious profit.[90] But before about 1040, they appeared quite rarely and were *special* links available only to a relative few with whom Cluny had or was forging particularly strong ties. The ties set up or confirmed by a simple gift were sufficiently important not to require other benefits. In the case of Cluny, a gift began an ongoing "partnership" with Saint Peter.[91]

But why was land the medium of the gift? On one level, this seems an ingenuous question. It is a commonplace to note that this was a society based on land; that kings, for example, used fiefs of land to reward their followers and pay their officials; that economic institutions of money and credit were unknown, little used, or avoided. Yet, at first glance, the unmovable nature of landed property remains the extraordinary fact about gifts to Cluny. For gift-exchange systems normally depend upon the exchange of portable goods: mats, precious copper slabs, even human beings. When Grierson applied the theory to the early Middle Ages, he did so in order to explain the movements of goods and coins. It is true that the land given to Cluny was sometimes treated as if it were a thing, an object, or a person. Land in Cluny's charters was usually referred to not as *proprietates*, which would have stressed the control that the holder had over it, but rather as *hereditates*, which stressed ancestral and social links.[92] But land was not portable; it could not be hoarded or

90. It is worthwhile pointing out that economic countergifts were also on occasion a feature of the gift nexus at Cluny: countergifts of some sort (sometimes not monetary, however) were a regular feature of the werpitiones. On the other hand, at Saint-Jean d'Angély and elsewhere, monetary countergifts were a regular feature of the relationship between donor and monastery. See below, Chapter 5 n. 77.

91. See the study by Thomas Head of Fleury and the *Miracula Sti. Benedicti* in "The Holy Dead and Christian Society: The Cult of the Saints in the Orléanais, 750–1215" (Ph.D. diss., Harvard University, 1985), pp. 367–88, which demonstrates that until the 1040s relics played a minor role in miracle stories; rather there was a well-developed "sense of both the saint's territory and of his relationships with those whom he aided and punished" (p. 360; see also pp. 367–88). McLaughlin, esp. pp. 183–84, discusses the ways in which donations created relationships with saints and monks.

92. The term "alod" was also rarely used, possibly for the same reason (al = all, od = own, possession, riches); but Gurevich has argued that this term had resonance with *ódal*, the inalienable, ancestral patrimony, and his point must be taken seriously; see Gurevich, "Représentations et attitudes," p. 529. Less convincing is his contrast between "les termes latins *hereditas* ou *possessio* avec

displayed; and the analogy quickly breaks down.[93]

It is therefore useful to see that in Mauss's original conception any object involved in a gift nexus was *immeuble*, however portable, because it was inalienable.[94] Annette Weiner's perceptive comments on Mauss have brought this issue to the fore. According to Weiner, the nature and the significance of the thing given—in the context of the culture in which it plays the part of gift—is of paramount importance. She calls attention, for example, to the distinction—in a clan with which Mauss was concerned—between *taonga*, that is, especially precious objects that were attached to its ancestry and identity and therefore ultimately inalienable and, on the other hand, *'oloa*, goods with purely secular meaning and easily given up.[95] We have already spoken of the interesting case of Flagy, where one group was associated with nearly every transaction, and which was used almost exclusively as a source of gifts. The Arlei did not use the place, Flagy, in their name, but clearly it was an element in their identity. Nevertheless, Flagy was exceptional. Most places were the sources of gifts and also of sales, exchanges, and werpitiones, shading from spiritual to secular significance even in the same generation. Land per se was not the equivalent of taonga.

And yet, land was something quite special by its very nature, and this in two nearly contradictory ways.[96] In the first place,

---

les termes germaniques *odal, epel*" (p. 525). In point of fact, the etymology of the word "alod" points more to emphasis on ownership than it does to descent. The documents of Cluny normally use the term *hereditas* rather than *alod* or *possessio*. Contrary to Henri Dubled, in "'Allodium' dans les textes latins du moyen âge" (*Le Moyen Age* 57 [1951]: 241–46), who was looking at Alsatian documents, Emily Z. Tabuteau has found in Norman charters that the terms *hereditas* and *alodium* were synonyms ("Ownership and Tenure in Eleventh-Century Normandy," *American Journal of Legal History* 21 [1977]: 104); but "inheritance" in Normandy might refer to land held from someone else (in feudal tenure); this was certainly true by the mid-eleventh century (p. 110). In either case, the terms implied permanence, i.e., "possessions over which the successive generations of a family had rights" (p. 112). In the Mâconnais, there was not the complication of land held in feudal tenure, since this was only rarely the case throughout the period under study here.

93. See Charles-Edwards, "Distinction," in Sawyer, where the uses of gifts of land are seen as clearly separate from those of objects.

94. Mauss, "Le don," p. 44; Cunnison's translation in *The Gift*, p. 7, is "indestructible property" for Mauss's *paraphernalia permanents* and "real property" for Mauss's *immeubles*.

95. Weiner, "Inalienable Wealth," esp. pp. 215–20.

96. It is remarkable, indeed, that anthropological literature, so richly filled

each parcel that came to the monks was transformed into the property of Saint Peter and at the same time stayed right where it was. Saint Peter became a neighbor. No doubt the grand annual tribute (*census*) of one thousand gold pieces, sent to Cluny by Fernando I in the second half of the eleventh century, also was transformed into the property of Saint Peter; but Fernando received prayers, not a neighborhood patron, in exchange.[97] That is, land, truly *immeuble*, remained in the sight of the donor or seller and indeed of the entire neighborhood (which was normally involved in its transfer) even as it was given away and afterward. This is true of all land. Moreover, as we shall see in Chapter 5, certain lands meant more than others, just as certain especially beautiful copper plates were treasured above all the rest by native Canadians. Even when the plates were confiscated to the museums of Canada, they continued to be invoked and given away at potlatch festivals—in the form of certificates!

---

with gifts of goods, less often speaks of gifts of land. Or rather, gifts of property, often following well demarcated lines of inheritance through lineage networks, are often treated as a part of kin relationships rather than as a part of gift exchange. Although not about gifts of land per se, an exceptionally useful study is Goodenough, *Property*. In Truk culture, there are gifts of land: *niffag* is a gift that obligates the receiver; *kiis* is given without compensation, generally by a man to his brother-in-law (p. 49). In general, however, participation in property is based on kin considerations; e.g., in property "corporations," maternal descent determines who is and who is not a member (p. 32). Annette B. Weiner, in *Women of Value, Men of Renown: New Perspectives in Trobriand Exchange* (Austin: University of Texas Press, 1976), shows older men lending land (a "yam exchange garden") to younger relatives so that the latter can make gifts of their labor in the garden. In this way, the younger men obtain rights to land; but they must also make "secret payments" (*pokala*), which give them access to "rights to control hamlet and garden lands" (p. 157). There are only rare instances in which a "fictive identity" is created to give land to someone outside the family, and this is only when all blood brothers or sons of blood sisters die out. Land is important for the identity of a family, but, in ways analogous to some of the Cluniac materials, "saying 'this is my land' does not have the same meaning as 'I control this land'" (p. 167).

97. BB 3441;IV:551–53 (c. 1070); BB 3509;IV:627–29 (7.1077). The money was used to buy clothes for the monks. Fernando's son, Alfonso VI, doubled the census to 2,000 gold pieces. See Charles Julien Bishko, "Fernando I and the Origins of the Leonese-Castilian Alliance with Cluny," in *Studies in Medieval Spanish Frontier History* (London: Variorum Reprints, 1980), paper 2, esp. pp. 23–30. See also Peter Segl, *Königtum und Klosterreform in Spanien: Untersuchungen über die Cluniacenserklöster in Kastilien-León vom Beginn des 11. bis zur Mitte des 12. Jahrhunderts* (Kallmünz: Lassleben, 1974), pp. 183–98. The work of Cowdrey suggests that requests for confraternity and for intercession increased after 1040 or so. This coincides with the period in which the donors to Cluny became more far-flung.

On the other hand, transfers of land also had an entirely different significance. They bestowed on Cluny the power of a seigneurial lord in a way that no amount of treasure by itself could have done. Whether handed over as gifts or in sales, parcels of land had the potential to create a relatively compact, consolidated "territory." This consolidation did not always happen, of course; nor was it always a consideration. That is why one must consider at what point on the continuum of motives a particular transaction falls. We have seen that, even in the tenth century, some distinction was maintained between predominantly social and predominantly economic land transactions. Bézornay, for example, was obtained almost entirely through purchase, significant in light of this distinction. But land obtained by gift was sometimes treated the same way. Though claims might originally overlap, and though memories might retain social associations for parcels of land, nevertheless, unlike discrete objects, land could be joined. Eventually the social meaning of Cluny's property would be outweighed by its other, more material and political, meanings. This transition was in fact already beginning in the period between 990 and 1010, with the provisions of the Council of Anse and the gradual decrease in the frequency of land exchanges.

The question of Cluny's property, then, is exceptionally complicated. For at times it is entirely unclear whether Cluny actually received anything tangible from a donation; redonations suggest that the first donation might have been a social gesture, important (to be sure), but not the same as a land transfer. At other times, the land was transferred in such a way that overlapping claims and associations were possible. And, finally, at times, the land indeed became the property of the monastery in the classical (and modern) sense. Throughout this book we have presented maps of Cluny's property. Aside from the many problems of representing tenth-century property with twentieth-century cartographic conventions, there is above all the problem of knowing what it is the maps show. Set in black and white, on flat paper, the maps of Cluniac property are by their very nature misleading. A more proper map would be drawn as if on water, in gentle flux, the light of ownership playing on it at many changing angles. Quite precisely, the property of Cluny was not a fixed entity. Its meaning, for Cluny and for those who associated themselves with Cluny, was now religious and social, now economic and political. With this in mind, it remains now to look at last at the nature and distribution of Cluny's property.

CHAPTER FIVE

Cluny's Property

"I, WICHARD, thinking of the enormity of my sins, give to God and his holy Apostles, Peter and Paul, and to Cluny, where venerable Father Lord Maiolus governs, a certain church dedicated in honor of the holy mother of God, Mary, which is in the pagus of Lyon, in the villa Cercié, on the river Ardières, with all that belongs to it, namely fields, meadows, woods, waters, mills, pastures, roads in and out, cultivated and uncultivated land."[1] The church at Cercié was one of approximately 150 churches received by Cluny between the time of its foundation and the death of Abbot Odilo in 1049. Churches were garnered in the course of 251 donations, quitclaims, redonations, and in one instance, that of Saint Desiderius at Sennecé-lès-Mâcon (ca. Mâcon-Nord), in a sale.[2] Some of these churches were handed over only in part; there was nothing unusual either for laymen or for Cluny to hold a fraction of the land and the revenues that supported a church. Cluny also received about twenty-four monasteries by the middle of the eleventh century. In fact, it is difficult to be precise about the number of churches and monasteries because these two categories were not always distinguished by

---

1. BB 1223;II:304–5 (2.967): ego Vuichardus . . . reminiscens peccatorum meorum enormitatem, dono Deo et sanctis apostolis ejus Petro et Paulo, et ad locum Cluniacum, quem domnus Maiolus, venerabilis pater, regere videtur, quandam ecclesiam in honore sanctae Dei genitricis Mariae dicatam, quę est in pago Lugdunensi, ac in villa Celsiaco sitam super fluvium Arderiam, cum omnibus suis apenditiis, campis scilicet, pratis, silvis, aquis, farinaris, pascuis, exitibus et regressibus, cultum et incultum." Cercié is dép. Rhône, ca. Beaujeu.
2. BB 751;I:708 (8.949): purchase of half of Saint Desiderius.

contemporaries. Rudolf III, for example, ceded to Cluny "the church or monastery [*aecclesiam sive monasterium]*" of Saint-Nicolas-sous-Bracon.³ And some churches eventually were transformed into monastic cells: Saint-Marie de Beaumont and Saint-Jean de Chaveyriat, which we will discuss below, began as churches, for example.

These churches and monasteries must be distinguished from monasteries *reformed* by Cluniac abbots and monks. Cluny's abbots were called upon to reorder the religious life of a number of monasteries in the light of their particular interpretation of the Benedictine rule.⁴ Some of these houses were in fact handed over to Cluny, but certainly not all. And, on the other hand, a monastery such as Souvigny was given to Cluny without a word about establishing the regular life there, appearing much like the transfer of a church.⁵

When monasteries and churches were ceded to Cluny, they became a part of the same gift nexus as its other property. For example, the half of the church at Sennecé-lès-Mâcon that was sold to Cluny in 949 was followed in the 960s by a gift of the whole (except for some of its revenues) by the bishop of Mâcon.⁶ Abbot Maiolus gave it away in precaria in the 970s; and about 1050 it was returned to Cluny in a quitclaim.⁷ There were other

3. *Rudolfinger*, no. 121, pp. 292–94, at p. 293 (=BB 2817;IV:21–23 [1029]). Formerly this church was known as Saint-Nicolas-de-Salins (dép. Jura, arr. Poligny). The editors of *Rudolfinger* call it "hl. Nikolaus zu Vaux" because the charter refers to the place "in loco qui recte Uallis vocatur."

4. For the tenth century, see the maps in Rosenwein, *Rhinoceros*, and the discussion there on pp. 42–56. The terminology suggested by Wollasch, *Mönchtum des Mittelalters*, pp. 149–58, to call monasteries that followed Cluny's monastic round the *ordo Cluniacensis*, and those "mit Cluny rechtlich verbundenen Klöster" (p. 154), the *Cluniacensis ecclesia*, has been adopted here.

5. The first donation of Souvigny is in BB 217;I:206–7 (3.920); the second in BB 871;I:824–26 (1.954). For the family of donors involved, see Genealogy 11. See, similarly, *Rudolfinger*, no. 121, pp. 292–94 (=BB 2817;IV:21–23 [1029]), where, in the only passage about the religious life, Rudolf III wants the monks at Saint-Nicolas, which he has just handed over to Cluny (p. 293) "tam pro nostra quam pro omnium salute Deo assidue preces et vota persolvant [to render prayers and vows to God both for our salvation and for the salvation of all]," hardly a prescription unique to Cluny's practices.

6. BB 751;I:708 (8.949); BB 1139;II:299–30 (Chaume, "Obs.," 963–68): "cum rebus et decimis et omnibus ibi pertinentibus securiter valerent . . . salvo servitio synodali et eulogiarum." The charter is a gift, in fact, of several churches near Mâcon, with the same conditions.

7. BB 912;II:24–25 (Chaume, "Obs.," 970–75), BB 911;II:24 (Chaume, "Obs.," c. 1050).

churches involved in quitclaims with Cluny: Saint-Germain at
Igé, Saint-Germain at Domange, Saint-Etienne at Combre, and
the monastery of Charlieu are instances.[8]

Yet churches and monasteries were different from other sorts
of property. They already belonged to a saint, and that saint was
served, either by a priest alone or with a small group of canons,
or by at least one monk. Churches and monasteries given to
Cluny were, like Cluny, the object of donations and hence of the
same sorts of social and religious impulses that brought largess
to Cluny itself. Did the property of these churches belong to
Cluny when they were ceded to it?

In the twelfth and thirteenth centuries the legal device of "in-
corporation" was elaborated to regularize the proprietary relationship between monasteries such as Cluny and the churches
that they held.[9] By then, too, monasteries in Cluny's ecclesia
normally did not thereby give up or, indeed, even share their
properties with Cluny. Some of them paid to Cluny a small
yearly tax that represented their subordination; but their property was their own.[10]

Matters were not so tidy in the tenth and eleventh centuries.
Saints, like men, could have overlapping claims. We began this
chapter with the donation of a church at Cercié by Wichard. The

8. Igé and Domange (both ca. Cluny): BB 856;I:810–11 (10.953); Combre
(dép. Loire, ca. Perreux): BB 897;II:12–13 (Chaume, "Obs.," c. 975); Charlieu
(dép. Loire, arr. Roanne): BB 730;I:685–87 (948–54). See also werpitiones of
churches in BB 356;I:334 (Hillebrandt, "Datierungen," c. 970); BB 520;I:506
(Chaume, "Obs.," c. 950); BB 764;I:720 (4.950) (partial church); BB 901;II:16
(Chaume, "Obs.," after 966); BB 1037;II:130–31 (10.957), etc.

9. Georg Schreiber, *Kurie und Kloster im 12. Jahrhundert*, Kirchenrechtliche
Abhandlungen, 65–68, 2 vols. (Stuttgart: Verlag Ferdinand Enke, 1910), 2:14–18;
Giles Constable, "Monastic Possession of Churches and 'Spiritualia' in the Age
of Reform," in *Religious Life and Thought (11th–12th centuries)* (London:
Variorum Reprints, 1979), paper 8, p. 311 and n. 47.

10. BB 4395;V:755–56 (12th cent.) gives a list of dues. See Giles Constable,
"Cluniac Tithes and the Controversy between Gigny and Le Miroir," *Revue
Bénédictine* 70 (1960): 591–624, and reprinted in *Cluniac Studies* (London:
Variorum Reprints, 1980), paper 8. Duby considered these dues important to the
economy of the monastery; see Duby, "Le budget de l'abbaye de Cluny entre
1080 et 1155: Economie domaniale et économie monétaire," in *Hommes et
Structures*, pp. 61–82, at 67. On the other hand, see the discussion in Jean Marilier, "L'expansion clunisienne dans la Bourgogne du nord aux XIe–XIIIe siècles,"
in *Consuetudines monasticae: Eine Festgabe für Kassius Hallinger aus Anlass
seines 70. Geburtstages*, ed. Joachim F. Angerer and Joseph Lenzenweger, Studia
Anselmiana 85 (Rome, 1982), pp. 217–28, where the property of Cluny's "obedi-
ences" in northern Burgundy is treated as the property of Cluny.

church was ceded along with all its land, in a way that made it almost indistinguishable from any other property donation. But there is evidence in other instances that the property of a saint was treated differently from other property.

Let us begin with the relatively simple case of Chevignes (ca. Mâcon-Sud). (For many of the churches mentioned here, see Map 5.) Land, not a church, was given to Cluny at this place by an illustrious donor, King Raoul, in 932.[11] Seven years later, Cluny's property there was confirmed by Louis IV d'Outre-mer.[12] At some point after that, the monks of Cluny them-selves constructed a chapel on the site. It was dedicated to Saint Taurin and "decorated with his holy relics." The monks "gave from their own domaines [ex suo indominicatu]" at the villa "Carnacus" (n. id.) a mansus (colonia) and everything that went with it, including three serfs; and they gave the church a field right outside its doors. All this was given as an endowment (ut . . . dotem acciperet); the church at Chevignes, although "per-taining" to Cluny, had a claim as well to its own land.[13] On the other hand, Cluny continued its own claim: in 955, King Lothar (the son of Louis IV d'Outremer) confirmed Cluny's immunity and stipulated that Cluny was to hold and possess Chevignes "and similarly other territory in their possession [terra proprie-tatis ipsorum] everywhere in perpetuity, firm stability, and secure freedom."[14]

The complexity of such an arrangement is revealed in a series

---

11. *Raoul*, no. 18, pp. 77–81 (21 June 932) (=BB 396;I:379–81). The other charters concerned with Chevignes are BB 499;I:483–85 (6.939; see n. 12 below), BB 780;I:733–34 (10.950; see below, n. 14), BB 2255;III:384–88 (994), BB 980; II:76–78 (10.995), BB 1108;II:201 (8.961), BB 1109;II:201–2 (8.961), BB 1277; II:356–57 (3.970), BB 2523;III:596 (c. 1000), BB 2569;III:629–30 (3.1003), BB 2570;III:630 (3.1003).
12. See *Recueil des actes de Louis IV, roi de France (936–954)*, ed. Philippe Lauer (Paris: Imprimerie nationale, 1914), no. 10 (6.939), pp. 30–32 (= BB 499; I:483–85).
13. BB 780;I:733–34 (10.950).
14. *Recueil des actes de Lothaire et de Louis V, rois de France (954–987)*, ed. Louis Halphen and Ferdinand Lot (Paris: Klincksieck, 1908), no. 7 (10.955), pp. 15–17 (= BB 980;II:76–78) at p. 16: "simulque cetera ubicumque locorum terra proprietatis ipsorum . . . ab eis in perpetuo teneatur ac firma stabilitate et secura libertate possideatur." Similarly, the monks of Cluny built a chapel at Solutré (ca. Mâcon-Sud; BB 408;I:393–95 [932–33]), where land had been given to them by Raoul shortly after his gift of Chevignes; *Raoul*, no. 19 (7.932), pp. 81–88 (= BB 397;I:381–82).

of donations having to do with the church of Saint-Jean de Chaveyriat (dép. Ain, ca. Châtillon-sur-Chalaronne). The church
probably came to Cluny in the 970s, although its revenues had
been donated to Cluny earlier.[15] During the last quarter of the
tenth century, Saint-Jean (for Saint John the Baptist) attracted a
number of donations from the Lyonnais.[16] Sometimes land was
donated to Saint-Jean alone, sometimes to Cluny and to Chaveyriat together. Sometimes the same people—the scribe Witold,
for example—were involved at one time in a gift to Cluny and
at another in a gift to Saint-Jean. Clearly contemporaries made
distinctions between places and saints. But the social uses of
landed gifts, which bonded groups and allowed for overlapping
claims, came into play here too.

Saint-Jean served, among other things, as a local necropolis. A
donation to it by Droho and Manasserius after its transfer to
Cluny endowed Saint-Jean alone with a piece of a field *in locum
sepulturę* for the soul of their brother Bernol.[17] Similarly,
Alsendis and Dodo gave Chaveyriat a field for the burial and the
salvation of the soul of Raulf.[18] These donors said nothing at all

15. Already in 971–72 there was a donation to Saint Peter of Cluny and
to Saint-Jean de Chaveyriat jointly (in BB 1308;II:384–85). Nevertheless, BB
1405; II:464 (10.974) shows Roclenus donating the church to Cluny. He was the
brother of Winibald, the husband of Teuza: see Genealogy 7: the Grossi, and
Bouchard, *Sword*, pp. 296, 298. He may have been the same as Count Alberic's
fidelis noster of the same name (see BB 1198;II:280–81, BB 1124;II:215–16, M
153:106). Interestingly, BB 653;I:608 (Chaume, "Obs.," 943–64) shows the parents of a certain Aymo giving him the church of Saint-Jean de Chaveyriat and
stipulating that if he died without heirs it should go to Cluny. Berna (Aymo's
mother?) and Bovo, levita (a witness to this transaction) are both associated with
Roclenus at Pouilly in BB 1535;II:584–85 (7.980). The *altare* and the tithes of
Saint-Jean had already been given to Cluny by Burchard, archbishop of Lyon (BB
1227;II:307–8 [5.967]).
16. The charters are incorrectly dated in BB. Chaume's redatings in "Obs.,"
have been adopted here. They are based on the identification of Witold, who
appears in BB 1281;II:359–60, BB 1054;II:149, BB 239;I:230–31, BB 414;I:400–
401, BB 2281;III:410–11, BB 2283;III:412, etc., and whose presence required
Chaume to reconsider to which King Rudolf and which King Conrad the charters
refer. Chaume also cast doubt on the dating of BB 442;I:430–31 ("En Marge 2,"
p. 51 n. 7; the presence of Droho in the same place, Bèzemême [dép. Ain, ca.
Virieu-le-Grand], in this and BB 414 points to similar dates). BB 1077;II:171–72,
BB 1120;II:211–12, BB 1225;II:306, BB 1868;III:102–3, BB 2278;III:407–8 are
redated by Chaume, "Obs.," to the period c. 980–c. 1003 on the basis of the
presence of the scribe, Johannes, sacerdos. BB 2447;III:528–29 was redated by
Chaume, "Obs.," on the basis of the witnesses, as was BB 2215;III:358–59.
17. BB 414;I:400–401 (Chaume, "Obs.," 994–1000).
18. BB 442;I:430–31 (Chaume, "Obs.," 994–1000).

about Cluny. On the other hand, a woman named Rotrudis gave land "to God, and Saint Peter of the monastery of Cluny, over which Lord Abbot Odilo presides, and to Saint Jean, precursor of the Lord, at Chaveyriat," but then she specified that the whole of the alod she was donating was to go to Saint-Jean.[19] At about the same time, Vulbertus and his wife did the same thing.[20]

The donation of one Archembald unflaggingly maintained ties between Saint Peter and Saint Jean. He gave a field "to God and his holy apostles Peter and Paul at Cluny, where Lord Abbot Maiolus presides, and to Saint Jean, precursor of the lord, at Chaveyriat." To the west and north, the land that he gave bordered on land "of Saint Peter and of Saint Jean." The purpose of his donation, was, like many others, to obtain burial at the church of Saint Jean; but Archembald, who reserved the usufruct of the land until his death, stipulated that afterward it was to "go to the place of Saint Peter and Saint Jean."[21]

Sometimes the two saints were so inextricably linked that the donors did not mention Chaveyriat at all; we would imagine that Cluny itself had been dedicated to Saint Jean if it were not for the presence of the scribe, Johannes, who also drew up charters for Chaveyriat.[22] Thus, in 989 the brothers Arnulf and Alberic gave a meadow "to the Lord God and to Saint Peter and to Saint Jean."[23] The same year Gerlannus gave a curtilis to the same trinity.[24] Boso and his wife, Constantia, wanted burial at Saint-Jean; nevertheless they did not think it necessary to give their land to Saint Jean but rather donated it to "the holy place

---

19. BB 2447;III:528–29 (Chaume, "Obs.," 997–1003).

20. BB 2215;III:358–59 (Chaume, "Obs.," 994–1005).

21. BB 1308;II:384–85 (7.971–72): "dono Deo et sanctis apostolis ejus Petro et Paulo, ad locum Cluniacum, ubi donnus abba Maiolus preesse videtur, et Sancto Johanni, precursori Domini, Chavariacensi, aliquid de alodo juris mei: hoc est campum in loco qui dicitur Montiliacus situm, qui terminatur . . . a sero et a cirtio [terra] Sancti Petri et Sancti Johannis. Hunc vero campum denominatum concedo ad jam dictum locum Sancti Johannis in loco sepulture . . . post meum quoque discessum, absque ullius contradictione ad Sancti Petri locum et Sancti Johannis perveniat." There is nothing that links this charter to the Bourbon family, and although the name Archembald was characteristic for it, it was common in other families as well.

22. BB note the invocation of Saint Jean but do not link it to Chaveyriat; see BB 1120;II:211–12, n. 1.

23. BB 1120;II:211–12 (Chaume, "Obs.," 989).

24. BB 1225;II:306 (Chaume, "Obs.," 989); see BB 2281;III:410–11 (Chaume, "Obs.," 994–1000).

Cluny [built] in honor of the blessed apostles Peter and Paul."[25]

Such a variety of attitudes, expressed at approximately the same time, and written up in some instances by the same scribe, indicates that the crucial issue to contemporaries was not how to give Cluny exclusive ownership of their land. The question for donors was, rather, how they could create links by means of a donation. Some people used the church at Chaveyriat as an opportunity to associate themselves in life and above all in death to a small but specific subset of the community of saints.

Like Saint-Jean de Chaveyriat, part of Beaumont-sur-Grosne (ca. Sennecey-le-Grand) was saint's land: the church there was dedicated to Sainte Marie. Wido, viscount of Clermont, and his wife gave it to Cluny in 980.[26] (We shall see below how important the family of the viscounts of Clermont were to Cluny.) The monks of Cluny appear to have sent at least one monk to live there almost immediately.[27] Beaumont was at first the object of the sort of pious gift giving that we have seen at Chaveyriat. Otbert and his sister gave land at Vieil-Moulin (ca. Sennecey-le-Grand) "to God and Sainte-Marie de Beaumont and to His holy Apostles, Peter and Paul at Cluny" for the soul of their mother and for her burial at Sainte-Marie.[28] Rodbert and his wife gave land to God and Sainte-Marie about the year 1000.[29] Similarly at this time, some neighbors gave donations to Sainte-

25. BB 2283;III:412 (Chaume, "Obs.," 994–1000): "Sacrosancto locum Cluniensi . . . dono, pro anima mea et in locum sepulture mee, ad locum Cavariaco, tres sextaradas de terra arabile . . . in pago Lucdunensi."

26. BB 1525;II:574–75 (5.980); for the counts and viscounts of Clermont, see below, Genealogy 9. I refer to the church as Sainte-Marie (rather than, as it would be today, Notre-Dame) because this is closest to the terminology of the charters.

27. The monk Lanbert (e.g., BB 2536;III:606) represented Cluny in several sales (see discussion below); the monk Isimbaldus (BB 2449;III:530) also lived at Beaumont.

28. BB 1636;II:671–72 (10.983). The documents for Beaumont are much more certainly dated than those of Chaveyriat, which makes an evolution in their purposes more apparent.

29. BB 2413;III:504 (dated 997–1031, but probably should be redated c. 1000 because of correspondence with the witnesses in BB 2449;III:530, concerning land also at "Corcellae" (l.- disp. near Beaumont). In BB 2449 (Chaume, "Obs.," c. 1000), Adelaida gave to "Domino Deo omnipotenti et Sancte Marie Virgini Belmontensi et omnibus sanctis."

Marie and God, for the salvation of their souls and/or for burial there.[30]

But between about 1004 and 1007 the transactions with Sainte-Marie became more frequently sales than donations. These, too, sometimes had social and religious as well as economic significance. Durannus and his wife, for example, sold to Lanbert, the Cluniac monk at Beaumont who acted as an intermediary, a *curtilis* and vineyard; in return they received money, but they also made the sale for the sake of their souls and for burial at Sainte-Marie.[31] On the other hand, the sheer number of sales in this short period of time suggests a campaign of consolidation. A different Durannus and his wife sold an alod near Beaumont to the monks of Cluny and to Sainte-Marie, accepting money from Lanbert.[32] Ardradus and his wife sold land in the same villa to the monks about the same time.[33] Trutbaldus and his wife sold land at Vieil-Moulin, receiving cash on the spot.[34] (At some point they also gave a *curtilis et vinea* "to God and Sainte-Marie de Beaumont and to his holy Apostles Peter and Paul at Cluny," in locum sepulturȩ).[35] Nadalis and his brothers sold a vineyard in the same place, and so on.[36]

The sales to Lanbert stopped about 1007, and there was no further activity concerned with Sainte-Marie until a series of

30. E.g., BB 2027;III:236–37 (Chaume, "Obs.," 994–1004), BB 2536;III:606–7 (1.1001).

31. BB 2644;III:682–83 (5.1007).

32. BB 2364;III:469–70 (Chaume, "Obs.," c. 1000–1007).

33. BB 2592;III:646 (5.1004); see BB 2027;III:236–37 (Chaume, "Obs.," 994–1004) for a donation by Ardradus's father to Sainte-Marie, in a document that speaks of Odilo (the abbot of Cluny) being in charge [*preest*] at Sainte-Marie.

34. BB 2593;III:647–48 (5.1004): "accepimus a te [Lanbert] precium de casa beati Petri Cluniacensis coenobii denariorum solidos xii et dimidium. Quapropter censuimus predictam vineam. . . . aeternaliter possidere fratribus commanencium loci Cluniasensi coenobii, ea scilicet racione, ut cellarium unum in loco Belmontense nobis abere liceat absque censu, quamdiu ipsi tantum vitales, Deo volente, abuerimus aures."

35. BB 120;I:134 (placed in Berno's abbacy by cartulary A: redated by Chaume, "Obs.," c. 930–40, on the basis of names of witnesses; but clearly to be grouped with BB 2593;III:647–48 [dated 1004] because of the same principals: Trutbaldus and his wife, Peropia, and their sons, Constancius and Isembardus, as noted in Hillebrandt, "Datierungen").

36. Nadalis: BB 2602;III:654–55 (10.1004–5); for more examples see BB 2640; III:680 (10.1006–7), BB 2638;III:678–79 (10.1006–7), BB 2645;III:683–84 (5.1007).

related donations were made there in 1021 or 1022. Four of them concerned land "in Sevoio," probably near Saint-Ambreuil (ca. Sennecey-le-Grand), and one, at Saint-Ambreuil itself, involved a man named Arembert, an important donor and witness at Sevoio.[37] Yet, although these donations did not mention Cluny, about the same time, probably about 1023, Otto-William, the count of Burgundy, quit his claim to, and made a donation of, the "taxes [*servitia*] and dues . . . from the men of Sainte-Marie de Beaumont who live at Sennecey-le-Grand and at 'Letua' [n. id.] and in every estate [*in tota potestate*] that belongs to that house of God [namely, Cluny]."[38] In short, at least the customary dues of Sainte-Marie were Cluny's.

Chaveyriat and Beaumont certainly owned their land. Contemporaries, for example, spoke of land with its borders on "terra Sanctae Mariae Belmontensis."[39] But Cluny owned it also. The evidence suggests that, as with Cluny's donors, overlapping claims were tolerated.[40] Yet there is a great difference between an Eve, for example, who invoked her claim to the land at Fontana at the moment that she quitclaimed it, and a church, whose claims to land would be buttressed by ideas about the community of God and his saints. Before 1049, Cluny's churches were its property; but it was property quite different from any other sort of land, however large or fertile. Sometimes it was, in a word, shared. Thus Waldemarus and his family could give land and a church in the diocese of Gap "for

37. BB 2752;III:776 (1021–22), BB 2755;III:778 (1021–22), BB 2756;III:779 (10.1021–22), BB 2758;III:780–81 (10.1021–22), BB 2759;III:781 (1.1022): with Arembert. BB 2757;III:779–80 (10.1021–22) concerns a "clausum qui vocatur Merlo," probably near the other properties. All concerned donations with reservation of usufruct; and all were drawn up by the same scribe.

38. BB 2277;III:407 (Chaume, "Obs.," c. 1023): "Noticia guerpitionis quam fecit comes Willelmus Deo et sanctis ejus apostolis Petro et Paulo. . . . [E]go Willelmus . . . veniens Cluniaco . . . feci guerpitionem simul et donationem . . . per deprecationem venerandae memorię domni Rainaldi, prioris, ceterorumque monachorum loci jam dicti, de omni querela servicii et consuetudinis quam exigere solebamus, ego et antecessores mei comites, ab hominibus Sancte Marię Belmontensis, qui manent in Siniciaco et in Letua et in tota potestate, quę ad supradictam Dei casam respicit." On Rainaldus, the prior of Cluny, see Maurice Chaume, "Les grands Prieurs de Cluny," *Revue Mabillon* 28 (1938): 149.

39. E.g., BB 2404;III:496 (10.997–98), BB 2628;III:671–72 (1.1006), BB 2752; III:776.

40. The overlapping could be quite complicated: land of Sainte-Marie de Beaumont held by a miles in benefice from one Ansedeus was exchanged with Cluny for other land in BB 3246;IV:366 (1049–1109?).

eternal possession" to "Saint Peter, glorious Prince of Apostles of the monastery at Cluny . . . and to Saint Mary at Ganagobie, a cell of that monastery."[41]

Yet, on closer inspection, the arrangements that Cluny made with houses that pertained to it could be as varied as any series of relationships.

The Property of Cluny's Monasteries

Romainmôtier

Romainmôtier, dedicated (like Cluny) to Saints Peter and Paul, was given to Cluny in 929.[42] The donor, Adelaide, wife of Richard le Justiciar and sister of Rudolf I, king of Burgundy, wanted the two houses to share one abbot, one rule, and one congregation: she envisioned monks shifting from one place to the other according to need. Yet there was so little contact between Cluny and Romainmôtier before the end of the tenth century that one scholar has proposed that Romainmôtier had been secularized, that is, used simply as a royal fisc, until 966.[43]

All this clearly changed under Odilo, who was recognized as the abbot of Romainmôtier and who took an active interest in its property. In 1011, for example, Rudolf III made redonations of some property to Romainmôtier "for the salvation of our soul and because of Odilo's petitions."[44] Odilo's importance for the

---

41. BB 2771;III:792–93 (10.1022–1023): "donamus, et ad possidendum perpetuum tradimus Sancto Petro apostolorum principi glorioso Cluniensis monasterii . . . et Beate Marie Canacopiensis suprataxati coenobii cellule." Compare a thirteenth-century charter for Ganagobie by the count of Forcalquier, remitting lands and customs "Deo et beatae Mariae de Ganegobie, et Villermo Anglico, priori, et fratribus ejusdem domus praesentibus et futuris in perpetuum." The sole mention of Cluny here was in the acknowledgment that Ganagobie belonged to the "ordo Cluniacensis" (BB 4424;V:795–97 [6.1206]).

42. BB 379;I:358–61 (6.929). This and the other monasteries included in this section were chosen because their charters for the tenth and early eleventh centuries were numerous enough to be of use.

43. J. P. Cottier, *L'abbaye royale de Romainmôtier et le droit de sa terre (du Vᵉ au XIIIᵉ siècle)* (Lausanne: Rouge, 1948), pp. 80–81. The first part of the cartulary of Romainmôtier, written in one hand, concerns charters in the main from the eleventh and twelfth centuries (the exception is Adelaide's donation to Cluny): see the introduction to *Romainmôtier*, p. xi.

44. *Rudolfinger*, no. 97 (3.1011), pp. 252–53 [= *Romainmôtier*, pp. 427–28]: "ob anima nostrẹ remedium nec non peticiones Odelonis venerandi abbatis reddimus deo et sancto Petro ad Romanum monasterium."

property of Romainmôtier is nicely illustrated by the gift nexus surrounding the villa Bannans.[45] Abbot Maiolus probably had given the advocacy (i.e., lay protectorship) of this property to Humbert, later known to historians as Humbert II of Salins. That, in any event was the way that Humbert's son, Galcher, miles of Salins, saw the matter. Indeed, Galcher testified that Abbot Odilo had renewed the gift, making it over to him.[46] In 1009/10 Rudolf III and Burchard, the archbishop of Lyon, at Odilo's request granted to Romainmôtier the *servitium* of dependents at Bannans.[47] Humbert quit his claim to some of these taxes, "for love of God and love of Saint Peter and Lord Odilo, abbot, and Lord Anselm, prior [of Romainmôtier]."[48] Later, about 1045, when Romainmôtier challenged his right to the advocacy, Galcher quit his claim in the presence of representatives sent by Abbot Odilo, who would have gone himself had he not fallen ill.[49] This is a neat example of give and take in the archives of Romainmôtier.[50] For our purposes, it demonstrates as well the active interest of Abbot Odilo in this process.[51]

45. Surveyed in Frédéric de Charrière, "Recherches sur le couvent de Romainmôtier et ses possessions," *Mémoires et documents, Société de la Suisse Romande*, 1st ser. (Lausanne: Marc Ducloux, 1841), 3:148–56, and more recently in Bernard de Vregille, *Hugues de Salins, archevêque de Besançon 1031–1066* (Besançon: Cêtre, 1981), pp. 21 and 185–87, and more fully in Vregille's 3-vol. study of the same title (Lille: Université Lille, 1976), 1:236–38, hereafter cited as Thèse. Bannans is dép. Doubs, arr. Pontarlier.
46. *Romainmôtier*, pp. 445–56, at 445: "Dicebat enim, quod S^tus. Maiolus dedisset Humberto, patri suo, sibi abbas Odilo."
47. *Rudolfinger*, no. 95 (1009–10), pp. 249–50.
48. Vregille, Thèse, 3:11*–12* (c. 1020).
49. Ibid., 3:72*–74* (c. 1045). For the date, see ibid., 1:238. The presence of Thibaud (Tetbaldus), count of Chalon, at the quitclaim would be explained by the origins of the land from both Romainmôtier and Saint-Marcel de Chalon. See *Romainmôtier*, pp. 461–62, at 461 (c. 1001, Fredoinus gave back precarial lands at Bannans): "reddidit S^to. Petro Rom°. monasterio, et S^to Marcello, martyre cabilonensi precarias . . . quia ipse ibi non poterat manere, propter inimicitias filiorum Walcherii, comitis."
50. The relationship between Romainmôtier and the family of Galcher continued; e.g., *Romainmôtier*, p. 446 (c. 1085): Galcher's son quits his claim to Chaux-d'Arlier; pp. 447 and 449: two donations by the same son.
51. It should be noted, however, that the family of Galcher was related to the tenth-century counts of Mâcon: Humbert I of Salins, Galcher's great-grandfather, was the brother of Leotald, count at Mâcon. The lords of Salins, therefore, from the first had important connections to the county of Burgundy. See the genealogy in Vregille, *Hugues de Salins*, p. 1. In the twelfth century, they were benefactors of Cluny directly; see BB 3769–BB 3776;v:121–27. These connections may help explain Odilo's interest in their case.

Many donations to Romainmôtier were made simply to Saint Peter "at that place."[52] But the intimate relationship between the property of Saint Peter at Romainmôtier and at Cluny remained intact. Thus Abbot Hugh called Romainmôtier *locus noster*.[53] When a question arose about how to use the revenues from the two salt pans that had been acquired under Romainmôtier's prior, Stephan (c. 1075–87), Hugh directed that the tax from one be used to adorn the church and the tax from the other be used to celebrate Stephan's *anniversarium*.[54] At Romainmôtier, the gift network included Cluny.

Paray-le-Monial

The monastery of Paray-le-Monial was originally (971) founded by Lambert, count of Chalon, "with the cooperation of Abbot Maiolus."[55] It was not under Cluny's jurisdiction, however, until 999, when it was formally handed over to Saints Peter and Paul by Lambert's son, Hugh, "so that [Abbot Odilo] and his successors might have firm authority to rule, govern, and order it according to the will of God, with all the churches, villae, mansi, mills, serfs and slaves of every sex and age, vineyards, fields, and roads in and out that pertain to it, wholly and completely."[56]

Paray, like Romainmôtier, had as its abbot the abbot of Cluny; on the spot was a prior. When the monks at Paray made an

52. E.g., the donation by Galcher, "filius Vualcherii filii Humbert": "trado domino et beato Petro," *Romainmôtier*, pp. 447–48; another version of the same donation: "trado dⁿᵒ. et beato Petro per manum Stephani, prioris predicti loci," p. 449. On the other hand, see p. 448: "ego Raynaldus dono et concedo domino deo ad locum, cui vocabulum est romano monasterio, et est constructus in honore bⁱ. Petri apostoli, in quo dominus Odilo abbas preesse videtur."
53. Ibid., p. 451.
54. Ibid., p. 451. On Prior Stephan, see Charrière, p. 247–48.
55. BB 2484 (5.999) recounts the history. See *Paray*, no. 2, pp. 2–3 (971). Originally, Paray was known as Orval.
56. BB 2484 (5.999): Hugh "tradit beatis apostolis Petro et Paulo et Cluniacensi monasterio, cui preest donnus Odilo, ita ut habeat, tam ipse quam etiam sui successores, firmam auctoritatem eundem locum regere, [gubernare] ac secundum Dei voluntatem disponere, cum omnibus inibi pertinentibus aecclesiis, villis, [mansis, farinariis, servis et ancillis, utriusque sexus atque etatis, vineis, campis, exitibus et regressibus,] totum ad integrum." The text in brackets is lacking in the summary in cartulary B; the *notitia* is found in its fullest extant form at the end of cartulary A.

exchange of mansi with Hugh de Busseuil and his father, the transaction was "mediated" by Paray's prior, Andrald, "at the command" (*praecepto*) of Abbot Odilo and of Hugh, the donor of the monastery. After 999, Hugh was both the count of Chalon and the bishop of Auxerre.[57] This explains the way in which he was referred to in a later notice, which spoke of a complex series of transactions concerning a certain mansus. The events were said to have taken place in "the time of Father Odilo and the noble count and bishop, Hugh, and of the prior, Lord Gonter." The mansus had been given to Paray, then taken back and given to a miles named Robert. Eventually Robert, "detained by a bodily infirmity" at Cluny, "gave the mansus again, destined for Paray, to God and his saints and to Lord Abbot Hugh [of Cluny]."[58] All these groups—Robert, Abbot Hugh, Paray, God and his saints—were seen as bound to one another. In the twelfth century, when Count William renounced all the *malae consuetudines* (unjust dues) that he had exacted "in terra Sancti," and returned the rights to Paray, he did so in the presence of Peter the Venerable, Cluny's abbot, and of Bernard, Cluny's prior.[59]

Yet, the complexity of property relations is highlighted by the fact that, during the same period, Paray was party to numerous land transactions without reference to Cluny. When the son of Hugh de Busseuil returned to Paray the mansus that his father had received in that exchange authorized by Abbot Odilo, it was given (without a word about the abbot of Cluny) "to the Lord God and to the aforesaid place," namely, Paray.[60] When Wicard de Vilers made a donation, it was "to God and that place, for his soul and burial."[61] This was, in fact, the usual formula, for, although Paray was dedicated to several saints, they were rarely

57. *Paray*, no. 96, p. 52. On Hugh, count and bishop, see Bouchard, *Sword*, pp. 106–7, 309–12.

58. *Paray*, no. 111, p. 58–59, at 59: "Unde isdem Rodbertus, post multos annos infirmitate corporis Cluniaco detentus, Deo et sanctis ejus et domno Ugoni abbati hunc mansum reddidit ad praelibatum Aureae Vallis locum." He added yet another gift above that, and he received 100 solidi in return; the transaction has the character of a quitclaim.

59. *Paray*, no. 209, pp. 108–9, at 108.

60. *Paray*, no. 97, p. 52.

61. *Paray*, no. 109, p. 58.

mentioned in the charters.⁶² At Paray, the gift network was therefore only occasionally linked to Cluny.

Sauxillanges

The same was true of Sauxillanges. There were already two churches at Sauxillanges when Acfred, duke of Aquitaine and nephew of William the Pious, gave this property, which had been ceded to him by God along with his title and his other worldly goods, back to God.⁶³ He set in place twelve brothers to praise the Lord there day and night and to pray and beg mercy for the sins of all; and he provided for them by specifying the land and serfs that pertained to Sauxillanges. Sometime after February 951, Pope Agapitus II wrote a letter to the churches of the Auvergne affirming Rome's special relationship with Sauxillanges, warning against any who might presume to disturb the monks there, and calling on Bishop Stephan of Clermont (about whom we shall have much to say later) to excommunicate anyone who violated its peace.⁶⁴ This was probably just after Stephan himself had entrusted the abbacy of Sauxillanges to Aymard, the abbot of Cluny.⁶⁵

There must have been someone ruling Sauxillanges on the spot under Aymard and Maiolus; but only under Odilo is there mention of a prior. In any case, the prior was unimportant.⁶⁶

---

62. On the various saints, see *Paray*, p. xiii. For the usual formula, see ibid., no. 80, p. 44; no. 81, p. 44; no. 82, pp. 44–45; no. 85, pp. 45–46, etc.

63. BB 286 (10.927) (= *Sauxillanges*, no. 13, pp. 47–51): "Acfredus, divina tribuente misericordia, Aquitanorum dux . . . reddo creatori meo Domino, regi regum et domino dominantium, de ipsa terra quam idem Dominus sua larga clementia parentibus meis et michi indignissimo largiri dignatus est." Elisabeth Magnou-Nortier ("Contribution à l'étude des documents falsifiés: Le diplôme de Louis le Pieux pour Saint-Julien de Brioude [825] et l'acte de fondation du monastère de Sauxillanges par le duc Acfred [927]" *Cahiers de civilisation médiévale* 21 [1978]: 313–38, esp. 323–38) has discovered several interpolations in this document, but the particular passage in question here is part of the original: Magnou-Nortier cites *Sauxillanges*, no. 82 (949), clearly authentic, which has nearly identical wording. William the Pious had originally founded the churches at Sauxillanges; see *Sauxillanges*, no. 146, pp. 135–37.

64. Zimmermann, no.125 (after 2.951), pp. 220–21 (= *Sauxillanges*, no.14, pp. 51–52; = JL 3662).

65. BB 792 (Chaume, "Obs.," after 2.951).

66. Under Aymard, a man named Ragnibert served in the abbot's stead: *Saux-*

The stewardship of Aymard was supposed to be absolute: according to Bishop Stephan, Sauxillanges was to be subject, either directly or under a subordinate, to Aymard's rule, order, and disposition.[67] Almost every donation charter from Sauxillanges mentions the name of the abbot, that is, the abbot of Cluny himself. In at least one instance, property was given to Cluny and Sauxillanges together: Abbot Odilo's father gave a donation to "the blessed Apostles, Peter and Paul, at Cluny and Sauxillanges into the hand and power of Abbot Odilo and Vivian [the prior of Cluny]."[68] When, in 998, Pope Gregory V drew up an inventory of property pertaining to Cluny, he not only included Sauxillanges, but also five major properties that came with it.[69]

Yet, in its own *local* context, it would seem that normally gifts given to Sauxillanges had nothing to do with Cluny, and that the abbot of Cluny wore a different hat there: he was, in fact, the abbot of Sauxillanges. It would be rash indeed to think that the property of Sauxillanges belonged to Cluny simply because Cluny's abbot was also its abbot.[70] For this is not at all what contemporaries said.

---

illanges, no. 428, pp. 326–28, at p. 327: "custodemque loci illius et provisorem subtus se fratrem Ragnibertum constituere voluit." Under Odilo and Hugh there was a prior Robert: ibid., no. 515, pp. 387–88 (abbacy of Odilo); no. 297, pp. 238–40 (abbacy of Hugh). See the calculations from the charters of Sauxillanges made by Dietrich Poeck, "*Cluniacensis ecclesia*: Cluny and its Monasteries" (Paper presented at the Twenty-second International Congress on Medieval Studies, Kalamazoo, Mich., 6–10 May 1987): Aymard was named in 23 charters, Maiolus in nearly 200 charters, Odilo in 160 charters. But there was a major change under Abbot Hugh, who was mentioned in only 26 charters.

67. *Sauxillanges*, no. 16, pp. 54–55: "quod quidem monasterium [i.e., Sauxillanges] domnus Aimardus, abba Cluniensis, tam per se quam etiam per sibi subditos ut pote sibi per omnia subjectum regit, ordinat atque disponit." The context is a donation charter by Stephan. The date is problematic: "anno xviii regnante Ludovico rege" places it in 972, but Aymard died in 964.

68. BB 2135;III:315–17 (BB gives 993–1048; Chaume, "Obs.," suggests 994–1008). In fact, it must be dated 3.999 because of the presence as witnesses of Rotbertus, prepositus, who was the prior of Brioude 957–March 999 (*Grand/Brioude*, p. lviii) and of Beraldus, decanus, who was the dean of Brioude March, 999–1011 (ibid., p. lix). The text is "affirmo ex meę possessionis jure beatis Petro et Paulo apostolis Cluniacensis seu Celsiniacensis cęnobiorum, in manum et potestatem Odilonis abbatis, necnon et Viviani."

69. See Table 9 and Map 5.

70. Poeck, in "Cluny and Its Monasteries," in fact concludes from his figures that, while Sauxillanges was dependent on Cluny in the tenth century, it became more and more independent in the course of the eleventh and twelfth centuries. Certainly Poeck has pointed to a significant change in modes of administration;

Thus, during Aymard's abbacy, one Gausbertus gave property to Aymard and the monks who lived at Sauxillanges, which (as he said) was established "in the name of the Trinity and in veneration of the holy mother of God and ever-virgin Mary, and no less in honor of the blessed Apostles Peter and Paul and John the Evangelist, and also John the Baptist and the twelve apostles." This particular donation was explicitly for prayers.[71] There was no mention of Cluny. Aymard was simply the abbot of the monks at Sauxillanges. Similarly Teobrandus gave two vineyards and a field "to the place called Sauxillanges, which is dedicated in honor of omnipotent God and His blessed Apostles Peter and John and where Lord Abbot Aymard rules with a band of monks subject to him."[72]

Nothing changed under Maiolus, who continued to act in a different capacity from "abbot of Cluny" when he was considered abbot of Sauxillanges. Ermenald gave a vineyard "to the holy church of the holy Apostles Peter and Paul and other saints who have been established there in worthy honor at the place called Sauxillanges, where Lord Maiolus rules as abbot."[73] It is true that the donation of Leodegarius and his wife, Benedicta, called Maiolus the abbot of Cluny, but this was simply to echo the words of Bishop Stephan about Aymard's role at Sauxillanges.[74] Similarly, in the time of Odilo, Benedictus gave a

but it is not a change in the gift network which, from the beginning, involved God, his saints, and the monks at Sauxillanges alone.

71. *Sauxillanges*, no. 17, pp. 55–56. Gausbertus called a man named Bertran his *senior*; Bertran's son was Stephan. We will return to Bertran and Stephan later, when we discuss the viscounts of Clermont. The connections between all of these donors suggest that a study (at least as long as the present work) might be made of the overlap and interaction between several gift-exchange systems. The groups centering on the viscounts of Clermont were involved in gift giving with many different monasteries, including Brioude, Saint-Flour, Conques, Cluny, and Sauxillanges. It would be well worth analyzing these ties in detail, to see if such prestation networks were interrelated, and whether they worked on the same or separate principles. What determined, for example, whether a gift went to one monastery or another?

72. *Sauxillanges*, no. 19, pp. 57–58.

73. *Sauxillanges*, no. 64, pp. 85–86: "Sacro sancte aecclesie sanctorum apostolorum Petri et Pauli et aliorum sanctorum qui ibi digno honore conditi sunt in loco qui vocatur *Celsinanias* monasterii, sub quo loco vel congregatione domnus Maiolus abba preesse videtur, ego in Christi nomine Ermenaldus et cedo domo supradictis sanctis vineam unam."

74. *Sauxillanges*, no. 88, pp. 101–2: "domnus Maiolus abba Cluniensi tam per se quam etiam per sibi subditos ut pote sibi per omnia subjectum regit, ordinat

vineyard "to the Lord God and Saint Peter and to the monastery that is called Sauxillanges, which is ruled under the governance of Lord Abbot Odilo."[75] And so on.

Saint-Jean d'Angély

Saint-Jean d'Angély (dép. Charente-Maritime) presents a different set of issues only at first glance. It was named as part of the property pertaining to Cluny quite late, during the abbacy of Hugh, in the papal privilege of Stephan IX (1058).[76] Thereafter it continued to be confirmed by popes. But the transfer to Cluny, which did not change the fact that Saint-Jean had its own abbot (one different from the abbot of Cluny), made almost no impact whatever on the nexus of gift giving and taking that Saint-Jean had with its neighbors. Gofred Ysembert and his sons, for example, gave part of their alod "to God and to Saint-Jean" about 1068, using the same formula that donors had used in the tenth century, when there was no question of Cluny's control over Saint-Jean.[77] When William Rufus conceded Saint-Jean's claims to half of the church at Tiers in 1098, "he relinquished it totally to Saint-Jean." Wido (Guy-Geoffrey),

---

atque disponit." See ibid., no. 16, pp. 54–55: "domnus Aimardus, abba Cluniensis, tam per se quam etiam per sibi subditos ut pote sibi per omnia subjectum regit, ordinat atque disponit."

75. *Sauxillanges*, no. 119, p. 121; see nos.120, 121, 122, etc. (pp. 121–27) with the same formula.

76. *Bull. Clun.*, pp. 15–16 (3.1058) (= JL 4385). Apparently earlier it had been reformed along Cluniac lines during the administration of Cluny's Abbot Odilo; see Ademar of Chabannes, *Chronicon* iii.56, ed. Jules Chavanon (Paris: Picard, 1897), p. 181.

77. *Angély*, no. 133;1:167 (1060–91, probably c. 1068). For tenth-century gifts see, e.g., no. 392;11:56; no. 393;11:57–58; no. 447;11:109. Examples of post-1058 gifts with the same or similar formulas: no. 136;1:169 (c. 1064); no.138;1:169–70 (c. 1080); no.139;1:170 (1068), etc. Some of the donations to Saint-Jean were at the same time sales (e.g., no. 138) with the formula *dono . . . et accipio x solidi*. No. 145;1:175–76 (1060–91; probably c. 1075) was a gift "propter quam plurimas injurias quas feci sancto Joanni et damna rerum suorum subjectorum" which was made "pro anima patris mei et matris proque mea, et pro animabus fratrum meorum," and for which the donor received fifty solidi. Such a transaction was clearly meant as a pious act and reveals a gift nexus more immediately involved in monetary give and take than Cluny's. See the remarks of Gregory, "Gifts to Men," pp. 648–49, about the uses of money in a gift economy. Money may be used in such a system exactly as any other object—such as yams, pigs, coppers —in an exchange.

duke of Aquitaine and count of Poitiers, gave back to Saint-Jean (not to Saint Peter) all the malae consuetudines that he had levied since his father's death.[78]

The radical separation between Saint Peter and Saint Jean by the end of the eleventh century is nowhere brought home more clearly than in the story of Aimericus Bechet.[79] His father had given the church of Notre-Dame de Genouillé to Saint Peter at Cluny, but Aimericus "took back the alms." Later he gave it to Saint-Jean, its abbot, and its monks. Cluny pressed its claim, but eventually accepted 200 solidi and dropped its suit. It is not so much the suit as Aimericus's decisive selectivity that is instructive. By the end of the eleventh century, saints did not so easily share a piece of property.

Yet the larger significance of this episode, and indeed of this entire parade of monasteries and their properties that we have been surveying, is that the gift network operating for each monastery must be analyzed individually. In most cases it was intensely exclusive and local. In some instances it intersected with other gift-giving networks and drew upon places and saints fairly far afield. And, of course, it could change over time.

One cannot, therefore, formulate a rule about when the property of a Cluniac monastery "belonged" to Cluny on the basis of the status of its abbot or prior. As we have seen, even when the abbot of a monastery was the same person as the abbot of Cluny, he might be acting in a separate capacity in each place. Nor can the question of ownership be neatly tied to the mode of affiliation, for it does not appear to have mattered if a monastery was given to Cluny to reorder or was listed as part of its ecclesia. Rather the question itself has to be posed differently. Property was part of a network of relations; the same piece could on the one hand signify a local gift to a local saint, and on the other, an appendage of the monastery of Cluny; and sometimes it could belong to both. It all depended on what relationship was to be stressed in any particular instance.

78. *Angély*, no. 11;1:31 (1058–87, probably c. 1082); no.300;1:322. Tiers is dép. Vienne, arr. Châtellerault.

79. *Angély*, no. 195;1:236 (1060–91, probably 1091). Genouillé is dép. Charente-Inférieure, arr. Rochefort.

Special Property

By 1049, Cluny had been involved in more than 3,000 land transactions. But all land is not equal. We are allowed a glimpse of the land that was most important to Cluny during this period in documents that list selected properties of Cluny: the confirmations of kings and popes and the inventory drawn up at the Council of Anse. A glance at Table 9 shows that, although there were discrepancies in these lists over the course of the tenth century, there was also a remarkable consistency, as new places were grafted onto old. At the end of that century, an unusually large number of pancartes for Cluny were drawn up in different contexts: first, in 994, twenty-two places were named by the Council of Anse; then, in 998, two confirmations of property were given by Rudolf III, king of Burgundy; and, in the same year, two privileges, one a very long inventory of seventy-eight places, were supplied by Pope Gregory V (see Map 5). The long list of Pope Gregory, which incorporated most of the places selected by the Council of Anse and many of the places named by Rudolf III, was repeated, with very few changes and only minor additions, by Pope Victor II in November 1055 and Pope Stephen IX in March 1058.[80] For more than fifty years, then, the places selected at the end of the tenth century remained of enduring importance, in any event in papal bulls. Of what significance are these lists?

Heretofore, we have spoken of transactions taking place in the tenth and eleventh centuries without invoking kings or popes. Indeed, Duby and others have shown how, in this period of many overlapping authorities, one cannot speak of any authority at all being in control.[81] The werpitiones in Cluny's documents reveal disputes and resolutions, they do not reveal the long arm

---

80. The bull of Pope Victor II is JL 4336 (= *Bull. Clun.*, pp. 13–14; = BB 3349;IV.:446 [6.1055]); the bull of Pope Stephen IX is JL 4385 (= *Bull. Clun.*, pp. 15–16; = BB 3354;IV:450 [3.1058]). The two bulls of Gregory V are Zimmermann, no. 348 (3.998), pp. 676–79, and no. 351 (4.998), pp. 682–86. The second of these is clearly genuine and has been used as the key text for Table 9. The first also includes a long list of places, but these are later interpolations into a simple confirmation concerning Romainmôtier.

81. See Georges Duby, "Evolution des institutions judiciaires," in *Hommes et structures*, pp. 7–60; Cheyette, "Suum cuique tribuere," pp. 287–99; Geary, "Vivre en conflit."

Table 9. Properties named in bull of Gregory V

Agapitus II [Zimmermann, no. 130 [3·954], pp. 229–31][1]	Council of Anse [BB 2255 [994]]	Gregory V[2] [Zimmermann, no. 351 [4·998], pp. 682–86][3]	Identification[4]
		in comitatu Matisconensi	(in the county of Mâcon)
1. abb. b. Martini		1. cell. Sti. Martini	1. St.-Martin-des-Vignes, S.-L., Mâcon[5]
2. abb. Sti. Johannis		2. cell. Sti. Johannis	2. St.-Jean-de-Mâcon, S.-L., Mâcon
3. Cauiniacas	3. Cavinias	3. Cauinias + ecc.	3. Chevignes, S.-L., Mâcon-Sud
4. Solustriacum	4. Solestriacum	4. Solestriacum + ecc.	4. Solutré, S.-L., Mâcon-Sud
5. Scotiolas	5. Scociolas	5. Escutiolas + ecc.	5. Ecussolles, S.-L., Tramayes
		6. Galliniacum + ecc.	6. Jalogny, S.-L., Cluny
		7. Rufiacum + ecc.	7. Ruffey, S.-L., Cluny
	8. Macerias	8. Macerias + ecc.	8. ? Mazille, S.-L., Cluny[6]
	9. Claromane	9. Graimannum	9. ? Clermain, S.-L., Tramayes[7]
	10. Peronnam	10. Petromniacum	10. Péronne, S.-L., Lugny
		11. Barieserenam	11. Bergesserin, S.-L., Cluny
12. Arpagiacum		12. Arpaiacum	12. Arpayé, Rhône, Beaujeu
13. Dabormiacum		13. Darboniacum	13. n. id.
	14. Besorniacum	14. Besorniacum	14. Bézornay, S.-L., Cluny
		15. St. Columbe, ecc.	15. Ste.-Columbe, S.-L., La Guiche
		16. Vitreriam	16. La Verrière, S.-L., La Guiche
		17. Burguliensem	17. ? Bourgogne, S.-L., Tramayes[8]
	18. Lordonem montem	18. castrum Lurdonum	18. Lourdon, S.-L., Cluny
19. quod Leodbaldus ... dereliquid[9]	19. Blanoscum	19. Blanuscum	19. Blanot, S.-L., Cluny
		20. Cottam	20. Cotte, S.-L., Cluny
21. Carilocensis, abb.	21. Carus Locus, mon.	21. Carus Locus, mon.	21. Charlieu, Loire, arr. Roanne
	22. Regniacum, mon.	22. Renniacum, cell.	22. Régny, Loire, arr. Roanne
23. St. Uictorem		23. ecc. Sti. Uictoris	23. St.-Victor-d'Aujoux, Rhône
	24. St. Uictorem ... supra Remis	24. cell. Sti. Uictoris	24. St.-Victor-sur-Rhins, Loire, St.-Symphorien

(Continued)

[Table 9—continued]

Agapitus II (Zimmermann, no. 130 [3.954], pp. 229–31)[1]	Council of Anse (BB 2255 [994])	Gregory V[2] (Zimmermann, no. 351 [4.998], pp. 682–86)[3]	Identification[4]
	26. Ivuirendam	25. ecc. Sti. Langulfi	25. St.-Gengoux-le-National, S.-L., arr. Mâcon
	27. Belmontem	26. Eguirandam + ecc. *in comitatu Cabilonensi*	26. Iguerande, S.-L., Semur-en-Brionnais [in the county of Chalon)
		27. Bellomonte, cell.	27. Beaumont-sur-Grosne, S.-L., Sennecey
		28. ecc. de Campiloco	28. Champlieu, S.-L., Sennecey-le-Grand
		29. Iuliacum + ecc. *in episcopatu Augustudunensi*	29. Jully-lès-Buxy, S.-L., Buxy [in the diocese of Autun)
	30. castrum Oiedellis	30. Oiadellis, cell.	30. Huillaux, Allier, Le Donjon
		31. ecc. + terr. quas Teotardus contulit[10]	31. Lenax, Allier, Donjon
		32. Magabrense, mon. *in comitatu Aruernensi*	32. Mesvres, S.-L., arr. Autun [in the county of Clermont)
		33. Siluniacum, mon.	33. Souvigny, Allier, arr. Moulins
		34. Firmitas, cell.	34. La Ferté, Allier, arr. Moulins
		35. Scurolias, cell.	35. Escurolles, Allier, Vichy
		36. Langiacus + ecc.	36. Langy, Allier, Vichy
		37. Ad Boscum, cell.	37. ? Bost, Allier[11]
		38. Riuis, mon.	38. Ris, Puy-de-Dôme, Thiers
		38a. Lussiaco	38a. Lussat, Puy-de-Dôme, Ennezat[12]
		39. Manrengum + ecc.	39. Maringues, Puy-de-Dôme, Thiers
		40. Ad Montes, cell.	40. ? Mons, Puy-de-Dôme, Riom[13]
41. Celsanicas		41. Celsinianense, mon. + terr.	41. Sauxillanges, Puy-de-Dôme, Issoire
		41a. Carniacum	41a. Charnat, Puy-de-Dôme, Thiers
		41b. Burniunculum	41b. Bournoncle-la-Roche, Hte.-Loire, Brioude
		41c. Abolniacum	41c. Bonnac, Cantal, Massiac
		41d. Ginniacum	41d. Gignat, Puy-de-Dôme, Issoire
		41e. Cardonetum	41e. St.-Allyre-de-Monton, Puy-de-Dôme[14]

(Continued)

[Table 9—continued]

Agapitus II [Zimmermann, no. 130 [3.954], pp. 229–31][1]	Council of Anse (BB 2255 [994])	Gregory V[2] [Zimmermann, no. 351 [4.998], pp. 682–86][3]	Identification[4]
		42. St. Florus, cell. + mansi	42. St.-Flour, Cantal
		43. Riliacum, cell.	43. Reilhac, Hte.-Loire, Langeac
		44. St. Salvator, capella in villa Saraciaco	44. Cerzat, Hte.-Loire, Lavoûte-Chilhac
		45. in Aniciensi civ., mansi + capella *in episcopatu Uiuariensi*	45. Le-Puy, Hte.-Loire (in the diocese of Viviers)
		46. Mizoscum, cell.	46. ? l.-disp. near Pailharès, Ardèche, co. St. Félicien[15]
		47. cell. de Rumpono monte	47. Rompon, Ardèche, la Voulte-sur-Rhône[R]
		48. Ad fontes, cell.	48. ? Fonts-de-Rochemaure, Ardèche, Rochemaure[R]
		49. Rioms, cell. *in episcopatu Uticensi*	49. Ruoms, Ardèche, Vallon-Pont-d'Arc (in the diocese of Uzès)
50. ecc. Sti. Saturnini[16]		50. mon. Sti. Petri & Saturnini + terr.	50. le Pont-St.-Esprit, Gard, arr. Uzès
		50a. Castro Coloncellas	50a. Colonzelle, Drôme, Grignan[R]
		50b. curte Tueleta *in Trecassino episc.*	50b. Tulette, Drôme, St.-Paul-Trois-Châteaux[R] (in the diocese of St.-Paul-Trois-Châteaux)
		51. St. Amandus, cell. *in episcopatu Arausico*	51. St.-Amand, Drôme, co. Montségur[R] (in the diocese of Orange)
		52. Poio Odoleno, cell.	52. Piolenc, Vaucluse, Avignon[R]
		53. mon. St. Pantaleonis *in Gapacensi episcopatu*	53. St.-Pantaléon-les-Vignes, Drôme, arr. Nyons[R] (in the diocese of Gap)
		54. St. Andrea, cell. *in patria Prouintia*	54. St.-André-de-Rosans, Htes.-Alpes, Rosans[R] (in the territory of Provence)
		55. Canagobiense, mon.	55. Ganagobie, Alpes de Hte.-Prov., Peyruis[R]
		56. curtem Valentiolam	56. Valensole, Alpes de Hte.-Prov., Digne[R]
		57. castro Sarrianis *in Ualentinensi episcopatu*	57. Sarrians, Vaucluse, Carpentras (in the diocese of Valence)

(Continued)

[Table 9—continued]

Agapitus II [Zimmermann, no. 130 [3.954], pp. 229–31][1]	Council of Anse (BB 2255 [994])	Gregory V[2] [Zimmermann, no. 351 [4.998], pp. 682–86][3]	Identification[4]
		58. Ales	58. Allex, Drôme, Crest-Nord^R17
		59. monte Syon in episcopatu Uiennensi	59. ? Montoison, Drôme, Crest-Nord^R18 (in the diocese of Vienne)
		60. Taderniacum, mon.	60. Ternay, Rhône, Lyon^R
61. "alodum, quem Uualdo... dedit"[19]		61. Causella, cell.	61. Chuzelle, Isère, Vienne^Rr
		62. Bracost	62. ? La Brachère, Isère, Sud-Vienne^Rr
		63. Insula + ecc. in episcopatu Lugdunensi	63. Ile d'Abeau, Isère, la Verpillière^Rr (in the diocese of Lyon)
		64. Taluzatis, cell.	64. Taluyers, Rhône, Lyon^R
65. St. Desiderius, ecc.[20]	65. Poliacum	65. Poliacum, cell.	65. Pouilly-lès-Feurs, Loire, Feurs^Rr
	66. Artadunum	66. Artedunum, cell.	66. Arthun, Loire, Montbrison^Rr
67. Ambertam	67. Ambertam, cell.	67. Anbertensem, cell.	67. Ambierle, Loire, Roanne^R
68. Sauiniacum	68. Saviniacum	68. Sauiniacum, cell.	68. Savigneux, Ain, St.-Trivier-sur-Moignans^Rr
69. Ambariacum		69. curtem Ambariacum	69. Ambérieux-en-Dombes, Ain, Châtillon-sur-Chalaronne^Rr
		70. ecc. Sti. Andeoli	70. St-Andéol-le-Château, Rhône, Lyon^R
		71. ecc. Adoratorium	71. Ouroux, Ain, Villeneuve^R
	72. Romanam	72. curtem de Romanis	72. Romans, Ain, arr. Trévoux^Rr
	73. Chavariacum	73. Cauariacum, cell.	73. Chaveyriat, Ain, Châtillon-sur-Chalaronne^Rr
		74. Luiniacum, cell.	74. 1.-disp, near Thoissey^Rr
75. Tosciacum	75. Tosciacum	75. Tussiacum + ecc.	75. Thoissey, Ain, arr. Trévoux^Rr
		76. omnes quas Vuichardus . . . contulit[21]	76. ? Chevroux, Ain, Pont-de-Vaux
		76a.	76a. ? Curtetrelle, Ain, co. Chevroux
		76b.	76b. Ozan, Ain, Pont-de-Vaux[22]
		77. Paterniacum, mon.	77. Payerne, Switzerland^R
		78. Romanum, mon.	78. Romainmôtier, Switzerland^R

(Continued)

(Table 9—continued)

1. In this table, the second list of Gregory V is taken as a standard; places named in the lists of Anse and Agapitus are not listed in their original sequence but rather are organized to show correspondences with Gregory V. Included in the list for Agapitus are only those places that reappear on the later inventories of Gregory V, Victor II (6. 1055; = JL 4336; = *Bull. Clun.*, p. 13), and Stephen IX (3. 1058; = JL 4385; = *Bull. Clun.*, p. 15). Places in Agapitus's bull that do not reappear later are Agiona (= Aine, ca. Lugny), Seneciascu(m) (= Sennecé-lès-Mâcon), Kaeidas (= ?Chiddes, ca. Saint-Bonnet-de-Joux), and "piscatoriam, quam Osam vocant" (= lake named Ozan, now 1.-disp, Ain, near Vésines and Asnières; not the same as, but close to, no. 76b). Agapitus's bull also mentions an "ecclesia sancti Abundi, quam Artaldus moriens . . . reliquit;" we know that an Artaldus gave Cluny Saint-Victor-d'Aujoux in BB 373;1:356–57. The ecclesia Sancti Abundi may have been part of this donation, since, in a confirmation by King Raoul, it is clear that Artaldus also gave donations "de aliis rebus" to Saint-Victor: *Raoul*, no. 18, pp. 77–81, at 80.

2. The order of this list is also the order of the lists in the papal bulls of Victor II and Stephen IX, both of which, in fact, are nearly identical to this pancarte of Gregory V, with a few additions. Thus the list of Gregory, drawn up on 22 April 998, was the standard one for more than fifty years. The real change came with Gregory VII; see Santifaller, no. 107, pp. 95–100.

3. Properties grouped together under one rubric by Gregory are indicated under the main rubric by a., b., etc. Where properties are not directly named but can be inferred from other evidence, the name is left blank in Gregory's column but is suggested in the identifications.

4. Based on identifications in consultation with Mme Quarré, or in Chaume, *Origines* II/3; Laurence Henri Cottineau and G. Poras, *Répertoire topo-bibliographique des abbayes et prieurés* 3 vols. (vols. 1 and 2, Macon: Protat, 1939; vol. 3, Paris, 1971); Dietrich Poeck, "Die Klöster der Cluniacensis ecclesia", draft of a study to be published in the series Münstersche Mittelalter-Schriften; *Rudolfinger*; Santifaller.

5. The modern place identification is followed by the département (normally abbreviated), followed by the canton (or arrondissement, if preceded by "arr."). The abbreviations are: ? = identification is uncertain; ecc. = church(es); mon. = monastery; mansi = *mansiones*; + = *cum*; cell. = *cella*; civ. = *civitas*; S.-L. = Saône-et-Loire; terr. = *terra(e)*. The superior symbol ʳ indicates a place that is mentioned in the confirmation of Rudolf III in *Rudolfinger*, no. 82, pp. 230–32; the superior symbol ᴿ refers to a place in his longer confirmation, *Rudolfinger*, no. 83, pp. 232–33. As Rudolf was king of Burgundy, his confirmations generally treated of places in the *pagi* of Lyon, Vienne, etc.

6. Either Mazille or "Maceria," near Neronde, ca. Mazille.

7. The bull of Gregory V is found in only two copies in cartulary C. Zimmermann reads here Graimannu(m) and its variant, Craimannu(m). On nonpaleographical grounds, it seems likely that Clairmannum is meant. See the following clusters of place names in the order that they occur in Gregory V and later pontifical confirmations for Cluny:

Gregory V	Victor II	Stephen IX	Gregory VII
Galliniacum	Galliniacum	Galliniacum	Galliniacum
Rufiacum	Rufiacum	Rufiacum	Rufiacum

(*Continued*)

(Table 9—continued)

Gregory V	Victor II	Stephen IX	Gregory VII
Macerias	Masilias	Masilias	Masilias
Graimannum	Clairmannum	Clairmannum	Clairmanum
Petromniacum	Barjeserenain	Barjeserenam	Barjeserenam
Barieserenam	Curtilias	Curtilias	Curtirias
Arpaiacum	Petromiacum	Petromiacum	Parronam

8. This identification is given by Chaume, *Origines* II/3;1157 n. 10. Santifaller gives Bourgueil, ca. Mont-Saint-Vincent; but the charters of Cluny consistently place Bourgueil in the Chaunois, as in BB 508,I:493–94, BB 761,I:717, etc.

9. "Hoc etiam quod Leodbaldus . . . dereliquid" = Blanot; See BB 283; I:278–79 (4.927).

10. The formulation in Gregory's bull, "illas etiam ecclesias et terras quas Teotardus clericus nuper contulit," is used (without the *nuper*) in subsequent privileges as well. In BB 2408; III:499–500, Teotardus, clericus, returned to Cluny "omnem terram ad locum Oiadellis pertinentem, et insuper omnem reliquam terram quam pater meus et mater mea . . . concesserunt." Additionally, he gave the "curtem de Lanat cum duabus ecclesiis, et quantum ad ipsam curtem aspicere videtur." BB 2408 should thus be dated before 4.998 rather than 997–1030.

11. Cottineau, 1:446 says Saint-Pierre *ad Boscum* is not identified, but the identification Bost is given in Jacques Hourlier, *Saint Odilon, Abbé de Cluny* (Louvain: Bibliothèque de l'Université, 1964), p. 212.

12. This identification is given in *St.-Flour*, no. 2, p. 4 n. 3.

13. This is the identification of Poeck, "Die Klöster der *Cluniacensis ecclesia*," and *St.-Flour*, Hourlier, *Odilon*, identifies it as Notre-Dame, near Maringues.

14. Also known as Saint-Allyre-sur-Veyre.

15. See Pierre Charrié, *Dictionnaire topographique du département de l'Ardèche* (Paris: Guénégaud, 1979), p. 437, for *Mizosco villa*.

16. The bull reads, "aecclesiam sancti Saturnini cum omni alodo, quem Geraldus archiepiscopus dedit." In BB 724,I:677–79 (8.948), Gerald gave Cluny his property at Uzès, namely at Pont-Saint-Esprit, with the church of Saint Saturninus, etc.

17. See J. Brun-Durand, *Dictionnaire topographique du département de la Drôme* [Paris: Imprimerie nationale, 1891], p. 6, cites BB 367; I:345–46 for the form *Alisium*, while the form *Ales* is cited as well, albeit from later documents. *Rudolfinger* suggests "Alais am Gardon" (dép. Gard], but this seems rather too far south.

18. Reading Monte Syon as Monte Ison, and following the identification in Brun-Durand, p. 233, citing BB 2466 = *Rudolfinger*, no. 83; but the editors of *Rudolfinger* have this place as n. id. (p. 433).

19. The text of the bull reads: "alodum, quem Uualdo veniens ad conversionem dedit." *Vualdo's conversion charter is not extant (as Zimmermann notes, p. 231 n. 8). But BB 635,I:592 is witnessed by Vualdo, monachus; and in BB 42;I:49 (1.891) a Vualdo, presbyter, sells land in the pagus of Vienne, at villa Caucilla [= Chuzelles] (including the church of Saint Mauricius], at Brociano subter, at Aucellatis (with the church of Saint Martin], at Lendatis (with the church of Saint Martin], and at Mossiaco (with the churches of Saint Mary and Saint Desiderius]. See also BB 23;I:27–28 (880?]. In the confirmation of Rudolf III for Vienne, Chuzelles is followed by Saint Desiderius (*Rudolfinger*, no. 83, pp. 232–33).

20. As listed in the bull of Agapitus, this church of Saint Desiderius is grouped with other places from the Lyonnais; perhaps, then, it refers to the church dedicated to that saint at Pouilly.

21. In BB 2282;III:411–12 (dated 994–1032, but by the interpretation here to be dated 994–98), Wichardus gave Cluny property in three villae in the Lyonnais: in villa Givrosio, villa Curtestrilo, and villa Osanno. Zimmermann, however, identifies the Wichardus of Gregory's list as the Wichard whose executors appear in BB 1619 (a donation of land at Taizé discussed in Chapter 2). However, Taizé is in the Mâconnais, whereas the bull of Gregory V is at this point enumerating property in the Lyonnais.

22. The port of Ozan, but not the villa, is confirmed in *Rudolfinger*, no. 83.

168

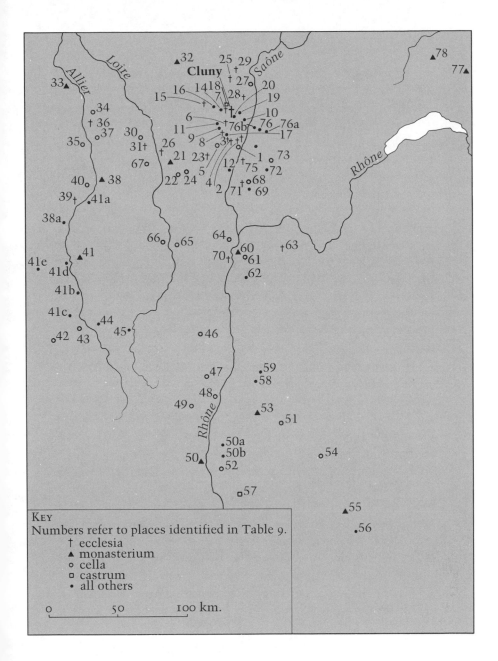

Map 5. Places inventoried by Gregory V (998)

Note: The following were consulted: Michelin Cartes 1:200,000 series; Institut géographique national, Cartes topographiques 1:50,000 and 1:25,000 series; J. Engel, *Grosser Historischer Weltatlas: Herausgegeben vom Bayerischen Schulbuch Verlag*, pt. 2: *Mittelalter* (Munich: Bayerischen Schulbuch Verlag, 1970), p. 80.

of kings or popes. Often enough, and increasingly as the tenth century came to an end, they did not involve even the local count. Donations, sales, and exchanges were drawn up by agreement between the parties involved and witnessed in most instances by families and neighbors. They were public documents; but it is anachronistic to speak of them as having "juridical" significance. What, then, was the force and meaning of royal and papal confirmations?

In the first place, the confirmations that Cluny received in the tenth century and the first half of the eleventh century were themselves gifts. Sometimes, indeed, they accompanied a donation of land, as, for example in 931, when King Raoul gave Cluny land at Chevignes and part of the fishery at Ozan at the same time that he confirmed Cluny's property at Blanot, its chapel of Saint-Victor-d'Aujoux, and its right to certain tithes.[82] Even when this was not the case, confirmations were always drawn up as the grant to a petition. Gregory V supplied his long inventory, for example, "because you have asked us to fortify your monastery with a charter of apostolic authority."[83]

Aside from their being themselves important items in the gift-exchange network with Cluny, these confirmations apparently supplied the inventory that the monks at Cluny wanted to see. That is, although on the one hand they were used as signs of hegemony, naming the properties that were thought to come under the authority of popes or kings, they also, more generally, named the properties that were important to Cluny. This is apparent in the fact that the confirmations were petitioned, and also in the fact that the same places were repeated, whether in royal confirmations or in papal bulls. Some of the places that Raoul, *rex Francorum*, confirmed in 931, for example, continued to appear in the papal bulls of the eleventh century. Indeed, the same information was apparently supplied to both kings and

82. *Raoul*, no. 18, pp. 77–81; Chevignes is ca. Mâcon-Sud; Ozan is dép. Ain, ca. Pont-de-Vaux (see *Raoul*, p. 77 n. 1); Blanot is ca. Cluny; Saint-Victor is dép. Rhône, ca. Monsols. On Cluny's tithes, see Giles Constable, *Monastic Tithes from Their Origins to the Twelfth Century* (Cambridge: Cambridge University Press, 1964), esp. pp. 57–83.

83. Zimmermann, no. 351, p. 683: "Et ideo quia postulastis a nobis, ut prefatum monasterium apostolicę auctoritatis serie muniremus." See ibid., no. 348, p. 677: "inclinati precibus tuis tibi ad regendum concedimus."

popes, as, for example, Raoul's reference to Leutbald as the donor of Blanot, which was repeated in the privilege of John XI that same year.[84] It is fair to say that papal and royal lists reflected the priorities of the monastery; that explains why the properties named at the Council of Anse were comparable to them.[85]

The intent of these confirmations must be understood within the gift network of which Cluny was a part. The places named were deemed especially important, and Cluny's claims were made more fully public through these documents.[86] A letter of Benedict VIII, naming the "enemies" (who, as we have seen, at other times were the "friends") of Cluny in 1021/23, was addressed to "all brethren and co-bishops in Burgundy, Aquitaine, and Provence."[87] Moreover, these confirmation lists emphasized relationships as well as property. Indeed, the bull of Gregory V, for example, sometimes neglected to name *places* altogether but included information about *donors*, as in the case of "all the churches, villae, and lands which Wichardus gave to Cluny on his deathbed," of which none was in fact named. The focus was on Wichardus, not on property per se.[88] In this instance, then, Gregory's list served above all to confirm a relationship rather than a title to property; the land proved Wichardus's tie to Cluny.

The letter of Benedict VIII similarly emphasized relationships, this time of enmity. Persecutors, said Benedict, were threatening the church at Trades, the seigneurie (*potestas*) at Laizé, and land at Huillaux; Warulf of Brancion and his brother Walter were holding onto land that Cluny had given in precaria to their uncle, and so on. Men were openly named, and they were to make satisfaction by the feast of Saint Michael (receiving the

84. Zimmermann, no. 64 (3.931), pp. 107–8 at p. 108: "Hoc etiam, quod Leodbaldus . . . reddidit . . ." (= JL 3584; = BB 391;I:372 [3.391]).
85. See Poeck, "Cluny and Its Monasteries"; Poeck makes the very interesting argument that Cluny was obliged to supply the proofs of its rights to properties that it wanted incorporated into a privilege.
86. See the discussion of "publicatio" in Fichtenau, *Urkundenwesen*, p. 80.
87. Zimmerman, no. 530 (4.1021–23), pp. 1007–10 (= JL 4013; = BB 2703; III:727 [9.1016]), at p. 1008: "omnibus fratribus et coepiscopis per Burgundia(m), Aquitania(m) et P(ro)uintia(m) constitutis."
88. See Table 9, n. 21.

absolution of God, of Saint Peter, and of the Pope); if they did not, they were to be excommunicated and cursed.[89]

A letter like that, understood alongside papal confirmations and the proclamations of the Council of Anse, did not have the purpose of making law or of bringing malefactors into court. The primary purpose of such documents was publicly to set Cluny apart from the world and to "sanctify" its most important holdings.[90] Long before the peace movement separated those who wielded weapons from those who did not, granting the unarmed (along with cattle and fields) immunity from violation, Cluny and certain special properties "subjected" to it were given a special status, "free from domination [ab dominatu] by any king, or bishop, or count, or any of the relatives of William [the Pious]."[91] These words, written in 931, and echoing the foundation charter of William himself, were repeated (with amplification) in tenth- and eleventh-century papal privileges and at the Council of Anse. Royal privileges stressed the antiquity of such immunity: they enumerated and renewed the provisions of charters of donation, "in the tradition of our blessed ancestors."[92] The force of these documents was not the threat of police power but of publicity.

89. Trades is dép. Rhône, ca. Monsols; Laizé is ca. Mâcon-Sud; Huillaux is dép. Allier, arr. Lapalisse. On monastic curses, see Little, "La morphologie des maledictiones."

90. Gurevich, *Categories*, pp. 236–37, has stimulating observations on the way in which the "sanctification" of property is a means of declaring its ownership.

91. Zimmerman, no. 64 (3.931), pp. 107–8 (= JL 3584; = BB 391;1:372): "liberum a dominatu cuiuscunque regis aut episcopi sive comitis aut cuiuslibet ex propinquis ipsius Uuilelmi." The Council of Anse spoke of Cluny's lands as being held *inviolabiter*. On the similar purposes of the peace councils (of which Anse was arguably one), see Hans Werner Goetz, "Kirchenschutz, Rechtswahrung und Reform: Zu den Zielen und zum Wesen der frühen Gottesfriedensbewegung in Frankreich," *Francia* 11 (1983): 193–240, with excellent bibliography. Privileges of various sorts for monastic houses were a regular feature of papal and regnal activity throughout the Middle Ages. There is a connection with this movement and the idea of privacy; see Philippe Ariès and Georges Duby, eds., *Histoire de la vie privée*, vol. 2: *De l'Europe féodale à la Renaissance* (Paris: Seuil, 1985), esp. pp. 25–29, 41.

92. *Rudolfinger*, no. 83 (998), pp. 232–33, at 233: "iustas et honestas peticiones, precepta regalia seu cartas vel donationes ab aliis fidelibus eidem Cluniacensi monasterio, quantum nostri in finibus regni habetur, factas in unum collecta corpusculum more patris nostri beate memoriae." On the two privileges for Cluny drawn up in 998 by Rudolf III, see Herwig Wolfram, "Lateinische Herrschertitel im neunten und zehnten Jahrhundert," *Intitulatio*, II: 142–44.

Particular properties were no doubt chosen to be on these lists for many reasons, but in nearly every case both prestige and economic interest were involved. Most of the properties for which Cluny petitioned confirmations were given by illustrious donors and invoked other illustrious associations. They generally involved property that belonged to a saint, property that was, in short, either a church or a monastery. Finally, such gifts were generous; they were doubtless of particular economic importance to Cluny. Some examples may serve to illustrate the way in which these factors worked together.

The first privilege that Cluny received coincided with the accession, in 927, of Odo to the abbacy of Cluny and to the simultaneous severing of ties between Cluny and Gigny, over which Abbot Berno had presided at the same time.[93] In that year, a confirmation of Cluny's properties was drawn up by Raoul, *rex Francorum*. Of all the possible properties that he might have mentioned (and already, in Berno's abbacy, at least thirty charters involving land in forty-one different places had been drawn up), three properties alone were singled out:[94]

> Let them [the monks of Cluny] hold in perpetuity the alod that Gerbaldus gave to that monastery; and let them similarly maintain perpetual rights to Blanot and its appendices . . . and also let them possess the curtis that is called La Frette, which Berno, by his own will took away from Gigny and turned over to Cluny (for both places were founded by him). Let them possess [La Frette] forever in just the way that [Berno] instituted, namely with the alod formerly belonging to Samson and with the dependents and the mansus that belonged to Larvin.[95]

93. It was rejoined with Cluny toward the end of the eleventh century; see Gregory VII (= JL 4974; redated by Poeck, "Clun. ecc.", 12.1076) in Santifaller, no.107.

94. These figures count charters dated in Berno's abbacy that have not been challenged by Chaume, "En Marge 1," "En Marge 2," or elsewhere.

95. *Raoul*, no. 12 (9.927), pp. 47–52, at p. 51 (= BB 285;1:281–82): "alodum, quem predicto monasterio Gerbaldus dedit, perpetuo teneant; Blanuscum similiter cum appenditiis suis, jure suo perpetuo vindicent; . . . curtem, simul que dicitur a la Fracta, quam prefatus Berno, de Gigniaco subtrahens, ad Cluniacum (per ipsum enim uterque locus fundatus est) licenter convertit, eo tenore quo ipse constituit, cum alodo quondam Samsonis et mancipiis et manso qui Larvini fuit, perhenni dominio possideant." Blanot is ca. Cluny; La Frette is ca. Montret.

Let us consider in turn each of the places named by Raoul. In 926, Gerbaldus gave land and peasants (*colonia* and *mancipia*) in the vicinity of Bruailles (ca. Louhans): at "Brilanga," Marcilly, Maumont, Culay, and Courcelles "for the salvation of the soul of my lord, the departed William [the Pious], and also for the salvation of his nephew, still living, also William, my lord, and for his family and all the faithful as well."[96] In this way, Girbaldus associated his donation with his relationship to William the Pious, the founder of Cluny.

Similarly, at Blanot, property including four churches was given to Cluny in 927 in a donation by Leutbald and Doda "pro anima domine meae Avane, necnon Vigelmi comitis [for the soul of my lady Ava and for that of Count William]" as well as for members of Leutbald's family and all Christian faithful.[97] This donation, once again, invoked Cluny's founders. Indeed, the land itself had been associated with William the Pious, with whom Leutbald's father, Warulf, had at one time shared it.[98]

The property at La Frette had an even richer network of associations. We do not have the original donation by Samson; but in 925 Berno went to La Frette to claim the land from Arnold Ayduin, who was Samson's brother, and who was also an *advocatus Sancti Petri*, that is, guardian of Saint Peter of Gigny.[99] Arnold quit his claim to the land, "which had been legally vested between [*inter*] Samson and Saint Peter for thirty years."[100] The following year, in his testament, Berno transferred the property to Cluny.[101] But the claims of Gigny remained; about eight years after Raoul's confirmation of Cluny's

96. BB 269;1:261–63 (5.926), places identified in *Raoul* follow Chaume, *Origines* II/3:1002 nn. 2–6.
97. BB 283;1:278–79 (4.927). But the words *Vigelmi comitis* were added by a second hand.
98. Ibid.: "sicut pater meus Vuarulfus cum Vuilelmo dividit, illam divisionem quę Vuilelmus accepit, hoc est duas partes, totum ad integrum Sancto Petro donamus."
99. BB 251;1:242–43 (5.925). Other property was also involved in this werpitio.
100. Ibid.: "xxx annis inter Samson et Sanctum Petrum de ipsis rebus et manopiis [mancipiis?] vestiti legaliter fuissent."
101. "Testamentum domni Bernonis Abbatis," *Bibl. Clun.*, cols. 9–10, dated 13 Jan.–9 Sept. 927 by Bautier and Dufour in *Raoul*, p. 49 n. 2. In addition to Raoul's confirmation of that year, one was issued as well by John X, text in *Raoul*, pp. 213–14.

possession of the property, Guido, the abbot of Gigny who had succeeded Berno there, made what was probably understood as a donation in precaria of the land at La Frette to Cluny. Of course, a life estate to a monastery is perforce a perpetual estate. The point was to maintain Gigny's own association with the property while at the same time giving it to Cluny in an act of gracious generosity.[102]

Be it known to all, present and future, that Lord Berno, venerable father, delegated to the monastery of Cluny by testamentary authority certain properties which he had once handed over to the monastery of Gigny. Therefore, I, Guido, the abbot of Gigny, willingly, with the consent of the lord brothers, draw up this document concerning these properties. I considered that he, our special father, dedicated and constructed both monasteries for one lord, that is, blessed Peter; and that he left behind [after his death] both the brothers at Cluny who serve that blessed Peter and those [who serve him] at Gigny, in a single brotherhood and with familial love; and moreover that he made his burial there [at Cluny]. Therefore . . . I hand over to Cluny this property, that is, the villa of La Frette, with all that pertains to it and with the whole alod that Samson gave to Gigny . . . on condition that wax worth twelve denars be given back in rent to Gigny every year on Saint Peter's day.[103]

102. BB 425;1:412–13 (dated 936 in *Raoul*, p. 49). The notation on the back of the original calls it a "precaria de Gigniaco"; the document begins with the formula that was common precisely for precarial donations in Cluny's charters: "Mos est lex, licet non spripta [sic; scripta]," etc. On this point, see Petitjean, p. 123 and n. 2.

103. BB 425;1:412–13: "Quapropter noverint omnes, tam futuri quam presentes, quia domnus Berno, venerabilis pater, quasdam res, quę Gigniaco monasterio fuerant ab ipso traditę, Cluniensi cenobio per testamentariam auctoritatem delegavit. Ego igitur Guido, predicti cenobii Gigniensis abbas, libenter com domnis fratribus ad ipsum consenciens, hanc auctoritatem de ipsis rebus facio. Consider[ans] videlicet quod ipse noster specialis pater utraque monasteria uni domino, id est beato Petro, dedicavit adque construxit, et tam ipsos fratres qui eidem beato Petro apud Cluniacum, quam istos qui Gigniaco deserviunt, in una fraternitate ac germana caritate dimisit, et insuper inibi sepulturam sibi locavit; hoc igitur ego attendens secundum auctoritatem quam prelibatus pater jam fecerat, predictas res, id est villam quę dicitur la Fracta, cum omnibus ad eam pertinentibus et cum omni alodo quem Sanson Gigniaco dedit, et cum dimidio prato quod Nonnus Saimo similiter dedit ad Cluniacum, ea ratione, ex fratrum consensu, trado ut per singulos annos cera xii denariorum pretio valens, missa Sancti Petri, pro vestitura Gigniaco reddatur." In his "Testamentum" Berno had prescribed that Cluny pay Gigny "per singulos annos census duodecim denariorum Gigniaco pro vestitura reddatur" (*Bibl. Clun.*, col. 11).

The property at La Frette was special, therefore, for a number of reasons. It was transferred from Gigny by Berno because of Cluny's poverty; clearly it was important because it supplied material wants.[104] But it also had the significance of intangible associations: with Berno's last act, with the *advocatus* of Saint Peter, and above all with the fraternal love (and rivalry) between Gigny and Cluny, both dedicated to the same saint.[105]

La Frette and the alod of Gerbaldus dropped off later lists. But Blanot remained: it was repeated, for example, in the inventory of Agapitus in 949, at the Council of Anse in 994, and in the list of Gregory V in 998 (see Table 9).

Special Property near Cluny

About 70 percent of the property named in the charters of Cluny was located in the pagus of Mâcon. Yet this was *not* the distribution of the places named in the papal privilege of Gregory V, which (as I have emphasized) was the model for subsequent bulls until the 1070s. There only 33 percent was in the Mâconnais. Table 10 summarizes the distribution in the list of Gregory V; it may be compared with the figures in Tables 11 (for the distribution of churches) and 12 (for the distribution of land).

Why was there a large discrepancy between de facto frequency and the chosen emphases of created lists? Let us begin to answer this question by looking first at properties in Cluny's neighborhood, using by way of example the frequently inventoried villa of Ecussolles.

There was already a church, dedicated to Saint Peter, at the villa of Ecussolles when Gauzfredus, *comes* (at Nevers?), and his wife, Eva, gave it to Cluny in 936. Gauzfredus gave it for the soul of his *senior*, William the Pious, and for William's son,

104. Berno, "Testamentum," *Bibl. Clun.*, col. 11: Berno explains why he transferred La Frette to Cluny, "quoniam ibi sepulturam mihi locavi. . . . Et certe pauperior est possessione, et numerosa fraternitate."

105. La Frette was very likely the subject of the bull of John X, about the same time as the confirmation of Raoul (927) and, indeed, addressed to Raoul among others, that spoke of the need to restore to Cluny what Abbot Berno had given to it from Gigny. The bull is printed in *Raoul*, pp. 213–14 (= *Bull. Clun.*, p. 2, where it is attributed to John XI).

Table 10. Distribution of properties in bull of Gregory V

Region	Total no. of places	%
Mâcon	26	33
Chalon	3	4
Autun	3	4
Auvergne	13	17
Viviers	4	5
Uzès	1	1
Saint-Paul	1	1
Orange	2	2
Gap	1	1
Provence	3	3
Valens	2	2
Vienne	4	5
Lyon	15	19

Note: Percentages are rounded to the nearest whole number; hence the total does not equal 100 percent.

Boso.[106] The donation was confirmed by Leo VII the following year, calling Gauzfredus a righteous man [*vir bonus*] and stipulating that "no man great or small may dare or presume to invade or molest or disturb" the place.[107] In the 960s and again in 980, Cluny acquired further property in the villa from a few people in the region who appear to have been related (the names Maalgerius, Maalgeldis, and Maalgodus are repeated in several donations) or closely associated (Ermenbert, for example, appears about 966 and again in 980).[108] After that time, transactions at Ecussolles ended, but the place was firmly enshrined from then on in confirmation lists. It had been donated, after all,

106. BB 446;I:434–36 (4.936). The church and land at Ecussolles was redonated in BB 449;I:438–40 (6.936), this time without reservation of usufruct, and here referred to as half of the church (*medietatem aecclesiae Sancti Petri*). On this Gauzfredus and Eva, *not* related to the couple in Genealogy 1, see Chapter 4, n. 43.

107. Zimmerman, no.74 (end of 936), pp. 126–28 (= JL 3598 [7.937]; = BB 479;I:464 [937]), at p. 127: "ut nullus homo parvus magnusve vel cuiuscomque dignitatis audeat vel presumat . . . invasionem vel molestiam aut inquietudinem facere."

108. BB 891;II:8–9 (Chaume, "Obs.," c. 966); BB 943;II:49 (Chaume, "Obs.," c. 966); BB 1194;II:277–78 (3.966); BB 1516;II:565–66 (3.980). A church of Saint Peter, which Chaume thought might be the one at Ecussolles, was sold by Bernardus and his daughter Gottestiva to Adamar and his wife, Vuandalmodis, in 975 (BB 1410;II:467–68 [1.975]); but the witness list—with the exception of the extremely popular name Bernardus—is quite different from the other witness lists for land at Ecussolles.

by a count, one, moreover, with links to Cluny's founder; it had a church dedicated to Saint Peter. It was probably also of economic importance.[109] To see this we must turn for a moment to a piece of evidence from a later period.

In the middle of the twelfth century, an inventory of the production of twelve deaneries (*decaniae*) belonging to Cluny was drawn up.[110] They were: Laizé, Beaumont, Malay, Saint-Hippolyte, Cluny (which, in the twelfth century, included Ruffey), Chaveyriat, Saint-Martin de Mâcon, Berzé, Arpayé, Montberthoud, Saint-Gengoux, and Lourdon. These were more inclusive than the names suggest: in the twelfth century, the deanery of Lourdon included the churches of Cotte, Merzé, Taizé, Prayes, Blanot, Donzy-le-Pertuis, and land at Dombine, Mailly, and Cruzille. These deaneries were productive enterprises: the one at Chaveyriat, for example, provided the monks with cheese, meat, and wine.

It is dangerous, of course, to apply the lessons of the mid-twelfth century to the early eleventh. It is very likely that cartulary B, in which this twelfth-century production inventory is found, was bound together with it precisely because Cluny had reorganized its finances at this time.[111] Nevertheless it is diffi-

109. Déléage cites BB 889;II:6–7 (Chaume, "Obs.," 969–94) for the appearance of the *obedientia*—an estate directly administered by a monk on the spot —of Ecussolles (p. 429 n. 6). Duby challenges the authenticity of the charter and the possibility of so early an obedientia (*Société*, p. 185, n. 53).

110. BB 4143;V:490–505 (1149–56). Alain Guerreau discusses it and assesses its economic implications in "Douze doyennés clunisiens au milieu du XIIe siècle," *Annales de Bourgogne* 52 (1980): 83–128, as does Georges Duby in "Un inventaire des profits de la seigneurie clunisienne à la mort de Pierre le Vénérable," in *Hommes et structures*, pp. 87–101; see also "Le budget de l'abbaye de Cluny entre 1080 et 1155: Economie domaniale et économie monétaire," in *Hommes et structures*, pp. 61–79, esp. 76–77.

111. This is the suggestion of Maria Hillebrandt. In fact, as Duby has shown in "Un inventaire," the twelfth-century inventory was part of the conservatively based economic reforms of Peter the Venerable, by which, after a period of "monetary economy," the monastery reorganized its sources of income, to base them once more on its domains. See BB 4132;V:475–82 (1147–48), which is the key document for Peter's economic reforms. The classic analysis of it is Duby, "Le budget," and now see Jean-Pierre Torrell and Denise Bouthillier, *Pierre le Vénérable et sa vision du monde: Sa vie—son oeuvre; l'homme et le démon*, Spicilegium sacrum Lovaniense: Etudes et documents, fasc. 42 (Leuven: Spicilegium Sacrum Lovaniense, 1986), pp. 43–48. See also Ulrich, *Antiquiores consuetudines cluniacensis monasteria* 3.5, in *PL* 149, cols. 738–40, a source dating from the second half of the eleventh century, which speaks of the *decani* of the monastery and the products they bring in each week. It seems very likely that

cult not to notice the close correspondence between the names of some of the deaneries and the names of some of the places mentioned at the Council of Anse and in the privilege of Gregory V.[112] We may recall the way in which the monks bought up land at Bézornay toward the end of the tenth century. Bézornay did not have a history of noble donors, nor was a church constructed there, yet it was enshrined on confirmation lists.[113]

Similarly, the land around the castle of Lourdon was bought and traded by the monks of Cluny in transactions that began in the 930s and came to an end by 966. By the end of the tenth century or the beginning of the eleventh, it had become an obedientia of the monastery.[114] It seems likely, then, that the places in the Mâconnais,—places like Ecussolles, Bézornay, and Lourdon—in particular, were included in the confirmation lists above all because of their economic importance. They had social meaning originally; but by the end of the tenth century, that significance had largely been lost.

Land beyond the Neighborhood

The distribution of the properties in the inventory of Gregory V also raises questions about property transactions far from the

the strategies of the later tenth century lay the groundwork for these deaneries, and afterward for those of the twelfth century.

112. See the list of twenty-three Cluniac deaneries in Burgundy that Déléage places at the end of the tenth century (in fact, very often, more properly to be dated some time in the eleventh) in Déléage, pp. 428–30: Bézornay, Jalogny, Lourdon, Chaveyriat, Chevignes, Cluny, Iguerande, Mazille, Montberthoud, Saint-Martin-des-Vignes, Thoissey, Ecussolles (citing BB 889;II:6–7; see n. 109 above), Romans, Jully-lès-Buxy, Gevrey-Chambertin, Laizé, Beaumont-sur-Grosne, Blanot, Péronne, Saint-Hippolyte, Arpayé, Ajoux, Saint-Gengoux-le-National.

113. But a charter probably from the abbacy of Hugh mentions a "clausula Salvamenti" at Bézornay (BB 3246;IV:366 [1049–1109]), and a church was already there in the privilege of Gregory VII (12.1075) (Santifaller, no. 107, p. 96): "Besorniacum cum ecclesia . . ."

114. BB 477;I:463–64 (9.937), an exchange; BB 488;I:473 (3.938), a partial sale, partial donation; BB 506;I:491–92 (1.940), an exchange; BB 485;I:470 (3.938), a donation; BB 1142;II:232–33 (11.962–63), an exchange; BB 1202;II:285 (966), a sale; BB 232;I:222–23 (my date: c. 940 because of rapprochement with BB 506), an exchange. In BB 2406;III:497–98 (and again in BB 2552;III:617), both c. 1002, Maiolus Poudreux quits his claim to "injustis exactionibus . . . in obedientia de Lurdono."

monastery. If the Mâconnais, Lyonnais, Autunois, and Chaunois were, in effect, Cluny's neighborhood, then how can one make sense of the fact that over 60 percent of the places listed by Gregory were either a leap to the southwest of Cluny, in the Auvergne region, or were beads on a string going down toward the southeast, roughly following the Rhône valley? In short, Gregory's list invites us to consider Cluny's far-flung relationships.

To understand the significance of these outlying regions properly, we would need to explore the specific social context for each place, precisely as we have tried to do for some groups and places in the Mâconnais. The purpose of what follows is, perforce, less grand. It is, first, to explain the distribution in Gregory's list by following out its geographical implications. Gregory's list emphasized properties outside of Cluny's "neighborhood" because they were given by important families with important and long-standing connections with Cluny. And, second, it is to reinforce this point by suggesting that, although many charters of donation to Cluny concern far-flung places, yet they represent a relatively limited number of social groups.[115]

The "Bosonids"

"In the name of the eternal Lord God, we, Hugh and Lothar, kings by grace of God . . . cede to the holy and venerable monastery of Cluny where Odo is now abbot, two *curtes* from our property in the county of Lyon, the one called Savigneux and the other Ambérieux-en-Dombes with everything that belongs to them."[116] Thus runs a donation charter, written at Pavia, by Hugh and his son, Lothar, kings of Italy in the 930s. Their gift of Savigneux and Ambérieux was included in the inventory of Gregory V for the Lyonnais. The obvious question that their do-

---

115. See Ulrich Winzer's "Zum Einzugsbereich Clunys im 10. Jahrhundert: Eine Fallstudie" (*Frühmittelalterlichen Studien*, forthcoming), which demonstrates that donations to Cluny from the Viennois, too, were dominated by a very few tightly interconnected groups associated with members of the higher nobility. I am grateful to Dr. Winzer for allowing me to read his paper prior to publication.

116. BB 417;1:403–4 (3.934).

nation raises is why anyone in Italy, even a king, should donate to a monastery more than three hundred kilometers away.

Hugh and Lothar represent the second and third generations, respectively, of a branch of the extended family that helped found Cluny and that made up some of its most important early patrons: the "Bosonids" (see Genealogy 8.).

The donations that Hugh and Lothar made of Savigneux and Ambérieux were part of a long series of donations—extending both backward and forward in time—made by members of this "family" in southerly regions.[117] Cluny was, in fact, something of a family enterprise right from the start. William the Pious founded Cluny with his wife, Ingelberga, daughter of Boso, king of Provence (879–87). Ingelberga herself gave Cluny the fisc of Romans, a large and most important piece of property that was named some ninety years later at the Council of Anse and in the privilege of Gregory.[118] Boso's brother, Richard le Justicier, a major power in Burgundy at the end of the ninth century, was not a donor to Cluny. But his son, Raoul, who was elected to the Frankish throne in 923, gave Cluny its earliest royal privilege (as we saw above) and donations besides. Richard's wife, Adelaide (who was, in addition, the sister of Rudolf I, whose family was, in its own right, among the great patrons of Cluny), gave Cluny the monastery of Romainmôtier, also invoking the name of William the Pious. This, too, was on Gregory's list.[119] The generation following Hugh of Italy continued the tradition of supporting Cluny: Manasses, archbishop of Arles, gave to Cluny four churches at Jully-lès-Buxy.[120] Again, this gift was listed by Gregory V. The property, however, was in the Chaunois, a

117. "Family" is a most problematic term, of course. The phenomenon that we are discussing concerns people who were related by blood and by marriage (particularly through females) in links that can be reconstructed by a modern historian. The question of whether this family was conscious of all or some or none of these links is quite a different matter. Bouchard rightly remarks that if modern reconstructions were all one needed, the entire early medieval aristocracy would appear as one extended family. But it seems that "subsets" of this particular family we call the Bosonids were aware of themselves as a social "cell," especially when the line descended through males. And it is also clear that females kept up certain family traditions, including that of endowing regular monasteries.

118. BB 205;1:193 (1.917).

119. BB 379;1:358–62 (5.929).

120. BB 726;1:681–83 (9.948).

Genealogy 8. "The Bosonids"

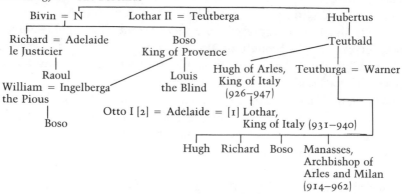

Note: This is a highly simplified genealogy; for a more complete table and discussion, see Poupardin, *Le royaume de Provence*, pp. 40–55, 142–43, 297–306; Chaume *Origines*, 1:544–45; and, most recently, Constance B. Bouchard, "The Bosonids; or, Rising to Power in the Late Carolingian Age," *French Historical Studies* 15(1988):407–431. Dr. Bouchard kindly allowed me to consult her work in manuscript. The early part of the family tree is the most murky: Boso is son of Count Bivin in *Annales Bertiniani*, A.D. 869, ed. Felix Grat, Jeanne Vielliard, and Suzanne Clémencet (Paris: Klincksieck, 1964), p. 167: "exsequente Bosone, filio Biuini quondam comitis." Richard is his brother (ibid., A.D. 882, p. 247 and n. 3): "Richardus, frater ipsius Bosonis." Teutberga is their maternal aunt (matertera) (ibid, A.D. 869, p. 167). Her brother is Hubertus, "clericus coniugatus et abbas monasterii Sancti Martini," who held the abbacy of Saint–Maurice d'Agaune as well (ibid., A.D. 864, p. 116: "Teotberga, soror eius"). Ingelberga is the sister of Louis the Blind, hence the daughter of Boso in BB 205;1:193–94. In BB 112; 1:124–28 she and William the Pious found Cluny. Teutbald is the son of Hubertus in *Annales Vedastini*, A.D. 880, MGH, SS 2: 198: "Teutbaldum, filium Hucberti." Manasses is "agnita regis Hugonis potentia" in Liudprand *Antapodosis* iv.6 in *Die Werke Liudprands von Cremona*, ed. Joseph Becker, 3d ed. (1915; repr., Hannover: Hahnsche Buchhandlung, 1977), p. 105.

reminder that the family had begun its ascent under the Carolingians with possessions in the north, and that the high aristocracy of the tenth century was still "international."[121]

121. Poupardin, pp. 42–43, has traced the origins of the Bosonids as a whole to the court of Louis the Pious. Richard le Justicier began his career as count of Autun, and his power rested there and in the areas around Chalon and Dijon. Warner, the father of Manasses, Richard, Hugh, and Boso, had been count of Troyes and viscount of Sens. See *Chronicon Sancti Petri Vivi Senonensis*, an. 924, in *Chronique de Saint-Pierre-le-Vif de Sens, dite de Clarius*, ed. Robert-Henri Bautier and Monique Gilles (Paris: CNRS, 1979), p. 72: "Warnerius vicecomes Senonum"; Flodoard, *Annales*, A.D. 925, in *Les annales de Flodoard*, ed. Philippe Lauer (Paris: Picard, 1905), p. 26 and n. 3.

The Rhône Valley

The generations-long support of Cluny by the Bosonids was not unusual. It begins to explain the donations that came to Cluny from regions far from the monastery. Just as in particular villae of the Mâconnais, so too in outlying regions, one or two groups tended to dominate all or most of the transactions. The difference is that gifts in the outlying regions were scattered over larger areas, and in most instances were from members of the very highest level of the aristocracy along with other groups that clustered around them.

The Uzège

There were only three donations to Cluny from the Uzège (albeit involving land in more than a dozen different villae) before 1049, all taking place between 946 and 952. The two most important of these were clearly related.[122] In the first, Gerald, the archbishop of Narbonne, gave Cluny the monastery and lands at Pont-Saint-Esprit (formerly Saint-Saturnin du Port) in August 948.[123] The donation immediately appeared on the inventory of Agapitus II in 949 and was repeated in papal bulls thereafter. Gerald was part of an important family in Provence, which would later be known as the Sabran. It was allied with the family of Rostagnus, the archbishop of Arles, who, indeed, was responsible for elevating Gerald to the archepiscopal office. Gerald was also associated with Hugh of Arles (see Genealogy 8); Jean-Pierre Poly thinks he was Hugh's *fidelis*.[124] Gerald's brothers, Amalricus and Bermondus, were counts.[125] A few years

122. The two that are related are BB 724;1:677–79 (dated c. 945 by Jean-Pierre Poly, *La Provence et la société féodale [879–1166]: Contribution à l'étude des structures dites féodales dans le Midi* [Paris: Bordas, 1976], p. 15) and BB 817; 1:770–72 (951–52). BB 693;1:647–48 (12.946) seems unrelated to these. It involves the inheritance of land belonging to Gyrardus and his wife that is eventually to end up in Cluny's hands.
123. BB 724;1:677–79 (c. 945). See Poly, *La Provence*, pp. 21 and 56, who calls him "pseudo-archbishop." But Geraldus called himself "indignus arciepiscopus" as did Gregory V (see above, Table 9, n. 16).
124. Poly, *La Provence*, pp. 21, 162 n. 186. Hugh often appeared in charters with Rostagnus; e.g., *Recueil des actes des rois de Provence [855–928]*, ed. René Poupardin (Paris: Imprimerie nationale, 1920), no. 42, pp. 78–80; no. 53, pp. 98–9.
125. BB 817;1:770–72 (951–52).

after Gerald's donation, a priest named Lucerius gave Cluny some land in the region around Uzès for the souls of (among others), Counts Amalricus and Bermondus, his *seniores*.[126]

The Valentinois

In the region of Valence, at some time during the abbacy of Maiolus, Arduin, praepositus, and his nephews, the brothers Arduin, levita, and Rostagnus, ceded to Cluny the church of Saint-Baudile at Allex.[127] The gift was one of those incorporated into the list of Gregory V. Rostagnus himself along with his wife, Letgardis, and his sons, including Ademar, Arnard, Odilo, and Rostagnus, gave Cluny property at Eurre and water rights at Allex.[128] In the next generation, Odilo and his wife and children gave more property at Eurre, while another Rostagnus, possibly the son of the first, along with his sons, Odilo ` and William, and his relatives (*cognati*) Monaldus and Wido, redonated the church of Saint-Baudile.[129] Monaldus and his wife, in their turn, gave Cluny the tithes of the church of Saint-Maurice, near Saint-Baudile; and Arduin, miles, gave to Cluny the land of his brother Monaldus in Allex on behalf of Monaldus's son, William, who was about to become a monk.[130] Arduin's nephew (*consobrinus*) Almannus, was present, which (as we shall see) may have significance for donations in the Vivarais. In short, there are seven charters in Cluny's archives that deal with the Valentinois; but in fact most of them involved several generations and subsets of the same family.[131]

126. Ibid.
127. BB 925;II:36–37 (954–994; Chaume, "Obs.," gives c. 990 because a Rostagnus continues to be alive in 1049–1109 [BB 3091;IV:264–65]; but we know from BB 367;I:345–46 [which I date about the same time as BB 925] that Rostagnus had a son named Rostagnus). Allex is dép. Drôme, ca. Crest.
128. BB 367;I:345–46 (dated wrongly in abbacy of Berno; see Chaume, "En Marge 2," p. 51 n. 7. It ought to be dated 954–94, along with BB 925;II:36–37). The subscriptio reads "S. Rostagni . . . S. uxoris ejus, nomine Leotgardis. S. filiorum eorum, videlicet S. Ademari, S. Arnardi, S. Odilonis, S. Rostagni, S. Jarentonis, S. Guigonis, S. Rostagni, S. Fulcherii, S. Stephani, S. Wicardi." Eurre is dép. Drôme, ca. Crest-Nord.
129. Odilo: BB 2993;IV:191 (1049–95); Rostagnus: BB 3091;IV:264–65 (1049–1109).
130. Monaldus and his wife: BB 3048;IV:237–38 (1049–1109); Arduin on behalf of Monaldus and William: BB 2984;IV:183 (Chaume, "Obs.," suggests 1055–60).
131. Prior to 1049, the only other charter concerned with property in the

The Vivarais

This general pattern was, of course, not invariable. In the Vivarais, for example, donations at Rompon and Ruoms, inventoried in Gregory's confirmation, appear to have been the work of groups unrelated to one another.[132] Yet the appearance of Rostagnus and Almannus, thus paired, as names of key witnesses to the donation of land at Rompon, suggests that this gift may be connected to those at Valence. Two later donations in the district of Viviers were the work of Armannus, bishop of Viviers 1015–37, and his family: land at Saint-Just and a church at Meysse or Saint-Vincent-de-Barrès.[133] Already before his elevation to the episcopacy, he had given Cluny land further south, near Saint-Paul-Trois-Châteaux.[134]

Conclusion

The donations along the Rhône, which were largely the work of a limited number of families, generally included a church or a monastery. (In the case of Rompon, it involved land on which a monastery was to be built.) Most of the time, confirmations were obtained for these properties; from the end of the tenth century onward, these lands and churches were numbered in official

---

Valentinois was BB 2921;IV:122–23 (1037), in which the monastery of Saint-Marcel-lès-Sauzet was given to the monks of Cluny by Ademar, the count of Valence. An earlier, apparently non-Cluniac, reform had been tried by Ademar's father, Lanbert; see BB 1715;II:735–38 (6.985).

132. Rompon: BB 1434;II:491–92 (7.976–77) with Almannus and Rostagnus in the witness list. A Bernard is also a witness, and it is tempting to associate him with the Bernard who, with his wife, Arimberga, gave Cluny a vineyard at Rompon c. 984, in BB 1707;II:729. Ruoms: BB 929;II:39 (954–94; Chaume, "Obs.," suggests a date after 998, but this is not convincing, since Maiolus is named as abbot and since the donation of Ruoms is confirmed in 998 by Gregory V [Chaume had looked only at the confirmations of Rudolf III of that year, in which Ruoms is missing]).

133. For Saint-Just (dép. Ardèche, ca. Bourg-Saint-Andéol), see BB 1988;III:200 (Chaume, "Obs.," 998–1015); here Armannus identifies himself as *levita*. For the two churches (both dép. Ardèche, ca. Rochemaure), see BB 2745;III:760 (c. 6.1020), with Armannus, *episcopus*, and his father, Geraldus. On Armannus, see *Gallia Christiana* 16, cols. 550–51. The donation was of the church at Meysse, but "si est de alodio Sancti Vincentii de Vivariensi, quod aliqui dicunt, episcopatu [but if it is an alod of the cathedral of Saint-Vincent de Viviers, as some say]" then the church at Barrès was to be substituted. Cf. Jean Régné and J. Rouchier, *Histoire du Vivarais*, 2 vols. (Largentière: Imprimerie Mazel et Plancher, 1914), 1:638 (pièces justif.) for a document recording the donation of the church at Meysse to the church of Viviers in 950.

134. BB 1988;III:200–1 (Chaume, Obs., 998–1015).

privileges among the things that pertained to Cluny. While in the Mâconnais a severe winnowing had to take place before the most "important" places could be named in inventories, the better part of donations to the south were enshrined there. Indeed, one might say that in almost every case, a donor family along the Rhône would have at least one property that it donated on a later inventory. There is little doubt that these were important families and that they had given important donations. The seemingly countless properties that Cluny received outside of its immediate vicinity were largely due to the generosity of a very finite, indeed tiny, group of aristocratic families.

The Auvergne

The same observation is true for the Auvergne. Between 909 and 1049, forty-three charters were drawn up transferring property to Cluny from that region. Yet almost every donor can be shown to fall into one of two groups, the first of which clustered around the viscounts (later counts) of Clermont, and the second of which was associated with the family that would later be known as the Bourbons. The most important donations of these groups were inventoried in confirmations such as that of Gregory V. The other donations were sufficient to swell the archives of Cluny, but, again, most originated in the context of this fairly circumscribed set of supporters. The first generation of these donors was connected to William the Pious; as with the Bosonids, the ties to Cluny begun at that point remained part of a group tradition.

The Viscounts and Counts of Clermont

As we have already seen, in 927, Acfred, the nephew of William the Pious, who now held his uncle's title, duke of Aquitaine, founded the monastery of Sauxillanges. He invoked his uncle in the pro anima formula, along with himself and other members of his family.[135] Witnessing the foundation were numerous viscounts, including Robert, the viscount of Clermont. A quarter century later, Robert's son, Stephan, bishop of

135. BB 286;1:282–87 (10.927).

Clermont, redonated Sauxillanges to Cluny (see Genealogy 9).[136]

The gift of Sauxillanges linked the salvation of the souls of Stephan and his family, of Acfred, "who offered his alod to omnipotent God, for which my father was executor," and of the two previous dukes of Aquitaine, William the Pious, and William the Younger.[137]

A few years later, in 955, a different Stephan and his wife, Ermengardis, gave to Cluny the church of Sainte-Marie at Huillaux along with the land attached to it and the relics of Saint Leotadus.[138] After the charter of the gift had been drawn up and signed, it was read aloud at a formal assembly consisting of William I, count of Poitiers and duke of Aquitaine (known in this capacity as William III) and the great men (*seniores*) of Auvergne. Among those confirming the provisions of the charter were Stephan, the donor; Stephan, the bishop; William, the count; Robert, the viscount (i.e., Bishop Stephan's father); and Robert, the abbot of Lembron, which had been founded by Bishop Stephan.[139]

Stephan and Ermengardis were probably also responsible for the gift to Cluny of land at Rougea.[140] Here were assembled

136. BB 792;I:743–44 (c. 951). Stephan was abbot of Conques during 942–84, the same time that he was bishop of Clermont. See *Conques*, no. 186 (4.946), pp. 160–62: "Stephanus abba episcopus . . ." In *Conques*, no.47 (c. 940–42), p. 49, he ceded the church of Roffiac to Conques.

137. BB 792;I:743–44 (c. 951): "tam pro salute animarum nostrarum [i.e., Stephan, his father, and his stepmother] quam etiam pro remedio Hacfridi comitis, qui ipsum alodium omnipotenti Deo obtulit, de quo etiam isdem pater meus ipsius elemosinarius extitit, vel pro anima Vuillelmi primi et maximi ducis, necnon et pro juniore Vuillelmo."

138. BB 825;I:779–81 (Chaume, "Obs.," 6.955). Huillaux is dép. Allier, arr. Lapalisse. Lauranson-Rosaz, pp. 113–14 and 145–46, identifies these donors as the protoseigneurs of Huillaux-Thiers.

139. BB 825;I:781: "Hec carta, jubente domno Stephano, lecta est in curte Eniziaco, ante domnum Willelmum comitem, in presentia domni Stephani, Arvernorum episcopi, die illo quando seniores Arvernici cum comite supranominato convenerunt eique se commendaverunt." Robert, *abbas*, gave property to Saint-Julian de Brioude; see *Brioude*, no. 108, pp. 124–25 (= *Grand/Brioude* 112 [942–57], pp. 29–30): "pro absolutione peccaminum meorum et pro redemptione animae meae, vel patris matrisve, et pro Stephano episcopo, *seniore meo*" (emphasis mine). The editors of *Gallia Christiana* 2, col. 481, identify him as the Robert who was the nephew of Bishop Stephan.

140. BB 872;I:826–27 (3.954). Rougea is dép. Puy-de-Dôme, ca. Belleville. There is, however, a problem in identifying the donors. At about the same time

Genealogy 9. Viscounts and counts of Clermont

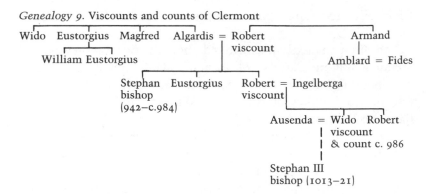

Note: The family is discussed in Lauranson-Rosaz, pp. 136–42. Stephan names his father, Robert; his mother, Algardis; and his step-mother, Hildegardis, in *Brioude*, no. 336, pp. 341–43 (= *Grand/Brioude* 448 [2.962], p. 141); Algardis discusses her own family in *Sauxillanges*, no. 82, pp. 96–98. In *Brioude*, no. 336, Stephan also names his uncles, Eustorgius, Magfred, Wido, Armand; Armand's son Amblard; Eustorgius's sons Eustorgius and William. Marcellin Boudet, in the introductory materials for *Saint-Flour*, p. cviii n. 4, suggests that Armand was an uncle on Stephan's mother's side, but this is disputed by Lauranson-Rosaz, p. 141, who argues for the relationships I have adopted here. Again, in *Brioude*, no. 336, Stephan names as his brothers Eustorgius and Robert. See also BB 792;1:743–44 (c. 951) and *Grand/Brioude* 333 (915–33), p. 94, with Rodbertus *vicecomes*. Amblard and his wife, Fides, were donors in *Brioude*, no. 140, pp. 155–56 (= *Grand/Brioude*, 148 [3.947], pp. 38–39). For Wido, see BB 1525;II:574–75 (5.980), where he is "gratia Dei Arvernice civitatis vicecomes," and where the donation (of Saint-Marie de Beaumont) is "pro anima avunculi mei Stephani, episcopi, ac pro genitore meo Roberto, pro genitrice etiam mea Ingelbergane, ac fratris mei Roberti." The copy of this document published in Etienne Baluze, *Histoire généalogique de la maison d'Auvergne*, 2 vols. (Paris: Dezallier, 1708), 1: preuves, p. 40, is of "l'original de cet acte dans le Tresor de l'abbaye de Clugny"; the names in the pro anima formula are the same as in the edition published in BB. Wido is styled *comes* in Sauxillanges, no. 340, pp. 262–63 (5.980–86) and in other documents cited in Lauranson-Rosaz, p. 91 n. 215.

Robert, the viscount, another Robert (probably the abbot), William (probably the count), and three other people who appeared at about the same time in connection with donations at Reilhac, namely Rodraud, Aynard, and Bertelaidis.[141] Rodraud's son,

---

there was a Stephan "dominus de castro Mezengo" who also had a wife named Ermengardis, and whom Lauranson-Rosaz (pp. 108–9) identifies as an uncle of Abbot Odilo (i.e., a brother of Odilo's father, Berald [see Genealogy 10]). Neither of these couples is to be confused with the parents of Viscount Dalmacius (I; c. 919–c. 947), who were also Stephan and Ermengardis (see the "Dalmacii" genealogy in n. 147). See Brioude, no.272, pp. 279–80 (= Grand/Brioude, 351 [8.919], p. 100) and Lauranson-Rosaz, pp. 124–26.

141. BB 873;1:827–28 (3.954) and BB 876;1:831–32 (3.954). Reilhac is dép. Haute-Loire, ca. Langeac.

Rostagnus, was present when Stephan and Ermengardis, in yet another gift, gave to Cluny their own share of the church of Saint Privatus at Reilhac.[142]

The other shares of the same church were donated to Cluny by Rodraud on the one hand and Gauzbert and his wife, Beringardis, on the other. Both gifts were witnessed by Viscount Robert, William, and another Robert, either the abbot or the viscount's son. Aynard and Bertelaidis were there as well.[143] These donations clearly took place within intersecting social circles.

The gift of the monastery of Ris was the work of the same groups. The cell constructed there was a project of Amblard, archbishop of Lyon.[144] Between the years 959 and 963, Amblard patiently obtained, mostly through purchase, the ten villae in the area of Thiers that would be given to Cluny along with Ris for its support.[145] There were various witnesses to these acquisitions, which took place at the rate of about one a year; but three witnesses remained constant: Eustorgius, Dalmacius, and Bertran. Eustorgius was the name of Bishop Stephan's uncle, brother, and nephew. Bertran was the lord [senior] of Rodraud, who, we saw above, was one of the donors of Reilhac.[146] Ber-

---

142. BB 1164;II:251–52 (Chaume, "Obs.," suggests 954–63; very likely it may be dated 3.954, to accord with the other gifts of the same church at that time). Present also were Count William and his wife, Adelaide. Lauranson-Rosaz, pp. 106 and 129–30, identifies Rodraud and his son, Rostagnus, as ancestors of the Beaumont family.

143. Rodraudus's donation: BB 873;I:827–28 (2.954); Gauzbert and Beringardis's: BB 876;I:831–32 (3.954).

144. BB 1450;II:503–6 (8.978). Marcellin Boudet, Saint-Flour, p. cxx, incorrectly identifies two archbishops of Lyon named Amblard, the first archbishop, 944–63, and the second, 974–78, separated by Burchard. But Gallia Christiana 4, cols. 72–79, has the more likely reconstruction: Burchard I was archbishop 949–956/7, Amblard (Boudet's Amblard I and II being the same person) was archbishop from 956/57 to c. 978, and Burchard II had the office from 979 to 1031. The problem is that a Burchard archiepiscopus gave the altare of Saint-Jean Chaveyriat to Cluny in "anno xxx Cohunradi regis" (BB 1227;II:307–8), which would put it at either 966 or 970, depending on how the regnal years were calculated. The editors of Gallia Christiana 4, col. 74, suggest deleting an x, making the regnal date anno xx, and the date of the charter 956 or 957.

145. BB 1068;II:162–63 (12.959); BB 1078;II:172–73 (1.960); BB 1115;II:206–7 (11.961); BB 1156;II:245–46 (6.963).

146. On the family of Bertran, the "Brioude" family, as Lauranson-Rosaz terms it, see Lauranson-Rosaz, pp. 127–28. It intersected with the family of Viscount Dalmacius and perhaps was linked by marriage as well (ibid., p. 126). The two families were closely associated in donations to Brioude. See, for example, Grand/Brioude 449 (936–83), pp. 142–43: "Sig. Dalmacii, vicecomitis . . . Sig-

tran, his son Stephan, and Dalmacius II, who was viscount and lay abbot of Brioude, were closely associated in a number of donations to Brioude.[147]

Who was Archbishop Amblard? As we have seen, Bishop Stephan's uncle, Armand, had a son named Amblard. In documents from Sauxillanges this Amblard was called a viscount; and in 963–64, surrounded by his fideles, he drew up a donation for Cluny of lands and churches near Clermont.[148] It seems almost certain that Amblard the archbishop was part of this family.[149]

---

num Stephani filii Bertrandi." (For the full witness list, see below, n. 158). Dalmacius II (see genealogy in n. 147) was abbot of Brioude from 936 to 983; see *Brioude*, no.28, pp. 51–52: "sub quo loco Dalmatius, gratia Dei vicecomes, rector praesse videtur temporibus Cuneberti praepositi." Stephan, son of Bertran, was associated with a different prior of Brioude, Joseph, in BB 876;1:831–32 (3.954). Bertran and his son seem also to be associated with Stephan and Ermengardis, e.g., BB 1115;11:206–7, with Stephan-Ermengardis and Bertran-Dalmacius as groups of witnesses. Bertran's wife was Emilgardis (or Emildis): see *Brioude*, no. 74, pp. 94–95 (= *Grand/Brioude* 76 [937], pp. 20–21; = Claude de Vic and Joseph Vaissette, *Histoire générale de Languedoc*, 15 vols. [Toulouse: Privat, 1872–93], 4:138–39). Lauranson-Rosaz, p. 128, has his wife named Ermengarde, but *Brioude*, no. 74, pp. 94–95, has "Signa Bertrandi et Emildis uxoris ejus, et Stephani eorum filii"). Their son, Stephan, was married first to Anna and then to Adelaiz; for Anna: *Brioude*, no. 293, pp. 300–301 (= *Grand/Brioude* 386 [4.943], p. 115); for Adelaiz: *Brioude*, no. 105, pp. 122–23 (= *Grand/Brioude* 109 [undated], pp. 28–29). Lauranson-Rosaz, p. 90 n. 212, connects the latter to the house of Anjou.

147. The viscomital family can be charted (in simplified form) as below, with the designations I and II added simply for the convenience of the modern reader. See Lauranson-Rosaz, p. 126.

Genealogy of the "Dalmacii"

Stephan = Ermengardis
(d. ?919) | (d. ?919)

Dalmacius I = Ingelberga
(d. 947) |

Dalmacius II
(d. 983)

148. BB 1167;11:254–56 (11.963–64); he was called viscount in *Sauxillanges*, no. 179, p. 160, and no. 753, pp. 536–37.

149. Lauranson-Rosaz, pp. 142–44, tentatively suggests that Archbishop Amblard was Viscount Amblard's uncle, the brother of Armand's wife, connecting Armand with the family of Nonette. Boudet (*Saint-Flour*, p. cxix) also suggests that the (two) Archbishop(s) Amblard probably "se rattacheraient à la famille du vicomte Armand." Certainly the social circles in which they made pious transactions were the same. See the list of principals and witnesses in

The generation of the two Stephans was not the end of these groups' relationship with Cluny. We have already seen that Wido, Bishop Stephan's nephew, gave Sainte-Marie de Beaumont to Cluny. The son of Stephan and Ermengardis, Teotard, redonated the church of Huillaux to Cluny, along with two churches at Ennezat that pertained to it.[150] He was present in 1011 when Wido, *miles et instaurator* of the monastery of Thiers, gave it to Cluny to be reformed specifically along the lines of Sauxillanges and Souvigny.[151] William V of Aquitaine, this Wido's lord, was present along with Stephan III, bishop of Clermont. Sometime later, Wido of Thiers gave Cluny land at Denone and Effiat, near Montpensier.[152]

The family of Abbot Odilo himself intersected with these groups (see Genealogy 10). We have already met Odilo's father, Berald, who made a donation to Cluny and Sauxillanges jointly.[153] The land that he gave had originally been acquired from the family of Viscount Dalmacius himself. The donation was witnessed by officials from Brioude. Indeed, the witness list for Berald's donation to Cluny/Sauxillanges closely followed the list of one of the donations of Dalmacius II to Brioude.[154] Odilo

---

Brioude, no. 63, pp. 83–84 (= *Grand/Brioude* 65 [3.927], p. 18), with Dalmacius, his wife, Ingelberga, and witnesses Bertrand, Eustorgius, Icterius, and Eldegerius; it compares closely with BB 1078;II:172–73 (960), concerned with the sale of land to support the monastery of Ris, among the witnesses of which were (in order) Iterius, Gerald, Dalmacius, Bertran, Eustorgius.

150. BB 2408;III:499–500 (997–1030; Lauranson-Rosaz suggests [p. 438 n. 143] after 1012). On Teotard, this friend and enemy of Cluny, whose donation is "pro perpetratis delictibus pluribus," see Lauranson-Rosaz, p. 438 n. 143, and also *Cartulaire de l'abbaye de Saint-Chaffre du Monastier*, ed. Ulysse Chevalier (Paris: Picard, 1884), no. 418 (4.993), pp. 157–58 and no. 420 (1.1016), pp. 159–60.

151. BB 2682;III:710–13 (9.1011). Lauranson-Rosaz, p. 147, suggests the possibility that Wido was married to Teotard's sister. For Wido's title, see the document in *Gallia Christiana* 2, Instrumenta col. 75.

152. BB 2006;III:217–19 (Chaume, "Obs.," 1011–31).

153. BB 2135;III:315–17 (3.999). See above, n. 68.

154. *Grand/Brioude* 449 (936–83), pp. 142–43. The lists follow:

Grand/Brioude	BB 2135
	. . .
S. Dalmacii vicecomitis	Dalmacius vicecomes
S. Stephani filii	Stephanus vicarius
	Ebo
Bertrandi	Bertrannus, fratres
	Dalmatius

Genealogy 10. The family of Odilo

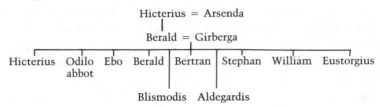

Note: On the family of Odilo, see Lauranson-Rosaz, pp. 133–35; *Saint-Flour*, pp. cxliii–cl; and Jacques Hourlier, *Saint Odilon, Abbé de Cluny* (Louvain: Bibliothèque de l'Université, 1964), pp. 28–30. Hourlier's identification of Odilo's mother as the "petite-nièce d'Hugues, marquis de Provence et roi d'Italie" (p. 30) would link her to the Bosonids; it is based on Baluze, 1:255, not always a trustworthy source. The genealogy here (much simplified) is based on information in BB 1838;III:82–83 (c. 991), BB 2135;III:315–17 (3.999), BB 2788;III:811–15 (9.1025), BB 2790;III:816 (1025), and *Brioude*, no. 320, pp. 325–26 (= *Grand/Brioude* 425 [957–83], p. 129). An Oddo is also important to the family: BB 2135, a donation by Berald, Odilo's father, was on behalf of his own soul, that of Oddo, whose land he was, in fact, donating, and for their fathers and relatives.

himself had been a canon at Brioude before coming to Cluny, and his father and mother had made a major donation there at that time.[155]

The Bourbons

The second important circle of support for Cluny in the Auvergne was formed by the family that would later become the lords of Bourbon (see Genealogy 11). The relationship with Cluny probably again grew out of the circle of William the Pious: Aimard was probably William's fidelis. In 915 he ceded the

Grand/Brioude	BB 2135
S. Geraldi	
S. Eldegerii	Ildegerius
S. Leotardi	
S. Achardi	
S. Bertrandi	Bertramnus
S. Stephani	
	Folconus
	Theotardus
	Gausfredus
	Ricolfus
	Eldigerius

155. *Brioude*, no. 320, pp. 325–26 (= *Grand/Brioude* 425 [957–83], p. 129). On Odilo at Brioude, see Jotsaldus *Vita Odilonis* i.1 (*PL* 142, col. 899); Jacques Hourlier, *Saint Odilon*, pp. 31–32.

Genealogy 11. The Bourbons

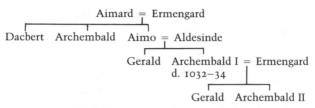

Note: Based on information in BB 871;1:824–26 (1.954), BB 906; 11:20 (redated by Chaume c. 975–80). See Max Fazy, *Les origines du bourbonnais,* 2 vols. (Moulins: Progrès de l'Allier, 1924), 2:25–47 and at p. 34, for the wife of Archembald I. The genealogy here is much simplified; a more complete reconstruction may be found in Devailly, p. 368, and also Lauranson-Rosaz, pp. 146–48.

monastery of Souvigny to Cluny.[156] Some thirty years later, his son, Aimo, gave Souvigny land at "Longvé"; shortly thereafter he redonated Souvigny to Cluny along with the land at Longvé.[157]

In the 970s Cluny received two donations in the vicinity of Châtel-de-Neuvre: one was from Hebreus and his wife, and one from his son.[158] In the latter, Archembald and Gerald served as witnesses. Similarly, they were present at the donation by one William, in 980, of land near Neuvy.[159] In 984 Ermengard, Archembald's wife, gave Cluny the church at Escurolles; the donation was witnessed by Dacbert and two Archembalds.[160] A later donation, from about 1030, also included Archembald and Ermengard, this time as witnesses.[161] Thus the association of

156. BB 217;1:206–7 (3.920); see Fazy, 1:23 and 2:22, where it is dated 915. On Aimard's relationship with William, see BB 112;1:124–28 (909), Cluny's foundation charter, where an Aimardus appears. Fazy, 2:19–20 asserts that Aimard was William's vassal and held Souvigny from him; and see Guy Devailly, *Le Berry du Xe siècle au milieu du XIIIe: Etude politique, religieuse, sociale et économique* (Paris: Mouton, 1973), p. 154.

157. Donation to Souvigny in BB 782;1:735–37 (11.950); donation of Souvigny to Cluny in BB 871;1:824–26 (1.954). See François Larroque, "Souvigny: Les origines du prieuré," *Revue Mabillon* 58 (1970): 1–24.

158. BB 905;11:19 and BB 906;11:20 (Chaume, "Obs.," suggests c. 975–80 for both).

159. BB 1512;11:562–63 (2.980).

160. BB 1696;11:720 (7.984).

161. BB 2007;111:219–20 (Chaume, "Obs.," suggests before 1031–34; he identifies Archembald as "Archambaud II de Bourbon, mari d'Ermengeard," but the problem seems one mainly of numbering). Ermengard mère was deceased by 954 (BB 871;1:824–26). Fazy, 2:42–43, explains why, in BB 2007, the name Ermengard was placed at the end of the witness list rather than at the beginning with Archembald: it had been added in different ink on the parchment, seemingly as

this family with Cluny was a family tradition. They were not in Cluny's immediate neighborhood, but other ties just as important bound them to the monastery.

The Outward Spread of Donations

If donations to Cluny generally came from intersecting circles of donors, nevertheless, this did not mean that the geographical distribution of donations to Cluny would remain forever fixed. On the contrary, as we have seen with the Bosonids and as remained true thereafter, great aristocratic families knew one another. Above all, through exchanges of women in marriage these families forged alliances and diffused their styles of benefaction. We can see how this worked by taking the instance of Agnes. She was the third wife of William V (the Great), duke of Aquitaine, who, in his own right, was a benefactor of Cluny; and she was the daughter of Otto-William, count of Burgundy, who also had a close association with the monastery.[162] Abbot Odilo gave Agnes the *potestates Sancti Petri* at Laizé in precaria.[163] This gift, like so many others given in precaria, was already associated with its recipient. As we have seen in Chapter 4, the church and land at Laizé had been given to Cluny by Leotald, the count of Mâcon, in the mid–tenth century.[164] Agnes was

---

an afterthought. For this couple, mentioned c. 1010–11, see Fazy, vol. 1, nos. 84, 91, and 96 (Ermengard alone) and Maurice Chaume, "Etudes Carolingiennes, III: D'où sortent les anciens sires de Bourbon?" *Annales de Bourgogne* 8 (1936): 101–5.

162. E.g., BB 2736;III:759–61 (Chaume, "Obs.," 1023–26), where Otto-William returns the *potestates* of Ambérieux-en-Dombes and Jully-lès-Buxy. BB 2742;III:765–66 speaks of Odilo "memor itaque familiaritatis et pie societatis . . . Willelmi [i.e., Otto-William]." See Constance B. Bouchard, "Laymen and Church Reform around the Year 1000: The Case of Otto-William, Count of Burgundy," *Journal of Medieval History* 5 (1979): 1–10. For William V (William III as count of Poitiers), see BB 2709;III:732 (5.1017) and, in general, Daniel F. Callahan, "William the Great and the Monasteries of Aquitaine," *Studia Monastica* 19 (1977): 321–42, esp. 336–40; Bernard S. Bachrach, "Toward a Reappraisal of William the Great, Duke of Aquitaine," *Journal of Medieval History* 5 (1979): 11–21, both with bibliography.

163. BB 2742;III:765–66 (Chaume, "Obs.," 1026–30), where Agnes identifies herself as the daughter of Otto-William and the wife of William, duke of Aquitaine. The fact is alluded to in Raoul Glaber, *Historiarum libri quinque*, iii, 2, ed. Maurice Prou (Paris: Picard, 1886), p. 57.

164. BB 768;I:723–24 (5.950). See Chapter 4.

Genealogy 12. The counts of Mâcon

Leotald, comes
(943–62)

|

Alberic II, comes [1] = Ermentrudis = [2] Otto-William, comes
(962–80)   (981–1026)

|

Agnes = William V

Note: A very simplified account based on the following: *M*, no. 7, p. 6 (a list of counts of Mâcon drawn up in the twelfth century); BB 1291;II:368 (1.971), a donation by Alberic and his wife, Ermentrudis; BB 2265;III:395–97 (9.994), Ermentrudis, comitissa, and Otto, comes, appear together as witnesses; BB 2742; III:765–66 (Chaume, "Obs.," 1026–30), where Agnes identifies herself as daughter of Otto-William and the wife of William, duke of Aquitaine. See Bouchard, *Sword*, pp. 261–72.

related to him indirectly, through the first marriage of her mother to Leotald's son, Alberic (see Genealogy 12). The connections set up by these marriages were part of a yet wider network. Duke William V exchanged each year precious gifts (*pretiosa munera*) with Sancho el Mayor, king of Navarre (1000–1035).[165] At the same time, Sancho began a relationship with Saint Peter at Cluny, becoming a special friend (*familiaris*) and a member of Cluny's *societas* for whom prayers were offered.[166] It is no wonder that the geographical patterns involved in land and church—and now, increasingly, monetary—transactions with Cluny should expand in the course of the eleventh century. For although families at that time, even at the level of the castellan, were putting down roots in one place and were opting for patrilineal dynastic strategies, nevertheless they sent

165. Adhemar of Chabannes, *Chronicon*, iii.41, p. 163.
166. Odilo, *Epistola* 3 (*PL* 142, col. 942): "Sumus itaque ex indissolubili familiaritate et societate qua olim patri vestro [the father of the recipient of the letter, Garcia of Navarra, was Sancho el Mayor] probamur copulati." See Bishko, "Fernando I, pp. 3–9. Raoul Glaber reported about this time a vow by Christians (presumably in Spain) to send to Saint Peter at Cluny the spoils of a victory over the Muslims for use in constructing a *ciborium* over the main altar: Glaber, p. 110. In his *Epistola* 2 (*PL* 142, col. 942) Odilo promised that silver (possibly the spoils that were vowed) would be used to build an altar at Cluny to memorialize Sancho el Mayor, and Sancho, the bishop of Pamplona. In BB 2891;IV:89–95, at 90 (6.1033), Sancho el Mayor says that Cluny "clarius ceteris monasteriis Benedicti perfecta florebat regulari religione" in connection with recounting the reform of San Juan de la Peña by a group of Cluniac monks sent to Navarre. See Segl, pp. 181–83.

their sons off to distant parts to learn the military life.[167] Women were a particularly mobile part of a truly international system of exchange within the aristocracy. Agnes, who began as the daughter of the count of Burgundy, was the mother of Empress Agnes (wife of Henry III) and she herself went on, after the death of William V of Aquitaine, to become the countess of Anjou.[168]

Patterns of Property Distribution

We have looked at the distribution of Cluny's "special property"—the property named in papal and royal privileges—and we have explored the nature of its rather more far-flung gift networks. It is time now to look at the aggregate of its property transactions and to suggest some patterns.

Churches

Churches were relatively rare and significant gifts: between 909 and 1049, 3,021 transactions of land sans churches took place with Cluny; during the same period, only 261 churches and monasteries were given (or taken).[169] The important geographical shifts in gift giving took place after 994: local transactions of monasteries and churches became less frequent, while those from outside the neighboring pagi increased. See Table 11 for a summary of the changes by intervals of approximately a half-century.

Particularly significant in the table are the numbers for the pagus of Mâcon as compared with those under the category

---

167. See Georges Duby, "Les 'jeunes' dans la société aristocratique dans la France du Nord-Quest au XIIe siècle," in *Hommes et structures*, pp. 213–26. Someone like Sancho el Mayor, whose predecessors had been content with purely local ties, now sought to connect himself with groups outside of his immediate vicinity; see Richard A. Fletcher, *St. James's Catapult: The Life and Times of Diego Gelmírez of Santiago de Compostela* (Oxford: Clarendon Press, 1984), pp. 29–30.

168. On Anjou, see Olivier Guillot, *Le Comte d'Anjou et son entourage au XIe siècle*, 2 vols. (Paris: Picard, 1972), and Johnson, pp. 8–17.

169. Here churches and monasteries handed over for reform are also taken into account.

Table 11. Distribution of churches and monasteries

Pagus	909–53 No.	%	954–93 No.	%	994–1049 No.	%
Mâcon	39	49	35	37	14	16
Autun	3	4	11	12	16	19
Lyon	19	24	19	20	11	13
Chalon	3	4	4	4	4	5
Vienne	3	4	3	3	3	3
Auvergne	7	9	7	7	2	2
Other	2	3	10	11	29	34
Uncertain	4	5	5	5	7	8
Total	80		94		86	

Note: Because many charters can be dated by abbot only, it is useful here to divide the century and a half at 954 (accession of Maiolus as *coadjutor*) and 994 (death of Maiolus). Percentages, which refer to each column, are rounded to the nearest whole number; hence the totals are not exactly 100 percent. To the total here of 260 churches and monasteries should be added one more, date unknown.

"Other." While 49 percent of the churches and monasteries pertaining to Cluny were located in the Mâconnais in the earliest period, only 16 percent were from that region in the last period. Conversely, while at first only 3 percent were from regions other than those quite near to Cluny, in the first half of the eleventh century regions farther flung made up the single largest category, or 34 percent of the transactions.

The pattern was remarkably constant in Cluny's first century. Churches given to or taken from Cluny were then mainly in its "immediate" neighborhood—the Mâconnais, Autunois, Lyonnais—and in the regions where, as we have seen, certain noble families had special and long-standing ties with Cluny. Indeed, the primary boundaries of the gift nexus with Cluny were those of the Mâconnais and Lyonnais (see Map 1).

In the eleventh century a marked shift took place. Neighborhood ties, formed around gifts of churches, did not cease entirely; but increasingly they lost ground to transactions from farther afield. The pagi of Mâcon, Lyon, and Autun together now accounted (in terms of percentages) for what Mâcon alone had formerly contributed. The Auvergne, once a steady source of ecclesiastical gifts, was now almost dry. After the year 1000, the trend was for churches to come from areas still farther away.

Figure 5. Rendering of mid-eleventh-century Cluny II, the second church built at Cluny, and other monastic buildings, by Kenneth John Conant. The view is from the east. Courtesy of The Medieval Academy of America.

Table 12. Distribution of land

Pagus	909–53		954–93		994–1048		Uncertain date	
	No.	%	No.	%	No.	%	No.	%
Mâcon	392	72	935	73	787	70	32	44
Autun	17	3	83	6	65	6	6	8
Lyon	37	7	83	6	54	5	9	13
Chalon	34	6	38	3	47	4	5	7
Vienne	16	3	29	2	3	0	5	10
Auvergne	6	1	16	1	23	2	1	1
Other	17	3	26	7	58	5	0	0
Uncertain	27	5	74	6	82	7	14	19
Total	546		1,284		1,119		72	

Land

The geographical pattern formed by simple land transactions changed less markedly. Table 12 may be compared with that for churches. The shift over time revealed by this table is mainly one of quantity. The second half of the tenth century was the great age of expansion: then, on average, there were thirty-three land transactions per year. By contrast, in the period thereafter, there were about twenty-one transactions per year. The pancartes drawn up at the end of the tenth century attest to the consolidation that took place then and mark the end of a phase.

There was, however, another shift about the same time, at which the data in Table 12 barely hint. This was a change in the nature of the charter, and particularly in the precision and care given to questions of place. In the eleventh century, the long, descriptive charters of the past gave way to *notitiae*: brief statements recording the fact that a transaction had taken place.[170] These were rarely witnessed and, although naming specific locations, did not concern themselves so much with borders or neighbors. They did, of course, name the principals. Changes in notarial practices clearly account for much of this; and these new practices were not limited to the documents of Cluny.[171]

170. On the *notitia*, see the illuminating discussion in Fichtenau, *Urkundenwesen*, pp. 73–87.
171. The notitia was common in Austria and Bavaria, for example, already at the beginning of the tenth century (ibid., p. 85).

Table 13. Boundary information

	909–54		955–1009		1010–49	
	No.	*%*	*No.*	*%*	*No.*	*%*
Not given	320	52	960	48	382	69
Given	299	48	1,055	52	168	31

Note: Tabulated, as is Appendix B, Illustration B.1, for charters concerned with transactions of churches, partial churches, and land. The break at 1009/10 was arrived at after experimenting with other possibilities. Percentages are for each time period (column) and are rounded to nearest whole number.

Nevertheless, it is clear that these notarial transformations themselves were symptomatic of a sea change in sensibilities and values.[172] Part of that change downgraded the charter itself, with its emphasis on the rituals of transfer and on the people associated with the land. Using border descriptions as a rough and ready measure of this change, we may assign the date of about 1010 as the time it took effect (see Table 13). After 1010, then, boundary information was supplied in less than a third of the transactions that took place with Cluny; in the tenth century it had been included about half of the time. This suggests that the placement of the land vis-à-vis neighbors became less important than it once had been. Meanwhile, the names of donors increasingly came to be accompanied by surnames. These surnames, themselves (generally) derived from the name of a property that had become the seat of a newly defined, linear family, were part of the same shift in sensibilities. After about 1000, it became less important to be the neighbor of Saint Peter than to be an independent benefactor of Cluny. The birth of the seigneurie and the solidification of the patrilinear family thus had its effect on modes of piety.

If gifts to Cluny had no hau demanding to return home, nevertheless they bound households together. The bequest of William the Pious and Ingelberga to Saints Peter and Paul brought in its train gifts from their fideles, friends, and relatives, and from circles of people related, in turn, to these others. Many such

172. On the usefulness of this abbreviated form and its connection with the production of *libri memoriales*, see ibid., p. 84.

gifts, enshrined in documents from royal and papal chanceries, became the core of Cluny's special property, its ecclesia. They have given Cluny the image of an empire. But a better image would have Cluny be a point at which lines of affiliation converge. The same may be said of the property of "Cluniac" monasteries. They were sometimes drawn into Cluny's network of social ties, but often they constituted separate social magnets whose lines of attraction touched only tangentially those focused on Cluny, even when they shared its abbot.

Conclusion:
Saint Peter's Neighborhood

THE FUNDAMENTAL QUESTIONS posed in this book seem simple enough. Why did men and women outside the monastery walls choose to give land to those inside? And, in turn, why did those inside choose to accept it? The answer in each individual instance is no doubt particular, idiosyncratic, and personal. Yet some patterns may be discerned.

Gifts of land had two different, yet coexisting meanings: on the one hand they signified the transfer of property and rights over it; on the other hand they signified a relationship between the donor and the donee. For the most part, the latter meaning predominated in the period before 1049. To the current reassessment of this period—which emphasizes order alongside disorder, and which delineates structures for handling disputes alongside incessant feuds—must be added the significance of property transactions. These worked as a social glue. In an age of fragmentation and social dislocation, land transactions emphasized the connections and interrelations among people and between people and saints. In the Mâconnais, Saint Peter at Cluny was a particularly potent cohesive force.

Gifts of land were not given out indiscriminately or impersonally but rather to those who mattered, to those who were related to one another, either by blood or by alliance. In this society, gifts (of all sorts) helped to express relationships of love, of subordination, and of enmity: they compensated for crimes and tied together estranged families.[1] In this sense, donations to

---

1. E.g., BB 2946;IV:146–47.

Cluny were part of a repertory of familiar gestures; they had the significance of including Saint Peter in a circle of friends and family members.

Gifts to Cluny must therefore be understood as the expression of relationships that existed between the monastery and those outside. They cannot be taken in isolation from other transactions. Charters of donations, werpitiones, sales, precarial arrangements, and exchanges are all, among other things, the written vestiges of important moments in friendships and enmities, intended to reinforce the web of the social fabric. Their social significance emerges over time, for relationships were built up slowly. Indeed, of all the ways in this society in which people could make, break, and renew links both within and beyond this world, donations were perhaps the most patient and the least instantaneous. They worked bit by bit, over lifetimes and through generations. This is no doubt because they were part of a very local social fabric, composed largely of families and neighbors.

The local setting is important. The absence of central authority virtually required that neighborhood associations sustain what social cohesion there was. During the years 909–1049, most donations to Cluny came from its vicinity. These gifts brought together or recalled old owners of property, souls of the dead and living to be saved, neighbors, friends, families, the monks of Cluny, and, most important, God and his saints, Peter and Paul. Land so parceled out was not "lost." People remembered what had been given and who had given it. If questions arose, if memories needed jogging, the processes of redonations, quitclaims, and precarial donations reaffirmed (at the least) the old connections. Some land had symbolic meaning, being property to give, to sell, or to claim again. Within this landscape, charged with affective significance, Saint Peter was a familiar and regular landowner, a neighbor right in the midst of other neighbors. One charter called Peter and Paul the *principes terrae*.[2]

Peter was the prince of the Apostles, doorkeeper of heaven, and a powerful mediator between God and man. The latter was

2. BB 379;I:358–61.

true, without doubt, of all saints; and as we have seen, saints other than Peter drew donations in their own vicinity. Saint-Jean de Chaveyriat or Saint-Jean d'Angély are good cases in point. Indeed, the gift networks with these monasteries demonstrate that even when a monastery was part of Cluny's ecclesia, its property often belonged to its own saint, not to Cluny's Peter. But, clearly, Cluny's Peter was a particularly potent mediator.[3] His power was in part due to the fact that he was served at Cluny by monks whose observance of the religious life was extraordinarily appealing.[4] Saint Peter at Cluny was worthy of largess. He formed a decisive common point on numerous interrelated circles of gift giving. The purposes of these circles were manifold: to give and give again land that was itself originally God's gift; to establish a partnership with Saint Peter and the monks who served him; to be remembered in association with the land that was given; to be the neighbor of Saint Peter. These motives doubtless had their secular counterparts, which are more difficult to glimpse because of the nature of the sources left to us. Yet we can see, even in the documents of Cluny, examples of dowries, nuptial gifts, and gifts to brothers, sisters, and heirs.[5] On the other hand, more "secular" elements may also be found in the links with Cluny: the very act of gift giving created and defined relationships and statuses, both between the principals and within the community at large. In the context of these many meanings, it is not necessary to seek for concrete counter-gifts, such as donations in return for prayers or burial privileges. The gift in itself was its own reward. The arengae of the charters make abundantly clear the redemptive effects of gift giving alone.

3. Cluny was not the only institution dedicated to Saint Peter. In the Mâconnais alone there were at least five churches with this *patrocinium*: at Blanzy, Curtil-sous-Buffières, Jullié, Domange, and Saint-Pierre-de-Lanque. Blantiaco: BB 474;I:460–61 (5.937); Curtilis: BB 1577;II:622–23 (11.981–82); Juliaco (Juvuiliaco): BB 2914;IV:114–15 (3.1037); Lanco: BB 387;I:368–69 (9.930); Domanico BB 1124;II:215–16 (1.962). They do not appear to have commanded an outpouring of gifts. We know about them, of course, only because they were given or sold to Cluny. How many borders on terra Sancti Petri referred to property pertaining to these churches?

4. See Rosenwein, *Rhinoceros Bound*, pp. 101–12.

5. E.g., BB 9;I:11–12 (10.863?), BB 43;I:51 (4.891), BB 83;I:93–94 (3.904–5), BB 86;I:96–98 (10.904?), BB 96;I:107–8 (2.908), BB 99;I:110–11 (8.908), BB 105; I:117–19 (9.909), etc.

All this clearly applies to the local society near Cluny. But it seems at first blush a thin explanation for the donations that came from regions quite far from the monastery. Here two further factors must be emphasized: the duties and expectations of the fideles of William the Pious, his wife, and his sister; and the force of family traditions. The donations that Cluny received down the Rhône and into the Auvergne were, by and large, not the donations of "locals." They were donations from powerful men and women, many of whom had ties either with the founders of Cluny and/or family roots in Burgundy. These people, along with new groups that came in time to intersect with them, gave repeatedly and richly to Cluny. The lands, churches, and monasteries that they donated were so important as to merit repeated invocations in royal and papal privileges.

All this socially motivated gift giving went on at the same time as a different system—one in which property was accumulated *or* alienated—was also in place. Eventually this other system predominated. This was partly due to the attenuation of relationships, which time itself brought despite the best intentions. Antelmus's sisters remembered his gift to Cluny, and doubtless the Antelmus who was named after him remembered him as well. But the memory of his donation, long-lived as it was, disappeared after about 1040, as did mention of the villa Fontana associated with his name. It seems very likely that Fontana continued to exist, but since no fresh claims arose with regard to it, it lost its social significance and become incorporated into Cluny's "patrimony."

This, indeed, was the second reason that the system destroyed itself. Adding lands to lands, parcels to parcels, the monks serving Saint Peter created (sometimes apparently inadvertently, at other times quite deliberately) a seigneurie of grand dimensions. The work of consolidation got under way in a flurry of activity just at the close of the tenth century. This very process was also taking place among members of the lay aristocracy at the same time. Land, which had been used so freely as a means of social bonding, now (in the hands of castellans and in the hands of the monks of Cluny as well) took on the character of a seigneurie and a family inheritance. This change had wide ramifications. Names, which had been single and possible to identify only in association with other names, now (among those in the upper classes) increasingly were followed by a patronymic, derived often enough from family estates as much as from patrilineal descent.[6] Many villae, which once were simply regional districts, were absorbed into lordships. Newly powerful castellans tied to themselves through the bonds of vassalage a now weakened aristocracy; and they established the protection and the bondage of the banal seigneurie over an increasingly subject peasantry. Land was no longer broken up into gifts to support all family members and ensure their solidarity. It lost much of its social significance in this new context.

Yet the mid–eleventh century also marked the beginning of Cluny's most powerful and prosperous phase, when donations, particularly of churches and monasteries, poured in from places far from the Mâconnais.[7] There were still gifts from Cluny's neighborhood, of course; and there was still a system of give and take.[8] Yet other motives were also at work. There were many more requests for confraternity, for prayers, for special commemorations, than there had been before.[9] As Cluny ceased to be primarily a neighborhood phenomenon; as certain kinds of new social bonds were set in place in the Mâconnais; as land ceased to have above all a social meaning, and became instead the seat of economic and political power; and, finally, as lay ownership of churches came under criticism from reformers, the mean-

6. Maiolus Poudreux's son, for example, was Odo Poudreux. See BB 3367; IV:463 (c. 1060); but more usually surnames were taken from place names. A related development was the increased use of the *laudatio parentum* in charters, which apparently signaled a new kind of family approval: i.e., the approval of a real alienation of the patrimony. See White, *Custom, Kinship.*

7. There was a falling off in terms of sheer number of donation transactions after 1050. But this is possibly because complete mansi in one place were the usual donation after 1050, whereas previously donations had been often of scattered pieces.

8. There were more quitclaims in Hugh's time than there had been before. And some of the same local families—the Grossi are a prime example—were involved with Cluny well into the twelfth century: e.g., in BB 3753;v:106, BB 3754;v:107–8. See Bouchard, *Sword*, pp. 163–68.

9. See Cowdrey, "Unions and Confraternity." Take, for example, BB 3765; v:117–18, in which Grimaldus, miles, gives all that he has and asks in return for prayers and masses. It is precisely when the memory of benefactors once associated with particular properties had dimmed that the necrology of Marcigny was drawn up, with the original status of the donors now forgotten and their names memorialized as monks. See Neiske.

ing of donations to Cluny changed. With the arrival of a pope who claimed to act from the merits of Saint Peter himself, it became less and less important to be the neighbor of Saint Peter at Cluny.

Appendix A

SAS Data Sets

Illustration A. 1. Edit *SAS* data set: CLUNY.ONE

Command →	Screen 1
	Obs 4159

```
CHTRNUM:   991
FSTDATE:   956
SNDDATE:
CONFDATE:  00
CHTRTYPE:  011
ACTIVITY:  D
OUTCOME:   1
TERMDATE:
FSTPAGUS:  2
SNDPAGUS:
AGER:      IAONICO
VILLA:     CORTEPLACIA
CHURCHES:
BORDERS:   1
STPETER:   0
VIAPUB:    0
RIVER:     1
DONORETC:  0
NOTES:
```

Illustration A. 2. Edit *SAS* data set: PLACES.ONE

Command →			Screen 1

Obs 2001

PLVILLA:	MORGONO (MORGON)	PLPAGUS:	o
PLAGER:	MORGONO (F)		
PLCHRCH:		IDQUALTY:	2
CITY:	MORGON	DEPT:	69
CANTON:	BEAUJEU		
COMMUNE:	VILLIE	REFERENT: C:	1134 N.15
ALTCITY:		ALTDEPT:	
ALTCANT:			
ALTCOMM:		ALTREFNT:	
LATTUDE:	46 LATMINS:	8 LATSECS:	39
LONGTUDE:	4 LONGMINS:	40 LONGSECS:	51
ESTWST: E			
NOTES:			

Illustrations A.1 and A.2 represent the data-entry screens for the two SAS data sets used. The abbreviation "Obs" refers to the "observation," the meaning of which is explained in the Introduction. The variables are as follows.

Illustration A.1, data set CLUNY.ONE:

CHTRNUM = charter number. This corresponds to the number in BB.

FSTDATE = first date. This was entered by year only. If one date was given, such as 965, that was entered as FSTDATE. If a range of dates was given, such as 956–57, the first was entered as FSTDATE and the second as SNDDATE.

SNDDATE = second date. See remarks for FSTDATE.

CONFDATE = confidence in the date. A range of codes was elaborated for this. For example, oo was the code for a date given by BB that was not challenged by Chaume, "Obs" (code 03), or Hillebrandt, "Datierungen" (code 06), and so on. The first digit of this two-digit code was changed to 1 if the date was approximate.

CHRTYPE = charter type. The first two digits of the code for this indicated the type of property involved in each transaction—as, for example, land or a church—or whether the charter was rather a confirmation of a transaction already made. The third digit indicated whether Cluny was involved.

Thus, for example, 011 was a land transaction (code 01) that concerned Cluny (..1); code 111 was a transaction involving a church that concerned Cluny; 211 was a transaction involving a partial church that concerned Cluny. Code 210 was a transaction involving partial church that was published as part of Cluny's archives by BB but did not in fact appear to concern Cluny. A separate code was used for a transaction involving a monastery (05) and for a transaction that involved the foundation or reordering of a church or monastery (07).

ACTIVITY. Forty-seven different codes were used for this category, taken as far as possible from the principal active verb or key word indicating the activity or activities involved in the charter. Thus V = vendo, D = dono, C = cedo, W = werpitio, R = redo, DU = dono/with reserve of usufruct, and so on. Some charters involved more than one activity, in which case separate codes were used for each transaction. Some activities were hybrids, as indicated, for example, by a code such as XP = an exchange of land, at least one piece of which was held in precaria, that is, for the life of the donee. The way in which these ACTIVITY codes were grouped in order to arrive at the broad categories of Donation, Sale, and so on, is indicated in Appendix B.

OUTCOME. Essentially a category to indicate whether Cluny gained or lost land. Six codes were used: 0 = no gain or loss for Cluny; 1 = gain for Cluny ; 2 = loss for Cluny; 3 = not a question of gain or loss; 4 = gain for a "Cluniac" monastery or church; 5 = loss to a "Cluniac" monastery or church; 6 = unclear.

TERMDATE = terminal date. This turned out to be a useless category. It had originally been intended to indicate when a piece of land, church, monastery, and the like was no longer part of Cluny's property.

FSTPAGUS = first pagus. Variable for the pagi named in the charter. The code 2, for example, referred to the pagus of Lyon. The code 5 was used (in conjunction with SNDPAGUS) for the least frequently mentioned pagi. The code 6 was used if no pagus was mentioned.

SNDPAGUS = second pagus. Used in two instances: (1) where FSTPAGUS = 6 (i.e., where no pagus is mentioned), when it was possible to identify the pagus of the charter through nontextual means (e.g., by identifying the persons involved or the villae), the code number of the pagus was entered for FSTPAGUS and 6 entered for SNDPAGUS; (2) where FST-PAGUS = 5, SNDPAGUS was coded to identify the pagi involved.

AGER = the name of the ager, in precisely the form it appeared in the charter.

VILLA = the name of the villa, in precisely the form it appeared in the charter.

CHURCHES = the patrocinium of the church, as, for example, Petrus, entered in the nominative.

BORDERS. If the charter specified borders, this was coded 1. If not, it was coded 0. This was done for each villa separately in charters that involved more than one villa.

STPETER. If one or more pieces of land in any one villa in the charter had one (or more) border(s) with Saint Peter of Cluny, it was coded 1.

VIAPUB = via publica. If one or more pieces of land in any one villa in the charter had one (or more) border(s) on a road (whether a major road or a field path) this was coded 1.

RIVER. If one or more pieces of land in any one villa in the charter had one (or more) border(s) on a river, this was coded 1.

DONORETC. If one or more pieces of land in any one villa in the charter had one (or more) border(s) with land of the donor or land *de ipsa hereditate* this was coded 1. However, for exchanges, a further refinement was added: 1 = if *de ipsa hereditate*, 2 = if donor, 3 = if both.

NOTES. A field in which to write incidental observations, peculiarities of the charter, correspondences to other charters, and so on.

Illustration A.2, data set PLACES.ONE:
PLVILLA = the variable VILLA in data set CLUNY.ONE.
PLAGER = the variable AGER in data set CLUNY.ONE.
PLPAGUS = the variable FSTPAGUS in data set CLUNY.ONE.
PLCHURCH = the variable CHURCHES in data set CLUNY.ONE.

IDQUALTY = quality of identification. The codes indicate a range of quality (all of which ought to be qualified by a question mark!): 1 = undisputed and without (much) doubt; 2 = uncertain; 3 = only approximate location known, either because place has disappeared, has been absorbed, or only ager has been located; 4 = serious dispute among authorities; 5 = not identified; 6 = may be a number of places, including those that have disappeared; 7 = Valous identification corrected by Mme Quarré.

CITY = modern place name

DEPT = modern département

CANTON = French canton

COMMUNE = French commune

REFERENT = reference. The most frequently used sources were C = Chaume, *Origines*, II/3; D = Déléage, *Bourgogne*; Q = Mme Quarré's files.

ALTCITY = alternative modern place name. This category and the six that follow were used only if IDQUALTY 4 or 6 were coded.

ALTDEPT = alternative département.

ALTCANT = alternative canton.

ALTCOMM = alternative commune.

ALTREFNT = alternative reference.

LATTUDE = degrees latitude.

LATMINS = minutes latitude.

LATSECS = seconds latitude.

LONGTUDE = degrees longitude.

LONGMINS = minutes longitude.

LONGSECS = seconds longitude.

ESTWST = longitude east or west of the Greenwich meridien.

NOTES. A field in which to write incidental observations, further identifications, and so on.

Summaries of
Property Transactions

THE TABLE in Illustration B.1 shows the number of transactions involving land and churches and their distribution by kind of activity and by abbacy for the period 909–1049. Illustration B.2 uses the same data, but now counting charters rather than transactions. In rare instances, charters contain more than one kind of activity (e.g., a donation *and* a sale), in which case the charter is counted more than once.

In order to see a sample of the kinds of assumptions upon which these and other results reported in the text are based, Illustration B.3 shows the "SAS Job" that was written to produce these two tables.[1] (The same assumptions have not always been used throughout this book, but I have indicated the differences in those instances.) The following, in particular, should be noted: (1) the definition of abbacies by date; abbatial dates in Illustrations B.1 and B.2 are those generally accepted (Maiolus is sometimes shown with dates 954–994; see Introduction, note to Table 2). However, for the purposes of defining the variable ABBOT for SAS, it was necessary that dates not overlap. Therefore, rather arbitrarily, the dates for the abbacies given in the SAS Job (Illustration B.3) are: Berno (909–26), Odo (927–41), Aymard (942–63), Maiolus (964–93), Odilo (994–1048). In Illustration B.3 the abbreviations are: eq = equal to, ge = greater than or equal to, lt = less than, ne = not equal to; (2) the definition of

---

1. To the data produced by the SAS Job were added, in Illustrations B.1 and B.2, the names and dates of the abbots.

Illustration B.1

Appendix B, Illustration 1
Frequency of Transactions

ABBOT

TABLE OF ABBOT BY TRANSFER

ABBOT		DONATION	EXCHANGE	LOAN	OTHER	PRECARIA	SALE	WERPITIO	TOTAL
FREQUENCY / PERCENT / ROW PCT / COL PCT									
Berno (909–927)	1	35 / 1.07 / 66.04 / 1.44	14 / 0.43 / 26.42 / 4.18	0 / 0.00 / 0.00 / 0.00	0 / 0.00 / 0.00 / 0.00	0 / 0.00 / 0.00 / 0.00	0 / 0.00 / 0.00 / 0.00	4 / 0.12 / 7.55 / 2.58	53 / 1.63
Odo (927–942)	2	120 / 3.68 / 74.53 / 4.95	29 / 0.89 / 18.01 / 8.66	0 / 0.00 / 0.00 / 0.00	1 / 0.03 / 0.62 / 20.00	0 / 0.00 / 0.00 / 0.00	10 / 0.31 / 6.21 / 4.85	1 / 0.03 / 0.62 / 0.65	161 / 4.94
Aymard (942–964)	3	429 / 13.17 / 69.08 / 17.69	83 / 2.55 / 13.37 / 24.78	5 / 0.15 / 0.81 / 17.86	2 / 0.06 / 0.32 / 40.00	31 / 0.95 / 4.99 / 30.10	44 / 1.35 / 7.09 / 21.36	27 / 0.83 / 4.35 / 17.42	621 / 19.07
Maiolus (964–994)	4	836 / 25.67 / 72.32 / 34.47	129 / 3.96 / 11.16 / 38.51	13 / 0.40 / 1.12 / 46.43	1 / 0.03 / 0.09 / 20.00	39 / 1.20 / 3.37 / 37.86	92 / 2.82 / 7.96 / 44.66	46 / 1.41 / 3.98 / 29.68	1156 / 35.49
Odilo (994–1049)	5	950 / 29.17 / 79.63 / 39.18	78 / 2.39 / 6.54 / 23.28	9 / 0.28 / 0.75 / 32.14	1 / 0.03 / 0.08 / 20.00	33 / 1.01 / 2.77 / 32.04	58 / 1.78 / 4.86 / 28.16	64 / 1.96 / 5.36 / 41.29	1193 / 36.63
Unknown (909–1049)	6	55 / 1.69 / 75.34 / 2.27	2 / 0.06 / 2.74 / 0.60	1 / 0.03 / 1.37 / 3.57	0 / 0.00 / 0.00 / 0.00	0 / 0.00 / 0.00 / 0.00	2 / 0.06 / 2.74 / 0.97	13 / 0.40 / 17.81 / 8.39	73 / 2.24
TOTAL		2425 / 74.46	335 / 10.29	28 / 0.86	5 / 0.15	103 / 3.16	206 / 6.32	155 / 4.76	3257 / 100.00

Illustration B.2

Appendix B, Illustration 2
Transactions Summarized by Charter

ABBOT

TABLE OF ABBOT BY TRANSFER

FREQUENCY PERCENT ROW PCT COL PCT	DONATION	EXCHANGE	LOAN	OTHER	PRECARIA	SALE	WERPITIO	TOTAL
1 Berno (909–927)	21 0.96 72.41 1.27	7 0.32 24.14 4.29	0 0.00 0.00 0.00	0 0.00 0.00 0.00	0 0.00 0.00 0.00	0 0.00 0.00 0.00	1 0.05 3.45 0.98	29 1.32
2 Odo (927–942)	82 3.73 77.36 4.97	15 0.68 14.15 9.20	0 0.00 0.00 0.00	1 0.05 0.94 20.00	0 0.00 0.00 0.00	7 0.32 6.60 3.65	1 0.05 0.94 0.98	106 4.82
3 Aymard (942–964)	272 12.38 70.47 16.47	42 1.91 10.88 25.77	5 0.23 1.30 18.52	2 0.09 0.52 40.00	13 0.59 3.37 22.81	36 1.64 9.33 18.75	16 0.73 4.15 15.69	386 17.57
4 Maiolus (964–994)	620 28.22 73.90 37.55	61 2.78 7.27 37.42	13 0.59 1.55 48.15	1 0.05 0.12 20.00	20 0.91 2.38 35.09	90 4.10 10.73 46.88	34 1.55 4.05 33.33	839 38.19
5 Odilo (994–1049)	613 27.90 78.29 37.13	37 1.68 4.73 22.70	8 0.36 1.02 29.63	1 0.05 0.13 20.00	24 1.09 3.07 42.11	57 2.59 7.28 29.69	43 1.96 5.49 42.16	783 35.64
6 Unknown (909–1049)	43 1.96 79.63 2.60	1 0.05 1.85 0.61	1 0.05 1.85 3.70	0 0.00 0.00 0.00	0 0.00 0.00 0.00	2 0.09 3.70 1.04	7 0.32 12.96 6.86	54 2.46
TOTAL	1651 75.15	163 7.42	27 1.23	5 0.23	57 2.59	192 8.74	102 4.64	2197 100.00

Illustration B.3.

SAS Job

```
1    DATA TEMP;
2     SET CLUNY.ONE;
3
4     if CHTRTYPE   ne  '011'   and
5        CHTRTYPE   ne  '111'   and
6        CHTRTYPE   ne  '211'         then delete;
7
8     if OUTCOME    ne  '1'     and
9        OUTCOME    ne  '2'           then delete;
10
11    if FSTDATE    ne    .     and
12      (FSTDATE    lt   909    or
13       FSTDATE    ge  1049)         then delete;
14
15
16
17
18    if FSTDATE    ge   909    and
19       FSTDATE    lt   927          then ABBOT = 1; * Berno;
20    else
21    if FSTDATE    ge   927    and
22       FSTDATE    lt   942          then ABBOT = 2; * Odo;
23    else
24    if FSTDATE    ge   942    and
25       FSTDATE    lt   964          then ABBOT = 3; * Aymard;
26    else
27    if FSTDATE    ge   964    and
28       FSTDATE    lt   994          then ABBOT = 4; * Maiolus;
29    else
30    if FSTDATE    ge   994    and
31       FSTDATE    lt  1049          then ABBOT = 5; * Odilo;
32    else
33    if FSTDATE    eq    .           then ABBOT = 6; * Unknown;
34    else                                 ABBOT = 7; * ???;
35
36    if ACTIVITY   eq  'C'     or
37       ACTIVITY   eq  'CO'    or
38       ACTIVITY   eq  'CU'    or
39       ACTIVITY   eq  'D'     or
40       ACTIVITY   eq  'DD'    or
41       ACTIVITY   eq  'DE'    or
42       ACTIVITY   eq  'DEU'   or
43       ACTIVITY   eq  'DR'    or
44       ACTIVITY   eq  'DRR'   or
45       ACTIVITY   eq  'DU'    or
46       ACTIVITY   eq  'R'     or
47       ACTIVITY   eq  'RD'    or
48       ACTIVITY   eq  'S'     or
49       ACTIVITY   eq  'T'     or
50       ACTIVITY   eq  'TU'          then TRANSFER = 'DONATION';
51    else
52    if ACTIVITY   eq  'CA'    or
```

Illustration B.3. (cont.)

```
53         ACTIVITY    eq  'DA'     or
54         ACTIVITY    eq  'DV'     or
55         ACTIVITY    eq  'RA'     or
56         ACTIVITY    eq  'TA'     or
57         ACTIVITY    eq  'V'      or
58         ACTIVITY    eq  'VDD'    or
59         ACTIVITY    eq  'VU'            then TRANSFER = 'SALE';
60    else
61    if ACTIVITY      eq  'CP'     or
62         ACTIVITY    eq  'DP'     or
63         ACTIVITY    eq  'DPE'    or
64         ACTIVITY    eq  'DPX'    or
65         ACTIVITY    eq  'XP'            then TRANSFER = 'PRECARIA';
66    else
67    if ACTIVITY      eq  'DAX'    or
68         ACTIVITY    eq  'DEX'    or
69         ACTIVITY    eq  'DUX'    or
70         ACTIVITY    eq  'DX'     or
71         ACTIVITY    eq  'X'      or
72         ACTIVITY    eq  'XU'            then TRANSFER = 'EXCHANGE';
73    else
74    if ACTIVITY      eq  'I'             then TRANSFER = 'LOAN';
75    else
76    if ACTIVITY      eq  'J'      or
77         ACTIVITY    eq  'JD'     or
78         ACTIVITY    eq  'JV'     or
79         ACTIVITY    eq  'W'      or
80         ACTIVITY    eq  'WA'     or
81         ACTIVITY    eq  'WD'     or
82         ACTIVITY    eq  'WDA'    or
83         ACTIVITY    eq  'WDX'    or
84         ACTIVITY    eq  'WU'     or
85         ACTIVITY    eq  'WUA'    or
86         ACTIVITY    eq  'WX'            then TRANSFER = 'WERPITIO';
87    else
88    if ACTIVITY      eq  'O'             then TRANSFER = 'OTHER';
89    else                                     TRANSFER = '?????';
90
91    keep  CHTRNUM
92
93          ABBOT
94          TRANSFER;
95    proc  SORT    data = TEMP;
96      by  TRANSFER
97          ABBOT
98          CHTRNUM
99          ;
100
101    proc  FREQ data = temp;
102      table    ABBOT * TRANSFER / missing;
103      title1   'Appendix B, Illustration 1';
104      title2   'Frequency of Transactions';
```

```
105
106
107
108     proc  SORT    data = TEMP;
109       by  TRANSFER
110           ABBOT
111           CHTRNUM
112             ;
113
114     data  TEMP2;
115       set TEMP;
116       by  TRANSFER
117           ABBOT
118           CHTRNUM
119             ;
120       if  first.CHTRNUM  then  output;
121
122     proc  FREQ    data = temp2;
123         table   ABBOT * TRANSFER;
124         title1  'Appendix B, Illustration 2';
125         title2  'Transactions Summarized by Charter';
```

TRANSFER, which is limited to charters concerned with gains and losses of land, "proprietary" churches, and partial churches; monasteries and churches in which reform is envisioned are *not* included, nor are confirmations; (3) transfers are created by grouping together a number of transactions; the key problem here is the "hybrid" transaction, for example, one that contains both the verb *dono* and the verb *accipio*, and might be interpreted either as a donation or a sale. I have here rather arbitrarily designated this particular sort of hybrid transaction (ACTIVITY = DA) as a SALE. In the instance of PRECARIA I include all charters involving the transfer of a piece of land for a specified length of time. This is true even if the charter concerns land given out *ad medium plantum* (coded as ACTIVITY = DPE); or if it involves an exchange, but one in which the land is to be in the hands of the recipient for his or her lifetime (or some other specified time [coded XP]). However, in Chapter 3, in order to discuss exchanges more fully, I have included ACTIVITY = XP transactions among exchanges.

Eve's Marriages and Children

THE QUESTION of Eve's family is extremely problematic, and I present my conclusions simply as my best guess. To summarize briefly, the evidence suggests the following: Eve was first married to a man named Milo, who died at some time between 997 and 1026. Thereafter, she married a man named Witbert and called as her own at least some of his sons, namely Hugo, Jocerannus, Wichard, and possibly Gislebertus and Leotard.[1] Witbert died before 1031/39.[2] Eve next married a man named Gauzfred, probably the former husband of her sister Adelaida.[3] Gauzfred and Adelaida had had two sons, Girbaldus and Rotbert.[4] Eve and

1. BB 2090;III:283–84. This is dated with great certainty to the period 1031–48 by Hillebrandt, "Datierungen" on the basis of the roster of names of representatives of Cluny recorded as present in the charter. But BB 2911 (Chaume, "Obs.," 1039) has Eve married to Gauzfred, who consents to the donation. In BB 2090, Eve does not appear with a husband. This suggests that BB 2090 may be dated 1031–39. Here Eve's children are given as: Wichardus, Hugo, Jocerannus, G—— and Z——. This version represents, however, the copy by Lambert de Barive of the (presumably) original charter. Cartulary B, which also contains a copy of the charter, gives L—— as the last initial. For at least two reasons, cartulary B appears to give the better reading: first, it adds the name of Wichardus to the signatories of the charter, and second, it supplies many words and phrases missing from the original when Lambert de Barive made his copy. I propose to follow cartulary B and surmise that the two children represented by the initials are G[islebertus] (who figures in the witness list among the list of "seculars") and L[eotard] (using the initial in the redaction of cartulary B).

2. I.e, before the time of BB 2090. But, of course, this is an argument from silence. The name of Eve's husband may have been omitted because the land in question had nothing to do with him.

3. Gauzfred appears as her husband in BB 2911;IV:111–12 (1039), BB 603;I:566–67 (dated by me after 1031–39, i.e., after BB 2090 and with BB 2911). Hillebrandt, in "Datierungen," suggests that BB 603 should be dated before c. 1031.

4. BB 2678;III:707–8; see above, Chapter 2, n. 9.

Genealogy C.1. The family of Eve

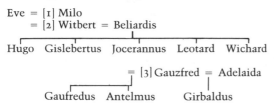

Gauzfred then had two sons together, Gaufredus and Antelmus. Sometime after 1031/39, Eve appeared with her husband, Gauzfred, and six sons: Girbaldus, Wichard, Hugo, Jocerannus, Gaufredus, and Antelmus.[5]

The argument that leads to these conclusions is as follows: Sometime between 997 and 1026, Eve gave a mansus and serfs in the villa "Jugis" (n. id) to God and Peter and Paul "for the salvation of the soul of my husband [*senior*] Milo, and my own."[6] Present at the donation were Witbert, Gislebertus, Arembert, Albuinus, Arleus, and Bernardus. Arleus and Bernardus were brothers (see Appendix D and Chapter 2), part of an important landowning family with close connections to Cluny. Witbert, whom I take to be the man who was soon to become Eve's husband, was already the stepfather of Gislebertus and Arembert and of two others, Ornadus and Bernard, besides; the argument for this depends on the following:

In the 990s, four brothers, Arembert, Gislebertus, Ornadus,

---

5. BB 603;I:566–67. The subscriptio (as recorded in cartulary A) reads: "S. Gaufredi, qui istum scamium fecit et ipse firmavit, et alios firmari rogavit. S. Eve, uxoris sue, et Girbaldi, filii sui. S. Vuicardi, filii sui. S. Hugonis, filii sui. S. Jotseranni, filii sui. S. Gaufredi, filii sui. S. Antelmi, filii sui. S. Gauzberti. S. Bernardi, fratris ipsius Gaufredi." I interpret this grouping to refer to "sets" of sons: Girbaldus (who was already alive when Gauzfred was married to Adelaida); Wichard, Hugo, and Jocerannus (who had been the sons of Witbert); and Gaufredus and Antelmus, placed together on the list as the sons of Gauzfred and Eve. I want to thank Constance Bouchard for help in deciphering the relationships here.

6. BB 2477;III:555. The charter must be dated during the reign of King Robert, or 997–1026. Chaume proposes 997 or 1003 on the basis of an identification of the Ava of this charter with the Ava in BB 2331;III:448–49 and BB 2625; III:669, an identification I find unconvincing. It must be noted, however, that it is upon a preponderance of circumstantial evidence—namely the witness list —that I base my own identification of the Ava of this charter with Eve, sister of Antelmus.

Genealogy C.2. The family of Beliardis

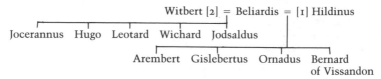

and Bernard of Vissandon, gave land to Cluny at Vetus Canava (near La Chaume) and at Château (both ca. Cluny).[7] They were the sons of a man named Hildinus and a woman named Beliardis.[8] In 995 or shortly thereafter, Witbert married Beliardis.[9]

Witbert had at least two sons with Beliardis, named Wichard and Jodsaldus, and probably three others, Jocerannus, Hugo, and Leotard.[10] On behalf of Witbert's soul, Beliardis and two of her

7. BB 3152;IV:312 = BB 311;I:307. The discussion of the brothers here and in Chapter 2 is based on ten charters. Those that are dated are BB 1639;II:674–75 (12.983), BB 2404;III:496 (997–98), and BB 1812;III:62–63 (989–90, but where the identity of the Witbertus may not be the same as "our" Witbert). There is also a charter in which Witbert was present as a witness for Eve, BB 2477;III:555 (998–1026). The undated charters are BB 320;I:313–14, BB 2209;III:355–56, BB 932;II:40–41, BB 2521;III:594–95, and BB 3152 = BB 311.

8. Hildinus is mentioned as the father of Ornadus, Gislebertus, Arembert, Bernard, and possibly others in connection with land at Ruffey in BB 1835;III:79, dated by BB c. 990 and redated by Chaume, "Obs.," c. 994, on the basis of its rapprochement with BB 2261;III:392, BB 2296;III:422–23 and BB 2686;III: 715–16. But Chaume is incorrect to say that the monk Dacfredus, who appears in BB 1835, ceases to appear in charters after 994. Hillebrandt, "Datierungen," dates his last appearance at 1004. Beliardis appears in BB 2293;III:420 (4.995). Here she, with the consent of her sons Ornadus, Gislebertus, Arembert, and Bernard, gives to Cluny some of her property in villa Vetus Canevas (= Vetus Canava) in the ager of Rufiaco (= Ruffey). BB 1835 refers to an exchange, in BB 667;I:620–21 (3.945), that concerned land at Ruffey and at Vetus Canava. The inescapable conclusion is that Beliardis and Hildinus had been married and had at least these four sons.

9. See BB 2296;III:422–23 (4.995). Here Ornadus, identified now as subdeaconus, and his brother Gislebertus appear in a charter along with (as witnesses) Arembert, Bernard, and Witbert. This charter also includes a Heldinus on the witness list. Thus, it is possible that Hildinus, father of the brothers, and Witbert, later to be the husband of Beliardis, are here represented. But, if order is important, it is odd that Heldinus's name is quite far down on the list, while Witbert's is close to Arembert and Barnard. The solution may be to regard the Heldinus here as the *nephew* of the four brothers: in BB 2324;III:443–44 (Chaume, "Obs.," 996–1013), Ornadus and his brothers name Hildinus and Icbertus their *nepotes*. Here, too, they mention that they have a sister named Eve.

10. Beliardis identifies Witbert as her husband and the father of Wichard and Jodsaldus in BB 320;I:313–14 (wrongly placed in Odo's abbacy; see Chaume "En Marge 2," p. 51 n. 7; perhaps c. 1000) and as the father of Wichard in BB 2209; III:355–56 (993–1048). In BB 320 she gives to Cluny land that came to her from

sons, Wichard and Jodsaldus, gave land to Cluny from Beliardis's paternal inheritance at villa "Canavas" (near La Vineuse). Two of Beliardis's sons, Arembert and Gislebertus, were present for the occasion. At another time, again on behalf of Witbert's soul, she gave to God, Saint Peter, and the monks at Cluny two mansi at "Vissandon" and a mansus at Buffières.[11] At the same time, she placated her son, Wichard, who made claim to this land, by giving him "in exchange" a mansus at "Vetus Curtis" (near Ravry). Beliardis's sons, Bernard and Hugo, were present at this transaction. About the year 1000, Witbert and his sons Hugo,

---

her father at villa Canavas on behalf of Witbert's soul. Since Witbert is not in the witness list, it is possible that he has died (this is Chaume's interpretation). But if so, we would have great difficulty in understanding how Eve came to name as her children sons who apparently were the sons of Witbert. There are many instances, however, when land is donated pro anima of a living person. A good example is BB 798;I:750, dated quite certainly January 951, where four brothers give the church of Saint Saturninus and much property to Cluny for the remedy of the souls of their mother and father, neither of whom was recorded as present. Yet in BB 802;I:754–56, dated quite certainly in March of the same year, the mother and father themselves give a donation.

That the Beliardis of BB 320 is the same as the Beliardis, mother of Gislebertus and Arembert, etc., is shown by the fact that these two figure in the witness list of BB 320. That the Witbert, husband of Beliardis, is the same Witbert who is the father or stepfather of Hugo, Bernard (of Vissandon), and Jocerannus, is shown by the presence of Hugo and Bernard in the witness list of BB 2209. In BB 2209 Beliardis gives Cluny land at Vissandon, which she says is from her paternal inheritance: "aliquid de mea hereditate quae mihi jure paterno evenit; et est sita in villa Vissando, scilicet duos mansos cum omnibus eisdem pertinentibus." It is likely that the Bernard who witnesses this is her son and that he is later known as Bernard of Vissandon. Chaume dated the charters of Bernard of Vissandon about 1070 on the basis of the appearance of that name on the witness list of a charter from that year (BB 3428;IV:539–40). Thus he redated to the last half of the eleventh century numerous charters that ought better to be grouped c. 1000, such as BB 3198;IV:339, BB 3151;IV:311–12, BB 583;I:556–57, BB 2098;III:291, BB 2521;III:594–95, none of which is dated by the scribe. In this I follow the suggestions in Hillebrandt, "Datierungen," where the range of dates c. 997–c. 1036/1039 is given for BB 583. The place Vissandon appears in the charters of Cluny for the most part between the years 960 and 990, rather than in the eleventh century. See BB 614;I:572–73, BB 932;II:40–41, BB 1083;II:176–77, BB 1289;II:366–67, BB 1951;III:168–69, BB 2209;III:355–56, BB 2235;III:371–72, BB 2392;III: 488. It is just possible for Bernard of Vissandon to have been born c. 980 and still to serve as a witness for a charter in 1070. Déléage, p. 455 n. 6, discusses Beliardis and her children and concludes that one of them is Bernard of Vissandon. However, it is probably more likely, as Constance Bouchard has suggested to me, that there were two Bernards of Vissandon, one living c. 1000 and the other c. 1070. Certainly Bernard is a common enough name to make this more than possible.

11. BB 320;I:313–14. We know that Beliardis had land at Vetus Canava; it is possible that "villa Canavas" is a scribal error for this place. In any event, the two locations were extremely close.

Gislebertus, Bernard, Jocerannus, and Leotard gave to Cluny some of their inheritance at Sainte-Cécile-la-Valouse, at Corchevet, and at Massilly (all ca. Cluny).[12] Arembert was present as a witness when the charter was drawn up. In a second charter, Witbert, who was described as very ill but who must have recovered if the interpretation of events here is correct, gave another donation to Cluny.[13] This time the gift consisted of a mansus at Ciergues and a vineyard at Vissandon, where (we know) Beliardis, too, had an inheritance. The children who were present at this transaction were Hugo, Gislebertus, Bernard, and Jocerannus. Also present as a witness was their brother Wichard.

It seems clear that sons got grouped in different ways in different transactions, depending in part upon the land involved. This helps to explain why, when Eve made a donation for the soul of Milo, only two of Witbert's stepsons—Gislebertus and Arembert—were present.[14] When Eve quit her claim to Fontana, at least three and possibly five of these sons were involved in the transaction: Wichard, Hugo, Jocerannus, G[islebertus] and L[eotard].[15]

It may be noted that the families of Witbert and his first wife, Beliardis, intersected with the family of Antelmus at several places before Witbert and Eve's marriage: at Vissandon, Ciergues, Sainte-Cécile, Buffières, and "Grandmont" (see Map 2). It

12. BB 2521;III:594–95. This is dated in BB (probably because of its similarity to BB 932;II:40–41, which was in the cartulary of Maiolus in cartulary A) c. 1000. BB 2521 was copied both by Lambert de Barive and by the redactors of cartulary B, who put it in the abbacy of Hugh. Chaume dates it c. 1050–60 because he identifies the Bernard, son of Witbert, as Bernard of Vissandon.

13. BB 932;II:40–41: Witbert is "in maxima infirmitate positus." This charter is dated in the time of Maiolus (954–94) by BB; Chaume, "Obs.," redates it to c. 1060, again because of the presence of Bernard of Vissandon.

14. There is still the difficulty of whether the Eve who donated the villa Jugis on behalf of Milo is the Eve who was the sister of Antelmus. In BB 2351;III:461, Milo is one of the witnesses, alongside Antelmus, for the donation of land at Lournand to Cluny. The two may be read together as a group, since preceding them on the list are Oddo, the donor, followed by the Grossi brothers: Maiolus, Israel, Bernard, and Bernard's wife, Emma. Milo and Antelmus form the next group along with Aydoard, who is probably Milo's brother. In BB 1933;III:151–52 (992–93) we find Engela, mother of Achinus, Aydoard, Wido, Milo, Sivuald, and Bernard. And in BB 2428;III:516–17 (uncertain date between 997 and 1031 [the reign of King Robert]; Chaume, "Obs.," suggests 996–1015), Eve appears as the wife of Milo; here she and Wido (Milo's brother) gave land "pro salute animae memorati Milonis."

15. BB 2090; see Chapter 2 on this quitclaim.

is also clear that Witbert was associated with the same neighborhood family, the Grossi, as Antelmus. The Grossi, then, form
a sort of bond or liaison between Antelmus's group and Witbert's group; if there is a family connection, it is possibly
through Beliardis, the *soror mea* of Oddo.[16] This may help to
explain how the two families appear "merged" by the 1030s.[17]

16. BB 350;I:330–31; and see Appendix D. Note that in BB 2406;III:497–98,
Oddo appears on the witness list with Milo, miles. This is probably the same
Milo as Eve's second husband.

17. There remains the problem that in no charter do we find Witbert and Eve
identified as husband and wife. Is it possible that Eve and Witbert were never
married but rather that Eve took on "his" children as her own because of the
associations of their respective families? The charters reveal a network of social
relations so close that they may perhaps only be explained by Duby's hypothesis
(in "Lignage, noblesse et chevalerie," in *Hommes et structures*, p. 405) of six
ancestral progenitors for 80 percent of the upper class in the Mâconnais c. 1100.
Whether family or neighbor (and, if Duby is correct, this was much the same
thing), these groups were intimately involved with one another.

APPENDIX D

The Family of Arleus

THE GENEALOGIES for Arleus (discussed in Chapter 2) were constructed from the following evidence. A charter of 980 concerns
Oda and her husband, Dado.[1] On the witness list are (among
others) an Arleus who consents, and Sevuinus (= Siguinus). This
allows us to group this charter with another charter where Oda,
her son Upertus, his sister Aia, and his nephews (or in the more
likely interpretation, her nephews) Arleus and Siguinus are involved.[2] Thus Oda was either of the generation of Arleus's
father, or of his grandfather. She may be found in a charter from
962 along with an "Arleus qui consensit" and (her husband)
Dado.[3] Oda's daughter Aia appeared in 963 along with the *ele-
mosinarii* Sendelemus, Dado, Arleus, Engelemus (= Ingelelmus),
and Teutbertus.[4] That same year, Dado and Oda appeared again
with Arleus.[5]

Ingelelmus, his wife, Emma, and his sons Arleus and Bernardus appear together in a charter from about the year 1000 along
with Arleus *consanguineus*.[6] Two of Arleus's other brothers and
his sister are mentioned in a charter from 990–91: Ornadus,
presbyter; Achard (who, elsewhere, is termed *clericus*; and

1. BB 1522;II:571–72 (980), concerned with Flagy.
2. BB 155;I:156–57 (Chaume, "Obs." c. 980), concerned with Flagy.
3. BB 1135;II:225–26 (8.962), concerned with Merzé.
4. BB 1157;II:246–47 (5.963), concerned with Varanges and "Mailly" (l.-disp.,
near Carrière des Moines).
5. BB 1158;II:247–48 (5.963), concerned with Massilly.
6. BB 2338;III:453–54 (Chaume, "Obs.," 996–1007, because that latter date
reflects the last dated charter in which Ingelelmus is found), concerned with
Flagy.

[226]

Teza.[7] Siguinus is identified as Achard's brother in another charter from the 990s.[8] In another, possibly later, document, Gaufredus, Wichard, and Achard are identified as brothers.[9] Elsewhere Achard is called *de Marziaco* (= Merzé); his wife is Emeldis; his sons, Gausfred, Jocerannus, and Otto; and his daughter, Rocelina, who is married to Hugo Burdinus.[10] Achard was also married to a woman named Tetsa (but the order of his marriages, the one to Tetsa, the other to Emeldis, is unclear); she gave land at Flagy and Massilly to Cluny on behalf of his soul.[11] Her brother Gilinus witnessed.

The wife of Siguinus was Alexandra, and his children were Soffredus, Wichardus, Gauzerannus, Lambert, and Simphorianus.[12] Soffredus's wife was Ingeltix, and his children were Ildinus and Leotaldus.[13]

The connection between this group and the group represented by Maiolus, Israel, and Bernard is clear, since Arleus called Gauzerannus of Uxelles his *senior*. That connection may account for the similar names that appear in the two families. The name

7. BB 1865;III:100−101 (990−91), concerned with Flagy. For Achard as clericus, see BB 2140;III:320.

8. BB 2290;III:417−18 (3.995), concerned with Flagy and Massilly.

9. BB 3155;IV:313−14 (?1049−1109), concerned with *Cavaniacus* (probably Chevagny-sur-Guye, ca. la Guiche), and BB 3255;IV:371 (?1049−1109: also concerned with *Cavaniacus*, and giving the name of their mother, Emma); see also BB 2867;IV:64−65 (1031−48; narrowed by Chaume, "Obs.," c. 1040−45 [= BB 2022;III:233]); concerned with Varanges, Merzé, and Tillouzot, ca. Flagy and Massilly. There is clearly a problem with dates, and three possible solutions: (1) Arleus, son of Ingelelmus, lived a very long time (witnessing charters from the 960s to 1049 or thereafter); (2) the Arleus who appears in the documents from the 960s is an earlier member of the family with the same name; or (3) the charters placed in the cartulary of Saint Hugh (1049−1109) must be dated back to the abbacy of Odilo (994−1049). These are not mutually exclusive alternatives, but I think the evidence supports a date before 1049 for BB 3155 and BB 3255.

10. BB 3290;IV:390−91 (?1049−1109), very possibly belonging to Odilo's abbacy; concerned with Merzé. See also BB 2036;III:243.

11. BB 173;I:165−66 (probably 990−91). The document is in cartulary A under the abbacy of Berno, but this is clearly incorrect, as Chaume already observed in "En Marge 1," p. 44 n. 4.

12. BB 2427;III:515−16 (997−1031, the reign of Robert; narrowed by Chaume, "Obs.," to 997−1020 on the basis of the activities of Siguinus), concerned with Merzé; BB 2120;III:305−6 (Chaume, "Obs.," 1022−30), concerned with Flagy. For a donation by Lambert of land not at Flagy, see BB 1804;III:56−57 (5.989). Lambert's death is the occasion of BB 2120.

13. BB 2647;III:685 (8.1007), no villa named. Soffredus is called the *consobrinus* (son of a brother) of Achard in BB 2036;III:243.

Tetsa, Achard's wife, is also the name of his sister (here, to make the distinction plain, spelled Teza); and it is in addition the name of the daughter of Oddo, for whom see Chapter 2, n. 26. If this Oddo is the same as the Oddo who is the brother of Beliardis (see Appendix C), then we can understand why Beliardis, too, had a son named Ornadus, who became, like Ornadus, presbyter, a clericus. There is circumstantial evidence: Achard, clericus, is a witness at the werpitio of Oddo and his sister Beliardis; and the sons of Beliardis, Ornadus and Arembert, are present along with Arleus (it is unclear which one) and Ildinus when Anselardus gives a donation of land at "Dariaco" (near Merzé) and at Cotte.[14] Eve, mother of the "second" Arleus, gave the other half of the land at Cotte in 1005–6.[15] Present here were Arleus, Wichard, clericus (= the son of Siguinus), and Eldinus (= Ildinus).

14. BB 2343;III:456–57 (Chaume, "Obs.," c. 1000).
15. BB 2625;III:669.

Transactions at La Chize

SOME OF THE charters relating to La Chize (see Chapter 3) can be dated only approximately. They have been rather arbitrarily assigned to a decade here. The charters that concern Cluny and La Chize are, by decade, 940–49: BB 615;I:573–74 (942–54), BB 571;I:550–51 (942–54), BB 636;I:593 (943), BB 638;I:594–95 (943), BB 645;I:600–601 (943) (five total); 950–59: BB 760;I:716–17 (950), BB 1072;II:166–67 (959–60) (two total); 960–69: BB 935;II:42–43 (954–78), BB 1117;II:208–9 (961–62), BB 1190;II:274–75 (965–66), BB 1203;II:286 (966), BB 1259;II:341–42 (969), BB 1260;II:342 (969) (six total); 970–79; BB 1361;II:429–30 (974), BB 1453;II:508 (978), BB 1485;II:538 (979), BB 1486;II:539 (979), BB 1487;II:540 (979), BB 1489;II:541 (979) (six total); 980–89: BB 1545;II:593–94 (980), BB 1554;II:601–2 (981), BB 1625; II:662 (982–83), BB 1724;II:747 (986–87), BB 1769;III:29–30 (Chaume, "Obs.," 987–95) (five total); 990–99: BB 131;I:141–42 (Hillebrandt, "Datierungen," 985–1000 or somewhat later), BB 3283;III:387–88 (Hillebrandt, "Datierungen," 985–1000 or somewhat later), BB 1767;III:28 (987–96), BB 1855;III:95 (990–91); BB 1930;III:149 (992–93), BB 1936;III:153 (992–93), BB 1967; III:185 (993–94), BB 133;I:142–43 (dated by the present author c. 990–96),[1] BB 1954;III:171 (Chaume, "Obs.," 994–96),

1. The date 910–27, assigned to BB 133, because cartulary A placed it in the abbacy of Berno, was already challenged by Chaume in "En Marge 1," p. 44 n. 3. The document involves in part a donation by Petrus and his wife, Vualetrudis, of land at La Chize that bordered on the property of Odile and Odile's sons. In BB 1954 (Chaume, "Obs.," 994–96), Odile is found with her son Malguinus giving land at La Chize. In BB 1767 (987–96), Malguinus (Malvinus) and his brother

BB 345; 1:327–28 (dated c. 995 by Chaume in unpublished marginal notes), BB 2295;III:422 (995), BB 307;I:304–5 (Chaume, "Obs.," c. 995), BB 2433;III:519–20 (Chaume, "Obs.," c. 998) (thirteen total); 1000–1009: BB 2134;III:315 (Chaume, "Obs.," 994–1008), BB 2339;III:454 (Chaume, "Obs.," c. 996–1008), BB 2503;III:581 dated by the present author c. 975–87),[2] BB 2081; III:276–77 (Chaume, "Obs.," 1000–1010), BB 2662;III:696 (1008) (five total); 1010–19: BB 2320;III:441 (Chaume, "Obs.," 1005–20), BB 2183;III:341 (Chaume, "Obs.," 1005–20), BB 2706;III:729 (1016), BB 2124;III:308–9 (Chaume, "Obs.," c. 1019) (four total); 1020–29: BB 2019;III:230 (Chaume, "Obs.," c. 1020); BB 2739; III:763–64 (c. 1020), BB 2810;IV:13 (1028–29) (three total). There are also six charters for La Chize in the archives of Cluny that do not directly concern the monastery: BB 186;I:173–74 (911), BB 200;I:187–88 (916), BB 620;I:577 (943), BB 1234;II:324 (968), BB 2421;III:510–11 (996–1005), BB 2417;III:507 (Chaume, "Obs.," 1000–20).

Bernard are involved in an exchange of land with Cluny at La Chize. It seems reasonable to assign a date of about the first half of the 990s to BB 133.

2. In BB 2503, both the place and date are in question. Déléage, pp. 1050–51, and Chaume, *Origines* II/3:1103, have extensive lists for charters involving La Chize, but BB 2503, is not on either list. It involves the sale or donation of a *curtilis in Sed* by Beliardis and her son Gausfredus. The land borders on terra Rotberti and terra Ranaldi. Rotbert and Ranald were sons of David, presbyter, who was involved in many charters at La Chize from the late 960s to the 980s: BB 935;II:42–43, BB 1234;II:324 (2.968), BB 1260;II:342 (5.969), BB 1453;II:508 (11.978), BB 1486;II:539 (5.979), BB 1487;II:540 (5.979), BB 1724;II:747–48 (986–87). Ranald was the principal in BB 1769;III:29–30 (987–96). It seems likely, therefore, that Sed = Segia = La Chize. If Chaume, "Obs.," is correct in thinking that the absence of Rotbert in BB 1453 (dated with certainty at 11.978) puts the terminus ad quem for charter BB 935 (which *does* mention Rotbert) at 978, then the same should be true for BB 2503 (see Chaume, "Obs.," for BB 935). But the absence of Rotbert seems a fairly weak argument. In any event, the date c. 1000 proposed by BB for BB 2503 should be made earlier, perhaps c. 975–87.

Charters Redated in the Text

THE DATE changes here concern only the charters used in the text. They were suggested by grouping charters by place and by using the index of lemmatized names (for which see the Introduction above). The reader who is interested in further date changes should consult Maria Hillebrandt's forthcoming study.

Charter no.	Proposed date	Reference
BB 133;I:165–66	c. 990–96	Appendix E, n. 1
BB 173;I:165–66	c. 990–91	Chap. 2, n. 60
BB 232;I:222–23	c. 940	Chap. 5, n. 114
BB 298;I:299	c. 1000–1010	Chap. 3, n. 23
BB 299;I:300	c. 1000–1010	Chap. 3, n. 23
BB 311;I:307	c. 990–1013	Chap. 2, n. 36
BB 320;I:313–14	c. 1000	Appendix C, n. 10
BB 340;I:325	c. 990	Chap. 3, n. 23
BB 367;I:345–46	954–94	Chap. 5, n. 128
BB 603;I:566–67	after 1031–39	Appendix C, n. 3
BB 924;II:35	c. 1013	Chap. 2, n. 49
BB 942;II:47–48	6.980	Chap. 4, n. 37
BB 1164;II:251–52	3.954	Chap. 5, n. 142
BB 2098;III:291	c. 1000	Appendix C, n. 10
BB 2114;III:301	c. 1000	Chap. 3, n. 23
BB 2135;III:315–17	3.999	Chap. 5, n. 68
BB 2282;III:411–12	994–98	Table 9, n. 21
BB 2408;III:499–500	before 4.998	Table 9, n. 10
BB 2413;III:504	c. 1000	Chap. 5, n. 29
BB 2477;III:555	1013–26	Chap. 2, n. 39
BB 2503;III:581	c. 975–87	Appendix E, n. 2
BB 2521;III:594–95	c. 1000	Appendix C, n. 10
BB 3151;IV:311–12	c. 1000	Appendix C, n. 10
BB 3152;IV:312	c. 990–1013	Chap. 2, n. 36
BB 3155;IV:313–14	before 1049	Appendix D, n. 9
BB 3198;IV:339	c. 1000	Appendix C, n. 10
BB 3255;IV:371	before 1049	Appendix D, n. 9
BB 3290;IV:390–91	before 1049	Appendix D, n. 10

Select Bibliography

Manuscript Sources

Paris, Bibliothèque nationale
    Nouv. acq. lat. 1497 = cartulary A
    Nouv. acq. lat. 1498 = cartulary B
    Nouv. acq. lat. 2262 = cartulary C
    Nouv. acq. lat. 766 = cartulary D
    Coll. Bourg. 76 (original charters of the 9th–10 c.)
    Fonds lat. 17715 (original charters of the 9th–10th c.)
    Nouv. acq. lat. 2154 (original charters of the 10th–11th c.)

Printed Sources

Ademar of Chabannes. *Chronicon*. Edited by Jules Chavanon. Paris: Picard, 1897.

Annales Bertiniani. Edited by Felix Grat, Jeanne Vielliard, and Suzanne Clémencet. Paris: Klincksieck, 1964.

Annales Vedastini. MGH, SS, 2:196-209.

Athanasius. *Vita S. Antonii*. In *PG* 26:838–976. In English, *The Life of Saint Antony*. Translated by Robert T. Meyer. New York: Newman Press, 1950.

Augustine. *Civitas dei*. Corpus Christianorum. Series Latina, 47–48. Turnhout: Brepols, 1955.

Bibliotheca Cluniacensis. Edited by Martin Marrier and André Quercetanus [Duchêne]. R. Fovet, 1614. Reprint. Mâcon: Protat, 1915.

Bullarium sacri ordinis cluniacensis. Edited by Pierre Symon. Lyon: Jullieron, 1680.

Cartulaire de l'abbaye de Conques en Rouergue. Edited by Gustave Desjardins. Paris: Picard, 1879.

Cartulaire de l'abbaye de Lerins. Edited by Henri Moris and Edmond Blanc. 2 vols. Paris: H. Champion, 1883.

Cartulaire de l'abbaye de Saint-Chaffre du Monastier. Edited by Ulysse Chevalier. Paris: Picard, 1884.

Cartulaire de Brioude. Edited by Henri Doniol. Clermont-Ferrand: Thibaud, 1861.

Cartulaire de Romainmôtier. Edited by Frédéric Charles de Gingins-La-Sarra. Mémoires et Documents, Société de la Suisse Romande, 1st ser., vol. 3. Lausanne: Ducloux, 1844.

Cartulaire de Saint-Jean d'Angély. Edited by Georges Musset. Archives Historiques de La Saintonge et de L'Aunis 30 and 33. 2 vols. Paris: Picard, 1901–3.

Cartulaire de Saint-Vincent de Mâcon. Edited by M.-C. Ragut. Mâcon: Protat, 1864.

Cartulaire de Sauxillanges. Edited by Henri Doniol. Clermont-Ferrand: Thibaud, 1864.

Cartulaire du prieuré de Paray-le-Monial. Edited by Ulysse Chevalier. Paris: Picard, 1890.

Cartulaire du prieuré de Saint-Flour. Edited by Marcellin Boudet. Monaco: Imprimerie de Monaco, 1910.

Chronicon Sancti Petri Vivi Senonensis. In *Chronique de Saint-Pierre-le-Vif de Sens, dite de Clarius.* Edited by Robert-Henri Bautier and Monique Gilles. Paris: CNRS, 1979.

Codex Laureshamensis. Edited by Karl Glöckner. 3 vols. 1929–36. Reprint. Darmstadt: Hessische historische Kommission, 1975.

Corpus consuetudinum monasticarum. Edited by Kassius Hallinger. 10 vols. Siegburg: Schmitt, 1963–83.

Flodoard. *Annales.* In *Les Annales de Flodoard.* Edited by Philippe Lauer. Paris: Picard, 1905.

Gallia Christiana. 16 vols. Paris, 1715–1865.

Glaber, Raoul. *Historiarum libri quinque.* Edited by Maurice Prou. Paris: Picard, 1886.

Grand cartulaire du Chapitre Saint-Julien de Brioude: Essai de restitution. Edited by Anne M. Baudot and Marcel Baudot. Clermont-Ferrand: Imprimerie générale, 1935.

Jotsaldus. *Vita Odilonis.* PL 142:897–940.

Liudprand. *Antapodosis.* In *Die Werke Liudprands von Cremona.* Edited by Joseph Becker. 3d ed. 1915. Reprint. Hannover: Hahnsche Buchhandlung, 1977.

Monumenta Vizeliacensia: Textes relatifs à l'histoire de l'abbaye de Vézelay. Edited by R. B. Huygens. Corpus Christianorum. Continuatio Mediaevalis 42. Turnhout: Brepols, 1976.

Odilo. *Epistolae.* PL 142:939–43.

Odo of Cluny. *De vita Sancti Geraldi.* PL 133:639–710.

Orderic Vitalis. *Historia ecclesiastica.* In *The Ecclesiastical History of*

234 | Select Bibliography

Orderic Vitalis. Edited and translated by Marjorie Chibnall. 6 vols. Oxford: Clarendon Press, 1969–80.

Papsturkunden, 896–1046. Edited by Harald Zimmermann. Österreichische Akademie der Wissenschaften, Denkschriften 174. 2 vols. Vienna, 1984.

Patrologiae cursus completus: Series latina. Edited by Jacques-Paul Migne. Paris, 1844–88.

Quellen und Forschungen zum Urkunden-und Kanzleiwesen Papst Gregors VII. Edited by Leo Santifaller. Pt. 1. Studi e testi 190. Vatican: Biblioteca Apostolica Vaticana, 1957.

Recueil des actes de Lothaire et de Louis V, rois de France (954–987). Edited by Louis Halphen and Ferdinand Lot. Paris: Klincksieck, 1908.

Recueil des actes de Louis IV, roi de France (936–954). Edited by Philippe Lauer. Paris: Imprimerie nationale, 1914.

Recueil des actes de Robert Ier et de Raoul, rois de France (922–936). Edited by Jean Dufour and Robert-Henri Bautier. Paris: Klincksieck, 1978.

Recueil des actes des rois de Provence (855–928). Edited by René Poupardin. Paris: Imprimerie nationale, 1920.

Recueil des chartes de l'abbaye de Cluny. Edited by Auguste Bernard and Alexandre Bruel. 6 vols. Paris: Imprimerie nationale, 1876–1903.

Regesta Pontificum Romanorum ab condita ecclesia ad annum post Christum natum MCXCVIII. Edited by Philippe Jaffé with Samuel Loewenfeld. 2d ed. by William Wattenbach. 2 vols. Leipzig: Veit, 1885–88.

Traditiones Wizenburgenses: Die Urkunden des Kosters Weissenburg, 661–864. Edited by Karl Glöckner and Anton Doll. Darmstadt: Hessische Historische Kommission, 1979.

Ulrich. *Antiquiores consuetudines cluniacensis monasteria.* PL 149: 639–778.

Die Urkunden der Burgundischen Rudolfinger (888–1032). Edited by Theodor Schieffer and Hans Eberhard Mayer. MGH, Diplomata et acta. Regum Burgundiae e stirpe Rudolfina. Munich: MGH, 1977.

Modern Sources

Where several papers or articles from a collection have been consulted, the individual articles are cited in the footnotes while the collection as a whole is cited here.

Appadurai, Arjun, ed. *The Social Life of Things: Commodities in Cultural Perspective.* Cambridge: Cambridge University Press, 1986.

Ariès, Philippe, and Georges Duby, eds. *Histoire de la vie privée.* Vol. 2: *De l'Europe féodale à la Renaissance.* Paris: Seuil, 1985.

Autenrieth, Johanne, Dieter Geuenich, and Karl Schmid, eds. *Das Verbrüderungsbuch der Abtei Reichenau (Einleitung, Register, Faksimile)*. MGH. Libri Memoriales et Necrologia, n.s. 1. Hanover: Hahnsche Buchhandlung, 1979.

Bachrach, Bernard S. "Toward a Reappraisal of William the Great, Duke of Aquitane (995–1030)." *Journal of Medieval History* 5 (1979): 11–21.

Baluze, Etienne. *Histoire généalogique de la maison d'Auvergne*. 2 vols. Paris: Dezallier, 1708.

Bange, François. "L'*ager* et la *villa*: Structures du paysage et du peuplement dans la région mâconnaise à la fin du haut moyen âge (IXe–XIe siècles)." *Annales: ESC* 39 (1984): 529–69.

Barraclough, Geoffrey, ed. *The Times Atlas of World History*. London: Times Books, 1978.

Barruol, Jean. "L'influence de St. Mayeul et de sa famille dans la renaissance méridionale du XIe siècle d'après une documentation nouvelle du Cartulaire d'Apt." In *Cartulaire de l'église d'Apt (835–1130?)*, edited by Noël Didier, pp. 67–86. Paris: Dalloz, 1967.

Berlow, Rosalind Kent. "Spiritual Immunity at Vézelay (Ninth to Twelfth Centuries)." *Catholic Historical Review* 62 (1976): 573–88.

Berman, Constance Hoffman. *Medieval Agriculture, the Southern French Countryside, and the Early Cistercians: A Study of Forty-Three Monasteries*. Transactions of the American Philosophical Society 76, pt. 5. Philadelphia: American Philosophical Society, 1986.

Berthelier, Simone. "L'expansion de l'ordre de Cluny et ses rapports avec l'histoire politique et économique du Xe au XIIe siècle." *Revue archéologique*, 6th ser., 11 (1938): 319–26.

Bishko, Charles Julien. "Fernando I and the Origins of the Leonese-Castilian Alliance with Cluny." In *Studies in Medieval Spanish Frontier History*. London: Variorum Reprints, 1980.

Black-Michaud, Jacob. *Cohesive Force: Feud in the Mediterranean and the Middle East*. New York: St. Martin's Press, 1975.

Blair, John, and Philip Riden. "Computer-Assisted Analysis of Medieval Deeds." *Archives* 15 (1982): 195–208.

Bloch, Marc. *Feudal Society*. Translated by L. A. Manyon. Chicago: University of Chicago Press, 1961.

Bossy, John, ed. *Disputes and Settlements: Law and Human Relations in the West*. Cambridge: Cambridge University Press, 1983.

Boüard, Alain de. *Manuel de diplomatique française et pontificale*. Vol. 2: *L'act privé*. Paris: Picard, 1948.

Bouchard, Constance B. "The Bosonids; or, Rising to Power in the Late Carolingian Age." *French Historical Studies* 15 (1988): 407–31.

———. "Family Structure and Family Consciousness among the Aristocracy in the Ninth to Eleventh Centuries." *Francia* 14 (1987): 639–58.

———. "Laymen and Church Reform around the Year 1000: The Case of Otto-William, Count of Burgundy." *Journal of Medieval History* 5 (1979): 1–10.

———. *Sword, Miter, and Cloister: Nobility and the Church in Burgundy, 980–1198.* Ithaca, N.Y.: Cornell University Press, 1987.

Brun-Durand, J. *Dictionnaire topographique du département de la Drôme.* Paris: Imprimerie nationale, 1891.

Bullough, Donald A., and Robin L. Storey, eds. *The Study of Medieval Records: Essays in Honour of Kathleen Major.* Oxford: Clarendon Press, 1971.

Callahan, Daniel F. "William the Great and the Monasteries of Aquitaine." *Studia Monastica* 19 (1977): 321–42.

Chagny, André. *Cluny et son empire.* Revised edition. Lyon: Emmanuel Vitte, 1938.

Charrié, Pierre. *Dictionnaire topographique du département de l'Ardèche.* Paris: Guénégaud, 1979.

Charrière, Frédéric de. "Recherches sur le couvent de Romainmôtier et ses possessions." *Mémoires et documents, Société de la Suisse Romande.* 1st ser., 3:148–56. Lausanne: Marc Ducloux, 1841.

Chaume, Maurice. "En Marge de l'histoire de Cluny." *Revue Mabillon* 29 (1939): 41–61; 30 (1940): 33–62.

———. "Etudes Carolingiennes, III: D'où sortent les anciens sires de Bourbon?" *Annales de Bourgogne* 8 (1936): 101–5.

———. "Les grands Prieurs de Cluny." *Revue Mabillon* 28 (1938): 147–52.

———. "Observations sur la chronologie des chartes de l'abbaye de Cluny." *Revue Mabillon* 16 (1926): 44–48; 29 (1939): 81–89; 29 (1939): 133–42; 31 (1941): 14–19, 42–45, 69–82; 32 (1942): 15–20, 133–36; 38 (1948): 1–6; 39 (1949): 41–43; 42 (1952): 1–4.

———. *Les origines du Duché de Bourgogne.* 2 parts. Part II in 3 fascicles. Dijon: E. Rebourseau, 1925–31. Reprint. Aalen: Scientia Verlag, 1977.

Cheyette, Fredric. "Suum cuique tribuere." *French Historical Studies* 6 (1970): 287–99.

Cheyette, Fredric L., and Claudie Duhamel-Amado. "Organisation d'un terroir et d'un habitat concentré: Un exemple Languedocien." In *Habitats fortifiés et organisation de l'espace en Méditerranée médiévale*, edited by A. Bazzana, P. Guichard, and J. M. Poisson, pp. 35–44. Table ronde, Lyon, 4–5 May 1982. GIS—Maison de l'Orient, 1983.

Clammer, John, ed. *The New Economic Anthropology.* New York: St. Martin's Press, 1978.

Codere, Helen. *Fighting with Property: A Study of Kwakiutl Potlatching and Warfare, 1792–1930.* Monographs of the American Ethnological Society 17. New York: J. J. Augustin, 1950.

Constable, Giles. "Cluniac Tithes and the Controversy between Gigny and Le Miroir." *Revue Bénédictine* 70 (1960): 591–624. Reprinted in *Cluniac Studies*. London: Variorum Reprints, 1980.

——. *Medieval Monasticism: A Select Bibliography*. Toronto: University of Toronto Press, 1976.

——. "Monastic Possession of Churches and 'Spiritualia' in the Age of Reform." In *Religious Life and Thought (11th–12th Centuries)*. London: Variorum Reprints, 1979.

——. *Monastic Tithes from Their Origins to the Twelfth Century*. Cambridge: Cambridge University Press, 1964.

Cottier, J. P. *L'abbaye royale de Romainmôtier et le droit de sa terre (du Ve au XIIIe siècle)*. Lausanne: Rouge, 1948.

Cottineau, Laurence Henri and G. Poras. *Répertoire topo-bibliographique des abbayes et prieurés*. 3 vols. Vols 1 and 2, Mâcon: Protat, 1939; vol. 3, Paris, 1971.

Cowdrey, Herbert Edward John. "Legal Problems Raised by Agreements of Confraternity." In *Memoria: Der geschichtliche Zeugniswert des liturgischen Gedenkens im Mittelalter*, edited by Karl Schmid and Joachim Wollasch, pp. 233–54. Münstersche Mittelalter-Schriften 48. Munich: W. Fink, 1984.

——. "Unions and Confraternity with Cluny." *Journal of Ecclesiastical History* 16 (1965): 152–62.

Dalton, George, ed. *Tribal and Peasant Economies: Readings in Economic Anthropology*. Garden City, N.Y.: Natural History Press, 1967.

Davies, Wendy, and Paul Fouracre, eds. *The Settlement of Disputes in Early Medieval Europe*. Cambridge: Cambridge University Press, 1986.

Déléage, André. *La vie rurale en Bourgogne jusqu'au début du onzième siècle*. 2 vols. text, 1 vol. maps. Mâcon: Protat, 1941.

Delisle, Léopold Victor. *Inventaire des manuscrits de la Bibliothèque nationale: Fonds de Cluni*. Paris: H. Champion, 1884.

Devailly, Guy. *Le Berry du Xe siècle au milieu du XIIIe: Etude politique, religieuse, sociale et économique*. Paris: Mouton, 1973.

De Vic, Claude and Joseph Vaissette. *Histoire générale de Languedoc*. 15 vols. Toulouse: Privat, 1872–93.

Dormeier, Heinrich. *Montecassino und die Laien im 11. und 12. Jahrhundert*. Schriften der MGH 27. Stuttgart: Hiersemann, 1979.

Dubled, Henri. "'Allodium' dans les textes latins du moyen âge." *Le Moyen Age* 57 (1951): 241–46.

——. "Quelques observations sur le sens du mot *villa*." *Le Moyen Age* 59 (1953): 1–9.

Duby, Georges. *The Early Growth of the European Economy: Warriors and Peasants from the Seventh to the Twelfth Century*. Translated by Howard B. Clarke. Ithaca, N.Y.: Cornell University Press, 1974.

——. *Hommes et structures du moyen âge: Recueil d'articles*. Paris: Mouton, 1973. Many of these articles are in English in *The Chival-*

rous Society, translated by Cynthia Postan. Berkeley: University of California Press, 1977.

_____. *La société aux XIᵉ et XIIᵉ siècles dans la région mâconnaise.* 2d rev. ed. Paris: J. Touzot, 1971.

_____. *Les trois ordres ou l'imaginaire du féodalisme.* Paris: Gallimard, 1978.

Duparc, Pierre. "Confréries du Saint-Esprit et communautés d'habitants au moyen-âge." *Revue historique de droit français et étranger,* 4th ser., 36 (1958): 349–67. Published in English in *Lordship and Community in Medieval Europe: Selected Readings,* edited by Fredric L. Cheyette. New York: Holt, Rinehart and Winston, 1968.

Etaix, Raymond, "Le lectionnaire de l'office à Cluny." *Recherches augustiniennes* 11 (1976): 91–153.

Fabiani, Luigi. *La terra di S. Benedetto: Studio storico-giuridico sull' Abbazia di Montecassino dall' VIII al XIII secolo.* Miscellanea cassinense 33–34, 42. 3 vols. Montecassino, 1968–80.

Fazy, Max. *Les origines du Bourbonnais.* 2 vols. Moulins: Progrès de l'Allier, 1924.

Febvre, Lucien. "Une enquête: La succession des circonscriptions." *Annales: ESC* 2 (1947): 201–4.

Fechter, Johannes. "Cluny, Adel und Volk: Studien über das Verhältnis des Klosters zu den Ständen (910–1156)." Diss., Tübingen, 1966.

Fichtenau, Heinrich. *Arenga: Spätantike und Mittelalter im Spiegel der Urkundenformeln.* MIÖG, Erg. 18. Graz: Böhlaus, 1957.

_____. *Lebensordnungen des 10. Jahrhunderts: Studien über Denkart und Existenz im einstigen Karolingerreich.* Monographien zur Geschichte der Mittelalters, 30, pts. 1 and 2. 2 vols. Stuttgart: Hiersemann, 1984.

_____. "Die Reihung der Zeugen in Urkunden des frühen Mittelalters." *MIÖG* 87 (1979): 301–15.

_____. *Das Urkundenwesen in Österreich vom 8. bis zum frühen 13. Jahrhundert.* MIÖG, Erg. 23. Vienna: Böhlaus, 1971.

Finley, Moses I. *The World of Odysseus.* New York: Viking Press, 1954.

Firth, Raymond. *Elements of Social Organization.* 1951. 3d ed. Boston: Beacon Press, 1963.

_____. "The Place of Malinowski in the History of Economic Anthropology." In *Man and Culture: An Evaluation of the Work of Bronislaw Malinowski,* edited by Raymond Firth, pp. 209–27. London: Routledge and Kegan Paul, 1957.

_____. *Primitive Economics of the New Zealand Maori.* New York: Dutton, 1929.

_____. *Primitive Polynesian Economy.* 1939. 2d ed. London: Routledge and Kegan Paul, 1965.

Fleming, Robin. "A Report on the Domesday Book Database Project." *Medieval Prosopography* 7 (1986): 55–61.

Fletcher, Richard A. *St. James's Catapult: The Life and Times of Diego Gelmírez of Santiago de Compostela*. Oxford: Clarendon Press, 1984.

Foster, Charles Wilmer. *Final Concords of the County of Lincoln from the Feet of Fines Preserved in the Public Record Office A.D. 1244–1272*. Vol. 2. Lincoln: Lincoln Record Society, 1920.

Fournial, Etienne. "La souveraineté du Lyonnais au Xe siècle." *Le Moyen Age* 62 (1956): 413–52.

Freed, John B. "Reflections on the Medieval German Nobility." *American Historical Review* 91 (1986): 553–75.

Ganahl, Karl Hans. "Hufe und Wergeld." *Zeitschrift der Savigny-Stiftung für Rechtsgeschichte, Germanistische Abteilung* 53 (1933): 208–46.

Garand, Monique-Cécile. "Copistes de Cluny au temps de saint Maieul (948–994)." *Bibliothèque de l'Ecole des Chartes* 136 (1978): 5–36.

——. "'Giraldus levita,' copiste de chartes et de livres à Cluny sous l'abbatiat de saint Odilon (+ 1049)." In *Calames et cahiers: Mélanges de codicologie et de paléographie offerts à Léon Gilissen*, edited by Jacques Lemaire and Emile Van Balberghe, pp. 41–48. Brussels: Centre d'étude des manuscrits, 1985.

——. "Le scriptorium de Cluny carrefour d'influences au XIe siècle: Le manuscrit Paris B.N. nouv. acq. lat. 1548." *Journal des savants* 4 (1977): 257–83.

Gathercole, Peter. "*Hau, Mauri*, and *Utu*: A Re-examination." *Mankind* 11 (1978): 334–40.

Geary, Patrick J. *Aristocracy in Provence: The Rhône Basin at the Dawn of the Carolingian Age*. Philadelphia: University of Pennsylvania Press, 1985.

——. "Echanges et relations entre les vivants et les morts dans la société du haut moyen âge." *Droit et Cultures* 12 (1986): 3–17.

——. *Furta Sacra: Thefts of Relics in the Central Middle Ages*. Princeton: Princeton University Press, 1978.

——. "Sacred Commodities: The Circulation of Medieval Relics." In *The Social Life of Things: Commodities in Cultural Perspective*, edited by Arjun Appadurai, pp. 169–91. Cambridge: Cambridge University Press, 1986.

——. "Vivre en conflit dans une France sans état: Typologie des mécanismes de règlement des conflits (1050–1200)." *Annales: ESC* 41 (1986): 1107–33.

Genicot, Léopold, ed. *Les actes publics*. Fasc. 3 of *Typologie des sources du moyen âge*. Turnhout: Brepols, 1972.

Giry, Arthur. *Manuel de diplomatique: Diplômes et chartes—chronologie technique—éléments critiques et parties constitutives de la teneur des chartes—les chancelleries—les actes privés*. Paris: Hachette, 1894.

Goetz, Hans-Werner. "Kirchenschutz, Rechtswahrung und Reform: Zu den Zielen und zum Wesen der frühen Gottesfriedensbewegung in Frankreich." *Francia* 11 (1983): 193–240.

Goodenough, Ward H. *Property, Kin, and Community on Truk.* Hamden, Conn: Archon, 1966.

Graesse, Johann G. T., F. Benedict, and H. Plechl. *Orbis Latinus: Lexikon lateinischer geographischer Namen des Mittelalters und der Neuzeit.* 3 vols. Braunschweig: Klinkhardt und Biermann, 1972.

Gregory, C. A. "A Conceptual Analysis of a Non-Capitalist Gift Economy with Particular Reference to Papua New Guinea." *Cambridge Journal of Economics* 5 (1981): 119–35.

——. "Gifts to Men and Gifts to God: Gift Exchange and Capital Accumulation in Contemporary Papua." *Man* 15 (1980): 626–52.

Grierson, Philip. "Commerce in the Dark Ages: A Critique of the Evidence." *Transactions of the Royal Historical Society,* 5th ser. 9 (1959): 123–39.

Guerreau, Alain. "Douze doyennés clunisiens au milieu du XIIᵉ siècle." *Annales de Bourgogne* 52 (1980): 83–128.

Guillot, Olivier. *Le Comte d'Anjou et son entourage au XIᵉ siècle."* 2 vols. Paris: Picard, 1972.

Gurevich, Aron J. *Categories of Medieval Culture.* Translated by G. L. Campbell. London: Routledge and Kegan Paul, 1985.

——. "Représentations et attitudes à l'égard de la propriété pendant le haut moyen âge." *Annales: ESC* 27 (1972): 523–47.

Hannig, Jürgen. "Ars donandi: Zur Ökonomie des Schenkens im früheren Mittelalter." *Geschichte in Wissenschaft und Unterricht* 3 (1986): 149–62.

Head, Thomas. "The Holy Dead and Christian Society: The Cult of the Saints in the Orléanais, 750–1215." Ph.D. diss. Harvard University, 1985.

Head, Thomas, and Richard Landes, eds. *Essays on the Peace of God: The Church and the People in Eleventh-Century France.* In *Historical Reflections/Réflexions Historiques* 14 (1987).

Heath, Robert G. *Crux imperatorum philosophia: Imperial Horizons of the Cluniac "Confraternitas," 969–1109.* Pittsburgh, Pa., Pickwick Press, 1976.

Herlihy, David. *The Social History of Italy and Western Europe, 700–1500: Collected Studies.* London: Variorum Reprints, 1978.

Hillebrandt, Maria. "The Cluniac Charters: Remarks on a Quantitative Approach for Prosopographical Studies." *Medieval Prosopography* 3 (1982): 3–25.

——. *Studien zu den Datierungen der Urkunden der Abtei Cluny.* Münstersche Mittelalter-Schriften. Forthcoming.

Horn, Walter, and Ernest Born. *The Plan of Saint Gall.* 3 vols. Berkeley: University of California Press, 1979.

Hourlier, Jacques. *Saint Odilon, Abbé de Cluny.* Louvain: Bibliothèque de l'Université, 1964.

Hunt, Noreen. *Cluny under Saint Hugh, 1049–1109*. London: Edward Arnold, 1967.

Huyghebaert, N., and Lemaitre, Jean-Loup, eds. *Les documents necrologiques.* Fasc. 4 of *Typologie des sources du moyen âge occidentale,* edited by Léopold Genicot. Turnhout: Brepols, 1972.

Iogna-Prat, Dominique. *Agni immaculati: Recherches sur les sources hagiographiques relatives à saint Maieul de Cluny (954–994).* Paris: Cerf, 1988.

———. "Continence et Virginité dans la conception clunisienne de l'ordre du monde autour de l'an mil." In *Académie des Inscriptions et Belles-Lettres: Comptes rendus, 1985.* Pp. 127–46. Paris: Boccard, 1985.

Jeanton, Gabriel. *Pays de Mâcon et de Chalon avant l'an mille: Notes de géographie historique.* Dijon: Rebousseau, 1934.

Jedin, Hubert, Kenneth S. Latourette, and Jochen Martin, eds. *Atlas zur Kirchengeschichte.* Freiburg: Herder, 1970.

Jobert, Philippe, *La notion de donation: Convergences 630–750.* Publication de l'Université de Dijon. Paris: Société Les Belles Lettres, 1977.

Johansen, J. Prytz. *The Maori and His Religion in Its Non-ritualistic Aspects.* Copenhagen: Musksgaard, 1954.

John, Eric. *Land Tenure in Early England: A Discussion of Some Problems.* Leicester: Leicester University Press, 1960.

———. "'Secularium prioratus' and the Rule of Saint Benedict." *Revue Bénédictine* 75 (1965): 212–39.

Johnson, Penelope. *Prayer, Patronage, and Power: The Abbey of la Trinité, Vendôme, 1032–1187.* New York: New York University Press, 1981.

Jorden, Willibald. *Das cluniazensische Totengedächtniswesen vornehmlich unter den drei ersten Äbten Berno, Odo und Aymard (910–954): Zugleich en Beitrag zu den cluniazensischen Traditionsurkunden.* Münstersche Beiträge zur Theologie 15. Münster: Aschendorf, 1930.

Landau, Peter. *Jus Patronatus: Studien zur Entwicklung des Patronats im Dekretalenrecht und der Kanonistik des 12. und 13. Jahrhunderts.* Vienna: Böhlau, 1975.

Larroque, François. "Souvigny: Les origines du prieuré." *Revue Mabillon* 58 (1970): 1–24.

Lauranson-Rosaz, Christian. *L'Auvergne et ses marges (Velay, Gévaudan) du VIIIe au XIe siècle: La fin du monde antique?* Le Puy-en-Velay: Les Cahiers de la Haute-Loire, 1987.

LeClair, Edward E., Jr., and Harold K. Schneider, eds. *Economic Anthropology: Readings in Theory and Analysis.* New York: Holt, Rinehart and Winston, 1968.

Lévi-Strauss, Claude. "Introduction à l'oeuvre de Marcel Mauss." In *Sociologie et anthropologie,* by Marcel Mauss, pp. ix–lii. Paris: Presses Universitaires de France, 1966.

Levy, Ernst. *West Roman Vulgar Law: The Law of Property*. Philadelphia: American Philosophical Society, 1951.

Lévy-Bruhl, Lucien. *Les fonctions mentales dans les sociétés inférieures*. Paris: Felix Alcan, 1910. Published in English as *How Natives Think*, translated by Lilian A. Clare, 1910. Reprint. Princeton: Princeton University Press, 1985.

Little, Lester K. "La morphologie des malédictiones monastiques." *Annales: ESC* 34 (1979): 43–60.

——. *Religious Poverty and the Profit Economy in Medieval Europe*. Ithaca, N.Y.: Cornell University Press, 1978.

Longnon, Auguste. *Atlas historique de la France depuis César jusqu'à nos jours*. 2 vols., text and plates. Paris: Hachette, 1907.

MacCormack, G. "Mauss and the 'Spirit' of the Gift." *Oceania* 52 (1981–82): 286–93.

McLaughlin, Megan Molly. "Consorting with Saints: Prayer for the Dead in Early Medieval French Society." Ph.D. diss. Stanford University, 1985.

Mager, Hans-Erich. "Studien über das Verhältnis der Cluniacenser zum Eigenkirchenwesen." In *Neue Forschungen über Cluny und die Cluniacenser*, edited by Gerd Tellenbach, pp. 167–217. Freiburg: Herder, 1959.

Magnou-Nortier, Elisabeth. "A propos du temporel de l'abbaye de Lagrasse: Etude sur la structure des terroirs et sur les taxes foncières du IXe au XIIe siècle." In *Sous la règle de saint Benoît: Structures monastiques et sociétés en France du moyen âge à l'époque moderne*, pp. 235–64. Proceedings of a colloquium held at l'abbaye de Sainte Marie de Paris, 23–25 October 1980. Geneva: Droz, 1982.

——. "Contribution à l'étude des documents falsifiés: Le diplôme de Louis le Pieux pour Saint-Julien de Brioude (825) et l'acte de fondation du monastère de Sauxillanges par le duc Acfred (927)." *Cahiers de civilisation médiévale* 21 (1978): 313–38.

Malinowski, Bronislaw. *Argonauts of the Western Pacific*. London, 1922. Reprint. New York: Dutton, 1961.

Marilier, Jean. "L'expansion clunisienne dans la Bourgogne du nord aux XIe–XIIIe siècles." In *Consuetudines monasticae: Eine Festgabe für Kassius Hallinger aus Anlass seines 70. Geburtstages*. Edited by Joachim F. Angerer and Josef Lenzenweger. Studia Anselmiana 85. Rome, 1982.

Mason, Emma. "The Donors of Westminster Abbey Charters, ca. 1066–1240." *Medieval Prosopography* 8 (1987): 23–39.

——. "Timeo Barones et Donas Ferentes." In *Religious Motivation: Biographical and Sociological Problems for the Church Historian*, edited by Derek Baker. Studies in Church History 15. Oxford: Blackwell, 1978.

Mauss, Marcel. "Essai sur le don: Forme et raison de l'échange dans les sociétés archaïque." *L'Année Sociologique* 1 (1923): 30–186. Published in English as *The Gift: Forms and Functions of Exchange in Archaic Societies*, translated by Ian Cunnison. New York: Norton, 1967.

Meekings, Charles Anthony Francis, with David Crook, eds. *The 1235 Surrey Eyre*. 2 vols. Surrey Record Society 31. Surrey: Sutton, 1979–83.

Miller, William Ian. "Avoiding Legal Judgement: The Submission of Disputes to Arbitration in Medieval Iceland." *American Journal of Legal History* 28 (1984): 95–134.

——. "Gift, Sale, Payment, Raid: Case Studies in the Negotiation and Classification of Exchange in Medieval Iceland." *Speculum* 61 (1986): 18–50.

Morrison, Karl F. "The Gregorian Reform." In *Christian Spirituality: Origins to the Twelfth Century*, edited by Bernard McGinn and John Meyenrdorff. Vol. 16 of *World Spirituality: An Encyclopedic History of the Religious Quest*. New York: Crossroad, 1985.

Murray, Alexander. *Reason and Society in the Middle Ages*. Oxford: Clarendon Press, 1978.

Nader, Laura, and Harry F. Todd, Jr., eds. *The Disputing Process: Law in Ten Societies*. New York: Columbia University Press, 1978.

Neiske, Franz. "Communities and Confraternities in the Ninth and Tenth Centuries." Paper presented at the Twenty-third International Congress on Medieval Studies, Kalamazoo, Michigan, 5–8 May 1988.

Newman, William Mendel. *Catalogue des actes de Robert II, roi de France*. Paris: Sirey, 1937.

Oexle, Otto Gerhard. "Gruppenbindung und Gruppenverhalten bei Menschen und Tieren: Beobachtungen zur Geschichte der mittelalterlichen Gilden." *Saeculum* 36 (1985): 28–45.

——. "Die 'Wirklichkeit' und das 'Wissen': Ein Blick auf das sozialgeschichtliche Oeuvre von Georges Duby." *Historische Zeitschrift* 232 (1981): 61–91.

Ortigues, Edmond, and Dominique Iogna-Prat. "Raoul Glaber et l'historiographie clunisienne." *Studi Medievali*, 3d ser., 26 (1985): 537–72.

Oursel-Quarré, Madeleine. "A propos du chartrier de Cluny." *Annales de Bourgogne* 50 (1978): 103–7.

Pacaut, Marcel. *L'Ordre de Cluny*. [Paris]: Fayard, 1986.

Parsons, Talcott, and Neil J. Smelser. *Economy and Society: A Study of the Integration of Economic and Social Theory*. 1956. Reprint. New York: Free Press, 1964.

Petitjean, Michel. "Remarques sur l'emploi de la précaire par l'abbaye de Cluny, d'après les chartes éditées par A. Bruel." *Mémoires de la Société pour l'Histoire du Droit et des Institutions des anciens pays bourguignons, comtois et romands* 41 (1984): 121–28.

Poeck, Dietrich. "*Cluniacensis ecclesia*: Cluny and Its Monasteries."

Paper presented at the Twenty-second International Congress on Medieval Studies, Kalamazoo, Michigan, 6–10 May 1987.

———. "Die Klöster der *Cluniacensis ecclesia.*" Draft of book to appear in Münstersche Mittelalter-Schriften.

———. "Laienbegräbnisse in Cluny." *Frühmittelalterliche Studien* 15 (1981): 68–179.

Polanyi, Karl. *The Great Transformation: The Political and Economic Origins of Our Time.* 1944. Reprint. Boston: Beacon Press, 1957.

Pollock, Frederick, and Frederic William Maitland. *The History of English Law.* 2 vols. 2d ed. 1898. Reprint. Cambridge: Cambridge University Press, 1968.

Poly, Jean-Pierre. *La Provence et la société féodale (879–1166): Contribution à l'étude des structures dites féodales dans le Midi.* Paris: Bordas, 1976.

Poupardin, René. *Le royaume de Provence sous les Carolingiens (855–933?).* Paris: Emile Bouillon, 1901.

Powell, James M., ed. *Medieval Studies: An Introduction.* Syracuse, N.Y.: Syracuse University Press, 1976.

Prinz, Friedrich. *Frühesmönchtum in Frankenreich: Kultur und Gesellschaft in Gallien, den Rheinlanden und Bayern am Beispiel der monastischen Entwicklung (4. bis 8. Jahrhundert).* Munich: Oldenbourg, 1965.

———. *Klerus und Krieg im früheren Mittelalter.* Stuttgart: Hierseman, 1971.

Radcliffe-Brown, Alfred Reginald. *Structure and Function in Primitive Society: Essays and Addresses.* 1952. Reprint. New York: Free Press, 1968.

Régné, Jean, and J. Rouchier, *Histoire du Vivarais.* 2 vols. Largentière: Imprimerie Mazel et Plancher, 1914.

Reilly, Bernard F. *The Kingdom of Castile under Queen Urraca 1109–1126.* Princeton: Princeton University Press, 1982.

Reynolds, Susan. *Kingdoms and Communities in Western Europe, 900–1300.* Oxford: Clarendon Press, 1984.

Richard, Jean. "La publication des chartes de Cluny." In *A Cluny: Congrès scientifique.* Fêtes et cérémonies liturgiques 9–11 July 1949. Dijon: Bernigaud and Privat, 1950.

Rosenwein, Barbara H. "Cartographic Patterns of Cluniac Monasticism." In *Monasticism in the Christian and Hindu Traditions: A Comparative Study,* edited by Austin B. Creel and Vasudha Narayanan. Lewiston, N.Y.: Edwin Mellen. In press.

———. *Rhinoceros Bound: Cluny in the Tenth Century.* Philadelphia: University of Pennsylvania Press, 1982.

Rosenwein, Barbara H., and Lester K. Little. "Social Meaning in the Monastic and Mendicant Spiritualities." *Past and Present* 63 (1974): 4–32.

Sackur, Ernst. *Die Cluniacenser in ihrer kirchlichen und allgemeinge-*

schichtlichen Wirksamkeit bis zur Mitte des elften Jahrhunderts. 2 vols. Halle an der Saale: Max Niemeyer, 1892–94.

Sahlins, Marshall. "The Spirit of the Gift." In *Stone Age Economics*, pp. 149–53. Chicago: Aldine-Atherton, 1972.

Samaran, Charles, and Robert Marichal. *Catalogue des manuscrits en écriture latine portant des indications de date, de lieu ou de copiste* 4, pt. 1. Paris: Centre national de la recherche scientifique, 1981.

Sankt Bonifatius: Gedenkgabe zum zwölfhundertsten Todestag. Fulda: Parzeller, 1954.

Sargent, Steven D. "Religion and Society in Late Medieval Bavaria: The Cult of Saint Leonard, 1258–1500," Ph.D. diss., University of Pennsylvania, 1982.

Sawyer, P. H., ed. *Medieval Settlement: Continuity and Change.* London: Edward Arnold, 1976.

Schieffer, Theodor. *Winfrid-Bonifatius und die christliche Grundlegung von Europas.* Freiberg: Herder, 1954.

Schlesser, Norman D. "Frontiers in Medieval French History." *International History Review* 6 (1984): 159–73.

Schmid, Karl. *Gebetsgedenken und adliges Selbstverständnis im Mittelalter: Ausgewählte Beiträge. Festgabe zu seinem sechzigsten Geburtstag.* Sigmaringen: J. Thorbecke, 1983.

Schmid, Karl, with Gerd Althoff et al., eds. *Die Klostergemeinshaft von Fulda im früheren Mittelalter.* 3 vols. in 5. Münstersche Mittelalter-Schriften 8. Munich: W. Fink, 1978.

Schmid, Karl, and Joachim Wollasch, eds. *Memoria: Der Geschichtliche Zeugniswert des liturgischen Gedenkens im Mittelalter.* Münstersche Mittelalter-Schriften 48. Munich: W. Fink, 1984.

Schreiber, Georg. *Gemeinschaften des Mittelalters: Recht und Verfassung, Kult und Frömmigkeit.* Münster: Regensberg, 1948.

———. *Kurie und Kloster im 12. Jahrhundert.* Kirchenrechtliche Abhandlungen, 65, 68. 2 vols. Stuttgart: Verlag Ferdinand Enke, 1910.

Segl, Peter. *Königtum und Klosterreform in Spanien: Untersuchungen über die Cluniacenserklöster in Kastilien-León vom Beginn des 11. bis zur Mitte des 12. Jahrhunderts.* Kallmünz: Lassleben, 1974.

Semmler, Josef. "Karl der Grosse und das fränkische Mönchtum." In *Karl der Grosse: Lebenswerk und Nachleben*, edited by Wolfgang Braunfels. 5 vols. Düsseldorf: Schwann, 1965.

———. "Pippin III. und die fränkische Klöster." *Francia* 3 (1975): 88–146.

Sherry, John F., Jr. "Gift Giving in Anthropological Perspective." *Journal of Consumer Research* 10 (1983): 157–68.

Tabuteau, Emily Z. "Ownership and Tenure in Eleventh-Century Normandy." *American Journal of Legal History* 21 (1977): 92–124.

———. *Transfers of Property in Eleventh-Century Norman Law.* Chapel Hill: University of North Carolina Press, 1988.

Torrell, Jean-Pierre, and Denise Bouthillier. *Pierre le Vénérable et sa vision du monde: Sa vie—son oeuvre; l'homme et le démon*. Spicilegium Sacrum Lovaniense: Etudes et documents, fasc. 42. Leuven: Spicilegium Sacrum Lovaniense, 1986.

Trexler, Richard C., ed. *Persons in Groups: Social Behavior as Identity Formation in Medieval and Renaissance Europe*. Medieval and Renaissance Texts and Studies 36. Binghamton, N.Y.: MRTS, 1985.

Valous, Guy de. "Le domaine de l'abbaye de Cluny aux Xe et XIe siècles." *Annales de l'Académie de Mâcon*, 3d ser., 22 (1920): 299–481. Also issued as *Le domaine de l'abbaye de Cluny aux Xe et XIe siècles: Formation, Organisation, Administration*. Paris: E. Champion, 1923.

——. *Le monachisme clunisien des origines au XVe siècle: Vie intérieure des monastères et organisation de l'ordre*. 1935. 2d ed. 2 vols. Paris: Picard, 1970.

——. *Le temporel et la situation financière des établissements de l'ordre de Cluny du XIIe au XIVe siècle*. Archives de la France monastique 41. Paris: Picard, 1935.

Van den Eynde, Damien. "Remarques sur la chronologie du cartulaire de Cluny au temps de Pierre le Vénérable." *Antonianum* 43 (1968): 217–59.

Van Engen, John. "The 'Crisis of Cenobitism' Reconsidered: Benedictine Monasticism in the Years 1050–1150," *Speculum* 61 (1986): 269–304.

Vidal-Naquet, Pierre. "Economie et société dans la Grèce ancienne: L'oeuvre de Moses I. Finley." *Archives européennes de sociologie* 6 (1965): 111–48.

Vregille, Bernard de. *Hughes de Salins, archevêque de Besançon, 1031–1066*. Thèse, Université de Besançon, 1976. 3 vols. Lille: Université Lille, 1976.

——. *Hughes de Salins, archevêque de Besançon, 1031–1066*. Besançon: Cêtre, 1981.

Ward, Jennifer C. "Fashions in Monastic Endowment: The Foundations of the Clare Family, 1066–1314." *Journal of Ecclesiastical History* 32 (1981): 427–51.

Wardrop, Joan. *Fountains Abbey and Its Benefactors, 1132–1300*. Cistercian Studies Series 91. Kalamazoo: Cistercian Publications, 1987.

Weinberger, Stephen. "Les conflits entre clercs et laïcs dans la Provence du XIe siècle." *Annales du Midi* 92 (1980): 269–79.

Weiner, Annette B. "Inalienable Wealth." *American Ethnologist* 13 (1985): 210–27.

——. *Women of Value, Men of Renown: New Perspectives in Trobriand Exchange*. Austin, Tex.: University of Texas Press, 1976.

White, Stephen D. *Custom, Kinship, and Gifts to Saints: The Laudatio Parentum in Western France, 1050–1150*. Chapel Hill: University of North Carolina Press, 1988.

_____. "Pactum . . . legem vincit et amor judicium. The Settlement of Disputes by Compromise in Eleventh-Century Western France." American Journal of Legal History 22 (1978): 281–308.

Winzer, Ulrich. "Zum Einzugsbereich Clunys im 10. Jahrhundert: Eine Fallstudie," Frühmittelalterlichen Studien forthcoming.

Wischermann, Elsa Maria. Marcigny-sur-Loire: Gründungs-und-Frühgeschichte des ersten Cluniacenserinnen priorates (1055–1150). Münstersche Mittelalter-Schriften 42. Munich: W. Fink, 1986.

Wolfram, Herwig, ed. Intitulatio II: Lateinische Herrscher-und Fürstentitel im neunten und zehnten Jahrhundert. MIÖG, Erg., 24. Vienna: Böhlaus, 1973.

Wollasch, Joachim. Mönchtum des Mittelalters zwischen Kirche und Welt. Münstersche Mittelalter-Schriften 7. Munich: W. Fink, 1973.

_____. "Parenté noble et monachisme reformateur: Observations sur les 'conversions' à la vie monastique aux XIᵉ et XIIᵉ siècles." Revue historique 264 (1980): 3–24.

Wollasch, Joachim, with Wolf-Dieter Heim, Joachim Mehne, Franz Neiske, and Dietrich Poeck, eds. Synopse der cluniacensischen Necrologien. 2 vols. Münstersche Mittelalter-Schriften 39. Munich: W. Fink, 1982.

Index

Passages concerned with an individual member of a family are indexed under that person's name; entries under a family name indicate general discussions of that family's activity. Names and places mentioned only in notes or tables are not indexed. All place names are département Saône-et-Loire unless otherwise indicated [in brackets]. Abbreviations are: ca. = canton, co. = commune, arr. = arrondissement, dép. = département, l.-disp. = place that has disappeared, n.id. = not identified, nr. = near

Library of Congress Cataloging-in-Publication Data

Rosenwein, Barbara H.
  To be the neighbor of Saint Peter.

  Bibliography: p.
  Includes index.
  1. Cluny (Benedictine abbey) 2. Church property—France—Cluny. 3. Bene-
fices, Ecclesiastical—France—Cluny. 4. Cluny (France)—Church history. I.
Title.
BX2615.C63R68 1989   333.3'22'094443   88-47912
ISBN 0-8014-2206-X (alk. paper)